ZAGATSURVEY.

2002

LONDON RESTAURANTS

**Edited and coordinated by
Sholto Douglas-Home, Susan Kessler
and Carol Diuguid**

**Published and distributed by
ZAGAT SURVEY, LLC
4 Columbus Circle
New York, New York 10019
Tel: 212 977 6000
E-mail: london@zagat.com
Web site: www.zagat.com**

Acknowledgments

Lisa Bauer, Deborah Bennett, Karen Bonham, Caroline Clegg, Ricki Conway, Alex, Louis and Tallula Douglas-Home, Ray Fine, Amanda Fox, Sandra and Michael Howard, Barbara Illias, Larry Kessler, Le Cordon Bleu, Pamela and Michael Lester, Margaret Levin, Jenny Linford, Ben and Sheila Miller, Zoe Miller, Becky Norris, Jean Oddy, Stephanie Pham-Quang, Zoe Price, Natasha Robinson, Anne Semmes, Clare Sievers, Alexandra Spezzotti, Annie Tobin, Peter Vogl, Susan and Jeffrey Weingarten, Sarah Westgate and Vanessa Whicker.

This guide would not have been possible without the hard work of our staff: Betsy Andrews, Phil Cardone, Jessica Fields, Natalie Lebert, Mike Liao, Dave Makulec, Laura Mitchell, Benjamin Schmerler, Robert Seixas, Daniel Simmons and Yoji Yamaguchi.

Contents

What's New

The good times keep rolling in London's restaurant scene, or so it would seem judging from the breathless pace of new openings. Despite gloom mongering from some quarters, the city's restaurateurs are falling over themselves to capture diners' attention with rousing new concepts.

• **Bumper Crop:** In the past few months alone, Hani Farsi has recreated the Italian legend Cecconi's in Mayfair, to instant success; Hakkasan, Alan Yau's Chinese newcomer, is making a splash in a former car park near Tottenham Court Road; Richard Neat, commuting from the French Riviera, is wowing Londoners with impressive New French cuisine at his Neat Restaurant in South Bank; and Aussie chef David Thompson has come to town to practice his unique brand of Thai cooking at Nahm in Christina Ong's Halkin Hotel in Belgravia. Meanwhile, true to his record of unveiling one major creation every decade, the legendary Mark Birley has inaugurated a private club, George, next door to Harry's Bar.

• **Hotel Honeymoon:** Not so long ago, hotel dining in the capital was the reserve of tourists and traditionalists. Then came Vong and La Tante Claire at the Berkeley, Nobu at the Metropolitan and Asia de Cuba at the Saint Martin's Lane Hotel. Now two of London's most celebrated chefs have major ventures planned in hotels: set to open at press time, Gordon Ramsay's New French venue in the revamped dining room at Claridge's already is attracting huge interest, as will Giorgio Locatelli's eaterie in the Churchill Hotel in Portman Square when it debuts in early 2002.

• **Luxury Life:** Londoners' love affair with glamorous settings also shows no sign of waning, with two revamped stalwarts poised to make a grand return as we go to press: the Greenhouse in Mayfair and Soho's Red Fort. In addition, respected restaurateurs Chris Bodker (Avenue, Circus) and Peter Gordon (ex Sugar Club) have openings on the horizon, in Theatreland and Marylebone, respectively, whilst A-Z Restaurants have plans for a new Memories of China in Chelsea and an Italian venue, Prezzemolo, in Fulham. Outside London, all eyes turn to a stylish new hotel in the Cotswolds, Cowley Manor, expected to open in the autumn.

• **Footing the Bill:** This year's newcomers enter an environment in which upward pressure on business rates means many will have to operate close to capacity in order to cover their overheads. And the fact that the average price for a meal in London has risen 6 percent to £30.85 in the past year suggests that owners increasingly are passing costs on to customers.

Still, Londoners have plenty to be proud of in their energetic dining scene – and ample reason to dive in, fork first!

Wimbledon, London   Sholto Douglas-Home
24 August, 2001

About This Survey

For more than 20 years, Zagat Survey has reported on the shared experiences of diners like you. Here are the results of our *2002 London Restaurant Survey,* covering some 1,296 restaurants in the London area. This marks the sixth year we have covered restaurants in London. We're pleased to report that each year the quality and diversity of the city's restaurants have improved. Today London must be included on any list of the best places to eat in the world.

By regularly surveying large numbers of avid local restaurant-goers about their collective dining experiences, we hope to have achieved a uniquely current and reliable guide. For this book, more than 3,700 people participated. Since the participants dined out an average of 2.5 times per week, this *Survey* is based on more than 482,000 meals annually.

Of the surveyors, 49% were women, 51% men; the breakdown by age is 17% in their 20s, 36% in their 30s, 21% in their 40s, 15% in their 50s and 11% in their 60s or above. In producing the reviews contained in this guide, our editors have synopsized our surveyors' opinions, with their exact comments shown in quotation marks.

Of course, we are especially grateful to our editor/coordinators: Sholto Douglas-Home, a London restaurant critic for 15 years, and Susan Kessler, Managing Director of Zagat Survey in the UK and a cookbook author and consultant for lifestyle publications.

To help guide our readers to London's best meals and best buys, we have prepared a number of lists. See Most Popular (page 10), Top Ratings (pages 11–16) and Best Buys (page 17). To assist the user in finding just the right restaurant for any occasion, without wasting time, we have also provided 43 handy indexes and have tried to be concise.

As companions to this guide, we also publish *Top International Hotels, Resorts & Spas,* as well as *Zagat Surveys* and Maps to more than 70 other markets. Most of these guides are also available on mobile devices and at **www.zagat.com**, where you can also vote and shop.

To join our **London Survey** or any of our other upcoming surveys, you can request a ballot by e-mailing customer service@zagat.com or using the pull-out card that's in this book. Each participant will receive a free copy of the next *Survey* when it is published.

Your comments, suggestions and even criticisms of this *Survey* are also solicited. There is always room for improvement with your help. You can contact us at london@zagat.com or by mail at Zagat Survey, 4 Columbus Circle, New York, NY 10019.

New York, NY
24 August, 2001

Nina and Tim Zagat

Key to Ratings/Symbols

Name, Address, Tube Stop, Phone* & Fax

Zagat Ratings

Hours & Credit Cards

		F	D	S	C
Tim & Nina's Fish Bar	◑Ｓ⊄	▽ 23	5	9	£9

Exeter St., WC2 (Covent Garden), 020-7123 4567;
fax 020-7123 4567

☑ Open seven days a week, 24 hours a day (some say that's "168 hours too much"), this "cheerful" and "chaotic" Covent Garden stalwart serving "cheap, no-nonsense" fish 'n' chips is an "ideal, dingy spot" for a "quick grease fix"; no one's impressed by the "tired, tatty decor" or "patchy service", but judging from its "perpetual queues", the food's worth it.

Review, with surveyors' comments in quotes

Restaurants with the highest overall ratings and greatest popularity and importance are printed in CAPITAL LETTERS.

Before each review a symbol indicates whether responses were uniform ■ or mixed ☑.

Hours: ◑ serves after 11 PM
Ｓ open on Sunday

Credit Cards: ⊄ no credit cards accepted

Ratings: Food, Decor and Service are rated on a scale of **0** to **30**. The Cost (C) column reflects our surveyors' estimate of the price of dinner including one drink and service.

F Food	**D** Decor	**S** Service	**C** Cost
23	5	9	£9

0–9 poor to fair	**20–25** very good to excellent
10–15 fair to good	**26–30** extraordinary to perfection
16–19 good to very good	▽ low response/less reliable

A place listed without ratings is either an important **newcomer** or a popular **write-in**. For such places, the estimated cost is indicated by the following symbols.

I	£15 and below	**E**	£26 to £35
M	£16 to £25	**VE**	£36 or more

---

* When calling from outside the UK, dial international code + 44, then omit the first zero of the number.

London's Most Popular

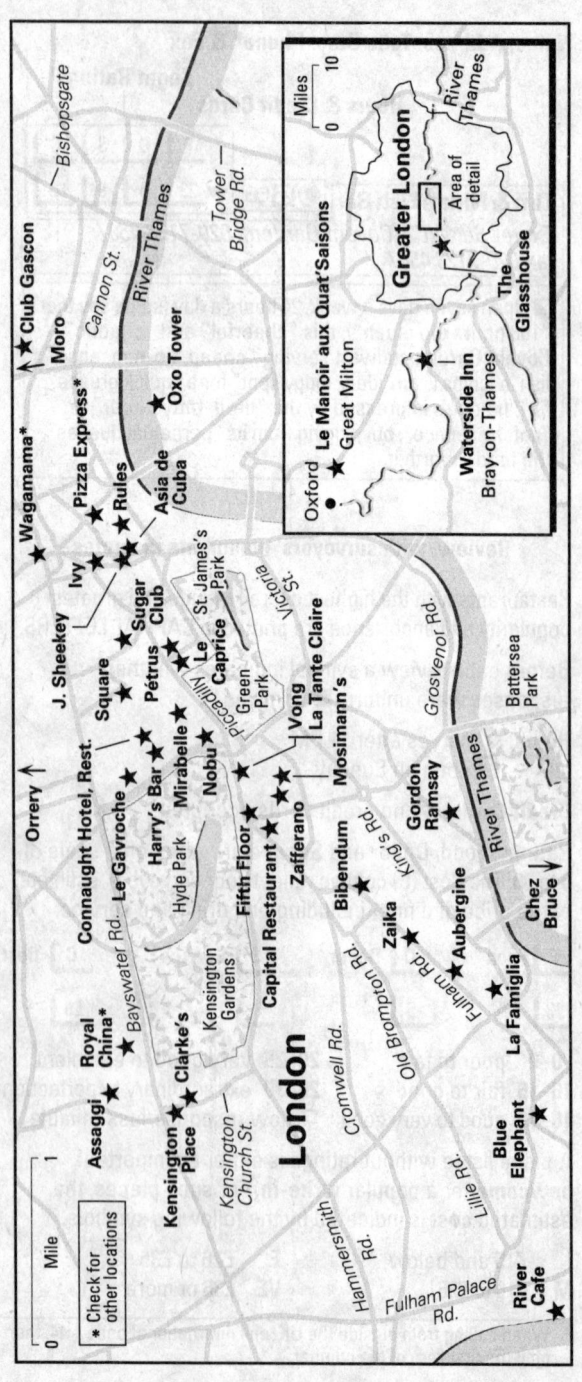

www.zagat.com

Outside London

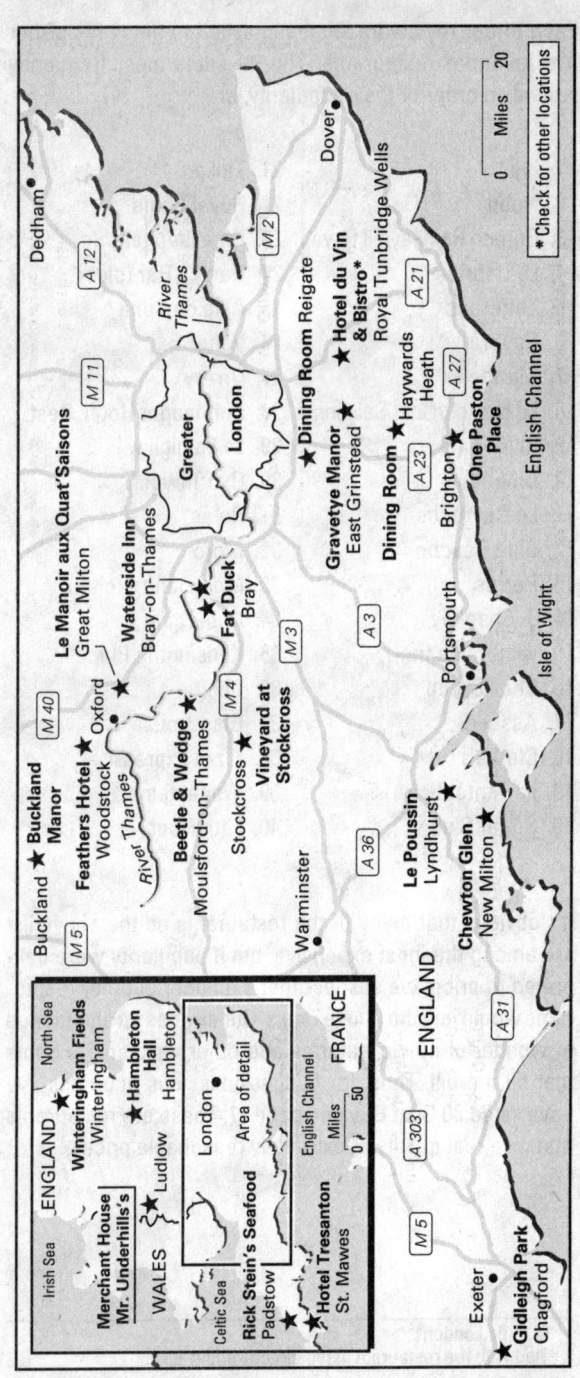

- Dedham
- A 12
- River Thames
- M 11
- Dover
- M 2
- ★ Hotel du Vin & Bistro* Royal Tunbridge Wells
- A 21
- ★ Dining Room Reigate
- Greater London
- ★ Dining Room
- ★ Gravetye Manor East Grinstead
- Haywards Heath
- A 27
- A 23
- ★ One Paston Place Brighton
- A 3
- Portsmouth
- English Channel
- Le Manoir aux Quat'Saisons Great Milton
- ★ Waterside Inn Bray-on-Thames
- ★ Fat Duck Bray
- M 3
- Isle of Wight
- ★ Buckland Manor
- ★ Feathers Hotel Woodstock
- Oxford
- M 40
- ★ Beetle & Wedge Moulsford-on-Thames
- ★ Vineyard at Stockcross
- M 4
- Stockcross
- River Thames
- Buckland
- M 5
- A 36
- Warminster
- ★ Le Poussin Lyndhurst
- ★ Chewton Glen New Milton
- ENGLAND
- A 31

Check for other locations
0 — Miles — 20

Inset map:
- Irish Sea
- North Sea
- ENGLAND
- ★ Winteringham Fields Winteringham
- ★ Hambleton Hall Hambleton
- ★ Merchant House Mr. Underhill's Ludlow
- WALES
- Celtic Sea
- ★ Rick Stein's Seafood Padstow
- ★ Hotel Tresanton St. Mawes
- London
- Area of detail
- English Channel
- FRANCE
- Miles 0 — 50
- ★ Gidleigh Park Chagford
- Exeter
- M 5
- A 303
- A 31

Most Popular

Each of our reviewers has been asked to name his or her five favourite restaurants. The 40 spots most frequently named, in order of their popularity, are:

1. Ivy
2. Nobu
3. Gordon Ramsay/68 Royal
4. Le Caprice
5. Zafferano
6. Square
7. Mirabelle
8. Le Manoir/Quat'Saisons †
9. River Cafe
10. Bibendum
11. Le Gavroche
12. Club Gascon
13. Pétrus
14. J. Sheekey
15. Waterside Inn †
16. Chez Bruce
17. Assaggi
18. Clarke's
19. La Tante Claire
20. Sugar Club*
21. Zaika
22. Royal China
23. Blue Elephant
24. Harry's Bar (club)*
25. Asia de Cuba
26. Vong*
27. Orrery
28. Connaught Hotel, Rest.
29. La Famiglia
30. Oxo Tower*
31. Rules
32. Moro
33. Mosimann's (club)
34. Aubergine
35. Kensington Place*
36. Capital
37. Glasshouse*
38. Pizza Express*
39. Wagamama
40. Fifth Floor

It's obvious that many of the restaurants on the above list are among the most expensive, but if popularity were calibrated to price, we suspect that a number of other restaurants would join the above ranks. Our city has an abundance of wonderful ethnic eateries and other inexpensive spots that fill the bill. Thus, for budget-conscious gourmets, we have listed 80 Best Buys on page 17. These are restaurants that give real quality at extremely reasonable prices.

---

† Outside London
* Tied with the restaurant listed directly above it

Top Ratings

Top lists exclude restaurants with low voting.

Top Food Ranking

28 Gordon Ramsay/68 Royal
27 Pétrus
    Le Manoir/Quat'Saisons †
26 Monsieur Max
    Nobu
    Defune
    Gidleigh Park †
    Le Gavroche*
    Square
    Waterside Inn †
    Clarke's
    Le Soufflé
    Parade
    John Burton-Race
25 Capital
    Chez Bruce
    Chewton Glen, Marryat †
    Aubergine
    Hambleton Hall †
    Miyama
    Pied à Terre*

    Zafferano*
    Oak Room MPW
    Tatsuso
    Assaggi
    Mosimann's (club)
    Foliage
    La Tante Claire
    Zaika
    Rick Stein's Seafood †
24 Harry's Bar (club)
    Four Seasons Chinese
    Gravetye Manor †
    Club Gascon
    Fat Duck †
    Vineyard at Stockcross †
    Connaught Hotel, Rest.
    J. Sheekey
    River Cafe
    Dorchester, Oriental
    Mark's Club (club)*
    Dining Room †

Top Food by Cuisines

British (Modern)
26 Clarke's
    Parade
25 Chez Bruce
24 City Rhodes
23 Richard Corrigan

British (Traditional)
24 Connaught Hotel, Rest.
23 Savoy Grill
22 Dorchester, Grill Room
21 Wilton's
    Guinea

Chinese
24 Four Seasons Chinese
    Dorchester, Oriental
    Royal China
23 Hunan
    Kai

Chophouses
22 Rib Room & Oyster Bar
21 Pope's Eye
    Smiths of Smithfield - Top Fl.
    Guinea
    Rules

Eclectic/International
23 Indigo
    Four Seasons, Lanes
22 Blakes
21 Savoy River Rest.
    Lanesborough Conservatory

Fish 'n' Chips
23 Two Brothers Fish
21 Nautilus Fish
    Sweetings
19 Rudland & Stubbs
18 Fish!

French (Classic)
26 Monsieur Max
    Le Gavroche
    John Burton-Race
25 Aubergine
    La Tante Claire

French (New)
28 Gordon Ramsay/68 Royal
27 Pétrus
26 Square
    Le Soufflé
25 Capital

† Outside London
* Tied with the restaurant listed directly above it

Top Food

Greek
23 Real Greek
20 Kalamaras Taverna
19 Daphne
17 Halepi
   Lemonia

Indian
25 Zaika
24 Sarkhel's
23 Vama
   Rasa
   Tamarind

Italian
25 Zafferano
   Assaggi
24 River Cafe
   Enoteca Turi
23 Neal Street Rest.

Japanese
26 Nobu
   Defune
25 Miyama
   Tatsuso
24 Cafe Japan

Mediterranean
24 Chives
23 Moro
22 Eagle
20 Rocket
19 Nicole's

Mexican/Tex-Mex/SW
20 Montana
17 Dakota
   Canyon
16 Idaho
14 Cafe Pacifico

Middle Eastern
23 Fairuz
22 Al Sultan
21 Beiteddine
   Al Hamra
20 Maroush

Modern European
25 Foliage
24 Ivy
23 Le Caprice
21 Brown's Hotel, Rest. 1837
   Le Pont de la Tour

North American
18 Christopher's
   Arkansas Cafe
16 Joe Allen
   Blues Bistro & Bar
15 PJ's Bar & Grill

Pizza
23 Pizza Metro
20 Basilico
   Red Pepper
   Eco
19 Spiga

Seafood
24 J. Sheekey
21 Wilton's
   Poissonnerie de l'Avenue
   Scotts
   Le Suquet

Spanish
21 Gaudí
   Cambio de Tercio
18 El Blason
   Meson Don Felipe
   Lomo

Thai
23 Vong
22 I-Thai
   Esarn Kheaw
   Patara
21 Blue Elephant

Vegetarian
23 Gate
   Rasa
22 Blah! Blah! Blah!
21 Lanesborough Conservatory
20 Food for Thought

Top Food by Special Features

Breakfast‡
21 Tom's Delicatessen
20 Kensington Place
19 Patisserie Valerie
   Cafe at Sotheby's
18 Bank Aldwych

Brunch
23 Le Caprice
21 Smiths of Smithfield - Top Fl.
   Ransome's Dock
20 Montana
   Villandry

‡ Other than hotels

Cheeseboard

28 Gordon Ramsay/68 Royal
26 Le Gavroche
Square
25 Pied à Terre
23 Orrery

Child Friendly

20 La Famiglia
18 Riccardo's
Fish!
14 Tootsies
13 Sticky Fingers

Hotel Dining

26 Nobu
Metropolitan
Le Soufflé
Hotel Inter-Continental
John Burton-Race
Landmark
25 Capital
Capital Hotel
Oak Room MPW
Le Meridien Piccadilly

In-Store Eating

22 Books for Cooks
Books for Cooks
21 Carluccio's Caffe
Fenwick
20 Fifth Floor
Harvey Nichols
19 Nicole's
Nicole Farhi
Cafe at Sotheby's
Sotheby's Auction House

Lunch Spots

26 Nobu
24 Club Gascon
Ivy
23 Moro
20 Drones

Meet for a Drink

20 Claridge's Bar
19 Avenue
18 Smiths of Smithfield - Top Fl.
17 Che
Oxo Tower Brasserie

Newcomers/Rated

24 Chives
23 Ubon by Nobu
22 Pug
21 Smiths of Smithfield - Top Fl.
20 Drones

Newcomers/Unrated

Cecconi's
Cinnamon Club
Hakkasan
La Trompette
Nahm

Offbeat

24 Club Gascon
22 Books for Cooks
19 Asia de Cuba
Les Trois Garcons
18 Spoon+

Olde England

24 Connaught Hotel, Rest. (1897)
22 Ritz (1906)
21 Wilton's (1742)
Rules (1798)
Sweetings (1889)

Outdoor

24 River Café
21 Smiths of Smithfield - Top Fl.
Le Pont de la Tour
19 La Poule au Pot
18 Spoon+

People-Watching

26 Nobu
24 Ivy
20 Drones
19 San Lorenzo
18 Spoon+

Private Clubs

25 Mosimann's
24 Harry's Bar
Mark's Club
20 Annabel's
19 Home House

Private Rooms

26 Nobu
Square
24 Connaught Hotel, Rest.
23 Mirabelle
21 FireBird

Pub Dining

22 Eagle
21 Guinea
Havelock Tavern
20 Churchill Arms
19 Salusbury Pub

Room with a View

21 Smiths of Smithfield - Top Fl.
Le Pont de la Tour
Putney Bridge
19 Windows on the World
Oxo Tower

Top Food

Sunday Lunch/Town
24 River Cafe
Ivy
23 Glasshouse
21 Wilton's
20 Belvedere

Sunday Lunch/Country
27 Le Manoir/Quat'Saisons
26 Waterside Inn
25 Chewton Glen, Marryat
Hambleton Hall
24 Fat Duck

Tasting Menu
28 Gordon Ramsay/68 Royal
26 Nobu
Square
25 Capital
24 Club Gascon

Tea
Brown's Hotel
Connaught Hotel
Lanesborough Hotel
Ritz Hotel
Savoy Hotel

Theatre District
24 J. Sheekey
Ivy
23 Richard Corrigan
22 Incognico
19 Asia de Cuba

Wine Bars
20 Cellar Gascon
Bleeding Heart
19 L'Estaminet
16 Ebury Wine Bar
Le Metro

Top Food by Locations

Belgravia/Chelsea/South Kensington/Knightsbridge
28 Gordon Ramsay/68 Royal
25 Capital
Aubergine
Zafferano
La Tante Claire

Bloomsbury/Marylebone
26 Defune
John Burton-Race
25 Pied à Terre
24 Royal China
23 Orrery

City/Clerkenwell
25 Tatsuso
24 Club Gascon
City Rhodes
23 City Miyama
Moro

Covent Garden/Soho
24 J. Sheekey
Ivy
23 Richard Corrigan
Neal Street
Savoy Grill

Kensington/Notting Hill
26 Clarke's
25 Assaggi
22 Chez Moi
bali sugar
Launceston Place

Mayfair/Piccadilly/St. James's
27 Pétrus
26 Nobu
Le Gavroche
Square
Le Soufflé

South Bank/Tower Bridge
22 Tentazioni
21 Le Pont de la Tour
19 Butlers Wharf Chop House
Oxo Tower
18 Bengal Clipper

Outside London
27 Le Manoir/Quat'Saisons
Great Milton
26 Gidleigh Park
Devon
Waterside Inn
Bray-on-Thames
25 Chewton Glen, Marryat
New Milton
Hambleton Hall
Hambleton

Top Decor Ranking

27 Les Trois Garcons
Amberley Castle †
26 Hotel Tresanton †
Opium
Mark's Club (club)
25 Criterion Brasserie
Ritz
Mallory Court †
Le Manoir/Quat'Saisons †
24 Momo
Blakes Hotel (SW7)
Gravetye Manor †
Cliveden, Waldo's †
Waterside Inn †
Mosimann's (club)
I-Thai
Pasha (SW7)
Lanesborough Conservatory
Savoy River Rest.
23 Vineyard at Stockcross †

Oak Room MPW
Gidleigh Park †
Home House (club)
Hambleton Hall †
Blue Elephant
Bishopstrow, Mulberry †
Chewton Glen, Marryat †
Gordon Ramsay/68 Royal
Connaught Hotel, Rest.
FireBird
Asia de Cuba
Ye Olde Cheshire Cheese
Oxo Tower
Palm Court
Windows on the World*
22 Putney Bridge
Spoon+
Rules
Belvedere
Dorchester, Oriental

Outdoors

Belvedere
Canyon
Coq d'Argent
Dan's
La Famiglia
Le Colombier
Le Pont de la Tour

Oxo Tower Brasserie
Ransome's Dock
Ritz
River Cafe
Rosmarino
Smiths of Smithfield-Top Fl.
Spoon+

Romance

Andrew Edmunds
Blakes Hotel (SW7)
Club Gascon
Criterion Brasserie
FireBird
Gordon Ramsay/68 Royal
Julie's

La Poule au Pot
Launceston Place
Lundum's
Mirabelle
Odin's
Richard Corrigan
Ritz

Rooms

Asia de Cuba
Aurora
Belvedere
Cecconi's
Cinnamon Club
Criterion Brasserie
Drones

Hakkasan
Lanesborough Conservatory
Les Trois Garcons
Momo
Prism
Ritz
Square

Views

Belair House
Blue Print Cafe
Cafe, Level Seven
Coq d'Argent
Foliage
Le Pont de la Tour
Neat Restaurant

Nobu
Oxo Tower
People's Palace
Putney Bridge
Smiths of Smithfield-Top Fl.
Thai on the River
Ubon by Nobu

---

† Outside London
* Tied with the restaurant listed directly above it

Top Service Ranking

26 Gordon Ramsay/68 Royal
  Chewton Glen, Marryat †

25 Le Gavroche
  Le Manoir/Quat'Saisons †
  Mark's Club (club)
  Waterside Inn †

24 Connaught Hotel, Rest.
  Le Soufflé
  Hambleton Hall †
  John Burton-Race
  Gidleigh Park †
  Capital
  Mosimann's (club)
  Mallory Court †
  La Tante Claire
  Square
  Savoy Grill

23 Annabel's (club)
  Four Seasons, Lanes
  Gravetye Manor †

Dorchester, Oriental
  Harry's Bar (club)
  Ritz*
  Lundum's
  Hotel Tresanton †
  Pétrus
  Vineyard at Stockcross †
  J. Sheekey
  Oslo Court
  Dorchester, Grill Room
  Clarke's
  Ivy
  Oak Room MPW
  Chez Moi

22 Claridge's Bar
  Merchant House †
  Lucknam Park †
  Savoy River Rest.
  Lanesborough Conservatory
  Le Caprice

---

† Outside London
* Tied with the restaurant listed directly above it

Best Buys

Top Bangs for the Buck

List derived by dividing the cost of a meal into its ratings.

1. Soup Opera
2. Soup Works
3. Pret à Manger
4. Starbucks
5. Coffee Republic
6. Costa Coffee
7. Caffè Nero
8. Aroma
9. Maison Bertaux
10. Troubadour
11. Little Bay
12. Churchill Arms
13. Busaba Eathai
14. Arkansas Cafe
15. Food for Thought
16. Ravi Shankar
17. Ed's Easy Diner
18. Costa's Grill
19. Chutney's
20. Tom's Delicatessen
21. Wagamama
22. Cranks
23. Patisserie Valerie
24. Great Nepalese
25. Jenny Lo's Tea House
26. Pepper Tree
27. Books for Cooks
28. DKNY Bar
29. La Porchetta Pizzeria
30. Tuk Tuk Thai
31. Lahore Kebab House
32. Alounak
33. Carluccio's Caffe
34. Chelsea Bun
35. Mildreds
36. Duke of Cambridge (SW11)
37. Basilico
38. Pizza Express
39. Sporting Page
40. Giraffe

Additional Good Values

Anglesea Arms
Aperitivo
Belgo Noord
Bombay Bicycle Club
Cafe at Sotheby's
Cellar Gascon
Chelsea Ram
Chiang Mai
Eagle
Eco
Engineer
Esarn Kheaw
Fairuz
Four Seasons Chinese
Gate
Hakkasan
Harrods
Havelock Tavern
Ifield
itsu

Joy King Lau
Lee Fook
Lemonia
Made in Italy
Maroush
Meson Don Felipe
Nautilus Fish
Parisienne Chophouse
Pizza Metro
Randall & Aubin
Rasa
Red Pepper
Rocket
Rodizio Rico
Royal China
Salusbury Pub
Spiga
Tabla
Truc Vert
Zaika Bazaar

Restaurant Directory

London

		F	D	S	C
Abeno [S]	▽	16	12	18	£17

47 Museum St., WC1 (Tottenham Court Rd.), 020-7405 3211; fax 020-7405 3212

■ It "may be small", but this "humble spot" in Bloomsbury comes "highly recommended" on account of its "warm atmosphere" and "fascinating", "authentic" *okonomi-yaki* – "pancake-things" (a cross between a Spanish omelette and Japanese pizza) "cooked at your table"; N.B. a post-*Survey* refurbishment may outdate the above decor score.

	F	D	S	C
Abingdon, The [S]	18	15	14	£27

54 Abingdon Rd., W8 (High St. Kensington), 020-7937 3339; fax 020-7795 6388

◪ "Kensington types" convene at this "boisterous", "no-fuss" "hangout" with "the feel of a well-loved local pub", which loyalists laud as a "reasonably priced" source of Modern European fare that's "ok for a casual dinner", however a few lament "unpredictable" service.

	F	D	S	C
Adams Cafe	14	8	18	£18

77 Askew Rd., W12 (Ravenscourt Park/Shepherd's Bush), 020-8743 0572; fax 020-8743 0572

■ A "simple but delightful" formula engages those who know this "basic" Shepherd's Bush eaterie: it's a cafe by day, but by night it becomes a restaurant that "specialises in Moroccan" and "Tunisian food and wine"; if the interior "looks a little tired", the "charming staff" compensate.

	F	D	S	C
Admiral Codrington, The [S]	17	17	16	£26

17 Mossop St., SW3 (South Kensington), 020-7581 0005; fax 020-7589 2452

◪ "This is not your grandfather's pub" declare veterans of the "mad bar scene" in the front of this "buzzy" Modern European gastro-pub in Chelsea that also has a "serene dining room" at the rear complete with a "wonderful sliding roof" and an outside patio that's "a treat in good weather"; as for the cuisine, voters are divided ("not great" vs. "lovely").

	F	D	S	C
Admiralty, The ◐ [S]	18	18	16	£35

Somerset House, The Strand, WC2 (Temple), 020-7845 4646; fax 020-7845 4647

◪ Everyone agrees that this historic building on The Strand is a "fabulous site" for an eaterie, but many feel Oliver Peyton's "austere" French Regional cooking is "not all it's cracked up to be", complaining of "slow service" and a "pricey" menu; still, the food's "fairly interesting", and the arrival of a new chef may further the kitchen's "flair."

Aix-en-Provence [S] ▽ 18 19 20 £39

(fka Room at the Halcyon)
Halcyon Hotel, 129 Holland Park Ave., W11 (Holland Park), 020-7727 7288; fax 020-7229 8516

◩ Ex-Ivy chef Nigel Davies has set up shop in the Halcyon Hotel's lower-ground dining room following a revamp (and a name change) that inaugurated a seasonal Provençal menu, "something different" from the previous regime's heavier French cooking; ensconced in leafy Holland Park, it boasts quite "nice atmosphere."

Alastair Little 22 14 18 £38

49 Frith St., W1 (Tottenham Court Rd.), 020-7734 5183; fax 020-7734 5206

◩ "He may be Little, but he's big on flavour" fawn fans of Alastair Little's "elegant" and "eccentric" "Soho classic" (since '85) that's home to "adventurous", "always enjoyable" Modern British cooking; style mavens tell another storey, though, lamenting the "austere" environs that inspire responses from "bland" and "poky" to downright "grim."

Alastair Little at Lancaster Rd. [S] 20 13 17 £33

136A Lancaster Rd., W11 (Ladbroke Grove), 020-7243 2220; fax 020-7792 4535

◩ Perhaps it's "not quite as cool as it thinks it is", but Alastair Little's second Modern British venue, a "small but intimate" Notting Hill eaterie, still finds plenty of supporters for its "confident and assured" cuisine; detractors, in equal numbers, disparage the room as "cramped" and the menu as "overpriced" and find the place is sometimes let down by "erratic" and "moody" service.

Alba 19 12 18 £31

107 Whitecross St., EC1 (Barbican/Moorgate), 020-7588 1798; fax 020-7638 5793

■ "In the food desert of the Barbican", this low-key Italian comes as an oasis of "passionate cooking" amid "cheerful" (if not elegant) surroundings; its ever-changing menu features "good-value Piedmont food", including "excellent" truffle dishes, and is nicely complemented by a "great wine list."

Al Duca [S] 19 15 16 £32

4-5 Duke of York St., SW1 (Green Park/Piccadilly Circus), 020-7839 3090; fax 020-7839 4050

■ "A consistent performer" with prices that don't require "re-mortgaging", this "efficient" St. James's Italian is "popular" with "office workers who do lunch" on its "well-cooked", "no-surprises" fare; its attempt at "sleek, sophisticated surroundings" "falls short", however, with style-watchers finding it "rather clinical" and "cramped."

Alfred 16 | 11 | 15 | £25

245 Shaftesbury Ave., WC2 (Tottenham Court Rd.), 020-7240 2566; fax 020-7497 0672

■ "Quirky" eats are available at this "steady, reliable" British eaterie in a "gastronomic backwater" at the top of Shaftesbury Avenue; the "canteen-like" cafe is "handy" for "lunchtime lingering with bangers 'n' mash" or as a "pre- or post-theatre spot."

Al Hamra ◐ [S] 21 | 14 | 16 | £31

31-33 Shepherd Mkt., W1 (Green Park), 020-7493 1954; fax 020-7493 1044

■ "When you can dine outside" "on a summer evening", "go hungry and with a lover" to this Shepherd Market Middle Eastern "godsend" that serves "great grub" "comparable to anything found in Lebanon"; "shame about the staff", however – in the "bazaar-like atmosphere" they can be "rushed" and "almost blunt."

All Bar One 11 | 12 | 10 | £14

48 Leicester Sq., WC2 (Leicester Sq.), 020-7747 9921; fax 020-7747 9920 [S]

126-128 Notting Hill Gate, W11 (Notting Hill Gate), 020-7313 9362; fax 020-7792 2104 [S]

7-9 Paddington St., W1 (Baker St.), 020-7487 0071; fax 020-7486 6960 [S]

289-293 Regent St., W1 (Oxford Circus), 020-7467 9901; fax 020-7636 8213 [S]

587-591 Fulham Rd., SW6 (Fulham Broadway), 020-7471 0611; fax 020-7385 2221 [S]

311-313 Fulham Rd., SW1 (Fulham Broadway), 020-7349 1751; fax 020-7349 9776 [S]

1 Liverpool Rd., N1 (Angel), 020-7843 0021; fax 020-7278 5869 [S]

44-46 Ludgate Hill, EC4 (St. Paul's), 020-7653 9901; fax 020-7248 0667

93A Charterhouse St., EC1 (Farringdon), 020-7553 9391; fax 020-7250 1234

42 MacKenzie Walk, E14 (Canary Wharf), 020-7513 0911; fax 020-7512 9278 [S]

Additional locations throughout London

◪ "They get a lot of flak," but their "predictable" pub grub "really isn't that bad" say defenders of this "inexpensive" chain of "late '90s–bland" wine bars that are also popular for Sunday brunches; critics call them the "Jekyll and Hyde of the bar world", with venues varying from "relaxing hangouts" to "vast, echoing barns full of squawking rabble."

Alloro 22 | 19 | 19 | £37

19-20 Dover St., W1 (Green Park), 020-7495 4768; fax 020-7629 5348

◪ This "attractive" Italian makes chums with its "beautifully balanced" meals, "professional service" and "bar that's fab for falling in love"; foes find that Zafferano's "overpriced", "short-menued" cousin "takes itself too seriously."

Alounak ◑ⓢ
20　11　14　£16

10 Russell Gardens, W14 (Olympia), 020-7603 1130
44 Westbourne Grove, W2 (Bayswater), 020-7229 4158;
fax 020-7792 1219

■ A "cosmopolitan" clientele crowds this "throbbing" Persian pair of "madhouses" in Olympia and Westbourne Grove offering "generous portions" of "authentically prepared", "delicious specialties", particularly the "stupendous meat dishes"; with a universally appreciated BYO policy, these "bustling" twins are "cheap" enough that most don't mind overlooking "bland decor" and "dour" staff.

Al San Vincenzo
21　12　17　£39

30 Connaught St., W2 (Marble Arch), 020-7262 9623

■ It may be "the size of a hotel room", but this "tiny", "unpretentious" Bayswater Italian cooks up "fantastic" fare that's far from room-service average; Neapolitan "home-cooked" "miracle" meals and "excellent wines" "seem to magically appear", proffered by "friendly staff" that make you feel "like one of the family."

Al Sultan ⓢ
22　14　17　£28

51-52 Hertford St., W1 (Green Park), 020-7408 1155;
fax 020-7408 1113

☑ Snacking film buffs deem this Shepherd Market Middle Eastern "decent" "for a nice bottle of wine and assorted Lebanese starters before or after a movie at the Curzon next door"; "clean, fresh" cooking and "professional service" are the main attraction, although its "simple surroundings" may be the reason frugal critics pan it as "too expensive."

Al Waha ◑ⓢ
–　–　–　M

75 Westbourne Grove, W2 (Bayswater/Queensway),
020-7229 0806

This Westbourne Grove Lebanese packs a lot of flavour into its small, intimate space split over two levels: its varied menu is overflowing with scores of mezze and main-course choices, all offered at reasonable prices; there are also pavement tables for outside dining, and it delivers locally.

Amandier
17　13　17　£40

26 Sussex Pl., W2 (Lancaster Gate), 020-7262 6073;
fax 020-7723 8395

Bistro Daniel
–　–　–　E

26 Sussex Pl., W2 (Lancaster Gate), 020-7262 6073;
fax 020-7723 8395

☑ Loyalists insist that Daniel Gobet "can't go wrong" with the "melt-in-your-mouth" French classics and "extensive wine list" at his "small, comfortable" eaterie in Bayswater; the less-enamoured find it a "letdown from his King's Road days" at La Ciboulette; N.B. the cellar bistro offers an open fire and lower-priced Provençal menu.

Amphitheatre, The ▽ | 14 | 16 | 14 | £36 |
Royal Opera House, Covent Garden, WC2 (Covent Garden),
020-7212 9254; fax 020 7212 9239

☑ The Royal Opera House's top-floor Modern British may be little-known as yet, but the lunchers and evening ticket-holders who've already discovered it are more enamoured with the "romantic, magical experience" of "dining on the balcony" than with Searcy's "cafeteria-style" cuisine.

Andrew Edmunds S | 20 | 18 | 17 | £28 |
46 Lexington St., W1 (Oxford Circus/Piccadilly Circus),
020-7437 5708

◼ "You know what you're going to get" at this "romantic" British-Eclectic "gem" in Soho, and "if you're short on height, pretension and money", "it's what you want": a well-priced, "interesting seasonal" menu, lots of "old-world atmosphere" – "charm, character", "candle wax" – and a decided "lack of legroom."

Anglesea Arms S | 18 | 14 | 13 | £20 |
35 Wingate Rd., W6 (Ravenscourt Park), 020-8749 1291;
fax 020-8749 1254

◼ "Get there early for a seat" at this "traditional London" gastro-pub in Shepherd's Bush offering "fab" Modern British fare with "more adventure than most", though "furnishings" of "stripped pine, bare boards and blackboards" are "predictably basic"; "service is terrible more often than not", and snobs snub the "cigarette-and-beer atmosphere."

Annabel's ◗ | 20 | 20 | 23 | £59 |
Private club; inquiries: 020-7629 1096,

☑ "Still permanently busy with the pretty people" (along with a few who're "past their sell-by date"), this "magical" Mayfair nightclub remains "great for an evening out" thanks to "impeccable service" and European cooking that's "amazingly good for a club"; "expense-account" prices mean some prefer to "go for the dancing, not the food."

Aperitivo | – | – | – | M |
41-45 Beak St., W1 (Piccadilly Circus), 020-7287 2057;
fax 020-7287 1767

On the former premises of Leith's Soho near Regent Street, this casual, friendly newcomer serves "generous portions" of Italian tapas-style dishes that go "beyond the ordinary" and are well-suited to speedy dining, particularly pre-theatre.

Aquarium S | 18 | 17 | 15 | £33 |
Ivory House, St. Katharine's Dock, E1 (Tower Hill),
020-7480 6116; fax 020-7480 5973

☑ With "interesting views over St. Katharine's Dock" and "lovely" first-come, first-serve seating on the waterside terrace, this "informal" seafooder has followers praising "fantastic" fish fare that's good for an after–sight-seeing bite near the Tower; finicky fanatics find it a "dull", "slow" flop.

Aquasia S   ▽ | 20 | 20 | 18 | £41 |

*Conrad International Hotel, Chelsea Harbour, SW10
(Fulham Broadway), 020-7823 3000; fax 020-7351 6525*

■ "The Riviera comes to London" with an unusual
Med-Asian menu and waterfront seating at Chelsea
Harbour's newest eaterie, inside the Conrad International
Hotel; it's a "bit out-of-the-way" but "deserves to be busier",
as it's "good for a hotel" and its "sophisticated" kitchen
will accommodate even an order for "a burger if you ask."

Arancia S   ▽ | 21 | 17 | 19 | £22 |

*52 Southwark Park Rd., SE16 (Bermondsey),
020-7394 1751; fax 020-7394 1044*

■ Though it "looks like a run-down cafe from the outside",
the interior of this "cosy, little gem in Bermondsey" is
"ideal for a romantic tête-à-tête" over an "interesting,
rustic" Italian menu that's "small" but nevertheless
includes "something to tempt everyone"; "save room
for the semifreddo", because at "miniscule" prices like
these, you can afford dessert.

Arcadia S | 16 | 16 | 17 | £27 |

*35 Kensington High St., W8 (High St. Kensington),
020-7937 4294; fax 020-7937 4393*

■ Chatty parrots and "beautiful dogs" are the "unusual"
regulars roaming this "reliable", "imaginative" Kensington
spot with an International menu, a "jewel to be shared
with close friends"; when surveyors note "exceptionally
attentive service", they're probably not referring to the
"great golden retrievers" who keep you company "while
you wait for the bill."

Archduke, The S | 12 | 12 | 14 | £19 |

*Concert Hall Approach, South Bank, SE1 (Waterloo),
020-7928 9370; fax 020-7928 0839*

■ "Neither good nor bad, but consistent" sums up
views on this "lively", if "unsophisticated", bistro serving
Modern British bites under the railway arches near
Waterloo; "moderately priced" and "convenient after a
Royal Festival Hall concert" or a spin on "the London
Eye", it's sometimes "swamped with casual customers."

Archipelago | – | – | – | VE |

(fka Birdcage)
*110 Whitfield St., W1 (Goodge St./Warren St.), 020-7383 3346;
fax 020-7383 7181*

At *Survey* time, Fitzrovia's "quirky" Birdcage "changed
ownership", started "trading under a different name" and
ushered in a new chef – whose New French cooking diners
can only hope will "rumble through the culinary jungle"
as in the old days – but it's retained the same "utterly
bizarre" decor; time will tell whether the new incarnation
enthralls; N.B. a lounge has been added downstairs.

ArdRí at the O'Conor Don ▽ 15 | 15 | 13 | £26

88 Marylebone Ln., W1 (Baker St./Bond St.), 020-7935 9311; fax 020-7486 6706

◪ Get "good pints of Guinness" and "wholesome" Irish-influenced "comfort" cuisine at this "cosy" first-floor dining room above a Marylebone pub; among the complaints: confused customers wish they'd clear up some of the "blarney" on the "overcomplicated" menu.

Ark [S] 17 | 16 | 17 | £31

122 Palace Gardens Terrace, W8 (Notting Hill Gate), 020-7229 4024; fax 020-7792 8787

◪ Revamped after its takeover by Bar Bourse in 2000, this "cheerful, relaxing" Kensington Modern Italian is "prettier than when it was" owned by Jean-Christophe Novelli; "crowded" with diners two-by-two, it's "perfect for a first date", and though "compelling servers" are "soft on the eyes", the cuisine can be "inconsistent."

Arkansas Cafe [S] 18 | 8 | 15 | £13

107B Commercial St., Old Spitalfields Mkt., E1 (Liverpool St.), 020-7377 6999; fax 020-7377 6999

■ Yankees yip "yee-haw" for "real down-home" BBQ at this lunch-only, "rough 'n' ready" joint near Spitalfields Market, where American owner Bubba is said to serve the "best barbecue this side of the Atlantic" and the "best char-grilled burger" in town; N.B. it's not open for Saturday lunch.

Aroma [S]≠ 10 | 11 | 11 | £8

125 The Strand, Wellington House, WC2 (Charing Cross), 020-7836 8852; fax 020-7836 8202

37 Bedford St., WC2 (Charing Cross/Covent Garden), 020-7836 8816; fax 020-7836 8820

1 Wrights Ln., Kensington, W8 (High St. Kensington), 020-7937 1605; fax 020-7937 1641

21 James St., W1 (Green Park), 020-7487 2685; fax 020-7487 2686

168 Piccadilly, W1 (Green Park/Piccadilly Circus), 020-7493 0250; fax 020-7493 0278

273 Regent St., W1 (Oxford Circus), 020-7499 6822; fax 020-7499 6823

187 Tottenham Court Rd., W1 (Tottenham Court Rd.), 020-7637 3346; fax 020-7637 3350

132 Brompton Rd., SW3 (Knightsbridge), 020-7581 9920; fax 020-7581 7927

138A Kings Rd., SW3 (Sloane Sq.), 020-7581 2718; fax 020-7581 2802

60 Fleet St., EC4 (Chancery Ln.), 020-7583 5959; fax 020-7583 5962

Additional locations throughout London

◪ "Bright and breezy", "cheap and cheerful" as the fast-food behemoth that owns them, this "mainstream" McCoffee chain serves "good coffee" in "colourful cups" and "ok sandwiches"; the unimpressed ask "can we blame McDonald's" for the "disappointing" brews and "inedible" edibles at these "run-of-the-mill" shops?

Aroma Chinese [S] | 18 | 10 | 14 | £20

11 Gerrard St., W1 (Leicester Sq.), 020-7439 2720;
fax 020-7437 0377 ◐
39 Gerrard St., W1 (Leicester Sq.), 020-7439 0534
118 Shaftesbury Ave., W1 (Leicester Sq.), 020-7437 0377;
fax 020-7437 0377 ◐

◪ Whilst the "extensive" multiregional Chinese choices at this trio of "efficient" Chinatown/Soho eateries include "nice noodles" and "good fish", culinary critics find the "basic" cooking "a bit soulless"; the "bright, modern environment" is "ideal" "with a crowd", though "very attentive" service can err on the side of "pushy."

Artigiano [S] | 18 | 18 | 17 | £32

12A Belsize Terrace, NW3 (Belsize Park/Swiss Cottage),
020-7794 4288; fax 020-7435 2048

■ "High standards" are "welcome" in Belsize Park, where this "chichi" Italian is one of the better options for dining; service varies from "witty" to "off", but "well-executed" cooking offers "consistent style and quality" amid decor so "smart" that diners "feel like they've been cast in the next *Star Trek* film"; N.B. the glass frontage folds open on warm days.

ASIA DE CUBA ◐ **[S]** | 19 | 23 | 16 | £44

St. Martin's Lane Hotel, 45 St. Martin's Ln., WC2 (Leicester Sq.),
020-7300 5588; fax 020-7300 5540

◪ The "kickin' scene" is "always an experience" at this hot spot inside Ian Schrager's "glamorous" St. Martin's Lane Hotel, where the "bizarre blend" of Asian and Cuban cuisines is "better than sex" to some; those less enchanted with the "expense" and "pretense" sniff that Philippe Starck's "wacky interior is perfect" "to see and be seen" in, but "you can't eat the pretty people."

Ask Pizza [S] | 14 | 13 | 13 | £16

145 Notting Hill Gate, W11 (Notting Hill Gate),
020-7371 0392 ◐
222 Kensington High St., W8 (High St. Kensington),
020-7937 5540; fax 020-7937 5540 ◐
219-221 Chiswick High Rd., W4 (Turnham Green),
020-8742 1323 ◐
121-125 Park St., W1 (Marble Arch), 020-7495 7760;
fax 020-7495 7760 ◐
48 Grafton Way, W1 (Warren St.), 020-7388 8108;
fax 020-7388 8112 ◐
1 Gloucester Arcade, SW7 (Gloucester Rd.),
020-7835 0840 ◐
345 Fulham Palace Rd., SW6 (Hammersmith/Putney Bridge),
020-7371 0392 ◐
300 King's Rd., SW3 (Sloane Sq.), 020-7349 9123 ◐

(continued)

(continued)
Ask Pizza
*160-162 Victoria St., SW1 (St. James's Park/Victoria),
020-7630 8228; fax 020-7630 8228
216 Haverstock Hill, NW3 (Belsize Park/Chalk Farm),
020-7433 3896; fax 020-7435 6490* ◗
Additional locations throughout London
■ If you have to ask, you must not get out much, since
this Italian chain is "dotted everywhere"; with "no
pretensions" toward greatness, it's just "perfect for what it
is": "reasonably scrummy pasta" and "solid pizza for the
not-very-fussy" served "quickly" in "airy" venues "before
the cinema" or "with the kids."

ASSAGGI | 25 | 17 | 21 | £42 |
39 Chepstow Pl., W2 (Notting Hill Gate), 020-7792 5501
☑ The fact that it's "extremely difficult to get a table" in its
"tiny", "unassuming" Notting Hill room speaks volumes
about this "all-around Italian pleaser" where "authentic",
"spectacular" fare is prepared with "passion and care" and
"service is entertaining and kind"; "the monthlong wait to
get in is worth it" for "sheer joy" that's "so simple, so fresh,
so perfect", although frugal foodies find it "sooo expensive."

Atlantic Bar & Grill ◗**S** | 15 | 18 | 13 | £37 |
*20 Glasshouse St., W1 (Piccadilly Circus), 020-7734 4888;
fax 020-7734 5400*
☑ "Keep your tongue firmly in cheek" at this "cavernous",
"crowded" Modern British restaurant/bar in Piccadilly
that's "had its heyday" but is still "cool" enough to feel
"like a movie set" packed with "beautiful people"; the
"loud" bar is loads of "fun", but it's also a "nice place to
spend a lot of money": "girlfriend loves it, wallet hates it!"

Atrium | 14 | 15 | 12 | £31 |
4 Millbank, SW1 (Westminster), 020-7223 0032; fax 020-7223 0010
☑ Though in an "odd setting" (the atrium of a Westminster
office block), this Traditional British dining room serves as
an unofficial "annex to Parliament", attracting a steady
stream of peckish politicians; whilst partisans proclaim it
"tries hard to do something a little different", oppositionists
counter it's "nothing to write home about" and warn the
service "can be slow" and "uptight."

Attica ◗ | – | – | – | E |
*14-16 Foubert's Pl., W1 (Oxford Circus/Piccadilly Circus),
020-7287 6983*
In danger of being overshadowed by its adjoining private
members' nightclub that's become an instant hot ticket,
this stylish, laid-back newcomer just off Carnaby Street
has a dark, moody interior – complete with smoked mirrors
and leather seating – and a punchy menu of Modern
European dishes, which patrons can watch being cooked
in the open kitchen.

AUBERGINE
25　20　22　£55

11 Park Walk, SW10 (Gloucester Rd./South Kensington), 020-7352 3449; fax 020-7351 1770

☑ "If you want to impress", surveyors suggest this "robustly elegant" Chelsea "classic" as a "top-class" option, thanks to William Drabble's "stunningly" "sublime" French cuisine; overall, the consensus is that it's "not missing Gordon Ramsay" (the since "decamped" chef who put it on the map), though there are more than a few complaints about "outrageous prices" and "condescending" attitude from its otherwise "extremely efficient" staff.

Aurora
19　19　17　£42

Great Eastern Hotel, 40 Liverpool St., EC2 (Liverpool St.), 020-7618 7000; fax 020-7618 7001

☑ Above Liverpool Street Station in the Great Eastern Hotel dwells Sir Terence Conran's "grown-up" Modern European dining room, a "grand", "airy" space with "sumptuous" architectural details (mosaic floors, stained-glass dome) that make it "terrific visually"; surveyors are of two minds regarding the menu, however ("fabulous", "well-prepared" vs. "no real depth"), but most agree "too many suits" in the crowd make it "better for business than romance."

Avenue ●S
19　18　16　£39

7-9 St. James's St., SW1 (Green Park), 020-7321 2111; fax 020-7321 2500

☑ Perfect for "people-watching" amid a "swirling cacophony" of "clinking and shouting", this big, "brash" St. James's "media hangout" dishes up Modern British cooking that's "surprisingly good" for a "trendy mass eaterie"; though the "gorgeous staff" "looks disappointed if you're not famous", it's a favourite of "City whiz kids at play" and "trainee Rupert Murdochs working their lunch breaks."

Axis ●
21　20　19　£41

One Aldwych Hotel, 1 Aldwych, WC2 (Charing Cross/ Covent Garden), 020-7300 0300; fax 020-7300 0301

☑ "A heaven of tranquillity compared to other Theatreland" haunts, this "hip" Eclectic–Modern British dining room in the One Aldwych Hotel boasts a "consistently" good menu and a "very smart" interior centred around a "modern mural"; the general consensus is it's "excellent for business" or "before the theatre", though quibblers quip the service can be "so slow you need to pack sandwiches."

Aykoku-Kaku
18　12　16　£30

Bucklersbury House, 9 Walbrook, EC4 (Bank), 020-7236 9020; fax 020-7489 8040

■ Something of a "relic from the '70s", this large City lunchtime favourite still produces "quality" Japanese fare, which is served up with "very fast service"; regulars happily overlook the "bland" decor for "genuine" sushi, "tasty" teppanyaki and set-price lunches in the canteen.

Ayoush S
13 | 20 | 14 | £25

59 James St., W1 (Bond St.), 020-7935 9839; fax 020-7935 1708

■ "You come for the" "North African atmosphere, with belly dancing" (on Friday and Saturday nights) at this exotic Mayfair eaterie, "rather than" the somewhat "disappointing" tagines and other Moroccan-Tunisian classics; still, given the "bizarre" (in a good way) decor and diverting entertainment, many find it a worthy destination; N.B. there's a private members' club in the basement.

Babe Ruth's S
9 | 11 | 10 | £20

172-176 The Highway, E1 (Shadwell), 020-7481 8181; fax 020-7481 9800

■ "Babe himself would have done better" fume those frustrated with this "formula" sports bar in Wapping, which strikes out with "little atmosphere", "mediocre service" and a "bland, boring", "overpriced" menu offering "poor attempts at American fare"; "distractions" for the kids such as a "mini–basketball court" keep parents "happy."

Back to Basics
▽ 18 | 9 | 15 | £25

21A Foley St., W1 (Oxford Circus), 020-7436 2181; fax 020-7436 2180

■ Fans feel fond of the "fantastic fish" at this Fitzrovian seafooder whose "somewhat plain interior doesn't do justice" to its "innovative combinations" of "extremely fresh" fare; though it's still little-known, selfish surveyors sigh this "small corner" spot is "getting too popular."

Bah Humbug S
20 | 21 | 18 | £25

The Crypt, St. Matthews Church, SW2 (Brixton), 020-7738 3184; fax 020-7733 1141

■ Nestled in an "atmospheric crypt" beneath Brixton's St. Matthew's Church, this Modern British "find" features "great" Vegetarian dishes and a few fish selections, and its "trendy" Bug Bar boasts live-music nights; though some find the red-velvet, candlelit "ambience slightly gloomy", most say "it's worth going" just for the "Gothic romanticism."

Balans S
15 | 12 | 16 | £20

187 Kensington High St., W8 (High St. Kensington), 020-7376 0115; fax 020-7938 4653 ●
60 Old Compton St., W1 (Leicester Sq./Piccadilly Circus), 020-7437 5212; fax 020-7734 2665 ●
239 Old Brompton Rd., SW5 (Earl's Court), 020-7244 8838; fax 020-7584 8778 ●
239 Brompton Rd., SW3 (Knightsbridge/South Kensington), 020-7584 0070; fax 020-7584 8778

☑ "A camp welcome" awaits groupies of this "groovy" cafe chain's "always busy" outposts and its "decent" Modern British "comfort food"; bashers bemoan "hit-or-miss" fare, suggesting the "spunky", "cute waiters have attitude problems"; still, they're "favourite late-night" "pop-ins" that are "great" for "all-day" "American-style breakfasts."

bali sugar [S] 22 17 19 £37

33A All Saints Rd., W11 (Westbourne Park), 020-7221 4477; fax 020-7221 9955

■ "Innovative", often "amazing" Pacific Rim "fusion" cooking makes for "enjoyable meals" at this "minimalist" Sugar Club sibling near Westbourne Grove, an "intimate", "romantically lit" spot that most find "charming" (if "a bit cramped"); whilst a few detractors say "some dishes work brilliantly, [but] others miss the mark", everyone agrees the rear garden courtyard is "great in summer."

Baltic ◐ [S] – – – E

74 Blackfriars Rd., SE1 (Southwark), 020-7928 1111

From the owners of Wòdka comes this airy, high-ceilinged Southwark newcomer sporting a gutsy Eastern European menu of dishes from the various Baltic nations and, of course, the obligatory list of iced, flavoured vodkas; its attractive bar makes a handy pit stop for visitors to the Tate Modern museum nearby.

Bam-Bou ◐ 17 22 14 £35

1 Percy St., W1 (Tottenham Court Rd.), 020-7323 9130; fax 020-7323 9140

◪ Whilst almost all agree the "brilliantly designed" interior of this "beautiful", "exotic" French-Vietnamese in a Fitzrovian townhouse "has special charm", sceptics assert it's "losing its allure" as a result of "expensive", "often-patchy" food served in "Lilliputian portions" by "slightly snarly staff"; proponents praise the "authentic flavours" of its "great" dishes and give the "good bar scene" a thumbs-up for "group nights out."

Bangkok Restaurant 19 12 14 £24

9 Bute St., SW7 (South Kensington), 020-7584 8529

■ "Still good after all these years", this "veteran" Thai pioneer, which opened in South Kensington in '67, remains "better than most" of its competitors thanks to its "genuine", "consistently" "tasty" cooking at "sensible prices"; though even fans complain of "cramped seating" and suggest the "unexciting decor" "needs a freshen-up", the fact that the place is "always busy" speaks volumes.

Bank Aldwych ◐ [S] 18 18 17 £35

1 Kingsway, WC2 (Holborn), 020-7379 9797; fax 020-7240 7001

◪ Those who "like it big and brassy" say this Aldwych "expense-accounter" "succeeds well" with its "satisfying" Modern British cuisine and "professional" service, but detractors declare the "bank has gone bust", decrying "mediocre" fare and an interior in need of "soundproofing"; still, for "power breakfasts", "business lunches" and "pre-theatre dinners", many report "good bang for the buck."

Bankside $\boxed{S}$ – | – | – | E

32 Southwark Bridge Rd., SE1 (London Bridge), 020-7633 0011
In a former office near the Tate Modern in Southwark, this
warm, easygoing restaurant and all-day-dining brasserie
has made a promising debut, serving "good" International
fusion cuisine that's deemed "excellent value for the money"
by early visitors (particularly the £10 set-price lunch); N.B.
there's live jazz on Saturday nights.

Bank Westminster &   17 | 18 | 16 | £35
Zander Bar ◐ $\boxed{S}$

45 Buckingham Gate, SW1 (St. James's Park),
020-7379 9797; fax 020-7240 7001
◪ This Bank Aldwych sibling near Buckingham Palace
boasts the longest bar in Europe (48 metres) and an airy
brasserie with decor wittily described as "*Barbarella* meets
the Savoy"; regarding the Modern British menu, whilst
some find the "great choice of fish" "enjoyable", others
think this "expense-accounter" should "concentrate on the
bar", which is "impossibly cool" and "busy" most nights.

Bar Bourse   16 | 13 | 15 | £27

67 Queen St., EC4 (Cannon St./Mansion House),
020-7248 2200; fax 020-7248 2211
◪ Supporters of this L-shaped basement restaurant/bar
call it quite a "nice" "City watering hole" boasting "good"
Modern British fare and a "place-to-be-seen" ambience;
contrarians counter it's "cramped" and "expensive for what
it is"; N.B. closed weekends.

Barcelona Tapas Bar   17 | 12 | 15 | £20

481 Lordship Ln., SE22 (Dulwich B.R.), 020-8693 5111;
fax 020-7721 8673 $\boxed{S}$
13 Well Ct., EC4 (Bank/Mansion House), 020-7329 5111;
fax 020-7729 8673
15 Botolph St., EC3 (Aldgate/Liverpool St.), 020-7377 5222;
fax 020-7721 8673
1A Bell Ln., E1 (Aldgate East/Liverpool St.), 020-7247 7014;
fax 020-7721 8673
◼ This "tightly packed" City trio (and a quieter Dulwich
outpost) "caters to all tastes – meat eaters, vegetarians" –
with a "vast selection of tapas" washed down with
"good Spanish wines" and served by "friendly" staff;
some report "inconsistent quality among the locations."

Bar Madrid ◐   13 | 12 | 13 | £22

4 Winsley St., W1 (Oxford Circus), 020-7436 4649;
fax 020-7323 3207
◪ Fine-dining aficionados find forays to this "friendly",
"feisty" "flamenco-and-fajitas" spot off Oxford Street
"disappointing", as the "eclectic (to say the least) menu" of
Spanish tapas and Tex-Mex tastes plays second fiddle to the
tequila, the sangria and the "let-your-hair-down" mood;
still, party people proclaim it's "lots of fun" for a "night out."

Base 🅂   ▽ 14 | 12 | 13 | £23
71 Hampstead High St., NW3 (Hampstead), 020-7431 2224;
fax 020-7433 1262

■ "Hugely appreciated" by those who "want to avoid the chains", this Hampstead venue features a daytime cafe on one side serving pastries and sandwiches, and a more formal restaurant on the other that serves "simple" Mediterranean dishes; N.B. a new chef took over during the *Survey* period.

Basilico 🅂   20 | 13 | 16 | £18
175 Lavender Hill, SW11 (Clapham), 020-7924 4070;
fax 020-7801 9693 ●
690 Fulham Rd., SW6 (Parsons Green), 020-7384 2633;
fax 020-7610 9145
515 Finchley Rd., NW3 (Golders Green), 080-0316 2656;
fax 020-7794 4062 ●

■ "Basil aplenty" is but one of the "tasty toppings" layered in "great combinations" upon the "huge, light" and "fresh pizzas" at this expanding chainlet of "cheap and cheerful" Italians; though there are a few table and counter seats, "more emphasis" is on "gourmet takeaway" and speedy delivery via a fleet of scooters.

Bayee House 🅂   ▽ 19 | 15 | 19 | £27
24 High St., SW19 (Wimbledon), 020-8947 3533; fax 020-8944 8392
100 Upper Richmond Rd., SW15 (East Putney), 020-8789 3161;
fax 020-8780 5638

■ "Whatever you choose, you can't go wrong" gush fans of the "slightly different", "well-presented" and "delicious" Szechuan/Peking dishes on offer at this Putney and Wimbledon pair; "although the decor is fairly basic", the "waitresses dressed in Chinese clothing" not only provide "very good service" but add a "little atmosphere" as well.

Beach Blanket Babylon 🅂   12 | 21 | 11 | £29
45 Ledbury Rd., W11 (Notting Hill Gate), 020-7229 2907;
fax 020-7313 9525

■ "Everyone should go at least once" "or twice" just for the "bonkers decor" exhort enthusiasts of this "wild, wacky" Notting Hill haunt that's "like eating in an amusement-park ride"; but "don't go there for" the "surly, unfriendly" servers or the "totally unmemorable" Mediterranean food, which wags wish "were half as good as the place looks."

Bedlington Cafe 🅂 ⌿   20 | 3 | 13 | £16
24 Fauconberg Rd., W4 (Gunnersbury), 020-8994 1965

■ "A greasy-spoon cafe" by day, this "cramped-but-convivial" Chiswick venue becomes a "well-run eaterie" in the evening serving "excellent Thai food" at "reasonable prices"; though the "basic" (to put it mildly) decor affords little beyond "tables and chairs", most find it "deserves patronage" for its "simple, heavenly" fare alone; P.S. the BYO policy is aided by "an off-license next door."

Beiteddine ◑ S
21 | 10 | 16 | £33

8 Harriet St., SW1 (Knightsbridge/Sloane Sq.), 020-7235 3969;
fax 020-7245 6335

■ This "upmarket joint" in Knightsbridge features a festival of "consistently good", "quality Lebanese foods" and a menu boasting "more dishes than a Chinese takeaway"; although a few find its less-than-palatial "looks depressing" and say "the tables are so close together it's impossible not to eavesdrop on your fellow diners", loyalists laud the "pleasant service" and efficient delivery.

Belair House S
18 | 19 | 16 | £35

Gallery Rd., Dulwich Village, SE21 (West Dulwich B.R.),
020-8299 9788; fax 020-8299 6793

■ Whilst "nothing in South London compares" to the "glorious setting" of this Georgian Grade II–listed building in Belair Park (near the Dulwich Art Gallery), some suggest the "stodgy" "decor needs to be more inviting"; a recent "change in menu" – to Classic French with Contemporary twists – instituted by new chef Zak Elhamdou may address complaints about the food not "quite hitting the mark."

Belgo Centraal ◑ S
15 | 14 | 14 | £22

50 Earlham St., WC2 (Covent Garden), 020-7813 2233;
fax 020-7209 3212

◪ "In spite of the itchy cassocks, the waiters are surprisingly pleasant" at this "bizarre" Belgian-themed basement eaterie in Covent Garden featuring "*Total Recall* [meets] *Mad Max*" decor and a "party atmosphere" encouraged by the "refectory seating arrangements"; "lost its appeal" sneer critics who feel they "could work on their food a bit more" (a "predictable" formula of mussels 'n' chips), but all appreciate the "excellent beer collection."

Belgo Noord ◑ S
16 | 16 | 15 | £22

72 Chalk Farm Rd., NW1 (Camden Town/Chalk Farm),
020-7267 0718; fax 020-7916 8036

◪ The Chalk Farm "original and best" location of the Belgian-themed chain, this "cosier" eaterie offers the same "*moules frites* par excellence" and "wonderful array" of Belgian beers, all served by "monks with muscles (joy!)"; critics complain, though, of "too much noise" and claim it's grown "complacent", content to "live off its reputation" rather than "concentrate on preparing better food."

Belgo Zuid S
15 | 17 | 14 | £21

124 Ladbroke Grove, W10 (Ladbroke Grove), 020-8982 8400;
fax 020-8982 8401

◪ "More beautiful than the other Belgos", this Belgian's "fabulous space" in Ladbroke Grove feels "like being in an upturned boat", with its timber panelling and long rows of wooden tables; "good *moules frites*" and other "filling" fare are "fun" to eat in this "beer heaven", though "if you can hear yourself think, you must be deaf!"

Belvedere, The 🅂　　　　　20 | 22 | 19 | £41

Holland Park, off Abbotsbury Rd., W8 (Holland Park),
020-7602 1238; fax 020-7601 4382

◪ "Reborn after a revamp", this "standout" spot in a "magic Holland Park setting" – now co-owned by celebrity chef Marco Pierre White – boasts an "elegant, spacious" interior and a "classy" new Modern European menu that devotees deem "good enough to justify the high prices"; others report "disappointing" cooking and "arrogant" service, concluding it's "better to behold" this undeniably "spectacular" venue "than to eat there"; N.B. check out the terrace.

Bengal Clipper ◗🅂　　　　　18 | 15 | 15 | £27

11-12 Cardamom Bldg, Shad Thames, SE1 (London Bridge/
Tower Hill), 020-7357 9001; fax 020-7357 9002

■ Located in "lovely" (if "not easily accessible") Butlers Wharf "at the foot of Tower Bridge", this is "not your run-of-the-mill curry house", thanks to "delicious" and "different" Indian and Bangladeshi dishes ("beware: spicy means spicy!") as well as Bengali specialties with a "refreshing focus on seafood", all served by "nattily dressed" waiters; though it may be a "little expensive", the set-price menus and "Sunday buffet are an excellent value."

Bengal Trader ◗　　　▽ 15 | 12 | 10 | £24

Butlers Wharf, 44 Artillery Ln., E1 (Liverpool St.),
020-7375 0072; fax 020-7247 1002

◪ This younger and lesser known Spitalfields sibling of Bengal Clipper is "cheaper" than the Butlers Wharf original, but a few feel its Indian-Bangladeshi cooking is "inconsistent" ("sometimes good, sometimes not"); still, some rate the place "nice for lunch in the City" thanks to competitively priced tasting, brunch and pre-theatre menus.

Benihana 🅂　　　　　　17 | 14 | 18 | £33

37 Sackville St., W1 (Green Park/Piccadilly Circus),
020-7494 2525; fax 020-7494 1456
77 King's Rd., SW3 (Sloane Sq.), 020-7376 7799; fax 020-7376 7377
100 Avenue Rd., NW3 (Swiss Cottage), 020-7586 9508;
fax 020-7586 6740

◪ "Amazing Japanese chefs" with "flying knives" still slice up "fresh, hot" and "exciting meals" at this teppanyaki-themed trio, in what most call a "hugely entertaining", "circus-like" atmosphere that's "fun for a group" and a "great show for kids"; the "novelty value" has faded for the jaded, though, who judge the tableside-"juggling" jollies "passé" – "you know what to expect" from this "formula."

Ben's Thai　　　　　　18 | 10 | 15 | £17

48 Red Lion St., WC1 (Holborn), 020-7404 9991
93 Warrington Crescent, W9 (Maida Vale/Warwick Ave.),
020-7266 3134; fax 020-7221 8799 🅂

(continued)

(continued)
Ben's Thai
283 Ballards Ln., N3 (Finchley Central), 020-8492 0201
■ They're "always full, and with good reason" assert admirers of these three "down-to-earth" eateries, "reliable" spots for "spicy", "authentic Thai-strength curries" at "good value"; the Warrington Crescent branch's pub is "wonderfully over-the-top."

Bentley's ◐ [S] — 18 | 16 | 18 | £35
11-15 Swallow St., W1 (Piccadilly Circus), 020-7734 4756; fax 020-7287 2972
◪ This "classy" Piccadilly "long-stayer" is a haven for "upper-crust" locals and tourists, who sup on "good seafood (at a price)"; iconoclasts who brand its Traditional British menu "boring" may bravo the recent addition of modern fish dishes, but the old guard hopes for "no change" to its institution of a "ground-floor oyster bar."

Beoty's ◐ — 16 | 13 | 21 | £32
79 St. Martin's Ln., WC2 (Leicester Sq.), 020-7836 8768; fax 020-7497 0355
◪ Fans of this "most friendly" French-influenced Greek in a Theatreland basement boast it's "a real beauty for service" with "old-fashioned dignity" (that's "quick if needed") and insist that its "good food" "never disappoints"; the derogatory deride it as a "dinosaur den", a "predictable" "has-been" that "needs a revamp in menu and decor."

Bertorelli — 16 | 14 | 15 | £28
11-13 Frith St., W1 (Leicester Sq./Tottenham Court Rd.), 020-7494 3491; fax 020-7437 3091 ◐
19-23 Charlotte St., W1 (Goodge St./Tottenham Court Rd.), 020-7636 4174; fax 020-7467 8902
44A Floral St., WC2 (Covent Garden), 020-7836 3969; fax 020-7836 1868 ◐
◪ These "unpretentious" spots offer "inexpensive", "robust Italian cooking" and "efficient service" at a "nice location" in Fitzrovia as well as a Theatreland spot that's "handy to the Royal Opera House"; whilst some say the "menu's getting a bit dull" and the "bored waiters" "lack enthusiasm", most maintain they're still "good for day-to-day" dining; N.B. the Soho branch opened post-*Survey*.

BIBENDUM ◐ [S] — 23 | 22 | 21 | £48
Michelin House, 81 Fulham Rd., SW3 (South Kensington), 020-7581 5817; fax 020-7823 7925
◪ It's "difficult to fault" this "class-act" Brompton Cross "institution" set in a 1911 Edwardian landmark (the Michelin Building), which for most is "still a great favourite" thanks to Matthew Harris' "fantastic" New French fare, the "stained-glass serenity" of its interior and "highly professional" staff; still, "staggering prices", "service slips" and a few "hit-or-miss" dishes leave a minority feeling "slightly disappointed."

Bibendum Oyster Bar [S] 20 17 17 £29

Michelin House, 81 Fulham Rd., SW3 (South Kensington), 020-7589 1480; fax 020-7823 7925

■ "A great spot to spend a relaxing afternoon" or have "the perfect light lunch", this "sophisticated" street-level Brompton Cross cafe is "faster, hipper and cheaper than the big Bibendum" upstairs, producing "notable seafood" dishes from a "good selection" of oysters and shellfish; it can be "difficult to find a seat" in its "characterful" room, but most "don't mind the queue", anticipating a "damn fine" meal; N.B. casual snacks are now available outside the front entrance.

Bice 19 15 18 £38

13 Albemarle St., W1 (Green Park/Piccadilly Circus), 020-7409 1011; fax 020-7493 0081

◪ One of an international chain spawned by the Milanese original, this "cavernous" Mayfair outpost strikes many as a "perfect lunch venue" for "business entertaining", with "reliable" Italian Modern cuisine (including "fine risotto"), "slick service" and a "lively-but-not-too-noisy" milieu; others find it "disappointing", though, balking at its "basement location" and "variable food and service."

Bierodrome [S] 13 13 13 £19

67 Kingsway, WC2 (Charing Cross/Holborn), 020-7242 7469; fax 020-7242 7493

678-680 Fulham Rd., SW6 (Parsons Green), 020-7751 0789; fax 020-7751 0678

44-48 Clapham High St., SW4 (Clapham North), 020-7720 1118; fax 020-7720 0288 ◐

173-174 Upper St., N1 (Highbury & Islington), 020-7226 5835; fax 020-7704 0632

71 St. John St., EC1 (Farringdon), 020-7608 0033; fax 020-7608 0003

■ There are now five "lively", "sassy" outlets of this expanding Belgian pub/restaurant chain, where the "head-banging choice of beers" is more of a draw than the "uninspired" menu of *moules frites* and the like; these "crowded" "echo boxes" may be "inferior to their big sisters" (Belgo Centraal, Noord and Zuid), but "at least they're cheaper", and there are "no monks' habits" on the "muscled waiters."

Big Easy [S] 13 12 13 £20

332-334 King's Rd., SW3 (Sloane Sq.), 020-7352 4071

■ "American expats" "homesick" for "huge portions" of "typical" States-themed food (with a Southern slant) such as "good steak" or "ok ribs" will find them at this "easygoing" "diner for families" on the King's Road; a haven for "messy eaters", it's a "children's favourite", but "don't go if you don't have them" say those in search of less "average", more "serious fare (or a quiet time)."

Bistrot 190 ◑Ⓢ 17 | 16 | 15 | £31
Gore Hotel, 190 Queen's Gate, SW7 (Gloucester Rd./
South Kensington), 020-7581 5666; fax 020-7581 5872
■ All agree this "lovely" bistro/bar in South Kensington is
convenient for a "pre-theatre dinner", as it's just around
the corner from the Royal Albert Hall and "opens early";
still, the dissatisfied deem it a "mediocre brasserie" where
there's "nothing special" about the "dull" Modern British–
French bistro food, "noisy" ambience and "erratic service."

Black & Blue Ⓢ 19 | 17 | 19 | £21
215-217 Kensington Church St., W8 (Notting Hill Gate),
020-7727 0004; fax 020-7229 9359
■ "Yanks head in droves" to this "welcome addition to
the London scene" in Kensington that's "one of the few
places" serving "great steaks (especially the T-bone)"
"cooked precisely according to customers'" preferences,
as well as "American-style hamburgers" and other "good
basics"; all in all, "solid, filling meals" at "affordable prices"
add up to real "bang for the buck."

Black Truffle 19 | 17 | 15 | £34
40 Chalcot Rd., NW1 (Chalk Farm/Primrose Hill B.R.),
020-7483 0077; fax 020-7483 0088
■ Loyalists "just love" the "delicious" fare at this "brilliant"
Modern Italian, which brings "a touch of class" to
Primrose Hill with its "compact, simply designed" interior
and "attentive, discreet" staff; though a few are "indifferent"
to its "charms", calling the service "inconsistent" and
"rushed", the majority rates it "a real find" for "excellent
value"; P.S. insiders say "sit downstairs" where it's "cosy."

Blah! Blah! Blah! ⌀ 22 | 12 | 17 | £21
78 Goldhawk Rd., W12 (Goldhawk Rd.), 020-8746 1337
■ "Even non-veggies will enjoy" this "quirky" Shepherd's
Bush "vegetarian haven" where the "innovative" dishes
are "full of complex tastes" and "visually satisfying" as
well, making some "forget what meat is!"; though it may
be "grim from the outside" (and, some say, "smoky" on
the inside), a "friendly, fresh-faced" staff will take your
mind off the "basic surroundings", N.B. it's BYO.

Blakes Ⓢ ▽ 22 | 21 | 16 | £33
31 Jamestown Rd., NW1 (Camden Town), 020-7482 2959;
fax 020-7284 3066
■ There's a lot that's "right about this place", a "great
local pub" and restaurant in Camden offering à la carte
lunches in the bar until 7 PM, at which point Eclectic-
International dinners like the signature duck ravioli are
served amid the "cosy, romantic atmosphere" of its "nice
upstairs dining room"; in clement weather, there's outside
dining on the pavement at front.

BLAKES HOTEL ◐ [S] 22 | 24 | 21 | £56

Blakes Hotel, 33 Roland Gardens, SW7 (Gloucester Rd./ South Kensington), 020-7370 6701; fax 020-7373 0442

◪ "You still feel like a beautiful person when you enter" this "sleek", "chic hideaway" in Blakes Hotel where Neville Campbell creates "delicious" and "innovative" Pacific Rim–accented Eclectic "concoctions", though a few surveyors snipe the somewhat "dated" decor is "becoming retro"; an "always-happening bar" and a "discreet", "sexy" setting have would-be Casanovas cooing it's "excellent for seduction", even though "shocked" wallet-watchers call the "dramatically" high "prices just plain silly."

Bleeding Heart Restaurant 20 | 17 | 18 | £33

Bleeding Heart Yard, Greville St., EC1 (Farringdon), 020-7242 8238; fax 020-7831 1402

Bleeding Heart Tavern

Bleeding Heart Yard, 19 Greville St., EC1 (Farringdon), 020-7404 0333; fax 020-7404 2727

■ "Finding it is always an adventure", but visitors to this French Contemporary "jewel" "tucked away" in Holborn say it's "worth the hunt" for its "reliable tucker", "tremendous wine list" and "pleasant" staff; the "buzzy, lively" bistro is "great" for a "quick working lunch", and the "dark", "intimate" downstairs is "the perfect place for conspiracies and affairs"; its nearby Tavern sibling serves spit-roasted Traditional British grills.

Bloom's [S] 15 | 7 | 11 | £20

130 Golders Green Rd., NW11 (Golders Green), 020-8455 1338; fax 020-8455 3033

■ The last bastion of the Bloom dynasty, this "never-changing" Golders Green kosher delicatessen continues to offer "good, home-cooked" "comfort food" served in cafe-like surroundings by famously surly waiters who "want to know why you haven't finished your dinner"; though some say the place is "living on its reputation", it remains popular for "late-night or early-morning snacks."

Bluebird [S] 17 | 18 | 15 | £36

350 King's Rd., SW3 (Sloane Sq.), 020-7559 1000; fax 020-7559 1115

◪ "Another [Sir Terence] Conran offering", this "light, airy", "trendy" venue in a "former garage" on the King's Road divides diners' devotions down the middle: half hail it as a "sophisticated" spot serving "simple, delicious" Med-inflected Modern British fare in a "lively atmosphere", whilst the others, citing "overpriced fare" that's "well below potential" and "ambivalent service", proclaim "this bird doesn't fly."

Blue Elephant ◖⧗ Ⓢ　　　21　23　19　£36
3-6 Fulham Broadway, SW6 (Fulham Broadway),
020-7385 6595; fax 020-7386 7665
■ Like "Alice going through the looking glass", visitors to
this "exotic" eaterie in Fulham "step into" "a dreamworld": a
recently refurbished "Thai-mixed-with-Disney" "jungle"
replete with "waterfalls" and "lush vegetation", where
"authentically dressed waiters" offer "luscious", "scrummy"
fare; though a few spoilsports call the "festive" decor
"cheesy" and the food "expensive", most find this "rain
forest" "paradise" "lots of fun" for "groups" and "great
for children"; the Blue Bar was recently added.

Blue Jade　　　　　　　　18　15　16　£22
44 Hugh St., SW1 (Pimlico/Victoria), 020-7828 0321;
fax 020-7630 9272
■ "If you like Thai, you'll like this" "quiet and relaxed"
Pimlico property proffering "reasonably priced", "authentic"
food ("choose the hot red curry"); add "friendly service"
to the mix of "great food" and "good value" and you've
got a spot that's "ideal for a quick lunchtime meal."

Blue Lagoon ◖⧗ Ⓢ　　　17　13　17　£24
284-286 Kensington High St., W1 (High St. Kensington),
020-7603 1231
■ Still relatively "new on the scene", this spacious, midpriced Thai over the road from the Kensington cinema
remains little-known, but those acquainted with it report
"very good" fare that's on its way to "fab"; even those who
feel "the food isn't spectacular" find "no disappointments",
and the "patient waiters" are appreciated.

Blue Print Cafe Ⓢ　　　　18　19　16　£36
Design Museum, Butlers Wharf, 28 Shad Thames, SE1
(London Bridge/Tower Hill), 020-7378 7031; fax 020-7357 8810
☑ "It's all about the view" of Tower Bridge from the
"fantastic" terrace of Sir Terence Conran's Eclectic
eaterie on the first floor of the Design Museum; whilst
some like the "innovative" cooking, many find the
"over-fussy, neurotic menu" "not as captivating" as the
"panorama" and quip that the staff follow a "blueprint
for bad service."

Blues Bistro & Bar Ⓢ　　　16　17　16　£24
42-43 Dean St., W1 (Piccadilly Circus/Leicester Sq.),
020-7494 1966; fax 020-7494 0717
■ For "a shopping pit stop" or "good-value, pre-theatre"
prix fixe, the American-International cooking at this Soho
bistro is just "fine"; however, surveyors sing the blues
over "lax" service and "tables too close together" that
"feel tacked onto the bar" – patrons guess this is why it's
"unbusy" despite the "great prices."

Boardwalk ◐ | 10 | 14 | 11 | £19 |

18 Greek St., W1 (Leicester Sq./Tottenham Court Rd.),
020-7287 2051; fax 020-7434 2088

■ More of a bar with live entertainment than a dining destination, this raucous Soho joint has a Cajun-American menu that's "excellent value for the money", though punters would like "bigger portions, please"; snooty sorts who "only ever go here late at night when nothing else is open" should be advised that its "excellent cocktails" make for a "very good happy hour."

Boisdale ◐ | 17 | 18 | 16 | £35 |

15 Eccleston St., SW1 (Victoria), 020-7730 6922;
fax 020-7730 0548

■ "Carnivores" "simply love the haggis", "great steak" and other meaty British dishes with a backdrop of live, "top-rate jazz" amidst the "tartan-rich red walls, old photos" and "dark wood" of this "whisky-and-cigar haven" on the Belgravia-Victoria border; a "boys' club" where "girls are welcome too", it "makes for a decadent" evening.

Bombay Bicycle Club | 21 | 16 | 17 | £24 |

95 Nightingale Ln., SW12 (Clapham South), 020-8673 6217;
fax 020-8673 9100

■ Cyclophiles pedal to Clapham for Indian "with a twist" at this "upmarket curry" joint that's "worth" the trip; the fare at this "institution" may be "a little expensive", but "a lot of thought goes into the preparation" and it's "cooked with British palates in mind", P.S. for eat-in or takeout, it's "quality all the way."

Bombay Brasserie ◐S | 19 | 19 | 17 | £34 |

Courtfield Rd., SW7 (Gloucester Rd.), 020-7370 4040;
fax 020-7835 1669

☑ Supporters say the South Kensington kitchen at this '80s survivor, the "first of the upscale Indians", still serves "enormous helpings" of "generally good" Anglicised grub in "palatial surroundings" featuring a conservatory "fit for a raj"; fussy foodies find it an "overcrowded, overpriced" place that's "living off the fumes of former glories."

Bonjour Vietnam ◐S | 13 | 11 | 13 | £22 |

593-599 Fulham Rd., SW6 (Fulham Broadway), 020-7385 7603;
fax 020-7610 2423

■ "If you can put up with the colour scheme" and "shabby decor" ("needs an upgrade"), this Asian venue on Fulham Broadway is somewhere "to go in a crowd" so as "to make the most of the set-menus", most notably the "great value" all-you-can-eat option at £14.50 (£10 at lunch); to purists, though, the "uninspiring" fare is "nothing close to Vietnamese food."

Books for Cooks
22 | 11 | 18 | £18

4 Blenheim Crescent, W11 (Ladbroke Grove/Notting Hill Gate), 020-7221 1992; fax 020-7221 1517

■ This "unique" "little treasure off Portobello Road" sells a wide range of cookbooks, but it also has a few tables for "simple" Eclectic dishes that "can be hit-or-miss depending on who's cooking"; it's a BYO, no-reserve "food-lover's womb": "learn how to cook, read how to cook and eat!"

Brackenbury, The S
21 | 14 | 17 | £31

129-131 Brackenbury Rd., W6 (Goldhawk Rd./Hammersmith), 020-8748 0107

■ "When local", stop into this "cosy" Modern British eaterie in Shepherd's Bush for "honest food without any delusions of grandeur"; the "workmanlike" fare might "not be very exciting" and the "simple decor" may be a bit "homely", but it's "the most reliable" joint in the neighbourhood.

Bradley's S
19 | 16 | 19 | £31

25 Winchester Rd., NW3 (Swiss Cottage), 020-7722 3457; fax 020-7435 1392

■ "Every area should have one", but the Swiss Cottage crowd is pleased that their own "good neighbourhood restaurant" remains "thankfully undiscovered"; the Modern British menu is long on "excellent fish", the "lovely" staff are "knowledgeable about wine" and though there's "not a lot of atmosphere", the "small, intimate" spot is "relaxing."

Brady's ⊽
▽ 22 | 14 | 17 | £20

513 Old York Rd., SW18 (Wandsworth Town B.R.), 020-8877 9599; fax 020-8333 0193

☑ "How a fish 'n' chip shop should be" state satisfied customers of this little-known Wandsworth diner providing "good, honest" meals "at very low prices"; whilst the fare may well have "gotten better this year", critical foodies still find it "forgettable", noting that it "needs a lick of paint."

Brasserie Rocque
14 | 12 | 12 | £31

37 Broadgate Circle, EC2 (Liverpool St.), 020-7638 7919; fax 020-7628 5899

■ Mid-division Med-Eclectic meals elicit scant enthusiasm at this popular place with outdoor dining next to Broadgate Circus' ice rink; since it changed hands over a year ago, it's beginning to look "a bit dated", with "bland corporate lunches" lapsing into "evenings tending toward the sleazy."

Brasserie St. Quentin S
17 | 16 | 17 | £32

243 Brompton Rd., SW3 (Knightsbridge), 020-7589 8005; fax 020-7584 6064

■ "When you most miss Paris", this "lively", "long-standing" French classic in Knightsbridge may be your "old-fashioned" tonic; "what it does, it does well", i.e. "unpretentious", "generous", meals served by "charming" staff, at "prices that are low compared to trendy restaurants du jour."

Break for the Border   8 | 8 | 8 | £20

5 Goslett Yard, WC2 (Tottenham Court Rd.), 020-7437 8595;
fax 020-7437 0479
8 Argyll St., W1 (Oxford Circus), 020-7734 5776

■ These "noisy", "fun" Tex-Mexers near Oxford Street are credited with "conveyor belt" food that receives few bravos, unlike the pair's "drinking and pulling" credentials: "brilliant for drunken group nights out" and "tequila-soaked parties."

Bridge, The   16 | 13 | 14 | £32

1 Paul's Walk, EC4 (Blackfriars), 020-7236 0000; fax 020-7329 9299

■ With "great views" across the Thames to the Globe Theatre and Tate Modern, this "newly discovered" City yearling has got off to a "good" start with an "interesting" Eclectic brasserie menu, but its long-term prospects should be boosted later in 2001 when the Millennium Footbridge re-opens adjacent to its glass frontage and riverside terrace.

Brinkley's S   13 | 14 | 12 | £27

47 Hollywood Rd., SW10 (Earl's Court), 020-7351 1683;
fax 020-7376 5083

■ The "chic crowd" "gets noisy" after several bottles from the "damn fine, well-priced wine list" at this "pleasant" Chelsea eaterie with a "very quaint" covered garden; its Modern British cooking is in less demand, however, than the fruit of the vine that "helps the food go down."

Brown's Hotel, Restaurant 1837 S   21 | 21 | 22 | £42

Brown's Hotel, 32 Albemarle St., W1 (Green Park),
020-7408 1837; fax 020-7518 4099

■ "Old-world ambience" meets "modern flair" in this "impressive yet comfortable" Mayfair hotel dining room where "elegant" Modern European cuisine is served in a "lovely, traditional" Edwardian/Jacobean setting; "well-presented", multi-course meals are perfect "for that special occasion", but be forewarned that all of this "fine formality" "doesn't come cheaply"; N.B. an exceptional list of vinos features many "interesting wines by the glass."

Brown's Hotel, The Library S   21 | 22 | 20 | £33

Brown's Hotel, 32 Albemarle St., W1 (Green Park), 020-7493 6020

■ "Quintessential English tea" "by the fireplace" during the afternoon in this "cosy, pampered" Mayfair hotel lounge is a "touristy" institution and a "great splurge"; now, in addition, it offers a wider range of "fast, convenient" dishes from a "good" International-Eclectic menu, which makes a fine alternative to the more formal 1837 dining room.

Browns Restaurant   15 | 15 | 15 | £24

82-84 St. Martin's Ln., WC2 (Leicester Sq.), 020-7497 5050;
fax 020-7497 5005 ◗ S
47 Maddox St., W1 (Oxford Circus), 020-7491 4565;
fax 020-7497 4564 ◗ S

(continued)

(continued)
Browns Restaurant
201 Castlenau Row, SW13 (Hammersmith), 020-8748 4486;
fax 020-8563 8601 S
9 Islington Green, Islington, N1 (Angel), 020-7226 2555;
fax 020-7359 7306 ◑S
8 Old Jewry, EC2 (Bank), 020-7606 6677; fax 020-7600 5359
Hertsmere Rd., E14 (Canary Wharf), 020-7987 9777;
fax 020-7537 1341 S

☑ No chain of fools, this "reliable" group of "regular haunts" is a "simple concept, excellently executed": British "comfort food" is served in "happy" "hangouts" "perfect" for "after work", "pre-theatre" or "lazy Sundays"; there is "variation between sites", however, with Central London having "become more bar than brasserie" and Kew and Barnes remaining "dependable" for families.

Buchan's S 17 | 15 | 18 | £27
62-64 Battersea Bridge Rd., SW11 (Sloane Sq.),
020-7228 0888; fax 020-7924 1718

☑ For a "different" "break from shopping", this "reliable" Battersea wine bar/eaterie serves "innovative Scottish fare"; loyal locals call it a "treasure" of "neighbourhood friendliness" that's "like dining in the comfort of a friend's house", but choosier sorts say that description applies only if your pal's place needs a "revamp."

Builders Arms S 16 | 15 | 13 | £19
13 Britten St., SW3 (Sloane Sq./South Kensington),
020-7349 9040

▧ "If you're in the mood for a pub, but not the stuffy atmosphere", fall into the arms of this "secluded" Chelsea gastro-pub for "typical nouveau British" grub; it's "a great spot for lunching" on signature Cumberland sausages or chicken-and-leek pie even if the "surly" servers and "odd weekend crowd" aren't particularly huggable.

Buona Sera ◑S 19 | 13 | 16 | £20
22-26 Northcote Rd., SW11 (Clapham Junction B.R.),
020-7924 1666; fax 020-7228 1114

▧ "Arrive early for a table" at Battersea's "enthusiastic" Italian and get "genuinely" "brilliant", "big, fat pizzas" and pastas at "cheap" prices in a room "so loud you don't have to worry if your companions are boring"; this "wicked" place is "great for groups."

Buona Sera at the Jam ◑S 15 | 16 | 13 | £20
289A King's Rd., SW3 (Sloane Sq.), 020-7352 8827;
fax 020-7352 8827

▧ If you're a "teenager", you'll love the King's Road Buona Sera sib; the pizzas and other Italian eats are "good", but the real "cool" fun is in "climbing the scaffolding" to "sit up high" at bunk-bed tables, though less-gymnastic jurors are just "not sure about coming down" again.

Busaba Eathai [S] 20 21 15 £17

106-110 Wardour St., W1 (Piccadilly Circus/Tottenham Court Rd.), 020-7255 8686; fax 020-7255 8688

◪ It's "difficult to remember the name but easy to remember the food" at this "buzzingly" "trendy" Soho spot where "delicious, fresh", "affordable" Thai is served at "shared tables" "with benches"; the gregarious gush that "the group-style eating promotes conversation amongst disparate" folks, whilst anti-social sorts sniff they "can't stand queuing" to sit amongst "strangers trying to ignore each other" in this no-reserve place.

Busabong Too [S] 19 13 17 £28

1A Langton St., SW10 (Fulham Broadway/Sloane Sq.), 020-7352 7414; fax 020-7352 7534

■ "Consistently good at a reasonable price", this "friendly" Thai feeds unfettered folks a "fantastic fusion of flavours" on two floors of a World's End townhouse; "upstairs is a must", as "you take your shoes off" and "lie down like Romans" – just remember to "leave the Jimmy Choos at home"; its nearby sibling, Busabong Tree, has closed.

Bush Bar & Grill ◐ [S] 19 20 17 £29

45A Goldhawk Rd., W12 (Goldhawk Rd.), 020-8746 2111; fax 020-8746 1331

◪ It's a hung jury over this "spacious", high-profile newcomer in Shepherd's Bush from the Woody's team: some claim it's "simply fantastic", with "lovely" Anglo-French cooking and "classy service", whilst others yawn that the fare is just "basic" and wonder how servers "find their way to work", since it seems they "can't get anything right."

Butlers Wharf Chop House [S] 19 17 17 £36

Butlers Wharf, 36E Shad Thames, SE1 (London Bridge/Tower Hill), 020-7403 3403; fax 020-7403 3414

■ "The view and the buzz make for a fun evening out" at Sir Terence's "brilliant location" near Tower Bridge; it's a "typical Conran" establishment where "staff that are friendly in a perfunctory way" serve "Trad English with spin" in a "smart", "casual atmosphere"; "if you can get an outside table, go", because it's "magical in summer."

Byron's [S] 19 17 19 £32

3A Downshire Hill, NW3 (Hampstead), 020-7435 3544; fax 020-7431 3544

◪ As "romantic" as the eponymous lord/poet himself, this "civilised" eaterie in a "charming" Hampstead townhouse serves "elegant and delicious" Modern British dishes that are "great for Sunday lunch"; warnings that "you leave slightly hungry" could be a thing of the past as, under the aegis of new head chef Andrew Bruce, the "little" meals may grow.

Cactus Blue ◑ S　　　 13 | 16 | 14 | £26
86 Fulham Rd., SW3 (South Kensington), 020-7823 7858;
fax 020-7823 8577

☑ "Fashion lemmings" and "singles" "never have a sad
time" at this "buzzing", "trendy" Chelsea cantina, though
opinions on the American Southwestern eats vary from
"creative" to "tasteless"; "nibble, ignore the mains" and
"head straight to sipping tequilas" and "superb cocktails"
for a "noisy night out with loud friends."

Cafe at Sotheby's　　　 19 | 17 | 17 | £23
Sotheby's Auction House, 34 New Bond St., W1 (Bond St.),
020-7293 5077

■ "After shopping on Bond Street", you won't have to
auction off your valuables to make a meal of the "interesting,
reasonably priced options" at this "quiet corner" in the
famous bidder's haunt; "healthy" Modern British dishes
that are "not carbohydrate filled" and a "stylish", "subdued"
setting (albeit with a "corridor feel") "score" with "serious
ladies who lunch."

Café Boheme ◑ S　　　 16 | 15 | 12 | £22
13-17 Old Compton St., W1 (Leicester Sq.), 020-7734 0623;
fax 020-7434 3775

■ "Great for filling the tank before hitting the clubs", this
"cheapish and cheerful" Soho charmer serves "reliably"
"good" French bistro fare; it may "not be as bohemian as
it would like", but because the late-nighter manages to be
"vibrant" and "relaxed" all at once, "here one feels good"
until 3 AM weekdays and 24 hours on weekends.

Café Delancey ◑ S　　　 14 | 14 | 14 | £22
3 Delancey St., NW1 (Camden Town), 020-7387 1985;
fax 020-7383 5314

☑ A "genuine brasserie feel" and "winning enclosed
courtyard" attract "trendy" locals to this "corner of
tranquillity in crazy Camden" for French bistro "food that
doesn't vary much" but is "tasty" and "convenient" "after
theatre" or for weekend brunch; gastro-snobs steer clear
of the "intellectual poseur" scene.

Cafe de Paris ◑　　　 13 | 16 | 14 | £36
3 Coventry St., W1 (Leicester Sq.), 020-7734 7700

☑ Those who go for the "exciting" "dancing" deem this
private Piccadilly nightspot "ok for the club, not really for
the restaurant"; open to non-members, the eaterie is "full
of tourists", but Londoners say "average" Modern European
edibles, "appalling service" and "rather tatty decor" "just
don't live up to its steep prices."

Café des Amis du Vin ◑   16 14 15 £27
11-14 Hanover Pl., WC2 (Covent Garden), 020-7379 3444;
fax 020-7379 9124

■ Oenophiles find this Covent Garden spot the "perfect, cosy bistro for a rainy afternoon" lingering over "solid" French fare and "great wines"; its "boozy" basement bar is popular with "discerning drinkers", and the "dark, intense" atmosphere is illicit enough to "give the impression that a lot of couples actually shouldn't be there" together.

Cafe Fish ◑ Ⓢ   17 13 15 £28
36-40 Rupert St., W1 (Piccadilly Circus), 020-7287 8989;
fax 020-7287 8400

◪ A "friendly and fresh" fishy "fueling station" for "pre-theatre or post-theatre", this "convenient" Soho seafooder serves "quick in-and-out" selections, including meals as part of budget dinner-and-a-show combos; though "pretty decor" featuring marine creatures goes over swimmingly well, afishionados fuss that the better bites seem to have "slipped the net."

Café Flo   13 12 13 £20
50-52 St. Martin's Ln., WC2 (Leicester Sq.), 020-7836 8289;
fax 020-7379 0314 ◑ Ⓢ
127 Kensington Church St., W8 (Notting Hill Gate),
020-7727 8142; fax 020-7792 1260 ◑ Ⓢ
25 Gloucester Rd., SW7 (Gloucester Rd.), 020-7589 1383;
fax 020-7581 0534 ◑ Ⓢ
676 Fulham Rd., SW6 (Parsons Green), 020-7371 9673;
fax 020-7371 5425 ◑ Ⓢ
11 Haymarket, SW1 (Piccadilly Circus), 020-7976 1313 ◑ Ⓢ
205 Haverstock Hill, NW3 (Belsize Park), 020-7435 6744;
fax 020-7431 7189 Ⓢ
334 Upper St., N1 (Angel), 020-7226 7916; fax 020-7704 2965 ◑ Ⓢ
38-40 Ludgate Hill, EC4 (St. Paul's), 020-7329 3900;
fax 020-7329 0698
149 Kew Rd., Richmond (Richmond), 020-8940 8298;
fax 020-8773 6205 Ⓢ

■ "Don't expect much and you won't be disappointed" by this "good-value" French cafe chain that's "harmless enough" but so "inconsistent from branch to branch" that eating here is like playing the "lottery on quality and taste"; its "formula-driven" bistro fare is "ok" "to stuff your face, not to impress your guests."

Cafe Japan Ⓢ   24 9 18 £23
626 Finchley Rd., NW11 (Golders Green), 020-8455 6854

■ Connoisseurs of the "raw and the cooked" give this "buzzing little Golders Green" Japanese "thumbs-up" for "authentic" sushi and "other exotic dishes beautifully served on interesting plates" "at acceptable prices"; "it's hard to get a table" in a room that's "a little cramped, basic and bright", but the "awesome" "food makes up for it."

Cafe Lazeez   17 | 14 | 15 | £25

21 Dean St., W1 (Leicester Sq.), 020-7434 9393;
fax 020-7434 0022 ◑🅂
93-95 Old Brompton Rd., SW7 (Gloucester Rd./
South Kensington), 020-7581 9993; fax 020-7581 8200 ◑🅂
88 St. John St., EC1 (Farringdon), 020-7253 2224;
fax 020-7253 2112

◪ The "attempt to create a Western touch in Indian"
dining at this trio in South Ken, Soho and Clerkenwell is
"good for people who like mellow taste when it comes to
spices", but not everyone appreciates the "unauthentic"
"spin" on "traditional dishes" or the "beautiful people" and
"horrendously loud music" that go with the Anglicised angle.

Cafe, Level Seven 🅂   15 | 19 | 14 | £21

Tate Modern, Bankside, SE1 (Blackfriars/London Bridge),
020-7401 5020

▥ Though there's art aplenty to see at Tate Modern,
"don't be in a rush" to get back to the galleries while
eating at its "busy", "efficient" seventh-floor cafe; if you
"relax", you'll "enjoy" "interesting and tasty" Modern
British cooking and "stunning views" across the Thames;
N.B. closed for dinner except Fridays and Saturdays.

Cafe Med   14 | 15 | 14 | £24

184A Kensington Park Rd., W11 (Notting Hill Gate),
020-7221 1150; fax 020-7229 5647 ◑🅂
320 Goldhawk Rd., W6 (Stamford Brook), 020-8741 1994;
fax 020-8741 9980 ◑🅂
22 Dean St., W1 (Tottenham Court Rd.), 020-7287 9007;
fax 020-7287 3529 ◑
21 Loudoun Rd., NW8 (St. John's Wood), 020-7625 1222;
fax 020-7328 1593 🅂
370 St. John St., EC1 (Angel), 020-7278 1199;
fax 020-7833 9046 🅂

◪ "Not exactly original" or "gourmet", "but well-executed",
the "simple, pleasant dishes" proffered by the numerous
links in this "dependable" Mediterranean chain include
what less-discriminating diners deem "outstanding fries"
and "wicked U.S.-style cheesecake"; picky patrons pooh-
pooh "bland food", "nondescript" interiors and "gloomy
service" at these "lifeless" "joints."

Cafe Pacifico ◑🅂   14 | 12 | 12 | £22

5 Langley St., WC2 (Covent Garden), 020-7379 7728;
fax 020-7836 5088

▥ Among the few "halfway decent Tex-Mex" options "in
town" ("we need more!"), this "cute", "noisy" Covent
Garden spot provides "good-size portions" of "well-
presented" fare that goes down well with "groups"; whilst
some complain it's "about as authentic as margaritas
made from a mix" ("go for the action, not eating"), a more
widespread complaint is that they "don't take bookings."

Cafe Rouge [S] 10 | 11 | 11 | £19

34 Wellington St., WC2 (Covent Garden), 020-7836 0998; fax 020-7497 0738
31 Kensington Park Rd., W11 (Ladbroke Grove), 020-7221 4449; fax 020-7792 3064
158 Fulham Palace Rd., W6 (Hammersmith), 020-8741 5037; fax 020-8563 2761
98-100 Shepherd's Bush Rd., W6 (Shepherd's Bush), 020-7602 7732; fax 020-7603 7710
227 Chiswick High Rd., W4 (Chiswick Park), 020-8742 7447; fax 020-8742 7557
15 Frith St., W1 (Tottenham Court Rd.), 020-7437 4307; fax 020-7437 4442
39 Park Gate Rd., SW11 (Clapham Junction B.R./Sloane Sq.), 020-7352 7924; fax 020-7924 3565
27-31 Basil St., SW3 (Knightsbridge), 020-7584 2345; fax 020-7584 4253
120 St. John's Wood High St., NW8 (St. John's Wood), 020-7722 8366; fax 020-7483 1015
18 Chalk Farm Rd., NW1 (Camden Town/Chalk Farm), 020-7428 0998
Additional locations throughout London

◪ Perhaps it "does what it's supposed to do" by "delivering" "formula", "no-frills" fare for a "safe, easy lunch", but Francophiles feel this "mediocre" chain of "French McDonald's" "wanna-be bistros" is "nothing to blush for"; "the most consistent thing is poor service" say critics of this "perfect example of a good idea gone wrong."

Cafe Spice Namaste 19 | 16 | 16 | £28

247 Lavender Hill, SW11 (Clapham Junction B.R.), 020-7738 1717; fax 020-7738 1666 ◐ [S]
16 Prescot St., E1 (Aldgate/Aldgate East), 020-7488 9242; fax 020-7488 9339

■ "Hoorah" haute-cuisiners holler for chef/cookbook author Cyrus Todiwala's new wave Indian pair in Clapham and in a City "no man's land near the Tower"; definitely "different from your average curry-house" nosh, his "inventive", "delicious" "concept" dishes come in "an eclectic range" "enjoyable" for "sharing in a big group", though "colourful, bizarrely inspired" decor can "detract."

Caffe Nero [S] ⊘ 14 | 12 | 14 | £10

Unit 1, 65-72 The Strand, WC2 (Charing Cross/Covent Garden), 020-7930 8483; fax 020-7930 8493
2 Lancaster Pl., WC2 (Covent Garden), 020-7836 6346; fax 020-7836 6356
29 Southampton St., WC2 (Covent Garden), 020-7240 3433; fax 020-7240 9766
79 Tottenham Court Rd., W1 (Goodge Street), 020-7580 3885; fax 020-7580 3014

(continued)

(continued)
Caffe Nero
225 Regent St., W1 (Oxford Circus), 020-7491 0763;
fax 020-7493 3743
62 Brewer St., W1 (Piccadilly Circus), 020-7437 1497;
fax 020-7437 3048
43 Frith St., W1 (Piccadilly Circus), 020-7434 3887;
fax 020-7734 8270
66 Old Brompton Rd., SW7 (South Kensington),
020-7589 1760; fax 020-7581 1610
1 Hampstead High St., NW3 (Hampstead), 020-7431 5958;
fax 020-7431 1691
Unit 1, Winchester House, EC2 (Liverpool St.),
020-7588 6001; fax 020-7588 7258
Additional locations throughout London
■ At 50-plus branches throughout Britian and growing, this empire of "excellent coffeehouses" is certainly not burning away; with "good-value", "quick" snacks of "delicious" coffee, "high-quality" Italian focaccia, panini and other "tasty, fresh" options winning "big fans", this is one formula that doesn't need fiddling.

Calzone 🅂 14 | 10 | 12 | £17
2A Kensington Park Rd., W11 (Notting Hill Gate),
020-7243 2003; fax 020-7243 2006 ●
335 Fulham Rd., SW10 (South Kensington), 020-7352 9797;
fax 020-7352 9798 ●
66 Heath St., NW3 (Hampstead), 020-7794 6775; fax 020-7794 1138
35 Upper St., N1 (Angel), 020-7359 9191; fax 020-7359 9192
☑ "Fast cooks" rustle up "good, basic pizzas", pastas and, yes, calzones at this "inexpensive" Italian foursome; the nutrition-minded "would love more healthy options like veggie pastas", and others say "take your earplugs" to these "small", "busy" spots.

Cambio de Tercio ●🅂 21 | 17 | 19 | £33
163 Old Brompton Rd., SW5 (Gloucester Rd.), 020-7244 8970;
fax 020-7373 8817
■ A "strong following of those in-the-know" cheer "*olé*" for this "buzzing South Ken Spaniard"; "authentic tapas" and other "classics" of Spanish cuisine offer "one delicious taste experience after another" served by "friendly" staff "fussing in a manner that makes you feel special" amid "funky decor" featuring bullfighting photos and paraphernalia.

Camden Brasserie ●🅂 17 | 14 | 17 | £25
216 Camden High St., NW1 (Camden Town/Chalk Farm),
020-7482 2114; fax 020-7482 2114
☑ "It's lasted because it's so consistent" assert long-time loyalists of this "loud-but-fun" Camden venue with "good" Med-British fare that can be "fab" for a snack "midweek or Saturday night"; a handful feels that, unless it gets an "update", the "overpriced nonsense" is "too boring" to dine upon more than once in a while.

Cantaloupe ◐ [S] 17 14 14 £23
35-42 Charlotte Rd., EC2 (Old St.), 020-7729 5566; fax 020-7613 4111
◪ "Popular" with Shoreditch "bohemians" seeking that "New York feel", this "lively" modern Mediterranean makes "simple, tapas-type" "nibbles" for a "lively" crowd grooving to house and funk in its "cool bar"; quieter foodies find the fare "dreadfully overrated" and warn that the DJ-induced "noise levels can make your teeth rattle."

Cantina del Ponte [S] 17 15 14 £31
Butlers Wharf Bldg., 36C Shad Thames, SE1 (Tower Hill), 020-7403 5403; fax 020-7403 4432
■ "Once you've found it", Sir Terence Conran's "old standard" Mediterranean on Butler's Wharf can be "lovely on summer evenings alfresco" with "stunning views of Tower Bridge and the Thames"; it seems that "nothing else sets it apart" from other rooms with a vista, however, since "overpriced" meals merit little mention and indoor diners decry decor that's "getting shabby."

Cantina Vinopolis [S] 18 17 15 £29
Vinopolis Museum, 1 Bank End, SE1 (London Bridge), 020-7940 8333; fax 020-7940 8334
◪ Under the railway arches of South Bank, this modern Mediterranean eaterie is a "vaulted" homage to the vine serving "varied and interesting but unpretentious" meals to match the 150-plus wines by the glass; it's "big" for "wild" "group nights out", though sipping, "not dining", is its focus; N.B. there's also a shop, bar and tasting tables on the premises.

Cantinetta Venegazzu [S] ▽ 15 14 16 £36
31-32 Battersea Sq., SW11 (Clapham Junction B.R.), 020-7978 5395; fax 020-7228 8946
■ This small Battersea Italian may be "fantastic in summer when you can be outside" on the patio, but interior "tables right next to each other" offer "no privacy whatsoever"; the few folks who've feasted from the "frequently changing" Venetian menu feel the "overpriced" offerings are "not as good as the bill suggests."

Canyon [S] 17 21 14 £30
Tow Path, Riverside, near Richmond Bridge (Richmond), 020-8948 2944; fax 020-8948 2945
■ A "perfect" riverside spot and "bright, sassy interior" get the thumbs-up at this "buzzy", "hip" Montana sibling in Richmond, and whilst the American Southwestern "fusion" menu splits votes ("first-rate" vs. "could be better"), "aloof", "slow" service is roundly condemned: "if they could just train their staff"; elderly diners can make use of a "fab golf buggy" to get them back to their cars.

CAPITAL RESTAURANT ◑ S   25 | 21 | 24 | £53
The Capital, 22-24 Basil St., SW3 (Knightsbridge), 020-7589 5171;
fax 020-7225 0011

■ "Away from the madding Harrods crowd", it's "bliss"
at this "chichi" but "low-key" dining room in Knightsbridge's
Capital hotel, where Eric Chavot's "superlative" New French
cooking "continues to be terrific"; matched by "remarkably
unstuffy service" in a "very romantic" small room, the
"wonderful flavours" are "pricey perfection" that fit the
bill "for Valentine's Day", "anniversary blowouts" and
other "special occasions."

Caraffini ◑   19 | 17 | 21 | £33
61-63 Lower Sloane St., SW1 (Sloane Sq.), 020-7259 0235;
fax 020-7259 0236

■ "Funny and always upbeat" staff make "you feel like a
lifelong friend" of this "lively" Italian near Sloane Square; its
dishes are "consistently good", and the ambience is so
"warm-hearted" that you'll have an "excellent meal" despite
"acoustics so bad it's hard to talk to your companion."

Caravaggio   18 | 16 | 15 | £34
107-112 Leadenhall St., EC3 (Bank), 020-7626 6206;
fax 020-7626 8108

◪ This "bright spot in the bleak City lunch scene" boasts
a rather "impressive" interior (a former bank) that "gets
quite hectic" thanks to the popularity of its "very good", if
"high-priced", Modern Italian cooking; the majority approves
of its "correct service", even if a handful suggests the place
"thinks too much about itself, not about the customer."

Carluccio's Caffe   21 | 16 | 17 | £20
3-5 Barrett St., W1 (Bond St.), 020-7935 5927;
fax 020-7487 5436 S
Fenwick, New Bond St., W1 (Bond St.), 020-7629 0699;
fax 020-7493 0069
8 Market Pl., W1 (Oxford Circus), 020-7636 2228;
fax 020-7636 9650 S

■ "See, a good meal in London doesn't have to be
expensive" boast boosters of this "promising" Italian
trio serving "fresh, well-cooked" fare "at good prices" in
"enjoyable", though "chaotic", settings; with branches in
Bond Street, St. Christopher Place and Oxford Circus, they're
"excellent when shopping" or "for Sunday brunch."

Casale Franco ◑ S   18 | 13 | 14 | £29
134-137 Upper St., N1 (Angel/Highbury & Islington),
020-7226 8994; fax 020-7359 1114

◪ "Decent" pastas and risottos, "delicious lobster" and
other seafood win praise for this cosy "osteria"-like Islington
Italian, but whilst fans find the plain surroundings "nice",
foes fume that the "tables are too close together"; opinions
are likewise split on the service ("very good" vs. "a shame"),
and some suspect it may have "gone off the boil."

Cassia Oriental ⬤　　　16　20　16　£33
*12 Berkeley Sq., W1 (Bond St./Green Park), 020-7629 8886;
fax 020-7491 8883*
◩ Advocates of this windowless Mayfair affair applaud the
"stylish" decor and the "fine" pan-Asian menu with "good-
value" fixed-price options, but critics complain that the
"beautiful decor is let down" by merely "average" fare and a
"cold", "hotel-like" ambience; still, retiring types who prefer
"not to be noticed" do appreciate the "cavernous" space.

Catch　　　　　　　17　16　16　£34
*158 Old Brompton Rd., SW5 (Gloucester Rd./
South Kensington), 020-7370 3300; fax 020-7370 3377*
◩ So "trendy" it feels like an "asylum for the PR industry",
this petite, youthful South Kensington seafooder shows
"great potential" with its "good-quality" fare according
to fans; "disappointed" dissenters, however, deem this
"catch too small", unable to "live up to its billing" or "prices."

Caviar Kaspia ⬤　　　21　18　19　£59
*18-18A Bruton Pl., W1 (Bond St./Green Park), 020-7493 2612;
fax 020-7408 1627*
■ "The place for Beluga" is what aficionados are calling this
smart Mayfair caviar specialist that also serves French and
Russian cuisines in a "civilised" setting; whilst cynics sneer
at the "pretentious" concept and the "funereal" ambience,
to fish-egg fanciers it's simply "great, great, great!"

Cecconi's　　　　　　–　–　–　VE
*5A Burlington Gardens, W1 (Green Park), 020-7434 1500;
fax 020-7434 2440*
This Italian legend from the '70s just off Bond Street has
been resurrected by Hani Farsi, the man behind Che, who
drafted the high-flying Giorgio Locatelli as consultant chef;
though prices are lofty, the prospects for this "popular"
spot "look hopeful", not least because the glamorous bar
has also taken off really well.

Cellar Gascon ⬤　　　20　20　18　£23
*59 West Smithfield, EC1 (Barbican), 020-7600 7561;
fax 020-7796 0601*
■ "Everything Club Gascon aspires to, at half the price"
insist supporters of this small, "good-looking", next-door
wine-bar sibling in Smithfield where "tiny, delicious
portions" of "excellent" Contemporary French cooking
are paired with "great" wines; cognoscenti counsel "do
not go there hungry" or if you're a "vegetarian", however.

Champor – Champor　　　–　–　–　M
62 Weston St., SE1 (London Bridge), 020-7403 4600
"Love the atmosphere" enthuse early visitors to this
Malaysian newcomer near London Bridge that can get
"quite mad" but boasts a well-priced menu of mix-and-
match flavours as well as a decor of murals and artefacts.

Chapel, The S
18 | 13 | 14 | £18

48 Chapel St., NW1 (Edgware Rd.), 020-7402 9220;
fax 020-7436 0456

■ Although it can be "a bit off-putting when you first enter", this "lively" gastro-pub in Edgware offers "a real surprise" to many with its "lovely" British dishes; the "no-rush" setting is "great for parties", though not surprisingly, some critics gripe that it gets too "loud and smoky."

Chapter Two S
21 | 18 | 20 | £33

43-45 Montpelier Vale, SE3 (Blackheath B.R.), 020-8333 2666;
fax 020-8355 8399

■ This Blackheath Village sequel to Kent's Chapter One is a "nice place for weekend jaunts", thanks to an "excellent-value" Modern European menu and "intimate" setting; whilst "they do pack you in", "attentive" staff help.

Charco's S
– | – | – | M

1 Bray Pl., SW3 (Sloane Sq.), 020-7584 0765

After a spell as Red River and then Bray Place, this bi-level Chelsea venue near King's Road changed hands post-*Survey* and after a swift makeover has gone back to using its more familiar name from the '80 and '90s; there's a well-priced Modern British menu that features tapas-style dishes.

Che ◗
17 | 18 | 17 | £40

23 St. James's St., SW1 (Green Park), 020-7747 9380;
fax 020-7747 9382

◪ A "grown-up" ambience and "widely spaced tables" make this St. James's eaterie an "excellent power lunch spot", even if the service is only "so-so"; whilst the Modern British cuisine is "decent" and "well-presented", sceptics sniff it's "not worthy of a revolution" and are apt to opt instead for the "cool" bar and cigar lounge downstairs.

Cheers ◗S
10 | 13 | 10 | £19

72 Regent St., W1 (Piccadilly Circus), 020-7494 3322;
fax 020-7494 2211

■ "Raise your glasses to a great sitcom" at this Piccadilly eaterie themed on the famous TV series that's a "fun" spot to imbibe; although boosters insist "office parties wouldn't be the same elsewhere", few are cheering the "badly done American diner" food, whilst many are vowing "not again."

Chelsea Bun S
15 | 9 | 12 | £13

70 Battersea Bridge Rd., SW11 (Clapham Junction B.R./
Sloane Sq.), 020-7738 9009
Limerstone St., SW10 (Earl's Court), 020-7352 3635 ◗

■ For a "first-class British fry-up", "you can't beat" this "old faithful" diner duo that's always "crowded" with regulars who come to "get the day off to a great start" or "nurse a hangover"; whilst "long waits" are to be expected, the service is "chipper" and "seems to go well with" the "everyday fare" that's "cheap, cheap, cheap."

Chelsea Kitchen ◑ S ≠   10 | 7 | 11 | £13
98 King's Rd., SW3 (Sloane Sq.), 020-7589 1330
■ "When you've spent all your money in the King's Road and need a good feed", this no-frills "London institution" in Chelsea serves "cheap", "large helpings" of "honest" diner grub in a setting as "cosy" as "mama's kitchen"; wags liken the fare to "prep-school food", but pragmatists point out that "you come for the price", after all.

Chelsea Ram S   18 | 14 | 13 | £19
32 Burnaby St., SW10 (Earl's Court/Fulham Broadway), 020-7351 4008; fax 020-7349 0885
■ "Ewe should make a visit" to this World's End haunt for "superb" British pub grub and a "great local atmosphere" ("council house meets mega-Sloane"); the lack of a "no-smoking area" gets the goat of some non-smokers, but regulars kid you not when they recommend this "casual, friendly" "neighbourhood venue."

Cheng-Du ◑ S   ▽ 14 | 12 | 14 | £23
9 Parkway, NW1 (Camden Town), 020-7485 8058; fax 020-7485 8058
▣ Not many know about this low-key Camden Chinese, but those who do appreciate its "reliable" Szechuan cuisine and "good-value" set menus that take the sting out of "expensive" à la carte prices; takeaway is an option for detractors disenchanted with the "lousy" atmosphere and "impossible" parking.

CHEZ BRUCE S   25 | 19 | 21 | £40
2 Bellevue Rd., SW17 (Wandsworth Common B.R.), 020-8672 0114; fax 020-8767 6648
■ "Perfect for posh nights out or cosy dinners", this "island of gourmet pleasure" by Wandsworth Common is the showcase for Bruce Poole's "sublime" Modern British–Classic French creations that are "cutting-edge", yet "unfussy"; though a few feel it "could do with a tart-up", the majority is pleased to find such "unpretentious" ambience and "friendly" service in a "top-notch" establishment.

Chez Gérard   16 | 15 | 15 | £29
119 Chancery Ln., WC2 (Chancery Ln.), 020-7405 0290; fax 020-7242 2649
Opera Terrace, The Market, 45 East Terrace, 1st fl., WC2 (Covent Garden), 020-7379 0666; fax 020-7497 9060 ◑ S
31 Dover St., W1 (Green Park), 020-7499 8171; fax 020-7491 3818 ◑ S
8 Charlotte St., W1 (Tottenham Court Rd.), 020-7636 4975; fax 020-7637 4564 ◑ S
9 Belvedere Rd., SE15 (Embankment/Waterloo), 020-7202 8470; fax 020-7202 8474 S

(continued)

(continued)

Chez Gérard

64 Bishopsgate, EC2 (Bank/Liverpool St.), 020-7588 1200;
fax 020-7588 1122
84-86 Rosebery Ave., EC1 (Angel), 020-7833 1515;
fax 020-7833 9118
14 Trinity Sq., EC1 (Tower Hill), 020-7480 5500; fax 020-7480 5588
☑ For a "quick" "basic French fix" (including "steak frites"
that "can't be beat"), these "chic", "low-key" brasseries
are "always a safe bet" for "middle-of-the-road dining"
as well as handy "pre-theatre" options; yet, "increasingly
bland" fare and occasionally "abrupt" service leave
regulars railing that the "standards have slipped."

Chez Liline 🅂   – – – E

101 Stroud Green Rd., N4 (Finsbury Park), 020-7263 6550;
fax 020-7272 9719
The "freshest" seafood straight from its sibling "fishmonger
next door" is the hook at this "fish-lovers' nirvana" in
Finsbury Park, with a "great-value" menu of "delicious",
Mauritian-inspired dishes that "you'd pay twice [as much]
for in the West End", nevermind the "modest" decor.

Chez Max   22 14 19 £39

168 Ifield Rd., SW10 (Earl's Court), 020-7835 0874;
fax 020-7244 0618
☑ "Excellent" French food is "the star" of this "noisy",
"eccentric" basement eaterie on the Chelsea-Fulham
border, where admirers are "always impressed" by the
"innovative" fare; reactions to the "entertaining owner" are
mixed, however: some find him "positively terrifying", whilst
others insist he's "worth the trip alone", adding "if you don't
feel hungry when he describes the food, you're not human."

Chez Moi   22 20 23 £42

1 Addison Ave., W11 (Holland Park), 020-7603 8267;
fax 020-7603 3898
■ "Excellent" service and "enjoyable" French-International
fare will make you "feel pampered" at this "old-fashioned"
Holland Park stalwart where the "high-camp interior"
comes straight "out of a time warp" and the "relaxing"
ambience is "perfect for romance"; for thrifty sorts who
find it a bit "expensive", there's a set-price lunch menu.

cheznico   22 20 21 £54

Grosvenor House Hotel, 90 Park Ln., W1 (Hyde Park Corner/
Marble Arch), 020-7409 1290; fax 020-7355 4877
☑ Now that "the stress on one's pocket has been alleviated"
by Nico Ladenis' switch to a "simplified", cheaper Classic
French menu, surveyors are split as to whether this "refined"
Mayfair hotel dining room is the "best value in town" or
simply "not what it used to be"; service elicits equally mixed
opinions ("exceptional" vs. "inattentive"), but most agree
that this spot still "has a sense of occasion about it."

Chiang Mai [S] 21 | 14 | 15 | £23

48 Frith St., W1 (Leicester Sq./Tottenham Court Rd.), 020-7437 7444; fax 020-7287 2255

■ "Refined Thai dishes" that "avoid the usual formula" are served by "friendly" staff in a "quiet", "calming" atmosphere at this "dependable" Soho eaterie; whilst even "real fans" concede that "decor's not one of its strong points", with "too many tables" squeezed into a "bite-size" room, they're glad that the small space "puts many [others] off."

China City ◐ [S] 15 | 9 | 11 | £20

White Bear Yard, 25A Lisle St., WC2 (Leicester Sq.), 020-7734 3388; fax 020-7734 3833

◩ Falling food and decor scores suggest that surveyors were unimpressed by a "recent restyle of the place and cuisine" at this spacious, "no-frills" Chinese spot located in the "middle of Chinatown", although many laud the "huge portions" of "passable, if not spectacular", fare as "great value"; gripers add the "brusque" service could stand some improvement.

China House ◐ [S] 18 | 21 | 17 | £23

160 Piccadilly, W1 (Green Park/Piccadilly Circus), 020-7499 6996; fax 020-7499 7779

◩ The "sky-high ceilings" and "elegant" decor at this "beautiful", "buzzy" Chinese in a converted bank on Piccadilly suggest prices that also reach the clouds, but in fact the "tasty" dumplings and noodle dishes are "very reasonable"; whilst sceptics call this high-profile spot "over-hyped" and "unremarkable apart from the location", it remains a popular standby for a "quick lunch."

Chinon 23 | 17 | 15 | £37

23 Richmond Way, W14 (Olympia/Shepherd's Bush), 020-7602 5968; fax 020-7602 4082

■ "Eccentric, but on its day, deeply satisfying", this "well-kept secret" near Olympia is where chef Jonathan Hayes prepares "out-of-the-ordinary", "addictive" Contemporary French dishes; the "bohemian" setting and "entertaining" service lend further charm to this "lovable local."

Chiswick, The [S] 19 | 13 | 17 | £30

131 Chiswick High Rd., W4 (Turnham Green), 020-8994 6887; fax 020-8994 5504

◩ Fans favour this Chiswick venue for its "very reliable", if "slightly repetitive", Modern British cuisine and "relaxed" atmosphere, but foes feel the menu's "promise is not matched" by "what arrives on the plate"; the "simple" decor leads some wags to advise bringing along an "attractive partner" because you'll find "nothing else to look at" here.

Chives | 24 | 15 | 19 | £36 |
204 Fulham Rd., SW10 (South Kensington), 020-7351 4747
☑ This youthful Chelsea addition to the Red Pepper stable (Green Olive, Purple Sage et al.) is off to a "good start", thanks to "young" chef Jun Tanaka's "excellent", "upmarket" Mediterranean cooking; some find the small, bi-level space a "pity", and the "spotty" service and "dreadful parking" also draw jeers, but most agree that this "happy find" is full of "potential."

Chor Bizarre ◐ S | 20 | 18 | 20 | £32 |
16 Albemarle St., W1 (Green Park), 020-7629 9802; fax 020-7493 7756
■ "Not as well known as it should be" according to enthusiasts, this Mayfair eaterie wins applause for its "consistent" efforts to "make Indian food interesting", as well as the "outstanding freshness" of its dishes; many are also sold on the "novel idea" of allowing diners to bid on the furniture and trappings in the "beautifully decorated" (albeit rather "kooky") room.

Choys ◐ S | 15 | 10 | 14 | £27 |
172 King's Rd., SW3 (Sloane Sq.), 020-7352 0505; fax 020-7352 0505
■ A "nice neighbourhood" choice for Chinese in Chelsea, this Szechuan and Cantonese specialist offers a midpriced menu that's "always dependable"; whilst many find the food and decor rather "boring", fans even recommend it as "a great place to take your parents."

Christopher's American Grill ◐ S | 18 | 16 | 16 | £37 |
18 Wellington St., WC2 (Covent Garden), 020-7240 4222; fax 020-7836 3506
Thistle Victoria Hotel, 101 Buckingham Palace Rd., SW1 (Victoria), 020-7976 5522; fax 020-7976 5521
☑ Surveyors are split over this "idiosyncratic" "old favourite" in Theatreland and its new "elegant, chic" Victoria sibling: the American "surf 'n' turf" formula leaves "dedicated carnivores" with their "taste buds aglow" (indeed, it's the top-rated North American in this *Survey*), but foes say the "high prices and low value" don't add up; opinions are similarly mixed about the service, but for most the "Manhattan"-esque settings are "always good fun."

Chuen Cheng Ku ◐ S | 16 | 7 | 11 | £18 |
17 Wardour St., W1 (Leicester Sq.), 020-7437 1398; fax 020-7434 0533
☑ When it comes to "great", trolley-borne dim sum ("served until 17.30"), fans boast that this "authentic" Chinatown Chinese is "as good as it gets", whilst the rest of the menu is "fun and filling"; yet foes find the fare merely "run-of-the-mill" and warn that when it gets busy, especially at lunch, "don't expect smiles" to accompany service.

Churchill Arms 🆂   20 | 14 | 13 | £14
*119 Kensington Church St., W8 (High St. Kensington/
Notting Hill Gate), 020-7727 4242*
▪ "Getting a table" is the "only problem" at this popular
dining room in a Notting Hill pub, where you "can't go
wrong" with the "bargain", "authentic" Thai dishes
and "Guiness to boot"; although the "unique", "unlikely"
setting is "cramped" and the service can be "rough", the
"price and quality" of the food smooth over most glitches.

Chutney Mary ◐🆂   19 | 19 | 18 | £33
*535 King's Rd., SW10 (Fulham Broadway), 020-7351 3113;
fax 020-7351 7694*
▪ For many, it's still "the done thing" to dine at this "self-
confident" Chelsea venue where "innovative", "consistent"
Indian cooking "rarely disappoints" and the "grand,
colonial" surroundings are "perfect for celebrating"; a
vociferous minority, however, contends that the food has
"lost its edge" and the service is "on autopilot", and that
therefore prices ought to be "a little more realistic."

Chutney's ◐🆂   20 | 10 | 13 | £14
*124 Drummond St., NW1 (Euston/Euston Sq.),
020-7388 0604*
▪ From fine "veggie Indian nosh" to a £5.45 eat-"all-you-
like" vegetarian buffet at lunch and all day Sunday, this
popular Euston eaterie offers "super food" at "remarkable"
"bargain prices"; its "filling" grub, like curries and
signature *rava dosai* accompanied by the eponymous
relish, is served in "lovely", albeit basic, surroundings.

Cibo 🆂   19 | 14 | 15 | £34
*3 Russell Gardens, W14 (Olympia/Shepherd's Bush),
020-7371 2085; fax 020-7602 1371*
▪ It's "not centrally located", but fans feel this "quiet",
"cosy" Italian near Olympia is "worth a trip" for "generous
portions" of "usually well-executed", "authentic" Tuscan
"staples" strong on seafood; however, "pompous staff"
that make "you feel forgotten" amidst the "average decor"
have sensitive sorts wondering why they bothered to
brave this "backwater."

Cicada   18 | 17 | 15 | £26
*132-136 St. John St., EC1 (Farringdon), 020-7608 1550;
fax 020-7608 1551*
▪ Those with savoir faire say this Clerkenwell Pan-Asian
serves "lovely" "food with flavour", including "excellent
starters"; but with its "great" minimalist decor, big plate-
glass windows, fireplace, patio and prominent bar, the
buzz is that it's more of a stylish watering hole for the
"hip" "who don't mind noise."

Cigala S　　　　　– | – | – | E
54 Lamb's Conduit St., WC1 (Holborn), 020-7405 1717;
fax 020-7242 9949
Hitting the right note in terms of "authentic" Spanish
atmosphere, this spartan-looking Bloomsbury "newcomer"
serves up "gutsy, peasant Spanish fare" well-matched
by an "interesting" Iberian wine list; there's a tapas bar
downstairs for quick or casual dining, but "book ahead",
as the place is often "over-crowded."

Cinnamon Cay S　　　　18 | 18 | 18 | £28
87 Lavender Hill, SW11 (Clapham Common),
020-7801 0932; fax 020-7924 5436
■ A "warm", "sweet" haven in Clapham, this "super place"
"tries hard" to deliver "delicious", "artistically presented"
Australasian dishes; with "friendly, helpful staff" and
"comfortable, interesting decor", it's an "excellent-value"
"South London find" "worth crossing the river for."

Cinnamon Club S　　　　– | – | – | VE
The Old Westminster Library, Great Smith St., SW1
(Westminster), 020-7222 2555; fax 020-7222 1333
After a long gestation, former PR Iqbal Wahhab has
opened the doors on this former public library near
Parliament to reveal an airy, elegant bi-level dining room
and stylish bar popular with politicos and lobbyists; head
chef Vivek Singh's wide-ranging, sophisticated Indian
cooking incorporates subtle French touches, courtesy of
consultant chef Eric Chavot from The Capital; N.B. they're
now serving an Indian Sunday brunch.

Circus ❶　　　　19 | 18 | 17 | £37
1 Upper James St., W1 (Piccadilly Circus), 020-7534 4000;
fax 020-7534 4010
■ At lunch when the media circus descends, this
"crisp"-looking Soho dining room feels "like an ad
agency reception"; a "somewhat limited" but "well-
prepared" Modern British menu is served in the "stark,
minimalist" eaterie, and a "trendy, upmarket clientele"
crowds the "dazzling" downstairs bar that's "straight
out of a James Bond movie."

City Miyama　　　　23 | 13 | 17 | £39
17 Godliman St., EC4 (St. Paul's), 020-7489 1937;
fax 020-7236 0325
◩ This discreet, little-known City Japanese near St. Paul's
Cathedral has a "sophisticated" menu that includes "great
sushi", signature shabu-shabu and several vegetarian
options; unfortunately, it suffers from a distinct "lack of
atmosphere" and, as wallet-conscious wags say, it "feels
like Tokyo, but more expensive."

City Rhodes   24 | 17 | 20 | £46
1 New Street Sq., EC4 (Blackfriars/Chancery Ln.),
020-7583 1313; fax 020-7353 1662
■ "Alone in its class" in Holborn, Gary Rhodes' "reliable
expense-accounter" proffers "splendid" Modern British
meals of "consistently high standard"; "don't let the suits
get you down" and ignore the "sterile decor" in its "very
businesslike" location, because the fare "is unbelievable";
N.B. head chef Adam Gray started in January '01.

Claridge's Bar S   20 | 22 | 22 | £28
Claridge's Hotel, Brook St., W1 (Bond St.), 020-7629 8860;
fax 020-7409 2210
■ Rendezvous with someone "glamorous" or "impress
visiting friends" with the "height of civilised living" at
this "utterly luxurious" "hideout" in the famously "classy"
Claridge's Hotel in Mayfair; "divine" Modern British
"nibbles" and "impeccably served cocktails" are "delicious"
in the "dark", "stylish" salon.

Claridge's Restaurant
Claridge's Hotel, Brook St., W1 (Bond St.)
See Gordon Ramsay at Claridge's.

CLARKE'S   26 | 19 | 23 | £46
124 Kensington Church St., W8 (Notting Hill Gate),
020-7221 9225; fax 020-7229 4564
■ Guests make "no stressful decisions" at Kensington's
Modern British "foodie essential": though "there is a little
more choice at lunchtime", "sheer culinary genius" Sally
Clarke cooks a "one-choice", four-course dinner that
"relies on seasonal goodies" for its "fresh, fresh, fresh"
appeal; "immaculate presentation is a feast for the eye",
to which the "gentle", "romantic" room plays understudy.

Clock Restaurant S   – | – | – | M
130-132 Uxbridge Rd., W7 (Boston Manor), 020-8810 1011;
fax 020-8405 5464
When it's time for a "treat", the few in-the-know drop in for
"regularly changing", "imaginative" Modern British dishes
at this "absolute gem" in Hanwell; "imaginative use of a
former bank" has transformed a place for saving money
into a "casually chic" eaterie where "money is well spent."

CLUB GASCON   24 | 19 | 19 | £44
57 West Smithfield, EC1 (Barbican), 020-7796 0600;
fax 020-7796 0601
■ "Foie gras is an art" at this "unique" Smithfield eaterie
where the "ambitious [Contemporary] French chef does
amazing things" in "baffling combinations" with the
"decadent" stuff; the "wide variety" of goose liver and other
"taster-size" dishes makes for a "stunning" "multi-course
feast" – and a "surprisingly large bill"; N.B. they've also
recently opened Comptoir Gascon, a delicatessen.

Coffee Republic ⊅   13 | 12 | 13 | £8

French Connection, 99-103 Long Acre, WC2 (Covent Garden), 020-7240 9725; fax 020-7240 9725 S
8 Pembridge Rd., W11 (Notting Hill Gate), 020-7229 6698; fax 020-7229 6698 S
197 Kensington High St., W8 (High St. Kensington), 020-7938 4261; fax 020-7938 4261 S
2 S. Molton St., W1 (Bond St.), 020-7629 4567; fax 020-7629 4567 S
80 The Strand, W1 (Charing Cross), 020-7580 4678; fax 020-7580 4678 S
39 Great Marlborough St., W1 (Oxford Circus), 020-7734 5529; fax 020-7734 5529 S
157 King's Rd., SW3 (Sloane Sq.), 020-7351 3178; fax 020-7351 3178 S
147 Fleet St., EC4 (Blackfriars), 020-7353 0900; fax 020-7353 0900
30-32 Ludgate Hill, EC4 (St. Paul's), 020-7329 2522; fax 020-7329 2522
47 London Wall, EC2 (Moorgate), 020-7588 2220; fax 020-7588 2220
Additional locations throughout London

■ "If you like it strong" and "hot", the "frothy coffee" "serves its purpose" at the many links in this "dependable" chain; these joints are "ok for caffeine" and "excellent for fat-free" pastries, but only "so-so" for "soggy sandwiches" served by "disorganised staff."

Collection, The ●S   15 | 17 | 14 | £37

264 Brompton Rd., SW3 (South Kensington), 020-7225 1212; fax 020-7225 1050

☑ "Its time has passed" according to critics of this "noisy", "suffocatingly smoky" Brompton Cross venue where "sign language is needed to converse", but defenders insist it "usually delivers" "good" Modern British cooking amidst "great atmosphere"; beyond the high-design "entrance that promises a lot", the bi-level interior "seems to lose the plot" according to some; N.B. the popular bar closes at 11 PM.

Como Lario ●   18 | 14 | 18 | £32

22 Holbein Pl., SW1 (Sloane Sq.), 020-7730 2954; fax 020-7244 8387

■ Focus isn't as much on the "up-to-scratch" fare as it is on the "great Italian festive spirit" at this "boisterous" Sloane Square spot, which is so "wonderfully friendly" that it's "sometimes too crowded" and "chaotic" for service not to be "somewhat erratic."

Condotti ●   17 | 16 | 17 | £20

4 Mill St., W1 (Oxford Circus/Piccadilly Circus), 020-7499 1308; fax 020-7491 2122

■ "Very reliable" and "reasonable", this "old favourite" in Mayfair is a "great place to grab a bite" of "good" pasta and "pizza that's a cut above"; "rather classy" for its category, it's particularly "useful after a hard day's shopping."

CONNAUGHT HOTEL, RESTAURANT S

24 | 23 | 24 | £57

The Connaught Hotel, Carlos Pl., W1 (Bond St./Green Park),
020-7499 7070; fax 020-7495 3262

■ "Step back into the golden past" at this "gilded" "haven of peace and excellence" in Mayfair's Connaught Hotel, where the "fabulous", "beautifully prepared" British-French "grand classic" cuisine is simply a "don't-miss", whilst "impeccable service" makes you feel that "everything is possible"; such "high standards" come at accordingly steep prices, however, so "have daddy pay"; N.B. after 26 years, head chef Michel Bourdin is set to retire at the end of 2001, when sous chef Jerome Ponchelle will don the top toque.

Conrad Gallagher ●S

– | – | – | VE

179 Shaftesbury Ave., W1 (Leicester Sq.), 020-7836 3111;
fax 020-7836 3888

After taking Dublin by storm, 30-year-old chef Conrad Gallagher makes his London debut with this huge, bi-level Theatreland newcomer featuring a glass-fronted, street-level bar and smart basement dining room serving punchy Modern Irish fare at top-end prices, along with a 400-strong wine list with an old world emphasis; there's also a private dining room.

Coq d'Argent S

18 | 20 | 16 | £40

No. 1 Poultry, EC2 (Bank), 020-7395 5000; fax 020-7395 5050

☑ "Groups of City power brokers noisily celebrate" the "stunning views" from Sir Terence Conran's Contemporary French aerie; this "fabulous rooftop rendezvous" is a "great venue to impress visitors" or "get some sun during lunch" on the terrace, but fussbudgets feel it's "overpriced" for "ordinary" fare and servers who think they are "grander than you."

Cork & Bottle ●S

16 | 13 | 14 | £19

44-46 Cranbourn St., WC2 (Leicester Sq.), 020-7734 7807;
fax 020-7287 1094

■ "An oasis in the middle of the tourist melee that is Leicester Square", this "cosy", "buzzy" wine bar boasts an "amazing", "20-plus-page list" of bottles and an "affordable" French-Med menu of "quick bites"; the basement setting is so "unpretentious" that many deem it downright "rickety" and suggest that the owner "do it up a bit."

Corney & Barrow

12 | 12 | 12 | £20

116 St. Martin's Ln., WC2 (Leicester Sq.), 020-7655 9800;
fax 020-7655 9816
44 Cannon St., EC4 (Mansion House), 020-7248 1700;
fax 020-7236 0074
3 Fleet Pl., EC4 (St. Paul's), 020-7329 3141; fax 020-7329 5155
16 Royal Exchange, EC3 (Bank), 020-7929 3131;
fax 020-7621 9209

(continued)

(continued)
Corney & Barrow
Lloyd's of London, 1 Leadenhall Pl., EC3
(Bank/Monument), 020-7621 9201; fax 020-7929 3947
37 Jewry St., EC3 (Aldgate), 020-7680 8550; fax 020-7680 6058
2B Eastcheap, EC3 (Monument), 020-7929 3220; fax 020-7929 7058
12-14 Mason's Ave., EC2 (Bank), 020-7726 6030;
fax 020-7726 6304
19 Broadgate Circle, EC2 (Liverpool St.), 020-7628 1251;
fax 020-7920 0106
9 Cabot Sq., E14 (Canary Wharf), 020-7512 0397; fax 020-7512 9852
Additional locations throughout London
■ "Bridget Jones meets the City boys" for "after-work drinks" at this "surprisingly good chain" of wine bars, and whilst "food is not the focus" here, the perky patrons can have some "nice bar nibbles" to go with a glass of "great wine"; dining diarists declare, however, "if you don't like crowds or noise, avoid it."

Costa Coffee S   13 | 12 | 12 | £8
44-48 New Oxford St., WC1 (Tottenham Court Rd.),
020-7580 5602; fax 020-7580 5602
69 Wigmore St., W1 (Bond St.), 020-7486 4131; fax 020-7486 4131
19 Goodge St., W1 (Goodge St.), 020-7637 5239;
fax 020-7637 5239
4 Grosvenor St., W1 (Bond St./Oxford Circus),
020-7499 2857; fax 020-7499 2857
112-114 Oxford St., W1 (Oxford Circus/Tottenham Court
Rd.), 020-7637 3459; fax 020-7637 3459
62 Shaftesbury Ave., W1 (Piccadilly Circus),
020-7734 3050; fax 020-7734 3050
56-58 King's Rd., SW3 (Sloane Sq.), 020-7591 0119;
fax 020-7591 0119
19 Hampstead High St., NW3 (Hampstead), 020-7431 5221;
fax 020-7433 1182
13 New Bridge St., EC4 (Blackfriars), 020-7356 0891;
fax 020-7356 0891
99 Gresham St., EC2 (Bank), 020-7600 2988; fax 020-7600 2988
Additional locations throughout London
☑ If "all [London's] coffee places blend into one after a while", perhaps it's the number of "busy" "locations that make a quick cup a plus point" at this "typical chain" offering "variable-quality", "American-style" brews and snacks amid a "lively Italian atmosphere"; penny-pinchers complain that it "costa too much" for "nothing special."

Costa's Grill ⊅   15 | 10 | 18 | £14
12-14 Hillgate St., W8 (Notting Hill Gate), 020-7229 3794
■ There are "no surprises" at this "dependably" "delightful neighbourhood" Greek-Cypriot in Notting Hill; if the fare is just "alright", it does "get cheaper and more cheerful with the passing years", and the garden is "great for sitting out in summer."

Cotto 21 14 16 £33

44 Blythe Rd., W14 (Olympia), 020-7602 9333; fax 020-7602 5003

◪ It's "not easy to find" this newcomer behind Olympia, but some say its "great" Modern British cooking is worth the search; others are "not very impressed" with the "overpriced" fare and are downright "disappointed" by the "cold", "bleak interior" and "slow service."

County Hall Restaurant [S] 19 20 16 £36

London Marriott County Hall, Westminster Bridge Rd., Queens Walk, SE1 (Westminster), 020-7902 8000; fax 020-7928 5300

◪ Views of Parliament across the Thames are "romantic", if somewhat "restricted", from this "pleasant" dining room serving "surprisingly good" Modern European meals in Westminister's Marriott Hotel; "rather inexperienced" staff move "slowly" through this "bit of a banqueting hall", but the "spacious" room is handy "for larger parties."

Cow, The [S] 18 15 16 £28

89 Westbourne Park Rd., W2 (Westbourne Park), 020-7221 5400; fax 020-7727 8687

■ Take "a second date" for a "rather illicit", "unexpected treat" at this "trendy Notting Hill hangout" upstairs from the "lively" same-named bar; daily changing "posh pub grub with seafood leanings" "seduces" a crowd "chockablock" with trendy locals who "relax" over "good conversation" amid its "friendly", "bohemian atmosphere."

Cranks ≠ 16 9 12 £13

5 Cabot Pl., E14 (Canary Wharf), 020-7513 0678; fax 020-7519 6792
5 Cow Cross St., EC1 (Farringdon), 020-7490 4870
8 Adelaide St., WC2 (Charing Cross), 020-7836 0660; fax 020-7836 0660
17 Great Newport St., WC2 (Leicester Sq.), 020-7836 5226; fax 020-7836 7120
23 Barrett St., W1 (Bond St.), 020-7495 1340; fax 020-7409 0671
9-11 Tottenham St., W1 (Goodge St.), 020-7631 3912; fax 020-7636 6113

◪ From its "beginnings in a humble cafe", this "easy, self-serve" Vegetarian institution has cranked itself into a "cookie-cutter", "canteen-like" chain; friends say it serves "consistently healthy", "hearty fare for moderate prices", but foes "fuss" it "overcharges for various permutations of boiled, mashed", "bland" veggies.

Creelers ▽ 21 14 22 £32

3 Bray Pl., SW3 (Sloane Sq.), 020-7838 0788; fax 020-7838 0788

■ A "quiet getaway from the hustle-and-bustle near King's Road", this "favourite" Eclectic-"Scottish secret" serves "modestly priced", "well-prepared" West Coast seafood and Gaelic dishes to a crowd that is made to "feel like family"; "pleasant" but still a bit "amateurish", this "homely" highlander has "not yet realised its great potential."

Crescent, The [S] ▽ 21 | 19 | 19 | £32

The Montcalm, 99 Fulham Rd., SW3 (South Kensington), 020-7225 2244; fax 020-7581 0547

■ "The mother of all wine lists" (including "great [selections] by the glass") is the claim to fame of this simple, bi-level vino bar in a "fashionable" location on Brompton Cross; it's a popular local hangout, even if the "interesting" Eclectic fare (in rather "small portions") doesn't set the world alight; P.S. the wine tastings offered monthly are "worth a try."

CRITERION BRASSERIE ◐ [S] 20 | 25 | 15 | £39

224 Piccadilly, W1 (Piccadilly Circus), 020-7930 0488; fax 020-7930 8380

◪ "It still glitters" rave reviewers enchanted with the "exquisite", "old-fashioned splendour" of this "Piccadilly oasis" gilded in "'20s decadence", though "all that gold" tends to outshine the kitchen's French-British cooking; widely disparaged is the "slow" "factory service" from "arrogant" staff, but even the most disgruntled concede that this "Marco Pierre White creation" is "perfect for before or after the theatre"; P.S. the "set lunch" is a "wonderful value."

Crivelli's Garden [S] ▽ 15 | 15 | 15 | £25

National Gallery, mezzanine level, Sainsbury Wing, WC2 (Charing Cross/Leicester Sq.), 020-7747 2869; fax 020-7747 2438

■ Though it "started well" according to those who know it, the masses have yet to discover this "surprising" spot in the Sainsbury Wing of the National Gallery, which boasts "great views" onto Trafalgar Square; part of the Red Pepper Group, it has two dining areas: one "for tea and cakes" and snacks, the other for more substantial Mediterranean cuisine; N.B. closed for dinner except on Wednesdays.

Cuba ◐ [S] 12 | 11 | 12 | £21

11-13 Kensington High St., W8 (High St. Kensington), 020-7938 4137; fax 020-7795 6064

■ "Drinking and salsa" dancing are the favoured activities at this Kensington eaterie that features an "excellent bar on Friday and Saturday nights", live music and Latin dancing lessons for the uninitiated; as for the "ok" Cuban edibles and tapas, they provoke less comment than the very generous happy 'hour' (which runs from midday to 8.30 PM).

Cuba Libre & Havana Bar ◐ [S] 12 | 14 | 12 | £21

72 Upper St., N1 (Angel), 020-7354 9998; fax 020-7354 9890

■ With "reliable", if "basic", Cuban cuisine to soak up the rum drinks, this "fun", colourful Islingtonian, one of the first Cubans in London, makes a "great place to have a party" (though pickier palates recommend "going for cocktails" and dancing only); a bust of Fidel Castro and other quirky touches enliven the "nice", Old Havana–style interior.

Cucina 🇸   19 | 13 | 16 | £30
45A South End Rd., NW3 (Belsize Park), 020-7435 7814;
fax 020-7435 7147
☑ "Hampstead's best local" may be this "sophisticated"
Pacific Rim–Modern British eatery, where a "good-looking"
interior is the backdrop for "fresh cooking" featuring an
"interesting" range of flavours; regulars assert "they try so
hard", even if there's a grumble or two about "iffy service."

Dakota 🇸   17 | 18 | 15 | £32
127 Ledbury Rd., W11 (Notting Hill Gate/Westbourne Park),
020-7792 9191; fax 020-7792 9090
☑ There's still a "great buzz" at this "cool" Notting Hill
sibling to Montana, Canyon et al., where the American
Southwestern menu is deemed "surprisingly good"
(especially the "fab brunch"), even if forward-looking types
fuss it's "not cutting-edge" enough; "smug", "absolutely
inattentive" service comes in for a bashing.

Dalchini 🇸   – | – | – | M
147 Arthur Rd., SW19 (Wimbledon Park), 020-8947 5966
The fact that it's "owned by the Sarkhel's" team is a plus
point for this new eatery with the novel concept of cooking
traditional Chinese dishes in an Indian style (i.e. with liberal
use of spices); in addition to the large basement with
takeaway service, there's a coffee bar/deli for snacks.

Dan's   16 | 15 | 17 | £35
119 Sydney St., SW3 (Sloane Sq./South Kensington),
020-7352 2718; fax 020-7352 3265
☑ "They're all so lovely" at this "rather clubby" Chelsea
stalwart where the regulars always "greet each other"; if
there's a sense the "dependable" British cooking "could try
harder", most find it satisfactory (it's "good – honestly"); P.S.
the "pretty conservatory and garden" are "nice in summer."

Daphne ◐   19 | 16 | 18 | £31
83 Bayham St., NW1 (Camden Town), 020-7267 7322;
fax 020-7482 3964
■ This "welcoming", "family"-run Greek "hidden" away
in Camden Town is "the sort of restaurant that puts one
in a good mood" according to admirers of its "homely"
"staple" dishes selected from a sensibly priced menu.

Daphne's ◐🇸   19 | 20 | 17 | £42
112 Draycott Ave., SW3 (South Kensington), 020-7589 4257;
fax 020-7225 2766
☑ "Rub shoulders with the beautiful set" at this "elegant"
(if "cramped") Brompton Cross Modern Italian that "after
all these years" remains "fun for people-watching" and is
"still a solid bet" for "appealing", "delicious" cuisine that's
"not cheap, but worth it"; as ever, some doubters "yawn"
it's "had its day" and object to the staff's "attitude", but
they remain in the minority: "just never fails!" cheer most.

Daquise S | 11 | 7 | 15 | £18 |
20 Thurloe St., SW7 (South Kensington), 020-7589 6117

■ "Please, never a makeover" plead "nostalgic" regulars of this "quaint", "unchanging" Polish "institution" outside the South Kensington tube station, an "oasis" where "authentic Polish" cooking (pork schnitzel, goulash and the like) goes down well amid the "time-warp decor"; equally endearing are its affordable prices offering "amazing value."

De Cecco | 20 | 14 | 16 | £29 |
189 New King's Rd., SW6 (Parsons Green), 020-7736 1145; fax 020-7371 0278

✓ "Bags of brio" and "excellent seafood" (try the lobster spaghetti) are the hallmarks of this "popular", "friendly" Parsons Green Italian "institution" where most "love the pictures on the wall", though a few affectionately suggest it could "be spruced up"; "a great standby" for "any occasion", it's no surprise the place is "always packed."

DEFUNE S | 26 | – | 20 | £39 |
34 George St., W1 (Bond St.), 020-7935 8311; fax 020-7487 3762

■ Those who were "put off by rather careworn" premises in Blandford Street should take another look now that this "authentic" Japanese has relocated post-*Survey* to new premises near Marble Arch; as far as the food is concerned, it's the "nearest to going to Japan" say connoisseurs, who rate it some of "the best, freshest sushi" and "fantastic sashimi" in town (rated second only to Nobu), prepared by theatrical, "jolly chefs"; not surprising, it "comes at a hefty price."

Del Buongustaio S | 21 | 15 | 17 | £31 |
283-285 Putney Bridge Rd., SW15 (East Putney), 020-8780 9361; fax 020-8780 9361

✓ "This is real Italian cuisine" assert friends of the "authentic" regional selections on a monthly changing menu at this "casual", "cramped" Putney Italian, which, despite an "unassuming exterior", can get "noisier than the Ministry of Sound"; acoustics aside, most find the fare "comforting" and "homely" and the staff "accommodating"; N.B. there's an adjoining pasticceria.

Delfina Studio Cafe | 16 | 17 | 13 | £30 |
Delfina Gallery, 50 Bermondsey St., SE1 (London Bridge), 020-7357 0244; fax 020-7357 0250

■ Inside a Bermondsey contemporary art gallery/artists' studio that was once a chocolate factory, this "usually packed" Modern British–Eclectic eaterie is "always a treat" for a meal before or after checking out the art, according to enthusiasts of its "interesting, fresh" cooking and "good-to-look-at" interior; N.B. lunch only.

Denim ◐ 🅂　　　　　　　10 | 16 | 10 | £26

4A Upper St. Martin's Ln., WC2 (Leicester Sq.),
020-7497 0376; fax 020-7497 0378

☑ "Good cocktails meet good people" at this "trendy"
"chill-out heaven" in Theatreland with a downstairs bar
for the "cool" "club" set and an upstairs Modern British–
Pacific Rim eaterie; the cuisine draws little comment beyond
this pointed suggestion: "you go for the drinks, not the food."

Depot, The 🅂　　　　　　17 | 19 | 17 | £27

Tideway Yard, Mortlake High St., SW14 (Barnes Bridge B.R.),
020-8878 9462; fax 020-8392 1361

☑ "If you can get a riverside table", this "low-key" Barnes
retreat is "a joyful place to be", but whilst the "view alone"
makes it worth a visit, the Modern British cooking gets a split
vote ("good" vs. "a bit up and down"); "nice staff" and
a "well-chosen" wine list tip the balance in its favour.

Dibbens　　　　　　　▽ 21 | 19 | 22 | £33

2-3 Cowcross St., EC1 (Farringdon), 020-7250 0035;
fax 020-7250 3080

■ This Smithfield spot draws little comment from surveyors,
but those who know it call it a "real gem" ("nice to dine
without the usual collection of men in suits"), where the
"relatively inexpensive" Modern British cooking comes
with "genuine, friendly service."

Dish Dash　　　　　　　18 | 18 | 16 | £21

57-59 Goodge St., W1 (Goodge St.), 020-7636 7474;
fax 020-7323 3077

☑ "Persian fun" pervades this "popular", "festive" eaterie
near Tottenham Court Road, a relative "newcomer" where
the "real key is knowing what to order" from the many
"delicious" and "interesting dishes" on an Anglo-Persian
menu that's "not as expensive" as some might expect; whilst
a few misanthropes "don't like sitting on the [shared]
benches", most find the setup "super for large groups."

Diverso ◐ 🅂　　　　　　16 | 15 | 15 | £33

85 Piccadilly, W1 (Green Park), 020-7491 2222; fax 020-7495 1977

■ "Eat Italian food – not something that imitates it" at this
quiet Italian on the edge of Green Park that locals consider
"good" for a "fast business lunch", thanks to its "original",
albeit "expensive", menu; more amorous types identify it
as ideal for "romantic" dining.

DKNY Bar　　　　　　　16 | 16 | 15 | £17

DKNY, 27 Old Bond St., W1 (Bond St./Green Park),
020-7499 6238; fax 020-7629 2796

■ "When faced with a heavy day's" "hard-core shopping",
Bond Street denizens make a beeline for this "clean" cafe
and juice bar inside DKNY serving "yummy" American-
style "refreshments"; consensus is, it's "perfect" for a
regenerative "break", though (surprise) it's "quite pricey."

Dôme　　　　　　　　　　　　11 | 12 | 11 | £17
8-10 Charing Cross Rd., WC2 (Leicester Sq.),
020-7240 5556; fax 020-7240 5565 S
32 Long Acre, WC2 (Covent Garden), 020-7379 8650;
fax 020-7379 8652 S
35A-B Kensington High St., W8 (High St. Kensington),
020-7937 6655; fax 020-7937 6644 S
57-59 Old Compton St., W1 (Leicester Sq./Piccadilly
Circus), 020-7287 0770; fax 020-7287 2172 S
194-196 Earl's Court Rd., SW5 (Earl's Court), 020-7835 2200;
fax 020-7835 0066 S
354 King's Rd., SW3 (Sloane Sq.), 020-7352 2828;
fax 020-7371 5855 S
Unit 2 Kingswell Ctr., 58-62 Heath St., NW5 (Hampstead),
020-7431 0399; fax 020-7421 4228 S
341 Upper St., N1 (Angel), 020-7226 3414;
fax 020-7704 6719 S
57-59 Charterhouse St., EC1 (Farringdon), 020-7336 6484;
fax 020-7336 6866
26 Hill St., Richmond (Richmond), 020-8332 2525;
fax 020-8332 1661 ◑S
Additional locations throughout London
■ "If you're passing" by and "hungry" for "a quick
bite", the many links of this ubiquitous chain hit the
spot with "simple", "cheap" French bistro fare that
presents "no surprises"; whilst less-sanguine surveyors
sigh the "formula" is "tired" ("hip, friendly" staff not
withstanding), supporters vote it a "tranquil" destination
to "spend an afternoon" with "coffee and the papers."

Don, The　　　　　　　　　　　– | – | – | E
The Courtyard, 20 St. Swithins Ln., EC4 (Bank), 020-7626 2606;
fax 020-7626 2616
From the team behind Bleeding Heart, this "welcome
newcomer" to the City boasts a ground-floor Modern
British restaurant and quieter basement brasserie,
both of which specialise in ports and sherries (fittingly,
considering that it's housed in the former headquarters of
famous port producer Sandeman); largely undiscovered
as of yet, this "friendly, relaxed" spot is gaining in
popularity, leading a few regulars to lament "sorry the
secret's out – but it deserves to be."

Don Pepe ◑　　　　　　　▽ 18 | 11 | 16 | £25
99 Frampton St., NW8 (Edgware Rd.), 020-7262 3834;
fax 020-7724 8305
■ Whilst it's still not widely known after a quarter-century
in business, loyalists insist "this is the place" for "hearty",
"authentic" Spanish paellas and other classic fare (most
notably, "good tapas"); it makes a fine venue to watch
"Spanish footie on the TV", and there are live guitar
performances most evenings.

Dorchester, Bar ◐ [S] 21 | 20 | 21 | £34

The Dorchester, 53 Park Ln., W1 (Hyde Park Corner/ Marble Arch), 020-7629 8888; fax 020-7317 6464

◪ "Excellent at any time of day", the "comfortable", "elegant" bar in Mayfair's famous Dorchester is "great for a classy, light bite" from an Italian menu that includes "nice snacks" ("historic club sandwich"); most evenings, the "always-good-fun" atmosphere is enhanced by a "jazz pianist" who tickles the ivories of what was once Liberace's bejeweled baby grand; a tip for would-be Casanovas: "good for impressing a new date."

Dorchester, Grill Room [S] 22 | 21 | 23 | £51

The Dorchester, 53 Park Ln., W1 (Hyde Park Corner/ Marble Arch), 020-7629 8888; fax 020-7317 6464

■ With a new chef, Henry Borsi, now ensconced at this "old-school" Traditional British dining room in Mayfair's Dorchester, its "lovely", "theatrical" setting (circa '31) remains an "all-time classic" for "superlative" cooking employing fine native ingredients in "splendid", time-honoured dishes "to keep the British end up"; "take your mum" to this "Sunday lunch favourite", and make sure the "dessert trolley groaning with goodies" stops at the table.

Dorchester, Oriental 24 | 22 | 23 | £53

The Dorchester, 53 Park Ln., W1 (Hyde Park Corner/ Marble Arch), 020-7317 6328; fax 020-7317 6464

■ Some of "the best Chinese food in London" (second only to Four Seasons) comes out of the kitchen at this "grown-up" eaterie in Mayfair's Dorchester, where chef Kenneth Poon's "refined" Hong Kong–style cuisine, "excellent" formal service and "sublime wine" selection are simply "exquisite" – and "exquisitely expensive"; those who feel a certain "lack of atmosphere" in the "elegant" main dining room might prefer booking one of three "fantastic private rooms" themed after Thailand, China and India.

Dover Street ◐ [S] 14 | 13 | 13 | £27

8-10 Dover St., W1 (Green Park), 020-7629 9813; fax 020-7491 2958

◪ It's a "hen-night heaven" with dancing to live jazz in the evenings and DJs in the "late-night" hours (until 3 AM), but this basement Mayfair "old favourite" is less beloved for its New French cooking, deemed "ordinary" at best; still, many find it hard to pass up its "cheap lunch" (£8 for two courses).

Down Mexico Way ◐ [S] 13 | 14 | 13 | £24

25 Swallow St., W1 (Piccadilly Circus), 020-7437 9895; fax 020-7287 1427

■ The "buzzing Latino atmosphere" is the "biggest attraction" at this Piccadilly "lively fiesta", a "jolly party venue" for those who like it "hot, hot, hot"; whilst the "huge portions" of "greasy" South American fare may not "match the real thing", "great cocktails" and "lots of Latin dancing" (with live bands and a house dance troupe) compensate.

Drones S　　　20　20　19　£44
1-3 Pont St., SW1 (Sloane Sq.), 020-7235 9555;
fax 020-7235 9566
■ "Marco's done it again" swoon surveyors smitten with this "slick", "comfortable" "good addition" to the Marco Pierre White stable, where the "great" Classic French cooking ("similar to Mirabelle") is "hard to fault" and the service "willing to please"; a disgruntled few "won't go again" ("huge disappointment"), but they're outnumbered by those who cheer "nice to have Drones back" after it "closed down" for a "fab refurb" last year.

Duke of Cambridge S　　20　15　17　£22
30 St. Peter's St., N1 (Angel), 020-7359 3066;
fax 020-7359 1877
☑ Seekers of a total "organic experience (beer, food)" visit this "buzzy" Islington gastro-pub that appeals to "genuine lovers of food" with its "ever-changing", seasonal "menu that never fails" and "relaxed, happy atmosphere"; loyal locals who find it's "all the better for" being in their neighbourhood imagine it might even "help push property prices higher."

Duke of Cambridge S　　19　16　17　£19
228 Battersea Bridge Rd., SW11 (Clapham Junction),
020-7223 5662
☑ "Not so much a pub with food as a restaurant with beer and drinks" summarise surveyors of this "very busy", recently refurbished gastro-pub that dishes out "great" Modern British cooking amid a "friendly atmosphere" (including a pleasant patio); denizens of Battersea boast "not everyone is lucky enough to have such a great local."

Eagle, The S⊅　　22　13　13　£20
159 Farringdon Rd., EC1 (Farringdon), 020-7837 1353;
fax 020-7689 5882
■ London's "original gastro-pub" in Clerkenwell "tries hard to live up to its reputation" for "unusual", "excellent-value" Mediterranean "flair food" served up in "funky", "informal" environs, and its enormous "popularity" is evidence of its success; the downside's "long waits for a table" and "crowded, smoky" conditions "louder than runway 2 at Heathrow", but nonetheless hardcore fans find it's "never a disappointment" – "if you can find a seat!"

East One　　　17　16　14　£21
175-179 St. John St., EC1 (Farringdon), 020-7566 0088;
fax 020-7566 0099
☑ It's "an old idea, but always great fun" insist those enchanted with the stir-fry concept (diners select their "own ingredients" for the "mad chefs" to prepare) at this Chinese wokery near Smithfield Market, which is considered "one of the better places that does the cooked-in-front-of-your-eyes thing."

Ebury Wine Bar & Restaurant S   16 | 14 | 16 | £24
139 Ebury St., SW1 (Victoria), 020-7730 5447;
fax 020-7823 6053

■ "A safe bet and still going strong", this "lovely little secret" on the Pimlico-Belgravia border remains a "pleasant" retreat for "experimental, but not intimidating" Modern British cuisine that mixes "warming" wine-bar classics with more "eccentric" options (like ostrich), whose trendiness belies the "dark", "traditional" decor; N.B. the front bar recently underwent a refurbishment.

Eco   20 | 16 | 15 | £20
162 Clapham High St., SW4 (Clapham Common),
020-7978 1108; fax 020-7720 0738 S
4 Market Row, SW4 (Brixton), 020-7738 3021;
fax 020-7720 0738

◪ This "bustling Clapham stalwart" and its Brixton sibling "could be slightly more comfortable", but nonetheless they win over most with their "fab", "interesting pizzas" heaped with "great" toppings; although service is generally "quick" once seated, expect to "wait" for a table because they get "sooo busy"; N.B. at press time, a Baker Street branch was in the works.

Ed's Easy Diner S   14 | 14 | 14 | £14
Pepsi Trocadero Ctr., 38 Shaftesbury Ave., W1 (Piccadilly Circus), 020-7287 1951; fax 020-7287 6998 ◑
12 Moor St., W1 (Leicester Sq./Tottenham Court Rd.),
020-7439 1955; fax 020-7494 0173 ◑
362 King's Rd., SW3 (Sloane Sq.), 020-7352 1956;
fax 020-7352 4660
Brent Cross Shopping Ctr., NW4 (Brent Cross),
020-8202 0999; fax 020-8202 7526 ◑
O₂ Ctr., 255 Finchley Rd., NW3 (Finchley Rd.),
020-7431 1958; fax 020-7431 9837

◪ It might be "as close to an American experience as Moscow is", but still, many consider this chain of U.S.-themed, '50s-style diners with "roadhouse decor" and golden-oldie hits on "the juke box" "fun places" for "fattening, fantastic junk food" ("delicious milk shakes", "gorgeous" burgers and fries); even critics who portray it as "pretty cheesy" concede "kids love it."

Efes Kebab House ◑   16 | 11 | 15 | £21
175 Great Portland St., W1 (Great Portland St.),
020-7436 0600; fax 020-7636 6293 S
80-82 Great Titchfield St., W1 (Oxford Circus),
020-7636 1953; fax 020-7323 5082

■ There's a "jolly atmosphere" – thanks in no small part to the "fun belly dancing" and cabaret – at this "noisy", "old-fashioned" West End duo that "offers well-cooked Turkish delights" at a "decent price"; its "decor's tired", but still plenty swear by it as "the perfect late-night stop."

El Blason
18 | 17 | 20 | £30

8-9 Blacklands Terrace, SW3 (Sloane Sq.), 020-7823 7383; fax 020-7589 6313

■ "El blooming good" enthuse fans of this "exceptionally friendly" ("owner knows all the neighbourhood gossip") Spaniard just off King's Road, which serves "tasty" tapas and classic dishes "at a reasonable price", though it also welcomes those who just "stop by for a drink"; regulars approve of the recent "great redo" of the interior.

Elena's l'Etoile
20 | 17 | 20 | £36

30 Charlotte St., W1 (Goodge St.), 020-7636 1496; fax 020-7637 0122

☑ Even though longtime hostess "Elena [Salvoni] rules with an iron hand" at this Fitzrovian brasserie, everyone receives an "exceptional welcome" (it's no wonder, then, that among the "interesting clientele" are "lots of regulars"); everyone agrees that this "very atmospheric place" "feels really French", but when it comes to the Gallic cuisine, opinions diverge: "always a treat" vs. "disappointing."

Elephant Royale S
– | – | – | E

Westferry Rd., E14 (Island Garden), 020-7987 7999; fax 020-7115 0073

Situated beside the entrance to the Greenwich foot tunnel in the Isle of Dogs, this colourful Thai debutante that's liberally decorated with Oriental foliage and artefacts offers an extensive, reasonably priced menu; there's also outside seating and a bamboo-lined, jazz-playing piano bar serving cocktails.

El Gaucho S ⇗
19 | 14 | 14 | £27

88 Ifield Rd., SW10 (Earl's Court/Fulham Broadway), 020-7823 3333; fax 020-8769 6586 ◗
Chelsea Farmers Mkt., 125 Sydney St., SW3 (South Kensington/Sloane Sq.), 020-7376 8514; fax 020-8769 6586

■ "Yee-haw! – giddy-up with some serious Argentine steaks" at this Pampas-themed pair of "friendly", "cute" and "cramped" "red-meat" havens in Chelsea Farmers Market and Chelsea (dinner only), where the "perfectly cooked" beef is so "tender and juicy" you hardly need "a knife"; everything comes in "hearty portions" and goes down better with plenty of red wine.

Elistano S
18 | 13 | 18 | £27

25-27 Elystan St., SW3 (South Kensington), 020-7584 5248; fax 020-7584 8965

☑ "Locals" "like the friendly, if disorganised, atmosphere" of this "modish" but "laid-back" Italian in Chelsea, claiming it's "reliable for an impromptu meal" of "good, homely" classic dishes paired with selections from a "nicely chosen wine list"; given its "beautiful-people" clientele and "good windows to admire the view outside", there's never a shortage of scenery.

Emile's
20 | 17 | 22 | £26

96-98 Felsham Rd., SW15 (Putney Bridge), 020-8789 3323;
fax 020-8785 7683

■ The Wandsworth Bridge Road branch "has closed,
very sadly", but this remaining Putney "local" is still
going strong, delivering a "great all-round package" of
"consistently good" Modern British–Eclectic cuisine at
"cheap prices"; admirers note the "great staff" here are
unusually "friendly" to boot.

Emporio Armani Caffe
15 | 16 | 14 | £23

Emporio Armani, 191 Brompton Rd., SW3 (Knightsbridge),
020-7581 0854; fax 020-7823 8854

■ "Small portions, high prices, but it is Armani" quip
customers of this "self-confident" in-store Italian cafe in
Knightsbridge, which might resemble a highly "tailored"
"train buffet car" but is considered by many as "a cut
above" and a shoppers' "quintessential stop" ("just a
quick snack, darling!").

Engineer, The 🖪
19 | 15 | 15 | £25

65 Gloucester Ave., NW1 (Camden Town/Chalk Farm),
020-7722 0950; fax 020-7483 0592

☑ "Glad I've been" say satisfied surveyors of this "cool,
relaxed" Primrose Hill gastro-pub noted for its "honest",
sometimes "inventive" Modern British–Eclectic cooking that
"tries the ecological route"; whilst the budget-minded
balk at the "pricey" menu, the majority calls it "perfect for
a girlie chat, romantic meal" or "late Sunday lunch" amidst a
"charming" setting (including a "gorgeous garden").

English Garden 🖪
19 | 17 | 17 | £41

10 Lincoln St., SW3 (Sloane Sq.), 020-7584 7272;
fax 020-7584 1961

☑ Following this "classy" bi-level Chelsea eaterie's
takeover a couple of years ago by the Richard Corrigan/
Searcy team, plenty of praise still abounds for its "heavenly"
Modern European cooking that's "always special" and
definitely "worth the money"; however, it's deemed "not
as good as it used to be" when it comes to the "frumpish"
decor and "slow service" (an assertion borne out by a
drop in ratings since the last *Survey*).

Enoteca Turi
24 | 19 | 21 | £33

28 Putney High St., SW15 (Putney Bridge), 020-8785 4449;
fax 020-8785 4449

■ "Putney's culinary tour de force" is this "outstanding
local" Modern Italian, according to devotees of Giuseppe
Turi's "enterprising", "*autentico*" cuisine, complemented
by a "superb wine" selection and served by a "welcoming
staff"; most agree that it's "much better post-revamp"
("refurbished, but same soul"), with its decor now looking
almost "as brilliant as the food."

Enterprise, The 🔲
17 | 18 | 15 | £28

35 Walton St., SW3 (South Kensington), 020-7584 3148;
fax 020-7784 2516

▨ Whilst some suggest it's "living on memories" of its
'90s "glory" days, this "lazy, warm" Chelsea gastro-pub
continues to reel 'em in with its "good ambience" and
array of "comfort food" from a "reliable" Modern European
menu; in the evenings it attracts a crowd of "wanna-be
Lovejoy types" ("perfect to catch a man on a Saturday
night"); P.S. it can be "very smoky", but the main gripe's
"can't book for dinner."

Esarn Kheaw 🔲
22 | 9 | 10 | £22

314 Uxbridge Rd., W12 (Shepherd's Bush), 020-8743 8930

■ "Even though the name is unpronounceable and the
decor kitschy", the "phenomenal", "adventurous"
Northeastern Thai cuisine ("clears the senses") at this
basic Shepherd's Bush canteen "makes up for it";
aficionados agree it's "one of the best" of its kind in
London, but just "don't expect overly friendly service
until they know you."

Exhibition Thai 🔲
∇ 16 | 14 | 15 | £30

19 Exhibition Rd., SW7 (South Kensington), 020-7584 8359;
fax 020-7741 0393

▨ The "new look works well" is the consensus on the
"charming revamp" of this "old local" Thai close to the
Natural History Museum in South Kensington, where
the introduction of "Western-style" food presentations
"also works well."

Fairuz 🔲
23 | 15 | 20 | £26

3 Blandford St., W1 (Bond St.), 020-7486 8108;
fax 020-7935 8581

■ This "quaint", "quiet" Marylebone Lebanese is voted
the top Middle Eastern eaterie in this *Survey*, a "sure bet"
for "excellent", "deliciously prepared" mezze followed by
"fresh and filling" classic dishes; a few grousers gripe
about "neglectful service", but most consider this to be an
"efficient, friendly" spot that "should be more expensive"
(just don't tell the owners).

Fakhreldine ●🔲
20 | 13 | 16 | £34

85 Piccadilly, W1 (Green Park), 020-7493 3424;
fax 020-7495 1977

Fakhreldine Express ●🔲

92 Queensway, W2 (Bayswater/Queensway),
020-7243 3177

▨ With a good view over Green Park through smoked
glass, this large, first-floor Lebanese eaterie replete with
Islamic decorative touches might "feel like a warehouse",
but those addicted to its "excellent" mezze and other
traditional dishes "love" it all the same; N.B. Fakhreldine
Express is primarily for takeaway.

Fatboy's Cafe S 14 | 11 | 15 | £18

*10A-10B Edensor Rd., W4 (Turnham Green), 020-8994 8089;
fax 020-8994 8089*
*431-433 Richmond Rd., Richmond (Richmond),
020-8892 7657; fax 020-8891 4707* ◗

■ Whilst they're somewhat "lacking in atmosphere"
("decor's a real step back in time"), this duo of "fun", basic
cafes in Chiswick and Richmond is considered "tops" for
"good, fast" Thai cooking at "great value" – hence they
get "very busy"; N.B. the Edensor Road venue is BYO.

Feng Shang Floating Restaurant S 17 | 19 | 18 | £31

*Cumberland Basin, Prince Albert Rd., NW1 (Camden Town),
020-7485 8137; fax 020-7267 2990*

☑ Aboard a colourful, Chinese junk–style houseboat
moored beside Regent's Park (and reached across a
drawbridge) is this attractive venue where "great" Chinese
fare and "polite service" satisfy seafaring surveyors; a tip:
it's "better for lunch than dinner – there's no view at night."

ffiona's ◗S 21 | 15 | 21 | £26

*51 Kensington Church St., W8 (High St. Kensington/
Notting Hill Gate), 020-7937 4152; fax 020-7937 4152*

☑ The "charming" attentions of "wonderful" Ffiona Reid-
Owen (she "sits at your table to take your order" and
"always makes great suggestions") are a major factor in
peoples' warm opinions of this "homey" Kensington eaterie
with a "comforting" menu of British "home cooking";
regulars are "afraid to let everyone in on this secret gem",
even if there are a few murmurs about the "rustic" interior
growing a bit "musty."

FIFTH FLOOR ◗S 20 | 18 | 17 | £39

*Harvey Nichols, 109-125 Knightsbridge, SW1
(Knightsbridge), 020-7235 5250; fax 020-7823 2207*

☑ "The 19th hole of a round of shopping", this "smart",
"slick" eaterie on the top floor of Knightsbridge's Harvey
Nichols department store "rarely disappoints", and a
new, "innovative" Modern British menu ushered in by
recently installed chef Simon Shaw is considered
"worth going for"; if a few dissenters deem it all "a touch
uninspiring" and "expensive", the "great bar" has its
fans: "pick up a man and have a lovely meal!"

Fifth Floor Cafe S 17 | 15 | 13 | £25

*Harvey Nichols, 109-125 Knightsbridge, SW1
(Knightsbridge), 020-7823 1839; fax 020-7823 2207*

☑ Admirers "would climb to the 10th floor" for a visit to this
"fun, trendy" Knightsbridge cafe inside Harvey Nichols
that's "wonderful any time of the day" for "unfussy" Med
snacks and light meals, with "fantastic" "people-watching"
and dining on the roof terrace to boot; snipers unimpressed
with the "huge queues" and "noise" ("Piccadilly Circus is
more relaxing") dismiss it as "too expensive."

Fina Estampa ▽ 18 12 14 £26
150-152 Tooley St., SE1 (London Bridge), 020-7403 1342;
fax 020-7403 1342

■ "Perfect for something different" suggest the few voters who know this old-fashioned ("like going back to the '80s") eaterie near Tower Bridge, which produces "delicious, exotic" Peruvian dishes, most notably seafood, and stands as perhaps the only outpost of Lima-style cuisine in London; "deserves to be better known."

FireBird 21 23 21 £43
23 Conduit St., W1 (Oxford Circus), 020-7493 7000;
fax 020-7493 7011

☑ Evoking memories of pre-revolutionary Russia with its "regal" decor, this Mayfair eaterie (sib to the New York original) proffers a "succulent" menu of "surprisingly light" fare, from caviar and blini to "big, beefy borscht"; admirers wonder "why's it empty?" and some sceptics set forth a possible answer: "not as hot as the name suggests" – "better enjoyed with a shot or two of vodka"; N.B. the new Room of Luxury is made to look like an Orient Express carriage.

First Floor S 16 21 15 £33
186 Portobello Rd., W11 (Ladbroke Grove/Notting Hill Gate),
020-7243 0072; fax 020-7221 9440

☑ The "Baroque setting" of this "charming, bohemian" Modern British dining room above a Portobello Road pub is "trendy, but not austere" after a redo not long ago that's deemed a success (the decor rating is up markedly since the last *Survey*); when it comes to the "imaginative" menu, however, opinions diverge: some say "wonderful", but others "nothing special"; P.S. there's a "great private room."

Fish! S 18 14 15 £27
41A Queenstown Rd., SW8 (Clapham Junction),
020-7234 3333; fax 020-7234 3343
92 Waterford Rd., SW6 (Fulham Broadway), 020-7234 3333
296 Upper Richmond Rd., SW1 (East Putney),
020-7234 3333
1 Lawn Terrace, Blackheath Village, SE3 (Blackheath B.R.),
020-7234 3333
Cathedral St., Borough Mkt., SE1 (London Bridge),
020-7234 3333; fax 020-7234 3343
36 Belvedere Rd., SE1 (Waterloo), 020-7234 3333;
fax 020-7234 3343
33 Westferry Circus, Hanover House, E14 (Canary Wharf),
020-7234 3333; fax 020-7234 3343

☑ "The Pizza Express of fish" best describes this "useful" school of eateries that's grown quickly thanks to its "tough-to-beat" formula of "fresh" seafood "prepared simply" in a "canteen" setting; whilst carpers crab the "concept soon stales", citing a "not-very-exciting menu" that "turns out expensive" as well as sometimes "slightly eccentric staff", at least it "does exactly what the name says."

Fishmarket | 18 | 16 | 15 | £36

Great Eastern Hotel, Liverpool St., EC2 (Liverpool St.), 020-7618 7200; fax 020-7618 7201

◪ "Stylish" and spacious it might be, but Sir Terence Conran's Bishopsgate seafooder inside the Great Eastern Hotel "lacks atmosphere" according to many (like "dining in a container"); its "good" seafood classics receive polite approval, "high prices" aside, leading admirers to imagine "if this weren't in the City, it'd be packed every night."

Floriana | 21 | 21 | 18 | £48

15 Beauchamp Pl., SW3 (Knightsbridge), 020-7838 1500; fax 020-7584 1464

◪ It's "hard to fault" Riccardo Mazzuchelli's Knightsbridge Modern Italian where "marvellous" fare matches the "excellent setting" and a "sense of occasion" makes for "special" "romantic" evenings with "that someone in your life"; still, some manage to do just that, saying the place has "lost its previous charm" and is deemed "overpriced."

Florians [S] | 21 | 16 | 19 | £33

4 Topsfield Parade, Middle Ln., N8 (Highgate), 020-8348 8348; fax 020-8292 2092

◪ Supporters of this "suburban" spot in Crouch End tout its "tasty [Modern] Italian food" served "in decent portions" along with "nice Sicilian wines" and report the kitchen is "more reliable than last year"; others applaud the "friendly" staff for giving it a "good try" but say they "wouldn't rave about" the "variable" and sometimes "too-complicated" cuisine; N.B. above ratings do not reflect a post-*Survey* chef change.

FOLIAGE | 25 | 21 | 21 | £52

Mandarin Oriental Hyde Park, 66 Knightsbridge, SW1 (Knightsbridge), 020-7235 2000; fax 020-7201 3811

■ The hotel may be the Mandarin Oriental, but the "superb cuisine" is Modern European at this "refreshing" spot where the "innovative" menu "emphasises luxury ingredients" for "maximum flavour" and the "comfortable" room's "huge window" makes "Hyde Park part of the decor"; though the staff strikes some as "slick" and "meticulous", others swear they're "so slow you should take pyjamas."

Food for Thought [S]⊘ | 20 | 9 | 12 | £13

31 Neal St., WC2 (Covent Garden), 020-7836 9072; fax 020-7379 1249

■ "Gorgeous value" is the most appealing quality of this Covent Garden Vegetarian, a basement barracks "for bean-munchers" that "can't be beat", given its "huge servings" of "inventive" fare that's "consistently yummy" yet "healthy"; whilst many "complain" about the "cramped", "crowded" quarters and "lousy decor", it's nevertheless "worth the queue"; P.S. night owls should note that the kitchen "closes far too early" (8 PM).

Footstool Restaurant ▽ 12 | 18 | 12 | £21
St. John's, Smith Sq., SW1 (Westminster), 020-7222 2779; fax 020-7222 5221
■ Church meets state beneath St. John's, Smith Square in Westminster as peckish politicos congregate in this "convenient" cafe, even though its "variable buffet" of Modern British–European lunch fare draws little comment; on those evenings when the nave above becomes a "popular concert" venue, "reasonable-value" prix fixe suppers are offered, but book early, as it "can be crowded."

Formula Veneta ◐ 16 | 13 | 16 | £34
14 Hollywood Rd., SW10 (Earl's Court), 020-7352 7612; fax 020-7352 8305
◪ Motor-racing enthusiast/"owner Gianni" Pauro and his "friendly staff" "are what make this" "mid-market" "neighbourhood" spot in Chelsea "a treat"; the "reliable [Modern] Italian food" may be "lacking in finesse" and may not "blow your socks off", but most call it "consistently tasty"; still, a few foes fume that "formula is the word" for the "fairly good cooking" and note that "too many tables overfill" the "too-noisy" room.

Fortnum's Fountain 16 | 16 | 15 | £24
Fortnum & Mason, 181 Piccadilly, W1 (Green Park/ Piccadilly Circus), 020-7973 4140; fax 020-7437 3278
■ "Discerning tourists", "out-of-town matrons" and "sherry-swashing ladies" "crowd" this "terribly British" all-day eaterie in Piccadilly's famous Fortnum & Mason "for a shopping break" or a "good lunch" "with the kids", so expect "to queue"; some say it's "a shame they keep taking old favourites off" the "modernised menu", but the "tutting waitresses" remain an "old-fashioned pleasure."

Four Regions ◐ [S] 18 | 18 | 17 | £27
County Hall, Riverside Bldg., SE1 (Waterloo/Westminster), 020-7928 0988; fax 020-7928 9060
■ The "nice location" of its "spacious" riverside dining room in Westminster's "prestigious" County Hall complex makes this Chinese "worth going to for the view alone", but "authentic" multiregional cooking has regulars returning to "order what [they] like"; in fact, some report that the "quality" cuisine makes it "easy to get into a rut" and chide the management to "change their menu more often."

FOUR SEASONS CHINESE ◐ [S] 24 | 11 | 15 | £25
84 Queensway, W2 (Bayswater), 020-7229 4320
■ "The legendary", "excellent crispy" "roast duck" at this Bayswater Chinese has hyperbolic supporters swearing they "know Far Easterners who fly to London just to eat" it; apocrypha aside, an otherwise "reliable" menu for those not in a fowl mood has proponents proclaiming "forget the decor and ambience" – this "always-busy" darling is "worth the wait."

Four Seasons Hotel, Lanes Restaurant 🇸
23 21 23 £47

Four Seasons Hotel, Hamilton Pl., W1 (Green Park/Hyde Park Corner), 020-7499 0888; fax 020-7493 6629

◪ "Excellent (for a hotel restaurant)" is how epicureans sum up the Eclectic cooking of Eric Deblonde, executive chef of this "grand" room overlooking Park Lane; his "attractively presented", "high-standard" cuisine "lives up to expectations of Four Seasons quality" and is "backed up by" "attentive service" (making it "great" "for business" or "a special occasion"), but some sigh the overall "effect is a bit like a chain."

Four Seasons Hotel, Quadrato 🇸
20 18 20 £44

Four Seasons Canary Wharf, 46 Westferry Circus, E14 (Canary Wharf), 020-7510 1999; fax 020-7510 1998

◪ Name and shape aside, there's nothing square about this Modern Italian in the Canary Wharf outpost of the Four Seasons chain; "not your run-of-the-mill hotel restaurant", it features an exhibition kitchen where "innovative" Northern dishes from an "extensive, changing" menu are prepared using "quality ingredients" and served by "friendly" staff; some sceptics scoff, though, that the "food tries too hard."

40° at Veronica's 🇸
▽ 16 12 17 £31

3 Hereford Rd., W2 (Bayswater/Queensway), 020-7229 5079; fax 020-7229 1210

◪ Chef-owner Veronica Shaw "specialises in British" recipes from the nation's distant culinary past at her small Westbourne Grove eaterie, where the cooking impresses some ("imaginative", "different") more than others ("mediocre", "overpriced"); present-day tastes are now accommodated too with a second menu of Modern British "nouvelle cuisine."

Fox & Anchor
15 10 12 £18

115 Charterhouse St., EC1 (Farringdon), 020-7253 5075; fax 020-7253 5089

■ "If a heroic English" "brekkie" and "an accompanying pint is your bag", this red-carpeted, velvet-seated veteran of a pub (opened in Smithfield in 1898) "is for you", provided "you make the effort" to get up early, as the fry-up starts at 7 AM; Traditional British lunches can be ordered from 10.30 AM, but be warned it's closed evenings and weekends.

Foxtrot Oscar
12 10 12 £25

Riverside Plaza, Chatfield Rd., SW11 (Clapham Junction/Wandsworth Town B.R.), 020-7481 2700 🇸
79 Royal Hospital Rd., SW3 (Sloane Sq.), 020-7352 7179; fax 020-7351 1667 🇸

(continued)

(continued)
Foxtrot Oscar
16 Byward St., EC3 (Tower Hill), 020-7481 2700;
fax 020-7481 2700 ◑

☑ "Huge portions" of Traditional American–British fare draw devotees to this trio of "basic" diners, but dissenters say the formula "needs an overhaul", citing "amateur service" and "boring" food from kitchens that "have stopped trying"; and whilst some say the year-old "one in Battersea is nice", others ask "how about an update" of the original Chelsea outpost's "dingy" decor?

Francofill 🟦 | 14 | 9 | 13 | £17 |
1 Old Brompton Rd., SW7 (South Kensington), 020-7584 0087;
fax 020-7591 0712

☑ "Good for a quick" meal, this "family-friendly" South Kensington bistro offers its own unique take on "French fast food" – the eponymous Francofill, a bread loaf stuffed with grilled meat and your choice of sauce; though fans say its "reasonable" prices mean "value for your money", others are "indifferent" to its "unpretentious cafe" fare.

Frederick's ◑🟦 | 20 | 20 | 19 | £38 |
106 Camden Passage, N1 (Angel), 020-7359 2888;
fax 020-7359 5173

■ "A classic" in its 32nd year, this "special-occasion destination" in Islington remains "true to expectations" thanks to "innovative" Modern British dishes "exquisitely presented" by "friendly" staff; the "gorgeous room" (adjoined by a "lovely" "garden oasis") has "regained its lustre" with a recent revamp of artwork; it may be "pricey", but "excellent value" makes this "real treat" "worth it."

Freedom Brewing Company   ▽ | 11 | 12 | 9 | £17 |
41 Earlham St., WC2 (Covent Garden), 020-7240 0606;
fax 020-7240 4422 🟦
14-16 Ganton St., W1 (Oxford Circus), 020-7287 5267;
fax 020-7287 2729

☑ Distinctive "functional decor" – plywood furniture, stainless-steel vats and bars – distinguishes this microbrewery duo in Convent Garden and near Regent Street; frequented more for their "quite interesting" selection of beers than their "pleasant-enough" British bar menu (mussels and chips, sausage and mash), both can be "quiet at lunchtime" but get extremely busy after work.

Friends ◑🟦 | 19 | 12 | 14 | £24 |
6 Hollywood Rd., SW10 (South Kensington), 020-7376 3890;
fax 020-7352 6368

■ It's all "very friendly" at this "nice Italian" in Chelsea, a "fun" "place for singles" in the evenings and "for [families with] children" on weekends; "excellent antipasti", generous "pasta portions" (some say "too big!") and "can't-be-beat" "thin-and-crispy" pizzas add up to "great value."

Fung Shing ◗ 🅂   20 | 10 | 14 | £26

15 Lisle St., WC2 (Leicester Sq.), 020-7437 1539;
fax 020-7743 0284

■ Boosters praise the "authentic", "delicious" Cantonese food "at excellent prices" offered by this Chinatown Chinese, as well as its "quiet", "understated" atmosphere and "friendly", "fast service"; though a few express "disappointment" that it's "not what it used to be", citing "drab", even "naff decor" and "typical" fare that's "no thrill", most maintain it's "generally very good."

Futures Café-Bar   ▽ 16 | 11 | 16 | £18

2 Exchange Sq., EC2 (Liverpool St.), 020-7638 6341;
fax 020-7377 1015

Futures Vegetarian Takeaway

8 Botolph Alley, EC3 (Monument), 020-7623 4529;
fax 020-7621 9508

■ "Always a winner", this City spot near Liverpool Street Station is "good for Vegetarian lunches" and has recently spruced up its menu; smokers shy away during the fume-free hours of 12-2 PM but feel more welcome at night, when it becomes a bar offering beers, wines, minerals and spirits; N.B. the Monument branch is takeaway and runs a popular delivery service.

Galicia ◗ 🅂   – | – | – | M

323 Portobello Rd., W10 (Ladbroke Grove), 020-8969 3539

"Tucked away at the end of Portobello Road", this Notting Hill Gate spot may look like "nothing special" but rustles up quite "good tapas" and other "traditional" Spanish dishes; a handful finds that "the quality of food is hit-or-miss," but "yummy" fare, "friendly service" and a "fun atmosphere" have most saying "olé!"

Garbo's 🅂   16 | 10 | 15 | £26

42 Crawford St., W1 (Baker St./Marylebone), 020-7262 6582;
fax 020-7262 6582

◪ "If you like Swedish food", you may find this Marylebone Scandinavian a "jewel" declare devotees of its "delightful" dishes (such as gravadlax that's "always good") and "simple" setting that looks like "your aunt's front room"; detractors beg to differ, however, citing "bland fare" and servers who "vont to be alone."

Garlic & Shots ◗ 🅂   11 | 13 | 14 | £19

14 Frith St., W1 (Leicester Sq.), 020-7734 9505;
fax 020-7734 8722

■ "Not for the faint-hearted", this "eccentric", Eclectic Soho haunt is "one of the most original restaurants" around, boasting a "bizarre atmosphere and a bizarre menu" on which "absolutely everything (including ice cream and beer) is smothered in garlic"; wags warn "vampires, beware" and advise mere mortals, just "don't talk to anyone for days!"

Gate, The
23 | 18 | 20 | £26

72 Belsize Ln., NW3 (Belsize Park), 020-7435 7733 🅂
51 Queen Caroline St., W6 (Hammersmith), 020-8748 6932;
fax 020-8563 1719

■ "Wonderful" is the word for this "laid-back bolt hole" for the "virtuous", an "unsung hero" in Hammersmith that "gives Vegetarianism a good name" by "concocting" a "variety" of "really original", "always-interesting dishes" from "quality ingredients"; "good service" from "pleasant staff" complements "delightful dining" that is "unbelievable value"; P.S. a "new one just opened in Belsize Park."

Gaucho Grill
21 | 17 | 16 | £31

19 Swallow St., W1 (Piccadilly Circus), 020-7734 4040;
fax 020-7734 1076 🅂
89 Sloane Ave., SW3 (South Kensington), 020-7584 9901;
fax 020-7584 0045 ◗🅂
44 Heath St., NW3 (Hampstead), 020-7431 8222;
fax 020-7431 3714 ◗🅂
1 Bell Inn Yard, EC3 (Bank/Monument), 020-7626 5180;
fax 020-7626 5181
29 Westferry Circus, E14 (Canary Wharf), 020-7987 9494;
fax 020-7987 9292 ◗

■ "Grab yer cowboy boots" and head off to one of these "noisy" chophouses, an expanding chain where the cows are "on the plates as well as the walls"; each is a "carnivore's heaven" with "huge slabs" of the "finest" Argentinean steak that's "so delicious you'll forget the words 'mad cow'" and forgive the "fun" but "tacky" decor; service splits surveyors – some say "charming", others "irritating."

Gaudí
21 | 18 | 18 | £36

63 Clerkenwell Rd., EC1 (Farringdon), 020-7608 3220;
fax 020-7250 1057

▣ Most maintain that the "outstanding", "creative", "delicious Spanish cuisine" and "attentive service" at this Clerkenwell spot would "make a Spaniard homesick"; still, some say the "location is a downside", the "bizarre decor" ("in the spirit of its namesake", architect and proto-surrealist Antoni Gaudí) is "a Daliesque nightmare" and the food is similarly "overblown"; "no tapas in sight" means others are "disappointed."

Gay Hussar
18 | 17 | 18 | £36

2 Greek St., W1 (Tottenham Court Rd.), 020-7437 0973;
fax 020-7437 4631

■ "Generous proportions" and a "genuine Central European feel" make this Soho stalwart "the place to go for a blowout" on "solid", "traditional Hungarian" dishes; a few say it's "lost its way" with "its heavy food" and carp about the "formal" feel, but most appreciate the "gracious service" and "lovely atmosphere" (though it's "not so good if your neighbour smokes").

Geale's Fish Restaurant S   15 9 12 £19
2 Farmer St., W8 (Notting Hill Gate), 020-7727 7528;
fax 020-7229 8632

☑ Partisans report that "the new owners" (since '99) of
this "scruffy"-looking spot in Notting Hill Gate (formerly a
"family affair" that opened in '39) have maintained its
"standard of" serving "real fish and chips" (though
"longtime customers remember much lower prices");
the disgruntled deride it as "not as good as it used to be",
a sentiment supported by falling food and service ratings.

George   _ _ _ E
Private club; inquiries: 020-7491 4433
The doyen of private clubs, Mark Birley, has created a new,
unusually relaxed Mayfair club next door to Harry's Bar with
an elegant dining room where an open kitchen prepares
simple, classic Modern European fare at prices lower
than any other Birley establishment; downstairs there's an
intimate, urbane bar with seductive alcoves and a giant
TV screen to maintain contact with the outside world.

George Bar & Restaurant S   ▽ 17 18 14 £18
Great Eastern Hotel, 40 Liverpool St., EC2 (Liverpool St.),
020-7618 7300

☑ "Sir Terence Conran's interpretation of a pub" in the
City's Great Eastern Hotel suits those who prefer their
taverns "without soiled carpets and a thick fog of smoke"
and scores points for "imaginatively prepared variations"
on "pub grub" that have enthusiasts exclaiming "who said
[Traditional] British food is boring?"; naysayers give a nod
to the "good idea" but still slam the "mixed-quality cooking."

Getti   13 12 13 £28
42 Marylebone High St., W1 (Baker St./Bond St.),
020-7486 3753 S
74 Wardour St., W1 (Leicester Sq./Piccadilly Circus),
020-7437 3319 ☾
16-17 Jermyn St., SW1 (Piccadilly Circus), 020-7734 7334;
fax 020-7734 7924

☑ A "good local standby", this quickly expanding "value-
for-your-money chain" offers "rustic" Modern Italian fare,
"pristine" settings and "centrally placed" locations in Soho,
St. James's and Marylebone; contrarians condemn its scoff,
saying you'd do better at a "cheaper spaghetti house",
and slam the "service [as] slow unless you are a regular."

Ginger S   _ _ _ M
115 Westbourne, W2 (Notting Hill), 020-7908 1990;
fax 020-7908 1991
This bright newcomer to the competitive Westbourne Grove
scene is a very reasonably priced Bangladeshi venue
that's off to a promising start since opening post-*Survey*;
N.B. the chef, Albert Gomes, comes from the respected
Sonargaon Hotel in Dhaka.

Giraffe S 16 | 14 | 16 | £17
6-8 Blandford St., W1 (Baker St./Bond St.), 020-7935 2333;
fax 020-7935 2334
46 Rosslyn Hill, NW3 (Hampstead), 020-7435 0343;
fax 020-7431 4090 ●
29-31 Essex Rd., N1 (Angel), 020-7359 5999; fax 020-7359 6158
■ "Chirpy", "spunky" staff set the tone at these "friendly"
eateries springing up around town (the latest in Islington),
which have a loyal following "from brunch to dinner" thanks
to "unique" International fare prepared with "lots of organic
ingredients" and a "quirky" "mix of interior styles" that
fosters a "lively atmosphere"; "children's favourites",
they're "not for the fussy" but "never a letdown."

Gladwins ▽ 20 | 15 | 18 | £38
Minster Ct., Mark Ln., EC3 (Bank/Monument), 020-7444 0004;
fax 020-7444 0001
☑ Caterer Peter Gladwin's spacious spot is "tough to
fault" according to supporters of its "imaginative" "but
expensive" International menu (although "bottled water is
included") served in "good surroundings" suited for
business meetings; the place provokes polar reactions in
others, though, who claim it's a "typical City restaurant"
that "can and should do better" with its "fixed menu";
N.B. lunch only, but can be booked for evening events.

Glaister's Garden Bistro S 16 | 15 | 14 | £26
36-38 White Hart Ln., SW13 (Barnes Bridge B.R.),
020-8878 2020
8-10 Northcote Rd., SW11 (Clapham South), 020-7924 6699;
fax 020-7924 5733 ●
4 Hollywood Rd., SW10 (Earl's Court/South Kensington),
020-7352 0352; fax 020-7376 7341 ●
☑ Fans of its "honest" Anglo-Franco cooking hoot "hooray"
for this trio of "bright bistros" (in Chelsea, Barnes and
near Clapham Junction), "unrushed, friendly" spots that
they say are "a cheap alternative to pub" dining and as
"good as any" competitor; the unconvinced "wouldn't go
out of the way", though, for the "over-ambitious menu" of
"mass-produced food"; P.S. the "lovely garden" in Chelsea
is "very pretty in summer."

GLASSHOUSE, THE S 23 | 20 | 21 | £39
14 Station Parade, Kew (Kew Gardens), 020-8940 6777;
fax 020-8940 3833
■ Part of the Chez Bruce/La Trompette/The Square group,
this "treasure" "just outside Kew Gardens BR" station
serves such "simply sublime", "subtly devised dishes"
that some swear they'd "sleep with the chef to find the
secret" of his "top-class", "inventive" Modern British
cooking; "outstanding service by a young team" and "classy
surroundings" add to the "brilliant", "blissful" experience.

Globe [S] 16 | 15 | 15 | £28

100 Avenue Rd., NW3 (Swiss Cottage), 020-7722 7200; fax 020-7722 2772

◩ "Useful after the cinema" nearby or a performance at the Hampstead Theatre next door, this "nice local eaterie" in Swiss Cottage hits the mark for most with an "imaginative" Modern British menu and a "lively, fun", "comfortable atmosphere"; others object to what they call "hit-or-miss" cooking and "spartan" decor, but all appreciate owner Neil Armishaw and his "friendly" staff for their "warm welcome."

Golden Dragon 🌙[S] 19 | 10 | 10 | £22

28-29 Gerrard St., W1 (Leicester Sq.), 020-7734 2763; fax 020-7734 1073

◩ There's "loads of [local] competition" for this large "buzzy", "authentic" Chinatown eaterie, but most reckon that it's up to the challenge, with "tasty", "good-value" Chinese fare (including "excellent dim sum") that's "well-prepared and promptly served"; dissenters declare "everything but the food is a letdown", especially the "rushed, blasé service" from "inattentive staff."

Good Earth 🌙[S] 18 | 15 | 16 | £28

233 Brompton Rd., SW3 (Knightsbridge/South Kensington), 020-7584 3658; fax 020-7823 8769

143-145 The Broadway, NW7 (Mill Hill), 020-8959 7011; fax 020-8959 1464

■ With outposts in Knightsbridge and Mill Hill, this "formal" Chinese duo has ardent admirers advocating its "sophisticated" "gourmet menu" of "fab" fare as "worth every penny" (though a few employ milder accolades like "standard" and "reliable"); even those who feel the "service could be better" say "the food keeps [them] coming back."

Goolies Bar & Restaurant [S] 18 | 16 | 16 | £27

21 Abingdon Rd., W8 (High St. Kensington), 020-7938 1122; fax 020-7937 6121

■ "An interesting crowd from far and near" – perhaps "giggling yuppies", perhaps even "actors from *The Bill*" – "ruin their diets" at this "hectic" Notting Hill venue that offers a "good", "exciting" British menu and "warm service"; recently "refurbished", the "decor is alive" with new colours, bringing a "twist of modern" to its "traditional feel"; in sum, it's "nice for a casual dinner."

Gopal's of Soho 🌙[S] 19 | 13 | 15 | £22

12 Bateman St., W1 (Tottenham Court Rd.), 020-7434 0840; fax 020-7434 0840

◩ "A firm favourite" for many, this Soho Indian's appreciated for "keeping up the high standards" of its "good curries" and other "traditional" dishes (such as "reliable tandoori chicken and naan") and for its "quick service"; still, a few mutter that the fare is "nothing unusual" and snipe that the "fraying-at-the-edges" decor "needs a fix."

Gordon Ramsay at Claridge's ◑ S　_　_　_　VE
Claridge's Hotel, Brook St., W1 (Bond St.), 020-7499 0099;
fax 020-7376 7170
Scheduled to open at press time, the much-heralded
renovation of this famed art deco dining room in Mayfair's
Claridge's Hotel coincides with the arrival of top chef Gordon
Ramsay – he'll split his time between here and his top-rated
Chelsea venue – and a New French menu broader than
any previous Ramsay offering; the space's redo brings big
changes: in addition to getting its own street entrance
and a more intimate room (just 65 seats), it now boasts a
chef's table in the kitchen, two private dining rooms, a
fumoir and a cocktail area; expect a long waiting list.

GORDON RAMSAY AT 68　　28　23　26　£66
ROYAL HOSPITAL ROAD
68 Royal Hospital Rd., SW3 (Sloane Sq.), 020-7352 4441;
fax 020-7352 3334
■ Now holding the No. 1 position for both Food and
Service, "enfant terrible" Gordon Ramsay's "stylish"
Chelsea venue has achieved pride of place in the pantheon
of "pricey", near-"perfect" London "icons"; "superb",
"spectacularly presented" New French fare and "inarguably
wonderful", "pampering service" from "warm" staff
combine to create the "quintessence" of "first-class" "fine
dining"; in fact, fanatic "followers" wax ecclesiastic in
their "worship" of its "divine" delights, insisting a visit to
this "heaven" is almost "a religious experience."

Goring Dining Room S　　20　20　21　£40
The Goring Hotel, Beeston Pl., SW1 (Victoria), 020-7396 9000;
fax 020-7834 4393
■ "Foreign visitors" and elderly "parents love" the "old-
world courtesy" of this hotel dining room in Victoria where
"morning, noon or night" the "pleasantly Traditional" British
cooking is just "right", i.e. "never outstanding, never
unsatisfactory"; proximity to Parliament, "well-spaced
tables" and several private dining rooms make it a "perfect
location" for "business" or "politics."

Granita S　　　　　　　　　20　14　17　£34
127 Upper St., N1 (Angel/Highbury & Islington), 020-7226 3222;
fax 020-7226 4833
☑ Certain surveyors say it's "still classy" "to see and be
seen" dining on "interesting, tasty" Modern European meals
in this "trendy Islington eaterie"; despite an "outrageous
bargain" lunch, others are "disappointed" by fare that "fails
to deliver" and an "overwhelmingly noisy", "minimalist"
room in which unimpressive "chairs and tables could very
well be from Ikea."

Great Eastern Dining Room | 18 | 19 | 17 | £34 |
54 Great Eastern St., EC2 (Liverpool St./Old St.), 020-7613 4545;
fax 020-7613 4137
■ "In the middle of nowhere" in Hoxton, diners discover "a buzzing atmosphere [full] of professional thirtysomethings" sunken into "designer" "chairs a little too comfy to take a third port"; though this destination for "surprisingly scrummy" Modern Italian fare is in "just too eastern a location" for a few foot-weary foodies, the "relaxed and classy" place is "still happening."

Great Nepalese ❶🅂 | 22 | 12 | 20 | £19 |
48 Eversholt St., NW1 (Euston), 020-7388 6737;
fax 020-7388 6737
■ Intrepid tasters testify that the "fresh", "flavourful" Nepalese-Indian provisions at this out-of-the-way Euston eaterie are "worth the trek"; if the decor is "not so nice", the servers are "oh-so-nice" ("they provide a welcome to everyone"), and the reasonable curries and other fare give "excellent all-round" "value."

Greek Valley | 15 | 10 | 18 | £21 |
130 Boundary Rd., NW8 (Swiss Cottage), 020-7624 3217;
fax 020-7372 2042
◪ "There is always some event taking place" with "fun dancing and plate-breaking" at this "friendly" St. John's Wood Greek taverna, a "longtime favourite" for "tasty", "cheap and cheerful" eats; "the owners are lovely people who make you feel like part of the family" at this "fun and comfortable" "local" haunt.

Green Cottage ❶🅂 | 20 | 10 | 17 | £21 |
9 New College Parade, Finchley Rd., NW3 (Finchley Rd./
Swiss Cottage), 020-7722 5305
■ "Delighted locals and visitors alike" "do not come for the decor but for wonderful food" that "has been constant for three decades" at this Finchley Road Chinese "veteran"; "it's the place in the area" for "quick pre-movie" "yummy" Cantonese, including a signature dish that fowl-lovers insist is "the best roast duck in town."

Greenhouse, The 🅂 | 21 | – | 19 | £42 |
27A Hay's Mews, W1 (Green Park), 020-7499 3331;
fax 020-7499 5368
■ Scheduled to reopen a few weeks after press time following a major renovation of its formerly "faded" premises, this Mayfair stalwart – approaching its 25th year – retains chef Paul Merrett and his "consistently good" Modern British cuisine, which, along with "very swish service", should help it remain a "top-notch" "business" venue that's also "excellent for Sunday lunch."

Green Olive S 19 | 16 | 17 | £33
5 Warwick Pl., W9 (Warwick Ave.), 020-7289 2469;
fax 020-7289 2463

☑ Red Pepper and the rest of the clan claim this "relaxed" "but trendy" Maida Vale venue as a cousin; some insist its "innovative" Italian cooking "matches quantity with quality", whilst others think the "overpriced", "mediocre" meals are the pits; service can be "friendly", but make sure you don't "get stuck in a corner" in the "drab downstairs."

Greens S 20 | 19 | 20 | £42
36 Duke St., SW1 (Green Park), 020-7930 4566;
fax 020-7930 2958

■ "It is like a favourite jacket" say loyalists who appreciate that "it feels so English" inside this St. James's seafooder; "for celebration or consolation", "sometimes you want predictability, not constant change", and "one invariably feels calmer and better after eating" a "very satisfying meal" of Traditional British "soul food" here.

Grenadier S 14 | 20 | 15 | £26
18 Wilton Row, SW1 (Hyde Park Corner), 020-7235 3074;
fax 020-7235 3400

■ As the bayonets and sabres on the walls suggest, this "lost piece of olde London" on a Belgravia mews was once the mess hall of the Duke of Wellington's guards; though there's "better pub grub available in the area", the "cosy" ambience is "perfect for taking tourists" "a step back in time" to when the in-house ghost was still an officer; P.S. they make a "good Bloody Mary."

Gresslin's S 19 | 15 | 19 | £33
13 Heath St., NW3 (Hampstead), 020-7794 8386;
fax 020-7433 3282

■ The "nice people" at this "likeable local" – "one of the few decent restaurants in Hampstead" – dish up "delicious", "attractively presented" Modern European meals, and it's a good thing the fare's so "fantastic", since diners must endure "silly highbacked bench seats" that "emphasise" the "awkwardness" of the layout.

Grissini S 18 | 17 | 18 | £42
Hyatt Carlton Tower, 2 Cadogan Pl., 1st fl., SW1 (Knightsbridge/ Sloane Sq.), 020-7858 7171; fax 020-7823 1708

☑ With a "stupendous" view over local gardens and acoustics that allow you to "hear yourself talk", it may be a "shame it's not busier" in the Hyatt Carlton Tower's Italian dining room; however, mealtakers put their money where their mouth is: those who've sampled the £16 "oustanding-value lunch" find the fare "fantastic", but "disappointed" dinner guests ordain it "il rip-off."

Groucho Club, The
15 | 16 | 16 | £35
Private club; inquiries: 020-7439-4685
■ Contrary to its namesake's famous remark, most media types do want to belong to a private club that would have them as members: "louche luxury" and a "lovely buzz" have kept this Soho "standard" "an 'in' spot" for "regulars" for more than 15 years; if the Modern British cooking is "frustratingly inconsistent", "let's be honest – it's not about the food, is it?"

Grumbles S
20 | 16 | 17 | £25
35 Churton St., SW1 (Pimlico/Victoria), 020-7834 0149;
fax 020-7834 0298
■ Pimlico's unprepossessingly "fun" wine bar prides itself on its constancy: the Anglo-French bistro menu full of "lovely, pleasant noshes" is indeed "reliable", and the joint "hasn't changed" its "way-old" decor in years; the set lunch for under £10 is eternally popular with workers in nearby offices.

Guinea, The
21 | 15 | 18 | £41
30 Bruton Pl., W1 (Bond St./Green Park), 020-7409 1728;
fax 020-7491 1442
■ In a "not-near-anything location" that's housed drinking establishments since the 1300s, this "hospitable" Mayfair gastro-pub is famed for its "unrivalled steak-and-kidney pie", a "real" Traditional British "treat"; this "great grill" may be priced for "tourists", but most meat eaters believe the "outstanding" fare is worth every guinea.

Gung-Ho ●S
20 | 14 | 17 | £30
330 West End Ln., NW6 (West Hampstead), 020-7794 1444;
fax 020-7794 5522
■ Hungry Hampsteaders are gung-ho about this "real local" Chinese "find" with "above average" Szechuan cooking and "a good wine list"; its "nice ambience" is aided by the "friendliest" servers "in town", whose "smiling and joking" help make a meal here a "great all-round" experience.

Hakkasan S
– | – | – | VE
8 Hanway Pl., W1 (Tottenham Court Rd.), 020-7927 7000;
fax 020-7907 1889
Housed in a former underground car park near Tottenham Court Road, this large, impressive-looking Chinese newcomer from the founder of Wagamama (Alan Yau) serves good-value dim sum lunch as well as modern, multiregional Chinese dishes; there are also two stylish bars, which serve light snacks and throb to the energetic beat of a resident DJ on Friday and Saturday nights.

Halepi ⏺Ⓢ   17 | 12 | 16 | £28
18 Leinster Terrace, W2 (Lancaster Gate/Queensway),
020-7262 1070; fax 020-7262 2083
48-50 Belsize Ln., NW3 (Belsize Park/Swiss Cottage),
020-7431 5855; fax 020-7431 5844
■ It "feels like eating with a big Greek family in their crowded living room" at this pair of "rustic", "jolly" Greek-Cypriot joints where "enthusiastic" service and "fresh", "consistently good" fare are appreciated as much as the "outstanding traditional guitarist" on weekends; since both the Hyde Park and Belsize Park venues get "fiendishly crowded", reviewers "recommend the takeaway service."

Harbour City ⏺Ⓢ   18 | 9 | 12 | £21
46 Gerrard St., W1 (Leicester Sq./Piccadilly Circus),
020-7439 7859; fax 020-7734 7745
☑ If you're looking for "dim sum to die for", "one of the best Chinatown" bets is this tri-level venue featuring a "fantastic" feast from noon until five Monday through Saturday; "Peking duck is good" too, but everything else is "a bit hit or miss", and if you're in a rush, be forewarned that "service is not so much slapdash as criminally slow."

Hard Rock Cafe ⏺Ⓢ   13 | 17 | 15 | £22
150 Old Park Ln., W1 (Green Park/Hyde Park Corner),
020-7629 0382; fax 020-7629 8702
☑ "Still crazy after all these years", this Hyde Park golden oldie in the famed pop chain continues to "pack 'em in" for "great fun" with "USA food", "good cocktails" and music memorabilia; even given "way-too-loud" tunes and burgers like "hard rocks", twisting teenybopping tourists shout it's only rock 'n' roll, but they like it, like it, yes they do.

Harrington Club ⏺   ▽ 19 | 20 | 19 | £42
Private club; inquiries: 020-7838 3000
■ Few surveyors have commented on South Kensington's "brilliant" new private club backed by Rolling Stone Ronnie Wood, but those in-the-know get satisfaction from the "wickedly devilish" Modern European, Thai-inflected menu; though there's no dress code, the "rock 'n' roll–grandiose setting", complete with spa, "has style" and, of course, isn't cheap; N.B. a new chef joined post-*Survey*.

Harrods   18 | 16 | 16 | £26
Harrods, 87-135 Brompton Rd., SW1 (Knightsbridge),
020-7730 1234; fax 020-7225 5903
☑ With over 20 eating options, it "depends where you go" within Knightsbridge's "crowded" Harrods store, but there's always an "excellent choice to suit both palate and wallet", from "great sushi" to pizzas from a "wood-burning" oven to "fun afternoon tea"; as for service, it "varies according to how busy it is" at this "Disneyland for foodies."

HARRY'S BAR   24 22 23 £58
Private club; inquiries: 020-7408 0844
■ "Get dressed up" "to be seen" in Mark Birley's "glamorous" private dining club in Mayfair that offers "absolutely wonderful Italian cooking", "fantastic service" and "great star watching"; lucky loyalists agree it's "well worth" the "membership fee" "to be able to book" a table in "the best power-lunch club ever."

Havana ◑🆂   12 15 12 £24
17 Hanover Sq., W1 (Bond St./Oxford Circus), 020-7629 2552;
fax 020-7491 2821
490 Fulham Rd., SW6 (Fulham Broadway), 020-7381 5005;
fax 020-7381 8591
■ "If you're in a Latin mood", these Cubans in Fulham and Mayfair offer a "nicely elegant" "fun atmosphere", "good happy-hour cocktails" and dance classes, but their Havana-accented cuisine gets the "thumbs-down"; snobs who find them "sleazy" prefer to salsa elsewhere.

Havelock Tavern 🆂≠   21 12 11 £20
57 Masbro Rd., W14 (Olympia/Shepherd's Bush), 020-7603 5374;
fax 020-7602 1163
■ Even those who've "eaten on many occasions" at this "reasonably priced", "bloody fantastic" Brook Green gastro-pub have "never had a dud meal"; the "wholesome", "tasty" Modern British cooking is "an absolute favourite" of many fanatical foodies, so it's almost "impossible" to find a seat here, and when you do, you'll suffer "continual interruptions from people asking for your table."

Helter Skelter 🆂   – – – E
50 Atlantic Rd., SW9 (Brixton), 020-7274 8600;
fax 020-7274 8600
In a "grotty" Brixton location on "the most unprepossessing of roads" is "an oasis of Modern British cooking" that's well "worth a whirl"; "mod music, menu and staff" leave a "lively, young clientele" "dizzy for more" of everything, including "fantastic" fish and meat, though the choices are "somewhat limited for vegetarians."

Henry J. Bean's 🆂   10 11 9 £17
195-197 King's Rd., SW3 (Sloane Sq./South Kensington),
020-7352 9255; fax 020-7376 5076
■ Party animals might enjoy "a lively night" in the "great outdoor beer garden" at this "fun", American-style Chelsea diner, though fare featuring "ok burgers" is "very expensive for what it is"; when the "cocktails take over" "on weekend nights", the crowd can get "obnoxious", but the "damn sexy barmen" compensate.

Hi Sushi
16 | 12 | 15 | £20

40 Frith St., W1 (Leicester Sq.), 020-7734 9688;
fax 020-7734 9882
16 Hampstead High St., NW3 (Hampstead), 020-7794 2828;
fax 020-7794 7328 S

☑ Cousins to Kensington's Koi, these "friendly" Soho eateries elicit wildly divergent responses: fans of the fare and fashionable decor describe "lovely, fresh and interesting sushi" served at "fun and comfy tables", whilst disillusioned diners call the "dry food" "nothing special" and the sunken tables "manoeuvrable" only if you are "stick-thin or a yoga guru."

Home
17 | 19 | 15 | £27

100-106 Leonard St., EC2 (Old St.), 020-7684 8618;
fax 020-7684 1491

☑ This "very hip" Modern British haunt near Old Street is only a few years old, but its retro decor gives it the feel of a "totally lovable" "'70s standby"; gastronomes grant its "groovy cocktails" and "good snacks" make it "better as a bar" than an eatery, since the "funky staff" are too "indifferent" and the joint is "too busy" for serious dining.

Home House ◐ S
19 | 23 | 19 | £40

Private club; inquiries: 020-7670 2100

☑ In an "outstanding" Portman Square building with an intriguing history, this "cool" private club is "so sumptuous" that members can "enjoy" "a whole evening" of "heaven on earth" within its high-ceilinged dining room, trendy bars, handsome garden, gym and even bedrooms; Modern European meals, though, are "variable in quality", and some warn "prepare to be fleeced."

Honest Cabbage S
17 | 13 | 15 | £24

99 Bermondsey St., SE1 (London Bridge), 020-7234 0080;
fax 020-7403 1119

■ As the name suggests, Alex Thompson's "buzzing, reliable" Bermondsey eatery serves a changing menu of "honest, wholesome" yet "interesting" Traditional British dishes from the "good old days"; "the price is right" too, making this "informal", basic place with its "down-to-earth" service a "great local" find.

House, The S
▽ 21 | 19 | 22 | £36

3 Milner St., SW3 (Sloane Sq.), 020-7584 3002;
fax 020-7581 2848

■ This "warm", "charming" Chelsea townhouse (now part of the Searcy-Corrigan group) is decorated "just like" an English country drawing room, serving as a "discreet", "romantic" backdrop for Graham Garrett's "interesting", "delicious" Modern British menu; if there's an occasional suggestion the "food still has some ways to go", all agree they're "trying hard."

House on Rosslyn Hill ◑ [S] 13 13 12 £24
34 Rosslyn Hill, NW3 (Hampstead), 020-7435 8037; fax 020-7431 3610
◪ A "rowdy crowd" frequents this "funky", "friendly" Hampstead brasserie to listen to "hip", "loud" live music some nights of the week and "to be seen but not to eat" International edibles that are dismissed as "absolute pants"; "scrappy" but "cool", it's a "great little place" "for drinks and starters and more drinks", or take the family for "kid-friendly Sunday lunch."

Hunan 23 13 19 £33
51 Pimlico Rd., SW1 (Sloane Sq.), 020-7730 5712; fax 020-7730 8265
■ "Don't antagonise [chef-owner] Mr. Peng by ordering from the menu", as "you'll never be disappointed" by "the boss's selection" at this Pimlico Chinese; "surprise after surprise" "just keeps coming" in a "dizzying display" of "delicious" dishes, though "there's nothing smart about" "premises that allow diners no elbow room."

Hush 16 19 15 £37
8 Lancashire Ct., W1 (Bond St.), 020-7659 1500; fax 020-7659 1501
◪ Diners "whisper" "shhh, don't tell all" about this "amazingly designed" "secret" off Bond Street, where Henry Harris oversees two different Modern British menus: "pretty good" fare is offered on the "expensive" first floor with its "wonderful bar", and "not hugely memorable" meals are served on the "chic" ground floor with its "great outdoor courtyard"; N.B. Strictly Hush is on the second floor for private dining.

Ibla 20 14 16 £35
89 Marylebone High St., W1 (Baker St./Bond St.), 020-7224 3799; fax 020-7486 1370
◪ "People should be flocking here" say fulsome fans of this "cool", "minimalist" Marylebone "gem" where the "focus" is on "fantastic" Modern Italian "flavours" that "keep getting better", though the jury is out as to whether you should "sit only in the front room" or be "careful to choose the back" in this "uncomfortable" place that feels a bit like "a morgue."

I Cardi [S] ▽ 15 17 18 £36
351 Fulham Rd., SW10 (South Kensington), 020-7351 2939; fax 020-7376 4619
■ An "ideal neighbourhood restaurant" should be "not too smart nor too scruffy" opine local Chelsea aficionados, and this newcomer strikes just that balance; its fare has "real Italian flair and attitude", and the room is "modern and chic", but it's low-profile enough as yet that few folks seem to know about the "great price-to-quality ratio" it offers.

Idaho Restaurant & Bar ◑ⓢ   16 | 18 | 15 | £32
13 North Hill, N6 (Highgate), 020-8341 6633;
fax 020-8341 5533
■ Like the U.S. destination itself, this "cool" Highgate
haunt (one of the posse that includes Montana) is an
"exciting, relaxing and fresh experience for all the senses";
"intelligent", "bold" American Southwestern cooking is
particularly "enjoyable at Sunday brunch" on the "nice
terrace", but because "there isn't a no-smoking section",
the air quality doesn't quite match that of its namesake.

Ifield, The ⓢ   19 | 17 | 16 | £26
50 Ifield Rd., SW10 (Earl's Court), 020-7351 4900;
fax 020-7351 1100
☑ With its "great atmosphere" and "happening bar",
Eddie Baines' Chelsea yearling is "always sure to be
seating" some of "the most beautiful ladies in town", and
the Modern British–Eclectic cooking they eat there "can
be good"; it can also be not so good, compelling critics to
comment that "the kitchen is still getting its act together."

Ikeda   20 | 14 | 19 | £37
30 Brook St., W1 (Bond St.), 020-7629 2730; fax 020-7628 6982
■ Japanese diners pining for a taste of home fill Mr.
Ikeda's diminutive, simply decorated Mayfair stalwart,
approaching its 25th year of "fantastic quality and range"
featuring "fine sushi" and signature tea ice cream; though
it's "a bit conservative" in style, the veteran does sport an
open kitchen so you can watch the chefs at work.

Ikkyu ⓢ   20 | 11 | 14 | £23
7 Newport Pl., WC1 (Leicester Sq.), 020-7439 3554;
fax 020-7773 4150
67A Tottenham Court Rd., W1 (Goodge St.), 020-7636 9280;
fax 020-7323 5378
☑ These two "authentic" Japanese eateries are under
separate ownership now, but both still provide "decent
sushi" as well as "adventurous" "variety for the non-sushi
fan" (albeit in premises that need "sprucing up a bit");
foodies favour the "excellent Tottenham Court Road" venue
and tend to "avoid" the Chinatown spot despite its all-
you-can-eat raw fish.

Il Convivio   21 | 19 | 18 | £39
143 Ebury St., SW1 (Sloane Sq./Victoria), 020-7730 4099;
fax 020-7730 4103
■ "The chef is a gastronomic master" claim hyperbolic fans
of this Pimlico-Belgravia "great night out", where "big
portions" of "excellent" pasta and other Modern Italian
dishes offer "good value"; the "bright, airy" room with its
electric glass roof may be "lacking a little warmth", however,
and service is not always convivial, according to some.

Il Falconiere ◐ 14 11 15 £27

84 Old Brompton Rd., SW7 (Gloucester Rd./South Kensington), 020-7589 2401; fax 020-7589 9158

◩ Kensington's "delightfully old-fashioned" bistro is a local "favourite" for "very reliable" Italian fare, even if culinary adventurers call it "slightly dull"; though the room is so "cosy" that "tables almost touch", "solicitous service" and good "value" make it a "restful, quiet place for business" or a "lovely lunch."

Il Forno [S] 16 13 15 £29

63 Frith St., W1 (Tottenham Court Rd.), 020-7734 4545; fax 020-7287 8624

■ Surveyors are "quickly becoming regulars" at this Soho hot spot in Claudio Pulze's empire, serving "simple" but "proper Northern Italian food", including signature pizza from the eponymous wood-burning oven; whilst the menu "does not offer a lot of selection", dishes are "well-prepared" and "reasonably priced", and the "perfectly balanced" atmosphere is "buzzy without being manic."

Il Portico – – – E

277 Kensington High St., W8 (High St. Kensington), 020-7602 6262

According to the "loyal clientele", it's "like eating out at a friend's house" at this unprepossessing Kensington Italian serving "reliable, upscale" fare in a "fun, delightful" atmosphere; there are tables outside underneath the cheerful green awning as well.

Imperial City 18 17 17 £31

Royal Exchange, Cornhill, EC3 (Bank), 020-7626 3437; fax 020-7338 0125

■ In an "unlikely location" in the vaulted cellar under the Royal Exchange is this spacious multiregional Chinese eaterie offering signature sweet-and-sour prawns and other "great food" at "reasonable prices" (by City standards); whilst the "service can wane at times", it's "dependable" enough for business dining to require reservations at lunch.

Inaho 21 14 16 £31

4 Hereford Rd., W2 (Notting Hill Gate), 020-7221 8495

■ As "authentic" as "hole-in-the-wall places in Tokyo" and Osaka, this "wonderful" Bayswater Japanese "hideout" "feels very much as if you are not in London"; "you can't swing your arms, let alone a cat" in this "tiny", "packed" 20-seater, but "sensational sushi" and other "innovative", "fresh" fare are worth the work to "book" an "uncomfortable chair."

Incognico ◐ 22 | 19 | 18 | £39

117 Shaftesbury Ave., WC2 (Leicester Sq.), 020-7836 8866; fax 020-7240 9525

■ "Everything's very slick" at this "clever" Classic French "extension of cheznico" (it's run by Nico Ladenis' daughter, Natasha), an "intimate" Theatreland eaterie where "not-too-fussy" meals move "from strength to strength"; its "buzzing atmosphere" and "bargain" prix fixe menus "more than compensate" for any discontent over "rough edges in service" and "tables too close together", leading the majority to conclude "this is a top-tier outfit."

Indigo ◐ S 23 | 20 | 20 | £37

One Aldwych Hotel, 1 Aldwych, WC2 (Charing Cross/ Covent Garden), 020-7300 0400; fax 020-7300 0401

■ "Overlooking a busy bar" on the mezzanine floor of the "superb", "modern" One Aldwych Hotel is an "elegant" "secret": this "chic", wood-and-steel dining room serving "unfailingly good" Eclectic fare all day; "reliably top-class" and "quick", it's the "perfect" "discreet" "business-lunch venue away from the tourists of Covent Garden."

Isola/Iso-Bar S 17 | 20 | 14 | £34

145 Knightsbridge, SW1 (Knightsbridge), 020-7838 1055; fax 020-7838 1099

Oliver Peyton has re-jigged things at this heavily stylised ("retro-land") Knightsbridge Italian, retaining the more casual downstairs dining area and converting the upstairs dining room into a chic bar; chef Bruno Loubet remains, offering a Modern Italian menu that features many of the popular dishes from the two former dining options, as does the "fabulous" wine list that stretches to over 400 bottles (80 by the glass).

Istanbul Iskembecisi ◐ S ⌿ ▽ 18 | 10 | 16 | £18

9 Stoke Newington Rd., N16 (Highbury & Islington/Liverpool St.), 020-7254 7291; fax 020-7254 7291

■ There's a wide selection of "fine" offerings at this "authentic" Turkish eaterie in Stoke Newington, and "everything on the menu is delicious", though carnivores in particular come for the "excessive meat-fests"; open from noon to 5 AM, it's "lots of fun" for eating in or taking out.

I-THAI S 22 | 24 | 19 | £54

Hempel Hotel, 31-35 Craven Hill Gardens, W2 (Lancaster Gate), 020-7298 9000; fax 020-7402 4666

■ "Dive into the world of minimalist" dining at this Hempel Hotel hideaway in Bayswater, where "imaginative" Italian-Thai-Japanese flavours are "amazing", "presentation is superb" and the only thing that's not "very calming" is the bill; N.B. post-*Survey*, this Japanese-backed hotel parted company with its famous founder, Anouska Hempel, which may lead to changes.

itsu [S] 19 | 17 | 15 | £25

103 Wardour St., W1 (Leicester Sq./Piccadilly Circus), 020-7479 4794
118 Draycott Ave., SW3 (South Kensington), 020-7590 2401; fax 020-7590 2403

■ The "dressed-up sushi looks like it's catwalking down the conveyor belt" in the "chichi atmosphere" of this "automated" Japanese duo in Chelsea and Soho; though "variety" and "authenticity are not to be expected", this "quicky" is a "funky, affordable" and "fashionable" (if "dizzying") way to deflower a "sushi virgin."

IVY, THE ◐[S] 24 | 22 | 23 | £44

1 West St., WC2 (Leicester Sq.), 020-7836 4751; fax 020-7240 9333

■ "If I were to choose my last meal" most surveyors would select this "slick machine" in Theatreland that, for the fourth year in a row, is "deservedly" voted London's Most Popular on account of "superior" Modern British–European cooking – "simple food done to perfection" – and "faultless service"; a handful assert it's "not at its peak now" and, as ever, frustrations abound about "surviving the booking process and weeks of waiting", but all in all, this "lively" venue with "ace star-spotting" still "has that special something."

Iznik [S] 19 | 15 | 16 | £20

19 Highbury Park, N5 (Highbury & Islington), 020-7704 8099; fax 020-7354 5697

■ For "all homesick Turkish expats", the succour of "tasty, homemade" fare, as well as the comforting presence of a "motherly hostess" and antiques, is "more than worth the trip" to this Ottomanesque Highbury eaterie; locals and "celebs" also enjoy all-day weekend dining here, such "a charming Turk iz Nik."

Jade Garden [S] 19 | 12 | 14 | £22

15 Wardour St., W1 (Leicester Sq./Piccadilly Circus), 020-7437 5065; fax 020-7429 7851

◪ This unassuming, bi-level Chinese is deemed "one of the few decent Soho" spots for "after theatre" or "pub"; the multiregional fare is "nothing special", but dim sum makes a "nice Saturday lunch", and although it can be "quite pricey" for "average" à la carte orders, the "superb fixed price" menus (£9 pre-theatre, £11 dinner) provide a "good" reason to "go for dinner."

Japanese Canteen [S] 15 | 9 | 11 | £15

5 Thayer St., W1 (Bond St.), 020-7487 5505; fax 020-7487 5505
9 Ludgate Broadway, EC4 (St. Paul's), 020-7329 3555; fax 020-7329 3555

(continued)

(continued)

Japanese Canteen

21 Exmouth Mkt., EC1 (Farringdon), 020-7833 3521; fax 020-7833 3521

◪ This Japanese trio "emulates Tokyo ramen shops", i.e. you "go in, eat, leave and there's no mucking about" within the "charmless", "clinical" places; though some savour bento boxes, most eaters insist that "the stuff compares poorly" with fare elsewhere; N.B. Exmouth Market has substantial seating, but the other shops are mainly takeaway.

Jason's [S] 20 | 15 | 17 | £38

Jason's Wharf, opp. 60 Blomfield Rd., W9 (Warwick Ave.), 020-7286 6752; fax 020-7266 4332

◪ "On the canal in Little Venice", this "unassuming", "quaint" place serves what seafood lovers say is "really fresh, wonderful fish" in-house and on two boats available for private charter; crabbier critics "do not like" the kitchen's catch, though, deeming dinner "only worth it for outdoor dining" "on summer nights."

Jen Hong Kong Cuisine ◑[S] 20 | 11 | 14 | £26

7 Gerrard St., W1 (Leicester Sq.), 020-7287 8193; fax 020-7734 9845

◪ "Pleasant for a lunch, but nothing special", this "typical Chinatown restaurant" offers an extensive menu of Hong Kong–style dishes; regulars who relish the signature crispy duck and "good, fresh fish" want this "local" to be "kept a secret", whilst "disappointed" diners wish to forget about it.

Jenny Lo's Tea House ≠ 18 | 10 | 17 | £16

14 Eccleston St., SW1 (Victoria), 020-7259 0399; fax 020-7823 6331

■ "The lucky ones living in the neighbourhood" of this "cheap" Chinese in Victoria wonder "why there can't be a chain" of them to relieve the "annoying" "lunchtime" "crowding"; "healthy" meals like "tasty noodles" are "served quickly" to those who queue up for a "shared table" and put up with an "irritating cash-only policy."

Jim Thompson's Flaming Wok [S] 15 | 19 | 13 | £24

243 Goldhawk Rd., W12 (Ravenscourt Park), 020-8748 0229; fax 020-8748 0866

141 The Broadway, SW19 (Wimbledon), 020-8540 5540; fax 020-8540 8728

408 Upper Richmond Rd., SW15 (East Putney), 020-8788 3737; fax 020-8788 3738

617 King's Rd., SW6 (Fulham Broadway), 020-7731 0999; fax 020-7731 2835 ◑

889 Green Lanes, N21 (Southgate/Wood Green), 020-8360 0005

◪ If hagglers "love" the "head-spinning" decor of this "wacky" Southeast Asian chain of "bazaars", they can take it home (it's all for sale); despite "massive portions", price tags on the "pale pastiche" of stir-fries are considered too high, and service can be "incapable."

Jin Kichi [S] | 21 | 11 | 17 | £28

73 Heath St., NW3 (Hampstead), 020-7794 6158

■ For "Japanese food served like it should be", this "scruffy" Hampstead yakitori house is an "authentic experience"; char-grilled dishes and other menu items are "unique" and "fantastic", and "waiters are really helpful"; daydreaming diners declare "just to think of" this "cramped but cute" place "makes me want to eat there."

Joe Allen ◑ [S] | 16 | 16 | 17 | £29

13 Exeter St., WC2 (Covent Garden), 020-7836 0651; fax 020-7497 2148

■ As "comfortable as an old shoe", this Theatreland "classic" is "so dated it's almost coming around again"; whilst "simple" British-American dishes like burgers and brownies are "no great shakes", the lively "atmosphere makes up for it" since, after curtain calls, the "dark, discreet" basement "fills with celebrities" swilling "expensive cocktails."

Joe's [S] | 18 | 18 | 18 | £29

126 Draycott Ave., SW3 (South Kensington), 020-7225 2217; fax 020-7584 1133

◪ Recently refurbished, this Brompton Cross bistro has heightened its "stylishness" so as to appeal even more to the folks "in fashion" who frequent it for daytime meals; if the Modern British menu is mainly just "ok" and the staff sometimes "weak", it can still serve as a "lovely place for a light shopping lunch."

Joe's Brasserie [S] | 15 | 13 | 14 | £26

130 Wandsworth Bridge Rd., SW6 (Fulham Broadway), 020-7731 7835; fax 020-7731 5897

■ "The only cure for Sunday morning" "in the heart of family-land" Fulham might be this "child-friendly", "nice, American-style brunch place" providing "good snacks and light meals" from an International selection; be forewarned that the staff in this "busy", "loud" joint get so swamped, for attention you may have to "strip nude and set your hair on fire."

Joe's Restaurant Bar | 16 | 14 | 13 | £28

Joseph Ettedgui, 16 Sloane St., SW1 (Knightsbridge), 020-7235 9869

◪ In the basement of the chic Joseph Ettedgui fashion store in Knightsbridge, this narrow eaterie inspires modest praise ("ok food, ok decor, ok service"), though the midpriced Modern British menu does include a few "perfect salads and delectable desserts"; for most, however, the place serves primarily as a popular meeting point–cum–pit stop after shopping.

JOHN BURTON-RACE [S] 26 21 24 £64

Landmark Hotel, 222 Marylebone Rd., NW1 (Marylebone), 020-7723 7800; fax 020-7723 4700

◪ Visitors "appreciate the high standards" and "great attention to detail" at the eponymous chef's Marylebone hotel dining room; "a gallant effort in an impossible location", this "benchmark" of "tradition" is "rather quiet but excellent", with "elegant, creative" French classics served by "attentive staff"; since "you need a bank loan" to afford it, perhaps it's best for a "special occasion."

Joy King Lau ◐[S] 20 9 12 £21

3 Leicester St., WC2 (Leicester Sq./Piccadilly Circus), 020-7437 1133; fax 020-7437 2629

■ An "almost entirely Chinese clientele" offers a "good sign" that this "no-frills" Chinatown place "has to be tried" for its "fantastic" fare, including "tasty dim sum"; despite "poor decor", at such "reasonable prices" "you don't mind coming back", "particularly for excellent-value" lunches.

J. SHEEKEY ◐[S] 24 22 23 £41

28-32 St. Martin's Ct., WC2 (Leicester Sq.), 020-7240 2565; fax 020-7240 8114

■ "The Ivy with a fish theme" is an apt take on this "well-hidden" Theatreland favourite that swims as strongly as its sibling when it comes to seafood (it rates No. 1 in the category in this *Survey*): its "superb" cuisine always "hits the mark", as does the "outstanding service" and "beautiful, yet understated" space (though there are a few quibbles that it's "laid out rather oddly"); the consensus is it's "a pleasure eating" at this "class act" that's "fiendishly good fun" and "getting harder to book at short notice."

Julie's [S] 17 22 17 £36

133-137 Portland Rd., W11 (Holland Park), 020-7229 8331; fax 020-7229 4050

◪ With its "warm", "dark" "multitude of dining rooms", this "truly romantic" Holland Park "hidey hole" feels perfectly "cosy for canoodling" "with someone else's wife"; though the "tired" Modern British dishes "need to catch up with London's food revolution", "all is forgiven" when you "sit in something resembling an updated coronation chair" to enjoy the "just gorgeous" (if slightly dated) "'70s" setting.

Julono [S] ▽ 18 20 19 £28

73 Haverstock Hill, NW3 (Chalk Farm), 020-7722 0909; fax 020-7428 9481

■ "Although a little off-the-beaten-track" in Haverstock Hill, this "friendly" feederie "has shown the way in terms of" Moroccan-Med meals; "handy and decent for couscous", it also features an "imaginative wine list" and the occasional belly dancer writhing to "good music"; "an attractive crowd" considers it "worthwhile" for "wonderful functions" in the basement lounge; N.B. lunch is only served weekends.

Just Around the Corner ● S   ▽ 14 | 12 | 14 | £23

446 Finchley Rd., NW2 (Golders Green), 020-7431 3300;
fax 020-7431 3300

◪ "The fact that you pay what you feel it deserves is novel, but nerve-racking" at this basic Finchley Traditional British–Classic French eaterie; whilst some claim it's "mediocre all-round", others suggest that "good food" and a "friendly owner" ensure its appeal as a "handy" local spot.

Justin de Blank   16 | 13 | 15 | £27

50-52 Buckingham Palace Rd., SW1 (Victoria), 020-7828 4111;
fax 020-7828 4666

◪ "Tasty" British brasserie fare, including some of the "best sausages in London", "will do" for a "simple", "pleasant lunch" at this Victoria venture named after its busy patron; if some outsiders find the "dreary place" "not very accommodating", "locals" enjoy it for "a drink after work."

Just St. James's S   14 | 18 | 14 | £37

St. James's & King Sts., SW1 (Green Park), 020-7976 2222;
fax 020-7976 2020

◪ For some, this Modern British newcomer in a former St. James's bank just might be "a nice addition to the scene" – after all, the "opulent" space is "already a Christie's canteen at lunchtime"; but most who "pay this much expect a total dining experience", and the "nothing-special" cuisine just "doesn't match the eloquence of the room."

Kai S   23 | 22 | 21 | £41

65 S. Audley St., W1 (Bond St./Marble Arch), 020-7493 8988;
fax 020-7493 1456

■ "Creative and special" servings "put Chinese on a higher plane" at this "high-end" Mayfair venue; "consistently excellent food and service" are "very expensive but worth it for a special night" out at this "romantic" rendezvous of which the "only real complaint" is "no separate smoking section"; a harpist plays two nights a week.

Kaifeng S   19 | 14 | 16 | £36

51 Church Rd., NW4 (Hendon Central), 020-8203 7888;
fax 020-8203 8263

■ "Relive your bar mitzvah" enjoying kosher Chinese nosh at this "amusing" Hendon venue; all of the cooking is "excellent" and "authentic", but expect "serious overpricing" – but just pay up, because dishes this delicious even "your bobbe never cooked"; N.B. closed Fridays.

Kalamaras Taverna S   20 | 10 | 18 | £27

66 Inverness Mews, W2 (Bayswater/Queensway),
020-7727 9122; fax 020-7221 9411

■ For "genuine" Greek "home cooking" and "a warm welcome", take a "step back in time to the '70s" at this "family-run" eaterie in a Queensway mews; its BYO policy and £16 prix fixe dinner "help if you want to take a group."

Kandoo ◐ S | – | – | – | M |

458 Edgware Rd., W2 (Edgware Rd.), 020-7724 2428

Here's a welcome, family-run addition to the ranks of Edgware Road eateries, boasting a "super ambience" and authentic Persian cuisine from a frequently changing menu that suits those on a "budget"; meals are served all day (midday to midnight), there's also a garden for summer dining.

Kastoori S | ▽ | 23 | 8 | 18 | £18 |

188 Upper Tooting Rd., SW17 (Tooting Bec/Tooting Broadway), 020-8767 7027

■ "It's definitely worth" the trip to Tooting for what the few voters who know it consider the "best veggie Indian in South London", with "good prices" to boot; fans "follow the advice of the friendly staff" and order "amazing", "unusual curries" and other Gujarati- and Ugandan-influenced "interestingly cooked vegetable" dishes to please even inveterate "steak-eaters."

Kennington Lane | ▽ | 22 | 21 | 18 | £34 |

205-209 Kennington Ln., SE11 (Kennington/Oval), 020-7793 8313; fax 020-7793 8323

■ "On the path to excellence" enthuse admirers of this starkly designed Modern European yearling that's become "a significant addition" to the Kennington area, thanks to cooking featuring "good ingredients imaginatively used" as well as a mostly French wine list; the in-the-know advise "ask for the set-price menu."

KENSINGTON PLACE ◐ S | 20 | 16 | 17 | £36 |

201-209 Kensington Church St., W8 (Notting Hill Gate), 020-7727 3184; fax 020-7229 2025

◪ "You always wonder whether your neighbour is famous" at this "brash, lively" Notting Hill eatery that's remained "popular after all these years", despite isolated reports that it "looks tired"; the "reliably" "delicious" Modern British cuisine attracts the "media" set, who crowd together "close enough to have a good look at the next table's food" and don't mind the "noisy acoustics" of this "echo chamber."

Kettners ◐ S | 14 | 16 | 14 | £24 |

29 Romilly St., W1 (Leicester Sq.), 020-7734 6112

◪ "Go on, treat yourself to a new carpet" urge surveyors struck by "the faded elegance" of this Modern Italian set in a Soho townhouse (perhaps the new owners will give it a "revamp"); given the "interesting champagne bar" and adjacent "cheap and cheerful" dining room serving pizzas and burgers, most find there's "nowhere better for children" and "pre-theatre eating", even if it's "nothing to write home about."

Khan's ◑Ⓢ | 16 | 9 | 10 | £18 |
13-15 Westbourne Grove, W2 (Bayswater/Queensway),
020-7727 5420; fax 020-7229 1835

■ With the "atmosphere of an Indian railway station in rush hour", this "madcap" Bayswater "mob scene" is an eternal crowd-pleaser thanks to its "huge portions" of "cheap, good" and "quick" Indian cooking "the way it's meant to be", never mind the "hit-or-miss" service; given that this "truly unique" spot went "non-alcoholic" a couple of years ago, however, some tipplers consider it best for "takeaway."

Khan's of Kensington ◑Ⓢ | 17 | 12 | 13 | £22 |
3 Harrington Rd., SW7 (South Kensington), 020-7584 4114;
fax 020-7581 2900

☑ "Just steps from the South Kensington tube" resides this "dependable, well-run" Indian "jewel" (not related to its Bayswater namesake), providing "modern", "flavourful" standards from a "regional" menu; a few sophisticates may sniff it's "Indian for the tourists", but even they concede it's a "pleasant place to visit" (especially considering the prix fixe lunch under £8).

Khun Akorn Ⓢ | ▽ 18 | 14 | 14 | £31 |
136 Brompton Rd., SW3 (Knightsbridge), 020-7225 2688;
fax 020-7225 2689

■ Considering its prime location next to Harrods, it's surprising that this pleasantly "unpretentious" Knightsbridge Thai isn't better known; nonetheless, its "delicious" standards (pad Thai, curries, etc.) and "fun", relaxed atmosphere (enhanced by the sarong-clad staff) ensure that it's well appreciated by the initiated.

King's Head, The Ⓢ | – | – | – | M |
1 The Green, Winchmore Hill, N21 (Winchmore Hill),
020-8886 1988

From a stable that includes The Queens and Builders Arms comes this Winchmore Hill "pub–cum–wine bar" overlooking a village green, which serves Traditional British gastro-pub fare in a homely setting that features an open wood fire for winter and walled garden in summer; early commentators report signs of "popularity."

Koi Ⓢ | 20 | 16 | 16 | £39 |
1E Palace Gate, W8 (Gloucester Rd./High St. Kensington),
020-7581 8778; fax 020-7589 2788

■ "Fab sushi" amid "bright", "lovely and tranquil" settings (complete with an aquarium of namesake koi) is what's on offer at this Kensington Japanese where there's also "top-marks" "teppanyaki cooked in front of you"; a warning to wallet-watchers: expect "ridiculously expensive" prices.

Kulu Kulu Sushi
17 | 9 | 12 | £19

76 Brewer St., W1 (Piccadilly Circus), 020-7734 7316;
fax 020-7734 6507

◪ "So fresh, so simple, so undiscovered, so cheap" marvel
epicureans enamoured with this "friendly", "low-key"
Piccadilly Japanese that gets "no points for visual charm"
but wins plenty with its "bargain sushi" delivered via
"*kaiten*" ("conveyor belt"); fans wonder "when will they
open a second branch?"

La Bersagliera ●◗S
15 | 6 | 14 | £22

372 King's Rd., SW3 (Sloane Sq.), 020-7352 5993

▪ There may be "no spaces between the tables" at this
"cosy, little" World's End trattoria, but no one minds the
close quarters too much given the "good, cheap Italian
cooking" on offer ("large, sumptuous pizzas", fresh
pastas and the like); even if they can be a bit "cheeky" at
times, the waiters know a thing or two about "welcoming
children"; N.B. at press time, a complete refurbishment
was in the works.

La Bouchée S
19 | 14 | 13 | £27

56 Old Brompton Rd., SW7 (South Kensington), 020-7589 1929;
fax 020-7584 8625

▣ "Ideal for low-key dates", this "real French bistro" in
South Kensington inspires "nostalgia" for the "Quartier
Latin of Paris" with its "amiable atmosphere" ("plenty of old
candles to pick the wax off") and "reliable", "good-value"
cuisine; all in all, it makes a "cosy escape from the London
rat race", though a few worry that a new chef and manager
might "ruin" this favourite that's been "unchanged for years."

La Brasserie ●◗S
16 | 16 | 14 | £28

272 Brompton Rd., SW2 (South Kensington),
020-7581 3089; fax 020-7581 1435

◪ "You could be in France" muse devotees of this
"charming", "cosmopolitan" Brompton Cross brasserie
serving "sound" Gallic "classics" with a "kid-friendly"
attitude; critics counter the "place is nothing special",
citing "predictable" fare and "erratic service" – "the feeling of
a French brasserie, but hardly a French man around!"

La Brasserie du
Marché aux Puces S
▽ 20 | 18 | 21 | £29

349 Portobello Rd., W10 (Ladbroke Grove), 020-8968 5828;
fax 020-7349 0575

▪ Handy for Portobello Road market shoppers, this
"unhurried", "unpretentious" French brasserie shines
thanks to its "interesting food" (including a popular
brunch menu for under £10) and "friendly", if "wonderfully
camp", service; the secret to its success may be that the
"patron and patronne really care about their customers."

La Brasserie Townhouse [S] ▽ 17 | 18 | 19 | £21

(fka Townhouse Brasserie)
24 Coptic St., WC1 (Holborn/Tottenham Court Rd.), 020-7636 2731; fax 020-7580 1028

■ "Tries hard and often succeeds" say voters who know this somewhat "underused" eaterie in a Bloomsbury townhouse that's "rather convenient for the British Museum"; its "contemporary" Modern French brasserie menu is a "swell value" (especially the prix fixe lunch for under £8), and in addition to a private dining room, it has four guest bedrooms.

La Cage Imaginaire [S] 18 | 18 | 20 | £30

16 Flask Walk, NW3 (Hampstead), 020-7794 6674

■ "Cute" and "delightful", this Hampstead eaterie (with 20 years' experience under its belt) boasts "good", "solid" New French cooking and "excellent service" amid a "pleasant" mews setting; all in all, it's "very sweet – like eating in Paris."

L'Accento Italiano ◐[S] 20 | 14 | 17 | £28

16 Garway Rd., W2 (Bayswater/Queensway), 020-7243 2201; fax 020-7243 2201

◪ It's "utterly reliable" for "decent Italian" classics in a "friendly, comfortable setting" (including garden seating) say supporters of this Bayswater trattoria, though there's a suggestion "they could change the menu a bit more"; still, "if you stick to the daily specials, it's worth the trip" to this "great neighbourhood local."

La Delizia ◐[S] 18 | 10 | 13 | £22

63-65 Chelsea Manor St., SW3 (Sloane Sq.), 020-7376 4111; fax 020-7795 1980

■ "Shame it's lost its alcohol license" (though a side benefit is that it's now "quite cheap"), but this "small", "casual" Chelsea pizzeria with quite "friendly staff" is "still worth" visiting for some of the "best pizzas in London"; it's also a "favourite" choice of neighbourhood denizens for "before-the-cinema" dining.

LA FAMIGLIA ◐[S] 20 | 17 | 18 | £36

7 Langton St., SW10 (Sloane Sq.), 020-7351 0761; fax 020-7351 2409

◪ "A certain glamour, a great location", "wonderful", "really Tuscan" cuisine and a "nice garden in summertime" "keep it popular" at this Chelsea "old favourite" Italian; still, the "not-enthralled" believe this "always-packed", "'60s-style trattoria" is "living on past glory", complaining of "unfriendly" service and a "kitchen that sometimes fails to cope."

La Finca
12 | 11 | 11 | £20

185 Kennington Ln., SE11 (Kennington), 020-7735 1061;
fax 020-7793 7663 ◐ S
96-98 Pentonville Rd., N1 (Angel/King's Cross), 020-7837 5387;
fax 020-7278 8221

■ "Good for quick tapas before salsa" or flamenco lessons, this Spanish duo is better loved for its Latin dancing (with DJs on Friday and Saturday nights) than for its basic but "tasty" small plates; in fact, some opt to just "drink there", choosing either the funky Kennington venue or its more traditionally Iberian-styled sib in Islington.

La Fontana ◐ S
20 | 17 | 21 | £40

101 Pimlico Rd., SW1 (Sloane Sq.), 020-7730 6630;
fax 020-7730 5577

■ Whilst "it's always a pleasure" visiting this "friendly", "family-owned" Pimlico Italian, where punters "go all the time" for risottos and other "solid" traditional dishes served with a "great personal touch", when "truffles (a specialty)" "are in season", fanatics insist the "cosy" place becomes one of "the best in London."

Lahore Kebab House ◐ S ⊬
21 | 6 | 12 | £14

2 Umberston St., E1 (Aldgate East/Whitechapel),
020-7481 9737; fax 020-7488 1300

■ "Never mind the decor" at this "noisy and jolly" Aldgate curry house, because its "yummy, spicy food" (including "some of the best kebabs on the planet"), chosen from an "excellent" Pakistani menu, belies the "humble" decor; another count in its favour is "good pricing", which makes it "fantastic value."

La Mancha S
17 | 15 | 16 | £24

32 Putney High St., SW15 (Putney Bridge), 020-8780 1022;
fax 020-8780 2202

■ Like a "trip to Barcelona", visits to this "crowded" Putney "find" "with the atmosphere of a bar in Spain" never fail to "satisfy" thanks to the wide selection of "great tapas" "cheaply" priced; even the few quibblers who find the nibbles "run-of-the-mill" appreciate its "authentic feel" and live guitarist.

LANESBOROUGH CONSERVATORY ◐ S
21 | 24 | 22 | £43

The Lanesborough, 1 Lanesborough Pl., SW1 (Hyde Park
Corner), 020-7333 7254; fax 020-7259 5606

■ "Bright, airy" and "delightful", this domed, "beautiful glasshouse" in Hyde Park Corner's Lanesborough hotel makes a "classy" destination for "excellent" Modern British–Eclectic cuisine, particularly during "dinner dances" with live jazz on weekend nights and "supremely elegant" Sunday brunches; it's also "heavenly" for tea, perfect for "out-of-towners" and a "good challenger to the Ritz"; P.S. watch out for "expense-account" prices.

Langan's Bistro 19 | 19 | 18 | £35

26 Devonshire St., W1 (Baker St.), 020-7935 4531; fax 020-7493 8309

◪ "Even without Peter, it's still an experience" extol enthusiasts of the late Peter Langan's "cheery" Marylebone restaurant where "decent" French cuisine is served up in an "intimate", artwork-bedecked dining room that looks "just like a bistro should"; nonetheless, a few dissenters who find the fare "a bit hit-or-miss" declare "the atmosphere is all."

Langan's Brasserie ◐ 19 | 19 | 19 | £39

Stratton St., W1 (Green Park), 020-7491 8822; fax 020-7493 8309

◪ As far as its loyal fans are concerned, this "clubby", "buzzing" Mayfair stalwart is "as flash as ever" thanks to the "consistently decent", sometimes "wonderful" British-French cuisine, "efficient" service and "great setting" (even if it could stand "a good coat of paint"); dissenters dismiss it as a "dinosaur of a brasserie" that's "lost its excitement", though even they concede you "still get to see famous people" here.

Langan's Coq d'Or [S] 17 | 16 | 17 | £36

254-260 Old Brompton Rd., SW5 (Earl's Court), 020-7259 2599; fax 020-7370 7735

■ The newest addition to the Langan's family is this "very pleasant" British-French "local" in Earl's Court that's somewhat less hectic than its siblings (they're "always able to squeeze us in with no notice"); among its finer features is a "great terrace", which is among the "best places" around for an outdoor "Sunday lunch."

Lansdowne, The [S] 19 | 17 | 14 | £27

90 Gloucester Ave., NW1 (Camden/Chalk Farm), 020-7483 0409; fax 020-7586 1725

■ "Get a sofa by the fire" at this "gastro-pub stalwart" in Primrose Hill where a "hip crowd" clamours for "hearty" Modern British–Eclectic fare with "delicious Spanish influences"; many prefer the "relaxed", "lovely" ground-floor bar, as the more formal upstairs dining experience can be marred by "shoddy service."

La Perla Bar & Grill [S] 13 | 15 | 16 | £21

28 Maiden Ln., WC2 (Covent Garden), 020-7240 7400; fax 020-7836 5088
803 Fulham Rd., SW6 (Parsons Green), 020-7471 4895; fax 020-7736 9309

◪ These Mexican twins in Covent Garden and Fulham have great appeal as "local bars" slinging "to-die-for margaritas" and "wonderful beer"; some support the "big portions" of "good food", but more are vexed by the "variable", "inauthentic" fare.

La Piragua ◐Ⓢ⌿   – – – E
*176 Upper St., N1 (Angel/Highbury & Islington), 020-7354 2843;
fax 020-7226 5480*
Carnivores crowd this "always fun" Islington South American that's "good for huge steaks and other meat dishes" and offers a "wide selection for vegetarians" as well, all at "unbelievable value"; though there's little in the way of decor, the ambience has "lots of character" and the "owner's a treat."

La Porchetta Pizzeria ◐Ⓢ   19 10 14 £15
*141-142 Upper St., N1 (Highbury & Islington),
020-7288 2488
147 Stroud Green Rd., N4 (Finsbury Park), 020-7281 2892;
fax 020-7281 2892*
■ "Seems to work best when crowded" say those who frequent this "manic" Finsbury Park pizza 'n' pasta purveyor and its Islington sib where, "if you can stand the decibels", you'll be rewarded by "superb pizzas" with unusual toppings; the combination of "large portions for very little" dough provides a "queue"-worthy experience.

La Porte des Indes ◐Ⓢ   20 22 18 £35
*32 Bryanston St., W1 (Marble Arch), 020-7224 0055;
fax 020-7224 1144*
◪ "Blue Elephant's sister" in Marylebone inspires devotion for its "delicious", "delicately prepared" Southern Indian fare with a French accent; the "fantastic setting", replete with "colonial" touches and a waterfall, makes this a "romantic" spot or "good for out-of-town visitors", but a few dissenters avow it's "too pricey" for "average" food.

La Poule au Pot ◐Ⓢ   19 22 18 £36
*231 Ebury St., SW1 (Sloane Sq.), 020-7730 7763;
fax 020-7259 9651*
■ "Romantic", "candlelit atmosphere" and "great outdoor" tables transform this Pimlico Green French bistro into a perpetual "first-date" "favourite"; the food's "authentic" and "lovely" and the service "attentive" at this "old standby" , and if "it's expensive for what you get", keep in mind that the "prix fixe lunch" provides "exceptional value."

L'Artiste Musclé ◐Ⓢ   12 13 14 £23
*1 Shepherd Mkt., W1 (Green Park), 020-7493 6150;
fax 020-7495 5747*
◪ This "Shepherd Market gem" is "still reassuringly cramped and smoky" after over 30 years, and whilst some feel the "unpretentious, wholesome [French] bistro cooking" is "too expensive for the quality", artists agree it's a "cheerful" spot for "sitting outside" and watching "Mayfair's own" go about their business.

La Rueda ◐ [S] 15 12 14 £25

102 Wigmore St., W1 (Bond St.), 020-7486 1718; fax 020-7486 1718
642 King's Rd., SW6 (Fulham Broadway), 020-7384 2684; fax 020-7384 2684
66-68 Clapham High St., SW4 (Clapham North), 020-7627 2173; fax 020-7627 2173

◪ For a "fun night out", with "dancing" and "amazing live entertainment" contributing to the "party atmosphere", these Spanish triplets are "real treats"; they're "great for groups" ordering tapas (estimated as "excellent" to "good" to "average"), though all the goings-on can get "noisy."

LA TANTE CLAIRE 25 21 24 £61

Berkeley Hotel, Wilton Pl., SW1 (Knightsbridge), 020-7823 2003; fax 020-7823 2001

■ "Brilliant flavours from a brilliant chef" cheer champions of Pierre Koffman's "supremely assured" "Classic French cuisine" in the Berkeley Hotel in Knightsbridge (where the "chic" setting is "not as warm as the old place" in Chelsea, according to some); from the "amazing bread" to the "extraordinary desserts", the meals come "close to perfection", aided by "charming waiters" and a "sommelier who knows his stuff"; P.S. though the "prices can get out of hand", the "prix fixe lunch is an outstanding bargain."

latitude ▽ 11 13 9 £28

163 Draycott Ave., SW3 (South Kensington), 020-7589 8464; fax 020-7584 6908

■ "Better as a bar" is the consensus on this Brompton Cross venue, and whilst the Modern British menu is "limited" in scope, it's rated a "great little place for informal meals with friends"; N.B. a new sushi menu is in the works.

La Trompette [S] – – – E

5 Devonshire Rd., W4 (Turnham Green), 020 8747 1836; fax 020 8995 8097

"Parking will be diabolical" predict those in-the-know of this promising, elegant Chiswick newcomer from the team behind The Glasshouse and Chez Bruce; early reports point to "attentive service" and "superb" New French dishes ("we were very pleased") from Ollie Couillaud, a former chef at The Square; "good drinks" are served at the limestone bar.

Launceston Place ◐ [S] 22 21 20 £40

1A Launceston Pl., W8 (Gloucester Rd.), 020-7937 6912; fax 020-7938 2412

■ With its "English country house atmosphere", this "intimate" Kensington townhouse offers a "very civilised" experience, perfect for "lingering" and "actually hearing your conversation", as well as a "consistently good" Modern British menu; "old-fashioned attentive service" helps keep it a "favourite", and if some find it a bit "twee", its future seems assured: it's "where I'll go when I'm older."

Laurent   ▽ 22 | 6 | 16 | £25
428 Finchley Rd., NW2 (Golders Green), 020-7794 3603
■ The "new owners" (from the Domino's pizza team)
have given this modest Golders Green venue a gentle
refurb, and whilst the "very satisfying" Tunisian cooking
remains "unapologetically excellent", frustrations at
the "small menu" focusing on couscous dishes should
subside when a planned menu expansion goes into effect.

Lavender, The   16 | 13 | 15 | £23
*193 Lower Richmond Rd., SW15 (Putney B.R.),
020-8785 6004; fax 020-7801 9227* ◖S
*171 Lavender Hill, SW11 (Clapham Common),
020-7978 5242; fax 020-7801 9227* S
24 Clapham Rd., SW9 (Oval), 020-7793 0770; fax 020-7801 9227 S
*112 Vauxhall Walk, SE11 (Vauxhall), 020-7735 4440;
fax 020-7801 9227*
☑ "The languid atmosphere draws the punters in" to this
mini-chain of pub/restaurants around South London that
satisfies supporters with "good, simple" Modern British–
Eclectic fare that's "nothing too adventurous", along with
its "friendly staff"; a few disparage the dishes as "stodgy",
but most agree these venues provide "a welcome break."

L'Aventure   S   22 | 20 | 18 | £40
*3 Blenheim Terrace, NW8 (St. John's Wood), 020-7624 6232;
fax 020-7625 5548*
■ "Charming proprietress" Catherine Parisot has presided
over this "jewel of a French bistro" in St. John's Wood for
more than 20 years; whether you choose the "romantic"
interior (which may need a "freshen-up") or the "pleasant
garden", the "authentic", "delicious" dishes delivered by
"exceptional staff" add up to a "special night out."

Le Bouchon Bordelais   S   ▽ 14 | 14 | 13 | £32
*5-9 Battersea Rise, SW11 (Clapham Junction B.R.),
020-7738 0307; fax 020-7564 6203*
Le Bouchon Lyonnais   S
*36-40 Queenstown Rd., SW8 (Clapham Common),
020-7622 2618; fax 020-7564 6203*
■ The "friendly", "relaxed" atmosphere at these Battersea
and Clapham bistros makes them "enjoyable" for a "casual
evening out"; the French fare is "consistently good" and
"reasonably priced", and there's also a "busy bar" scene.

Le Boudin Blanc   S   21 | 17 | 16 | £32
*5 Trebeck St., Shepherd's Mkt., W1 (Green Park), 020-7499 3292;
fax 020-7495 6973*
■ A "quaint", "pearl of a bistro" boast *les amis* of this
"romantic" ("candlelit but not slushy") spot in Mayfair
serving "reliable", "authentic" and "well-executed" French
fare at "brilliant value"; though service comments run the
gamut from "friendly" to "average" to "surly", all agree
it's a "great summer place."

Le Cafe du Jardin ◐ [S] 18 16 17 £33

28 Wellington St., WC2 (Covent Garden), 020-7836 8769; fax 020-7836 4123

◪ "Buzzy without being headache-inducing", this "pleasant", bi-level Covent Garden eaterie is "useful for pre-theatre dining" on "well-presented" Modern British–Eclectic fare (that a few bash as "boring") in a setting with "so many windows, the neighbourhood is the decor"; N.B. at press time a second location called Le Deuxieme was set to open in Covent Garden.

Le Café du Marché 21 19 18 £34

22 Charterhouse Sq., EC1 (Barbican), 020-7608 1609; fax 020-7336 7459

■ It's "somewhat hard to find, but well worth the effort" maintain loyalists of this "lively", "romantic" bistro near Smithfield; the "fab" French fare using "fantastic seasonal ingredients" makes this a "favourite" for "lingering lunches" or evenings that "feel like a dinner party."

LE CAPRICE ◐ [S] 23 21 22 £45

Arlington House, Arlington St., SW1 (Green Park), 020-7629 2239; fax 020-7493 9040

■ "The warmest greeting" and a "glamorous, urbane" atmosphere are part of the "special appeal" of this "stylish", popular Piccadilly sib of The Ivy, and if "the experience falls short of expectations" for the capricious, the "formula still works" for the steadfast: "wonderful" Modern British–European cooking, "professional" service and "celeb"-watching; P.S. "no slippage since the dynamic duo left" is the verdict after the departure of founders Chris Corbin and Jeremy King.

Le Colombier [S] 19 18 18 £39

145 Dovehouse St., SW3 (South Kensington), 020-7351 1155; fax 020-7351 0077

■ "Hard to beat" hail those who've come across this "hidden, authentic bistro", which boasts a "quaint" ambience indoors and a "lovely terrace" that's perfect for a "fine day"; the "great" Classic French fare "hits the right spot" and provides one of the "best buys" in Chelsea, whilst the "spirited service" also receives high marks.

Lee Fook ◐ [S] 19 10 16 £21

98 Westbourne Grove, W2 (Bayswater/Notting Hill Gate), 020-7727 0099; fax 020-7727 8773

◪ Few surveyors commented this time around, but those who did were divided over this slightly frayed Queensway Chinese: some find "fresh", "authentic" Cantonese fare in "generous portions" with "conscientious" service, whilst naysayers note it's "not so great" and remark on the "entertainingly rude" staff; your call.

Lee Ho Fook ●S
17 | 10 | 12 | £21

15-16 Gerrard St., W1 (Leicester Sq./Piccadilly Circus),
020-7494 1200; fax 020-7494 1700

▨ This "big", "venerable Chinatown institution" offers "consistent" Cantonese cooking, including "great duck" and "the best dim sum", but bashers bemoan the "offhand service" and conclude the place "doesn't elevate beyond the ordinary."

LE GAVROCHE
26 | 22 | 25 | £63

43 Upper Brook St., W1 (Marble Arch), 020-7408 0881;
fax 020-7491 4387

■ "Feel like a plutocrat from the moment you walk into" Mayfair's "gourmet Mecca" whose basement setting is "inviting and luxurious"; the "beautifully accomplished", "mind-blowing" Classic French cuisine from Michel Roux (son of Albert) comprises "innovative recreations of ageless classics", and the "cosseting service" ensures "everything runs like clockwork"; though a minority maintains this "stately old galleon is sinking slowly", more exclaim all this "excess of excess" is "worth every penny."

Le Mercury ●
15 | 11 | 15 | £19

140A Upper St., N1 (Angel/Highbury & Islington),
020-7354 4088; fax 020-7359 7186

▨ This "basic" Islingtonian still has "lots of character" according to admirers who also appreciate "surprisingly good" food from the "superb-value" Eclectic–French bistro menu; although sceptics beg to differ, reporting "variable" fare and "slipshod service", many keep it "in reserve as a fallback."

Le Metro S
16 | 15 | 16 | £22

L'Hotel, 28 Basil St., SW3 (Knightsbridge), 020-7591 1213;
fax 020-7823 7826

■ Little-known and commented upon, this Knightsbridge hotel basement wine bar/cafe (The Capital Hotel's "little sister") is a stone's throw from Harrods, and whilst it "could do with a makeover", those who know it say it's an "ok spot to pop into after work"; its Modern British menu is "nothing special", but it affords "good value."

Lemonia ●S
17 | 15 | 17 | £26

89 Regent's Park Rd., NW1 (Chalk Farm), 020-7586 7454;
fax 020-7483 2636

■ There's always a "celebration" at this "raucous", 22-year-old Greek in Primrose Hill where "freshly made", "delicious food" arrives in not-so-spartan portions; the "friendly atmosphere" at this "family-run" taverna makes for a "pleasant (and cheap) evening", and though a few sourpusses decry "dumbed-down" cooking, a chorus counters the "warmth is what does it."

Lemon Thyme [S] – | – | – | E

190 Castelnau Barnes, SW13 (Barnes B.R.), 020-8748 3437
The latest from the Red Pepper Group is this "nice-looking" Barnes venue that's made a "promising beginning", leaving some "impressed" with "great", albeit conventional, Italian cooking, whilst others have no time for "uncaring service."

Le Muscadet ▽ 17 | 10 | 15 | £34

25 Paddington St., W1 (Baker St.), 020-7935 2883; fax 020-7224 5429
◪ "Great [Classic] French" fare and "friendly service" are the hallmarks of this modest-looking Marylebone bistro; some find it "depressingly decorated" and "living in the past", but most deem it "worth a taxi ride", if not a long one.

Le Palais du Jardin ◐ [S] 20 | 19 | 16 | £36

136 Long Acre, WC2 (Covent Garden), 020-7379 5353; fax 020-7379 1846
◪ "The buzz continues and standards remain high" laud loyalists of this "elegant" Covent Garden brasserie with a "stylish bar area"; the "wide-ranging" French menu also pleases (try the"fantastic seafood" and "heavenly desserts"), though some upbraid the "slow service" and "expensive" tariff; N.B. its Chelsea sibling is no more.

Le Piaf [S] 14 | 12 | 12 | £21

75 Southampton Row, WC1 (Holborn), 020-7580 7800; fax 020-7580 9483
156 Chiswick High Rd., W4 (Turnham Green), 020-8995 1656; fax 020-8995 1401
16 Percy St., W1 (Tottenham Court Rd.), 020-7636 5289; fax 020-7637 1525
40 Wimbledon Hill Rd., SW19 (Wimbledon), 020-8946 3823; fax 020-8946 1965
146 Upper Richmond Rd., SW15 (East Putney), 020-8780 3833; fax 020-8780 3845
75-77 Dulwich Village, SE21 (North or West Dulwich B.R.), 020-8693 9331; fax 020-8697 9331
◪ "Tries hard" but "could do better" is the consensus on this French bistro–style chain that's "just right for cheap, simple" (if "a little stodgy") meals doled out in "good portions"; many surveyors find the offerings "disappointing", but others insist it makes quite a "good local."

Le Pont de la Tour ◐ [S] 21 | 22 | 18 | £48

Butlers Wharf Bldg., 36D Shad Thames, SE1 (London Bridge/ Tower Hill), 020-7403 8403; fax 020-7403 0267
◪ "The Tower Bridge view is the magic touch" of Sir Terence Conran's "stylish" Modern European riversider, which fans anoint "a winner" for its "excellent" cooking, "special outside terrace" and "never-fail bar"; foes find this "great venue" has "had its day", though, objecting to "supercilious service" and a crowd of "City types on expenses galore"; N.B. there's a new chef, Earl Cameron.

L'Escargot ◐ | 23 | 20 | 20 | £42

48 Greek St., W1 (Leicester Sq./Tottenham Court Rd.), 020-7437 6828; fax 020-7439 7474

■ "Definitely special" and "very upper-class", this "old, established Soho eaterie" hung with "great art" ("Picasso, Warhol") and spread over several floors is "still excellent after all these years" thanks to its "wonderful" Classic French cooking and "lovely", "unpatronising service"; "superb nights out" here start with a perusal of "all 50 pages" of the wine list and end with a "pricey" tab – though most agree "you get your money's worth."

LE SOUFFLÉ [S] | 26 | 21 | 24 | £52

Hotel Inter-Continental, 1 Hamilton Pl., W1 (Hyde Park Corner), 020-7318 8577; fax 020-7491 0926

■ "One of the best hidden secrets of London" is the Hotel Inter-Continental's formal dining room, where the "high-quality" New French cuisine "rivals the best in London" and the "elegant, but not obsequious" service is virtually "unbeatable"; but this "outstanding" (if "rather stiff") Hyde Park Corner stalwart that "never changes" is about to enter a new era: at press time it was set to "wish a happy retirement" to chef Peter Kromberg, who is turning in his toque after a quarter century in the kitchen.

L'Estaminet | 19 | 18 | 19 | £33

14 Garrick St., WC2 (Covent Garden/Leicester Sq.), 020-7379 1432; fax 020-7379 1530

■ Approaching its 10th year, this Covent Garden brasserie boasting "wonderful" Classic French cooking and "great service" remains a business diner's staple and an "excellent pre-*Buddy*" – as in the Strand Theatre's long-running musical – venue; for best "value", surveyors suggest the "fantastic £12" set-price, pre-theatre menu.

LES TROIS GARCONS | 19 | 27 | 21 | £48

1 Club Row, E1 (Liverpool St.), 020-7613 1924; fax 020-7613 5960

■ "Visually stunning" is an understatement when you're talking about this East End "newcomer", which ranks No. 1 for Decor in this *Survey* thanks to its "absolutely breathtaking" interior, an "Aladdin's cave" of stuffed, bejewelled animals ("lions in tiaras") and other "funky", "high-camp" furnishings, most of which are for sale; whilst for many the quite "good" Classic French cuisine can't compete with the "fantastic" surroundings, ardent admirers insist it's "tip-top."

Le Suquet ◐[S] | 21 | 16 | 17 | £39

104 Draycott Ave., SW3 (South Kensington), 020-7581 1785

◪ Eat "surrounded by people having a great time" at this Brompton Cross slice of the "South of France" sought out for its "super, simply prepared" "fresh fish" and "grand seafood platters"; it "tries hard and deserves to do well", though a minority crabs about "decor as shabby as the service."

Levant 16 17 18 £32
Jason Ct., 76 Wigmore St., W1 (Bond St.), 020-7224 1111; fax 020-7486 1216
◪ The "freshest, most delicious" "nouvelle" Levantine (Eastern Mediterranean–North African) cooking comes out of the kitchen at this "lovely, muted" spot in Marylebone; but whilst everyone appreciates the "pleasant" service, its basement "location turns off" some who find it "gloomy."

Lexington, The 17 14 15 £30
45 Lexington St., W1 (Oxford Circus/Piccadilly Circus), 020-7434 3401
◪ An "enjoyable cafe" in Soho, this Modern European succeeds on the strength of its "simple dishes done well" and "wonderful ambience" enhanced by live jazz; dissenters "disappointed" with the premises ("all a bit ramshackle") are outvoted by those who think it "great for a romantic meal."

Light House [S] ▽ 21 17 19 £33
75-77 Ridgway, SW1 (Wimbledon), 020-8944 6338; fax 020-8946 4440
■ Some of the "best food in Wimbledon" is at this "light, airy" beacon of Modern Italian "fusion" cooking, according to connoisseurs of its "clever and tasty" dishes featuring "unusual ingredients"; whilst the "minimalist" interior can get "noisy" on busy days, it's a "relaxing" spot nonetheless, thanks in part to the "lovely", "informal service."

L'Incontro ☾ [S] 20 17 18 £48
87 Pimlico Rd., SW1 (Sloane Sq.), 020-7730 3663; fax 020-7730 5062
◪ The design touch of David Linley shows in this "elegant" Pimlico Italian that's "worth a detour" for its "excellent, imaginative" cuisine with a Venetian bias; foes find it "too expensive" for "food that varies in quality."

Little Bay [S] 🚫💳 16 13 18 £14
228 Belsize Rd., NW6 (Kilburn Park), 020-7372 4699; fax 020-7372 8282
■ "Forget the location and basic decor", because this "budget gem" in Kilburn is "full all day, every day" with groupies of its "fab" Med fare, priced for "fantastic value" (especially the "outrageous bargain" of a set-price lunch for less than £6); to boot, service comes "with a smile."

Little Italy ☾ [S] 18 14 15 £28
21 Frith St., W1 (Leicester Sq./Tottenham Court Rd.), 020-7734 4737; fax 020-7734 1777
■ "Party the night away" at this "cramped", yet "beguiling" Soho Italian where the "jolly atmosphere" lasts "until the early hours of the morning", when it turns into a bar/club; its "huge, authentic pasta plates" and other dishes "like mama used to make" are "surprisingly good", but as for the "hospitable" service, is "there an Italian word for *mañana*"?

Livebait　18 | 14 | 15 | £32
21 Wellington St., WC2 (Covent Garden), 020-7836 7161;
fax 020-7836 7141 ☽
175 Westbourne Grove, W11 (Notting Hill Gate), 020-7727 4321;
fax 020-7792 3655 S
2 Northside, Wandsworth Common, SW18 (Clapham Junction
B.R.), 020-7326 8580; fax 020-7326 8581 ☽ S
2 Hollywood Rd., SW10 (Earl's Court), 020-7349 5500;
fax 020-7349 5501 S
43 The Cut, SE1 (Waterloo), 020-7928 7211;
fax 020-7928 2279 ☽
1 Watling St., EC4 (Bank/Mansion House), 020-7213 0540;
fax 020-7213 0541

◪ With the "traditional tiled decor" and "beautiful, fresh" seafood selection of a "fishmonger", this rapidly expanding chain's diverse menu affords "unparalleled choices for fish lovers"; critics carp it's all a little "too formulaic", however, citing "utilitarian" decor and "perfunctory" service, as well as a "pricey" bill ("will eat your wallet alive").

LMNT ☽ S　– | – | – | E
316 Queensbridge Rd., E8 (Highbury & Islington), 020-7249 6727;
fax 020-7249 6538

With an interior like a Hollywood stage set for a larger-than-life Egyptian comedy (over-stylised hieroglyphics, murals, sphinxes etc.), this "wild-and-wacky" former Hackney pub has hired Tom Ilic (ex-new end) as a consultant chef to its polished Modern British menu; P.S. "must see the loos to believe them."

Lobster Pot, The　21 | 17 | 19 | £38
3 Kennington Ln., SE11 (Kennington), 020-7582 5556

■ Part of the appeal of this "eccentric" Gallic seafooder in Kennington is its "dated", "kitsch" interior that's "like the cabin of a boat" (complete with portholes and "cramped" seating); "fun" atmosphere aside, though, its raison d'être is "excellent" (if "costly") fare, including some of "the best *soupe de poisson* outside France", served with plenty of "French charm."

L'Odeon　17 | 17 | 15 | £38
65 Regent St., W1 (Piccadilly Circus), 020-7287 1400;
fax 020-7287 1300

◪ Its always-"crowded", "stylish bar" is a favourite Piccadilly Circus "late-night haunt" and may be the most appreciated aspect of this New French eaterie in a "lovely space" overlooking Regent Street; whilst many voters appreciate its "good-for-the-price" menu, a vocal cadre of critics calls the place "over-hyped", dismissing the food as "nondescript" and service as "inattentive"; N.B. there's live jazz.

Lola's 🄂   20 | 19 | 19 | £35

The Mall Bldg., 359 Upper St., N1 (Angel), 020-7359 1932;
fax 020-7359 2209

▨ "Ideal for old-fashioned romantics" ("grab the table by
the arched window"), this "airy, spacious" former tram
shed in Islington is also "a great place for serious eating"
thanks to its "hearty", "high-quality" Eclectic cooking; the
less-enamoured may wonder "what is the fuss about?",
citing "uninspiring" food and "spotty service", but even
they concede there's a "lovely", "relaxed local feel to the
place" (enhanced by the tones of a "subtle pianist").

Lomo ◗🄂   18 | 14 | 14 | £23

222 Fulham Rd., SW10 (Earl's Court/Fulham Broadway),
020-7349 8848; fax 020-7349 8848

■ "If you're craving tapas", "potent sangria" and "fun on
high stools", this "lively" Fulham Road Spaniard makes an
attractive option given its "decent-size" small plates and
"reasonable prices"; of course many would "rather be in
Madrid", but the "friendly service" and "nice-looking
crowd" mean "this is almost as good."

L'Oranger   23 | 21 | 21 | £49

5 St. James's St., SW1 (Green Park), 020-7839 3774;
fax 020-7839 4330

▨ "Perfect for a meeting" or "for a quiet dinner", this
"elegant" St. James's New French "fine dining" room has
become a "West End classic" thanks to chef Kamel
Benamar's "exquisite" cuisine, the "great setting" and
"formal" yet "friendly" service; critics counter it's "safe
but unimaginative" and protest about "expense-account"
prices, though there is a more "affordable" (£20) set lunch.

Lou Pescadou ◗🄂   18 | 12 | 17 | £33

241 Old Brompton Rd., SW5 (Earl's Court), 020-7370 1057;
fax 020-7244 7545

▨ "Serious fish eaters" swear by this "informal" piscatorium
in Earl's Court, which provides "beautifully prepared",
"authentic French" seafood that fanatics deem "worth
every penny"; it has its share of detractors too, though,
who complain of "cheap-looking decor", an "arrogant"
attitude and merely "fair" food.

Luc's   16 | 12 | 14 | £30

17-22 Leadenhall Mkt., EC3 (Bank/Monument), 020-7621 0666;
fax 020-7623 0028

■ "One of the best quick City lunch places" around is
this "popular" Leadenhall Market brasserie where "old
French classics" are "efficiently served" in "lively", Gallic
atmosphere; just bear in mind that the closely placed "tables
make it unsuitable for confidential business"; N.B. lunch
only and closed weekends.

Luigi's of Covent Garden ◐ 18 | 14 | 18 | £34

15 Tavistock St., WC2 (Covent Garden), 020-7240 1789; fax 020-7497 0075

■ "It feels like New York in the '50s" at this "homey", "old-style Italian" in Theatreland where wise punters follow the "recommendations" of the "fatherly waiters" (who seem "as old as the pictures on the wall") when ordering from the menu of "home-cooked" "classics"; overall, it's a "reliable" option that's very "convenient for the theatre."

Lundum's [S] 20 | 22 | 23 | £36

119 Old Brompton Rd., SW7 (Gloucester Rd./South Kensington), 020-7373 7774; fax 020-7373 4472

■ "Jaded" Londoners who've tried it all are refreshed by visits to this "sweet", "family-run" Danish eaterie in a former South Kensington library that has "all the ingredients for a relaxing night out": "extremely nice", "cheerful" staff, a "superb" menu of "imaginative" Scandinavian dishes ("wonderful herring") and a "romantic", "charming" interior; by day, diners appreciate the £12.50 set-price lunch and "love the [£15.50] Sunday buffet."

Made in Italy ◐ [S] 17 | 12 | 12 | £22

249 King's Rd., SW3 (Sloane Sq.), 020-7352 1880; fax 020-7351 5098

◩ It "helps to speak Italian" at this "reliable neighbourhood" King's Road Italian offering a "limited, but decent-quality" selection of "good pizzas" (served on "trestle platforms") and pastas; however, both the "fun" but "noisy" atmosphere and the variable service irk some surveyors; N.B. lunch is served weekends only.

Maggie Jones's [S] 18 | 17 | 16 | £30

6 Old Court Pl., W8 (High St. Kensington), 020-7937 6462; fax 020-7376 0510

■ "Enter a time warp" ("baskets of dried flowers", "bottles dripping with wax") at this "quaint", "cosy" Kensington eaterie, where "good, honest" Traditional British "comfort fare" and "attentive service" from "hunky" (i.e. camp) waiters goes down a treat; "it's history – you've just got to go" urge devotees, though the less-sentimental note this "dusty" favourite might "need a revamp."

Ma Goa [S] 21 | 11 | 17 | £23

242-244 Upper Richmond Rd., SW15 (East Putney), 020-8780 1767; fax 020-8246 6878

■ The "truly authentic Goan food" cooked up at this "different", dinner-only Putney Indian receives a "warm endorsement" from regulars who relish the "really interesting", sensibly priced menu, which "proves curry is more than chicken korma"; its "friendly", "homely" interior occasionally hosts live music; N.B. a deli recently opened next door.

Maison Bertaux Ⓢ⌐

22 | 12 | 16 | £13

28 Greek St., W1 (Leicester Sq./Piccadilly Circus), 020-7437 6007

■ "A cup of tea and a slice of mille-feuille" from this Soho "landmark" (est. 1871), and "all is right with the world"; "may it never change" declare denizens of this "old-worldly pâtisserie" that feels a little "like being on a film set", for how ever would they do without the café au lait, "nice cakes" and some of the "best croissants in London"?

Maison Novelli ◐

20 | 15 | 16 | £41

29 Clerkenwell Green, EC1 (Farringdon), 020-7251 6606;
fax 020-7490 1083

☑ It's "Jean-Christophe at his best", gush groupies of this "relaxed" New French in "cool Clerkenwell", where the "top-notch" eponymous chef is credited with "serious", "classy food" (matched by the "encyclopaedic wine list"), albeit in "fairly ordinary surroundings"; that said, a few cynics are "bored with all that tall food" and suggest the place is "struggling to find its form", citing erratic service ("smooth" vs. "unobliging") and "scarily expensive" prices.

Malabar ◑Ⓢ

20 | 15 | 17 | £25

27 Uxbridge St., W8 (Notting Hill Gate), 020-7727 8800;
fax 020-7743 8350

■ "Being discovered slowly but surely", this "Notting Hill sleeper" lures in a "trendy", clad-"in-black" crowd with its "divine", "refined" curries (call it "nouvelle Indian") that "induce cravings at least once a fortnight"; add "bright", "stylish surroundings" and "attentive service", and what you've got is a "fantastic neighbourhood place"; P.S. regulars note "you'll need to book."

Malabar Junction ◑Ⓢ

▽ 22 | 16 | 18 | £26

107 Great Russell St., WC1 (Tottenham Court Rd.),
020-7580 5230; fax 020-7436 9942

☑ Set in a "lovely, soothing conservatory", this Bloomsbury eaterie is widely commended for its "authentic, well-presented" South Indian cooking infused with the "subtle flavours" of Kerala, and non-carnivores take comfort in the fact that "veggie and non-veggie" dishes are prepared in two separate kitchens; livelier sorts consider the wine bar/cafe "downstairs much more fun."

Mandalay

▽ 20 | 9 | 20 | £19

444 Edgware Rd., W2 (Edgware Rd.), 020-7258 3696

■ The extremely modest decor of this "lovely local" eaterie on Edgware Road belies the quality of its "great" Burmese cuisine, which reflects Indian and Chinese influences; but whilst its selection of curries and noodles may well "taste better than in" Myanmar, it's the "funny", "helpful" owner who captures surveyors' imaginations; N.B. the prix fixe lunch is under £6.

Mandarin Kitchen ◐ S　　22 | 9 | 13 | £28
14-16 Queensway, W2 (Bayswater/Queensway),
020-7727 9012; fax 020-7727 9468

◪ "A favourite amongst Chinese people" and "seafood lovers", this "authentic" Queensway Mandarin-Cantonese eaterie is where "everyone goes for lobster noodles" and other "wonderful" marine fare; frustrations abound about the "meaningless reservation" system (they're accused of "double-booking"), and the "dark", "time-warp decor" also has few admirers, but still the place is "always busy" thanks to its simply "delicious food."

Mandola S　　19 | 16 | 16 | £20
139-143 Westbourne Grove, W11 (Notting Hill Gate),
020-7229 4734

■ There's a "real cosy atmosphere" ("take your tie off!") at this "fun", "dimly lit" Bayswater "taste of Africa" featuring a "unique" menu of "hearty", flavourful Sudanese dishes that make for a "cheap" meal – not least because "you bring your own alcohol"; service can be "slow", although the "laid-back and friendly" approach is appreciated.

Manor ◐ S　　– | – | – | VE
6-8 All Saints Rd., W11 (Westbourne Park), 020-7243 6363;
fax 020-7243 6360

This sophisticated Notting Hill newcomer from Matthew Du Cann (who previously owned the site when it was Mas Cafe) is attracting early support for its International–Southern European menu from Adam van Schravendyk, who replaced the original chef sacked on the venue's opening day; downstairs is a slick cocktail bar.

Manzi's ◐ S　　19 | 15 | 17 | £33
1-2 Leicester St., WC2 (Leicester Sq./Piccadilly Circus),
020-7734 0224; fax 020-7437 4864

■ Everyone gets a "big welcome" at this "bright, busy" Piccadilly seafood "tradition" dripping in "old-world charm", a veteran that "hasn't changed" much since it opened in 1928; devotees deem its classics like "huge Dover sole" "first-class", even if the menu is a bit "tired"; P.S. regulars note "upstairs is quieter and less hectic than downstairs."

Mao Tai ◐ S　　22 | 18 | 18 | £35
58 New King's Rd., SW6 (Parsons Green), 020-7731 2520;
fax 020-7471 8992
96 Draycott Ave., SW3 (South Kensington), 020-7225 1964;
fax 020-7225 1965

◪ "Tasty, superb, gorgeous" gush surveyors smitten with this "excellent" Szechuan eaterie in a sophisticated Parson's Green setting, though there are more than a few grumbles from the mingy-minded about its "so-expensive" prices; Brompton Cross denizens welcome the addition of a second location on Draycott Avenue.

Marine Ices [S] 17 | 9 | 16 | £17

8 Haverstock Hill, NW3 (Chalk Farm), 020-7482 9003; fax 020-7482 9005

■ "Wow!" cry ice cream fiends about the "fabulous gelato" scooped out at this "well-worn" Chalk Farm Italian, which is "fab" with kids – and "without kids"; whilst its "pretty good" menu of pizzas and pastas has its defenders, the majority suggests "leave the main course and start with a sundae."

MARK'S CLUB 24 | 26 | 25 | £62

Private club; inquiries: 020-7499 2936

◪ "In a class of its own" insist initiates of Mark Birley's "elegant" Mayfair private dining club marked by "flawless, friendly service" and "high-standard" Traditional British food that's "unbelievably expensive" – "you may need to take out a mortgage" to pay; a few renegades wish "they'd change the menu", but most claim this "hedonistic power trip" is "the ultimate in luxury."

Maroush ☾ [S] 20 | 12 | 15 | £26

21 Edgware Rd., W2 (Marble Arch), 020-7723 0773; fax 020-7723 3161
68 Edgware Rd., W2 (Marble Arch), 020-7224 9339; fax 020-7723 3161
62 Seymour St., W1 (Marble Arch), 020-7724 5024; fax 020-7723 3161
38 Beauchamp Pl., SW3 (Knightsbridge), 020-7581 5434; fax 020-7723 3161

■ "Among the best Lebanese", this quartet near Marble Arch and in Knightsbridge serves "tasty" Middle Eastern fare that's "reasonably priced"; they're "great to just plop at the bar for lunch", and they're considered "as good as it gets" "after a night out."

Masala Zone [S] – | – | – | M

9 Marshall St., W1 (Oxford Circus), 020-7287 9966; fax 020-7287 8555

Spicy, competitively priced Modern Indian fare meets with widespread approval at this new, large Soho venture from the team behind Veeraswamy and Chutney Mary, where tribal art helps create an evocative atmosphere.

Mash 15 | 16 | 13 | £30

19-21 Great Portland St., W1 (Oxford Circus), 020-7637 5555; fax 020-7637 7333
266 Albemarle St., W1 (Green Park), 020-7495 5999; fax 020-7495 2999

◪ The "cool orange interior" ("like being in a Smash ad") at Oliver Peyton's "noisy" bar/restaurant off Oxford Street is "looking a bit tired now", but still "makes a gray day seem brighter", and it's been joined by a "bright, modern" Mayfair sibling; each venue has a "fun microbrewery" and Modern European–Med fare that divides diners – "tasty" vs. "ordinary" – whilst "haughty service" needles others.

Matsuri   22   17   19   £43

15 Bury St., SW1 (Green Park), 020-7839 1101;
fax 020-7930 7010

■ "Zero ambience, but worth a visit" is the scoop on this
"calm", "unfussy" Mayfair basement venue that provides
an "excellent introduction to Japanese food" with "top-
notch teppanyaki" and "good sushi"; some quarrel it's
"quite expensive", but Don Juans deem it "perfect for
impressing a first date."

Maxwell's ◗S   12   11   12   £21

8-9 James St., WC2 (Covent Garden), 020-7836 0303;
fax 020-7240 3562
76 Heath St., NW3 (Hampstead), 020-7794 5450;
fax 020-7435 5158

◪ This pair of "faux-American" diners in Covent Garden and
Hampstead is the place to go for "burgers in a time warp"
and "great desserts"; whilst a few critics say they're "tourist
traps" and "not worth a visit", most think they're still "good
for a family night out."

Mediterraneo ◗S   20   16   18   £31

37 Kensington Park Rd., W11 (Ladbroke Grove), 020-7792 3131;
fax 020-7229 7980

■ There's a "friendly" atmosphere at this "Notting Hill
charmer" (Osteria Basilico's sib) that earns plaudits for
its "well-thought-out" Modern Italian cuisine from a
"fantastic", albeit "small, menu"; it may be "noisy" and
"quite crowded", but the many regulars of this "sweet"
spot say they could "eat here every day."

Mela ◗S   –   –   –   M

152-156 Shaftesbury Ave., WC2 (Leicester Sq.), 020-7836 8635;
fax 020-7379 0527

Expect "upmarket Indian food" at bargain prices from a
regional, country menu at this little-known but promising
newcomer in a "great location" a stone's throw from
Cambridge Circus in Soho; other attractions are the bright,
colourful dining room (where the tandoor ovens are on
view) and lunch items for under £5.

Melati ◗S   20   9   16   £19

21 Great Windmill St., W1 (Piccadilly Circus), 020-7437 2745;
fax 020-7734 6964

■ "Addicting" and "authentic" Malaysian, Indonesian
and Singaporean fare has attracted admirers to this
"great" Soho spot for over 20 years; its wide range of
dishes is "dependably" "hot and spicy" and "reasonably
priced", and if the setting is a tad "cramped" and basic-
looking, the "efficient" service will get you in and out in
a timely fashion.

Memories of China **S**   20 | 15 | 17 | £38
353 Kensington High St., W8 (High St. Kensington),
020-7603 6951; fax 020-7603 0848 ●
67-69 Ebury St., SW1 (Victoria), 020-7730 7734
☑ "Interesting Chinese food not found anywhere else"
is the strong suit of this "upmarket" Belgravia and
Kensington duo deemed "excellent" by supporters; those
who'd rather forget them claim they "lack sparkle", citing
merely "competent" cuisine and a "stark", "impersonal"
atmosphere; N.B. at press time, change is afoot: a refurb
is slated for the Ebury Street location, its sib is set to move a
few doors down Kensington High St. and a new branch is
planned for Chelsea.

Memories of India ●**S**   19 | 11 | 16 | £27
18 Gloucester Rd., SW7 (Gloucester Rd.), 020-7581 3734;
fax 020-7589 6450
160-162 Thornbury Rd., Osterley (Osterley), 020-8847 1548
☑ Acolytes of this modestly decorated "neighbourhood"
Indian veteran in Kensington appreciate the "smiling
staff" and "very good" cooking starting with the "tasty
papadums", although antagonists tell of "kiddie-size
portions" and "pricey" tariffs; N.B. the Osterley outpost is
new and unrated.

Mesclun **S**   – | – | – | E
24 Stoke Newington Church St., N16 (Manor House),
020-7249 5029; fax 020-7275 8448
"Well-worth braving the scuzzy end of Church Street" say
intrepid surveyors who've discovered this "real find" in
Stoke Newington; the Modern British menu includes "top-
drawer fish dishes" and "fresh salads", and the service is
"pleasant without being sycophantic."

Meson Don Felipe   18 | 14 | 14 | £24
53 The Cut, SE1 (Southwark/Waterloo), 020-7928 3237;
fax 020-7736 9857
■ "The spot for intense talks over strong Rioja", this "buzzy"
Spanish "favourite" near Waterloo also offers a "plentiful"
array of "good" tapas and a "range of Iberian wines" to suit
your conversational needs; a "great Flamenco guitarist"
adds to the "fun atmosphere", but the lack of "elbow
room" rankles some.

Met Bar ●**S**   11 | 16 | 13 | £31
Private club; inquiries: 020-7447 5757
☑ "Celebrity-spotting can kill conversation" at the private
bar in Park Lane's Metropolitan Hotel that's "teeming with
trendies"; the jaded are unimpressed with the International
fare and balk at "sky-high prices" at this place that's become
a "parody of itself", but those whose expectations are well-
met maintain it's still "fun."

Metrogusto　　　　20 | 18 | 18 | £30
153 Battersea Park Rd., SW8 (Battersea Park B.R.),
020-7720 0204; fax 020-7720 0888
11-13 Theberton Street, N1 (Angel), 020-7226 9400;
fax 020-7226 9400 S

■ The "modern, smart" Battersea original ("odd location, but worth travelling") has been joined by a "warm" Islington sibling; the "good" Modern Italian menu offers a "proper choice of vegetarian dishes" accompanied by "interesting wines", though wallet-watchers warn it's "too dear."

Mezzo ◑S　　　　16 | 17 | 13 | £35
100 Wardour St., W1 (Leicester Sq./Piccadilly Circus),
020-7314 4000; fax 020-7314 4040

◪ "You need to be in the partying frame of mind" to get the most out of this "big, brash and noisy" basement bar/restaurant complex in Soho with a Modern European menu that some gauge as "good" and others opine is "totally unexciting" (maybe that's why staff are so "disinterested"); some say the live bands "are worth every penny of the extra £5 cost", but more conclude it's another "cookie-cutter offering from Conran."

Mezzonine ◑　　　　15 | 14 | 13 | £26
100 Wardour St., W1 (Leicester Sq./Piccadilly Circus),
020-7314 4000; fax 020-7314 4040

◪ On the ground floor of Mezzo is this "cheapish canteen" offering an "informal dining experience" with a "generally good" Thai menu; whilst the interior typifies Conran's "usual high standard", "slow service" and the "spillover" from the "jammed bar" into the dining area get low marks; P.S. it's often "incredibly noisy" at night thanks to a resident DJ.

Mildreds S⊭　　　　18 | 11 | 14 | £16
58 Greek St., W1 (Tottenham Court Rd.), 020-7439 2392;
fax 020-7494 1634

■ "Fantastic homestyle dishes" are still the hallmark of this "best Vegetarian around", a Soho stalwart that's "nice on a cold night" for a fix of "good organic food"; even though it "lacks atmosphere", it's still "great value."

Mimmo d'Ischia ◑　　　　20 | 16 | 19 | £39
61 Elizabeth St., SW1 (Sloane Sq./Victoria),
020-7730 5406

■ "Mimmo runs a good ship" salute maties of this "welcoming" Belgravia Italian that's "always full" and no wonder: "charming" staff serve "delicious" Traditional Italian fare in a "happy" atmosphere that attracts boatloads of "celebrities"; mutineers mutter that "prices exceed the quality", but on balance, this "venerable" venue that's pushing 30 "deserves its loyal following."

Ming ◑

35-36 Greek St., W1 (Leicester Sq./Piccadilly Circus),
020-7734 2721; fax 020-7437 0292

▽ 16 | 14 | 15 | £29

◪ It may be little-known, but it's adored by voters in-the-know for "reliably good" Chinese with "unusual dishes [served] in Western surroundings" in Soho; though a few are unimpressed by "expensive" fare that arrives in "small portions", more find it a "friendly" place that's "great for kids"; N.B. a £10 dinner menu is available pre-theatre.

Min's

31 Beauchamp Pl., SW3 (Knightsbridge), 020-7589 5080;
fax 020-7581 3777

▽ 19 | 24 | 18 | £29

◼ In a "seductive corner of Knightsbridge", this "romantic" townhouse comprising three floors offers a "low-key, simple" Modern British–Med menu skewed toward seafood; the "cosy" bar is "good for afternoon" snacking, whilst the "romantic" first-floor restaurant "makes a great date spot."

MIRABELLE ◑S

56 Curzon St., W1 (Green Park), 020-7499 4636;
fax 020-7499 5449

23 | 22 | 21 | £48

◼ "If you're going to push the boat out, there's no better jetty" than Marco Pierre White's "flagship" in a "stylish, airy" Mayfair space that's the perfect backdrop for its "top-class" Classic French cuisine, "expansive" "wine list that contains hidden bargains" and "crisp" "seamless" service; "without a stuffy dress code", this still is "a glamorous place for a special occasion", even though many feel "you pay too much"; the only problem: it's "so difficult to get a table."

Mission S

116 Wandsworth Bridge Rd., SW6 (Fulham Broadway),
020-7736 3322

▽ 21 | 17 | 21 | £35

◼ It's early days, but missionaries are relieved a "restaurant of true calibre has hit this area" of Fulham, where the "lovely owners" of this "great local" make sure you'll sup on "surprisingly good" Modern British cooking; those who find this mission impossible claim the menu is "pretentious"; N.B. closed Monday, lunch available weekends only.

Mitsukoshi

Dorland House, 14-20 Lower Regent St., SW1 (Piccadilly Circus), 020-7930 0317; fax 020-7839 1167

21 | 13 | 17 | £41

◪ Tired shoppers shout "thank goodness for the quality" Japanese fare, including "celestial" sushi served at this St. James's Asian department store; the basement venue vexes with its "total lack of atmosphere", but the savvy don't mind as they sit down to a set-price lunch for under £10.

Miyabi ▽ 24 | 18 | 19 | £28

Great Eastern Hotel, Liverpool St., EC2 (Liverpool St.),
020-7618 7100; fax 020-7618 7101

■ "One of London's finest for quality Japanese food" insist supporters of this "City gem" (part of Sir Terence Conran's empire) inside the handsome Great Eastern Hotel; especially esteemed are "excellent sushi" and sashimi, as well as its bento box takeaway/delivery service.

MIYAMA 🅂 25 | 14 | 21 | £42

38 Clarges St., W1 (Green Park), 020-7499 2443;
fax 020-7493 1573

■ Expect to be greeted by a host in native costume at this unobtrusive, simply decorated Japanese tucked into a Mayfair townhouse; "traditional food" (including teppanyaki specials) and old-fashioned service make for a "very nice" experience.

Mju ⌗ – | – | – | VE

Millennium Knightsbridge Hotel, 17 Sloane St., SW1
(Knightsbridge), 020-7201 6330; fax 020-7201 6302

A windowless room with a huge skylight inside the Millennium Knightsbridge Hotel is the setting of this newcomer from Sydney-based Tetsuya Wakuda, whose culinary creations feature seasonal Japanese flavours enhanced by classic French technique; there is no menu, as such, only a recitation of what the chef has prepared that day; N.B. it's also open for brunch at the weekend, and there is a bar area serving food.

MOMO ●🅂 18 | 24 | 17 | £38

25 Heddon St., W1 (Piccadilly Circus), 020-7434 4040;
fax 020-7287 0404

☑ "Take the theme-park atmosphere with a pinch of salt" and "savour" the "unrivalled originality" of this "beautiful", "Moroccan souk" off Regent Street that proffers a "wonderful" menu of "sensual" dishes, though those who report "mediocre" meals advise just "go for the" "transporting environment"; it's the "height of fun" thanks in no small part to the "fantastic, dancing staff" and "very hip" crowd; P.S. a "groovy downstairs [members'] bar adds to the excitement", and now the fully licensed Mô Tea Room serves lighter fare next door.

Monkeys 23 | 19 | 22 | £44

1 Cale St., SW3 (Sloane Sq./South Kensington),
020-7352 4711

■ "Keep it a secret" plead prime mates of this "charming" Chelsea Green "perennial" known for its "effusive" owners, a husband-and-wife team who appear "genuinely pleased you're there"; the Anglo-French fare is "delicious", "especially the game" dishes, and oenophiles go ape over a "proper" wine list.

Mon Plaisir ◗　　　20 | 18 | 18 | £34
21 Monmouth St., WC2 (Covent Garden/Leicester Sq.),
020-7836 7243; fax 020-7240 4774
■ Its "healthy disregard for fad foods" has pleased
patrons of this "comfortable" Soho bistro for over 50
years, and it's "still worth going" for "fantastic traditional
French", including an "excellent cheese board"; though
the "rushed" service isn't to everyone's liking, it works for
the pre-theatre crowd, who find the prix fixe menus to be
one of the "best deals in town."

MONSIEUR MAX S　　　26 | 18 | 21 | £41
133 High St., Hampton Hill, (Fulwell B.R.), 020-8979 5546;
fax 020-8979 3747
■ "*Vaux le détour*" out of town say those who know Max
Renzland's "cosy" Hampton Hill "gem" where "impeccable
standards are maintained" in the form of "superb service"
and "strong, gutsy" dishes from an "outstanding" Classic
French menu; there's just one problem: "the rest of London
has found out about it!"

Montana S　　　20 | 18 | 18 | £34
125-129 Dawes Rd., SW6 (Fulham Broadway), 020-7385 9500;
fax 020-7386 0337
☑ "I've died and gone to Southwestern heaven" drawl
devotees of this "relaxed, cosmopolitan" Fulham venue
that "offers an exciting, different" American fusion menu,
brought to table by "friendly" staff that aren't "in your face";
though a minority is "not impressed" ("bland", "expensive"),
most call it "a class act", noting especially its "nice brunch"
and "live music that doesn't intrude" (Wednesday–Sunday);
N.B. a new chef joined post-*Survey*.

Monte's　　　21 | 19 | 20 | £45
Private club; inquiries: 020-7245 0896
☑ It "now has a good buzz to it" following a "revamp" and
the installation of Jamie Oliver as consultant chef, though
this "posh" Knightsbridge private club "still feels old-
fashioned"; non-members can sample its "brilliantly"
"simple" Modern Italian cuisine at lunch (dinner is for
members only), and there's always the more casual upstairs
bar, the basement nightclub ("different night, different
atmosphere") and street-level cigar shop.

Montpeliano ◗S　　　18 | 16 | 17 | £38
13 Montpelier St., SW7 (Knightsbridge), 020-7589 0032
☑ There's "always a joyful ambience" at this long-standing,
"old-fashioned" Italian trattoria in Knightsbridge, according
to loyalists "addicted" to its "good, honest fare" and
"attentive" service ("nothing is too much trouble"); foes
fume it "panders too much to regulars", complaining of
"cramped" conditions and excessive "attitude" from the
staff, but all agree it's handy for "Harrods."

Monza ●S

21 | 14 | 21 | £35

*6 Yeoman's Row, SW3 (Knightsbridge), 020-7591 0210;
fax 020-7591 0210*

■ "The food more than makes up for the cramped dining" at this "buzzy", Formula One–themed Knightsbridge venue, where the "top-gear" Modern Italian cooking is served by "friendly" waiters who "negotiate the small gaps with style and wit"; "when crowded, the decibel level" is as "stratospheric" as a revving F-1 engine, but few seem perturbed: it's "organised chaos, but charming."

MORO

23 | 17 | 19 | £33

*34-36 Exmouth Mkt., EC1 (Angel/Farringdon), 020-7833 8336;
fax 020-7833 9338*

■ "Reservations still trade on the futures market" at this wildly "popular", yet "unaffected", Clerkenwell eaterie whose "winning formula" combines a "friendly", "lively atmosphere" with "refreshingly original" "Moorish food" (from Spain, North Africa and the Eastern Mediterranean); whilst budget-minded sorts suggest a "set-price menu would ease the wallet", there's always the more affordable option of eating tapas in its "great bar."

Moshi Moshi Sushi

17 | 10 | 13 | £20

*7-8 Limeburner Ln., EC4 (St. Paul's/Thames City), 020-7248 1808;
fax 020-7248 1807*
Unit 24, Liverpool St. Station, EC2 (Liverpool St.), 020-7247 3227
*Cabot Pl. East, level 2, E14 (Canary Wharf), 020-7512 9911;
fax 020-7512 9201*

◪ Though "conveyor-belt sushi" is "no longer original", this "fun" City trio of Japanese "craving satisfiers" is "superb for its type", offering an "always-delicious", colour-coded selection of circulating "fresh sushi"; whilst those on limited lunch hours grow frustrated with the sometimes "long queues at peak period", most find it's well "worth the wait."

MOSIMANN'S

25 | 24 | 24 | £56

Private club; inquiries: 020-7235 9625

◪ "If you get an invite to this private dining club, go!" advise admirers of Belgravia's "gourmet's paradise" quartered in an "old church", a "superb setting" for Anton Mosimann's "sublime" International cuisine ("the food is art") and "fantastic" service that "anticipates desires"; "special occasion, business or romance – take your pick", it's "wonderful all around", though "pity it's members-only."

Motcomb's S

17 | 15 | 17 | £36

*26 Motcomb St., SW1 (Knightsbridge/Sloane Sq.),
020-7235 6382; fax 020-7245 6351*

◪ Longtime loyalists are relieved that this "stately old-timer" in Belgravia has "kept the friendly" ambience following a total "redecoration"; its "non-fussy" Modern British menu remains as pleasingly retro as ever, which leads an avant-garde few to suggest the place is for the "oldsters."

Movenpick Marché [S] 11 10 10 £18
Portland House, Bressenden Pl., SW1 (Victoria), 020-7630 1733
◩ "Touristy, but good for a quick bite" is the consensus on this Victoria International "canteen" where the "concept" has diners choosing their own "stir-fry" ingredients to be "cooked in front" of them; many find it's "not as good as those in Europe" (it "would be brilliant if the food were fresher"), but it's hard to fault its convenience as a travellers' stop-off.

Moxon's ▽ 22 14 19 £34
14 Clapham Park Rd., SW4 (Clapham Common), 020-7627 2468; fax 020-7627 2424
◩ "Go away, it's mine" plead the few surveyors who know this modest-looking Clapham seafooder, fearing that "too many people might come" if word about it gets out; it's a "great local", open for dinner only and offering an "excellent" £12.50 prix fixe menu of fresh fare; N.B. the kitchen recently underwent a chef change.

MPW Brasserie [S] 14 13 13 £32
Posthouse, 215 Haverstock Hill, NW3 (Belfase Park), 020-7435 6080; fax 020-7435 5586
◩ "Shouldn't we expect more from MPW?" wonder voters who "had higher hopes for" this Marco Pierre White–overseen newcomer in Haverstock Hill's Posthouse, citing a "suburban feel", "ordinary" New French cooking and "slow service"; others are more supportive, reporting "innovative food" and an "excellent set menu", concluding with one telling point: "nothing else nearby!"

Mr. Chow ◐[S] 19 17 18 £42
151 Knightsbridge, SW1 (Knightsbridge), 020-7589 7347; fax 020-7584 5780
◩ "Nostalgic memories" pervade this Knightsbridge Chinese stalwart (est. 1968), where loyalists assert the "dated" atmosphere remains "charged with the good and the famous"; reports on the Beijing cooking are mixed, however, with admirers insisting it's "the best Chinese-orientated food" around and sceptics calling it "bland" and balking at "prices that defy belief."

Mr. Kong ◐[S] 21 9 13 £24
21 Lisle St., WC2 (Leicester Sq.), 020-7437 7341
◩ "Consistently good Cantonese food" and a kitchen open until the wee hours (last orders at 2.45 AM) are among the main attractions of this "authentic" Chinatown establishment, though even admirers admit its "decor is nothing to write home about"; the fact that walk-ups "face a long queue" suggests its "tasty" dishes are "well worth" the wait.

Mr. Wing ●S

18 | 20 | 17 | £33

242-244 Old Brompton Rd., SW5 (Earl's Court), 020-7370 4450; fax 020-7565 4578

■ Lots of "suggestive greenery" fills the interior of this "lovely" (if "a tad OTT") Earl's Court Chinese, which also boasts "quality" multiregional cuisine and "very kind service"; with the added benefit of live music, it's no wonder that it's "always A-1" as far as its admirers are concerned.

Mustards Smithfield Brasserie

16 | 13 | 16 | £28

60 Long Ln., EC1 (Barbican), 020-7796 4920; fax 020-7606 0720

■ "Just a stone's throw from the Barbican" is this two-level French bistro/wine bar overlooking Smithfield Market; it may look a bit "tired" these days, but nevertheless it remains a popular choice for Gallic–Modern British cooking that most characterise as "always reliable and enjoyable."

Nachos S

9 | 10 | 12 | £19

212 Fulham Rd., SW10 (Fulham Broadway/South Kensington), 020-7351 7531; fax 020-7349 0633

■ "Tex-Mex for the novice" and plenty of slushy margaritas to wash it down are what's on offer at this "cheap", festive Fulham Road joint with "friendly staff" and the "typical atmosphere" of a south-of-the-border "imitation" in London; however, more deeply "disappointed" diners complain the edibles (fajitas, nachos, etc.) are "as plastic as the decor."

Nahm S

– | – | – | VE

Halkin Hotel, Halkin St., SW1 (Hyde Park Corner), 020-7333 1234; fax 020-7333 1100

Following the departure of Stefano Cavallini and an elegant revamp of Christina Ong's sleek Belgravia hotel dining room, famous Australian chef David Thompson has arrived to unveil an ambitious menu of unique Thai dishes, which are helping propel this sophisticated newcomer into the front line of London dining; N.B. the name means 'water' in Thai.

Naked Turtle S

16 | 16 | 18 | £31

505 Upper Richmond Rd. W., SW14 (Richmond), 020-8878 1995; fax 020-8392 1388

■ There's an "uplifting atmosphere" at this "lively" Modern British–Eclectic eaterie in East Sheen; among the specialties of its South African chef are exotic dishes like kangaroo, crocodile and emu, provoking a range of remarks from "terrific" to "weird"; N.B. it has live jazz and a new bar area.

Nam Long Le Shaker ●

15 | 15 | 14 | £33

159 Old Brompton Rd., SW5 (Gloucester Rd./South Kensington), 020-7373 1926; fax 020-7373 6043

■ "Once you have battered your way past all the Gucci and Prada handbags" at the bar (dispenser of "lethal cocktails"), the Vietnamese cooking is "not half bad" at this "exciting" South Kensington venue with the "real energy" that comes with a "young, very Euro" crowd.

Nancy Lam's Enak-Enak ▽ 20 | 11 | 18 | £29

56 Lavender Hill, SW11 (Clapham Junction B.R.), 020-7924 3148; fax 020-7241 6710

■ Celebrity chef Nancy Lam is "loud and rude but incredibly adorable" as she serves up "delicious", "home-cooked" Indonesian–Far Eastern fare at her "small", "cosy" Lavender Hill venue; they "don't do lunch", but for "an entertaining dinner", this is "an experience" (though booking's essential).

Nautilus Fish 21 | 8 | 14 | £18

27-29 Fortune Green Rd., NW6 (West Hampstead), 020-7435 2532

■ "Fish want to end up at this fish heaven" in West Hampstead, a basic, compact stalwart that stacks up as "one of the best" fish 'n' chip shops "in town", known for its particularly "fresh" fare fried in matzo batter; given the unpretentious surroundings, it's "hardly [a place for] a night out", but nonetheless, it remains a "great favourite."

Navajo Joe ◐ [S] 13 | 11 | 12 | £22

34 King St., WC2 (Covent Garden), 020-7240 4008; fax 020-7240 4009

■ "Well, the nachos are ok" and the rest of the American Southwestern–Mexican menu "is reasonable", yet most are attracted by the "lively bar" and "good happy hour" at this rowdy Covent Garden haunt that makes a "good meeting place"; "sit upstairs and watch from the balconies."

Neal Street Restaurant 23 | 18 | 21 | £44

26 Neal St., WC2 (Covent Garden), 020-7836 8368; fax 020-7240 3964

■ "Maybe you'll even see Antonio Carluccio himself" at the celebrity chef's "unpretentious" Covent Garden eaterie, which specialises in the "most amazing mushrooms" from an Italian menu packed with "wow tastes"; detractors deem it "an '80s power restaurant that hasn't moved on", complaining of experiences that "don't quite add up to" the "expensive" "price tag"; N.B. there's a new chef de cuisine in the kitchen, Flavio Giacoletto.

Neat Restaurant ◐ [S] – | – | – | VE

Oxo Tower Wharf, Barge House St., SE1 (Blackfriars/Waterloo), 020-7928 4433; fax 020-7928 8644

Neat Brasserie ◐ [S] – | – | – | E

Oxo Tower Wharf, Barge House St., SE1 (Blackfriars/Waterloo), 020-7928 5533; fax 020-7928 8644

After conquering Cannes with his lauded Riviera eaterie, Richard Neat's new Southbank venture a few floors below Oxo Tower restaurant arrives as one of London's most significant post-*Survey* openings, comprising a classy restaurant serving Neat's ambitious, self-assured New French cooking at top-end prices, and a less-formal brasserie with a similar, but less high-brow menu that's also marginally cheaper; both spaces have river views.

New Culture Revolution　　　15　11　13　£16
157-159 Notting Hill Gate, W11 (Notting Hill Gate),
020-7313 9688 **S**
442 Edgware Rd., W2 (Edgware Rd.), 020-7402 4841 **S**
305 King's Rd., SW3 (Sloane Sq.), 020-7352 9281 **S**
43 Parkway, NW1 (Camden Town), 020-7267 2700
42 Duncan St., N1 (Angel), 020-7833 9083 **S**
☑ "Fresh, healthy" and "cheap" North Chinese fare
"swiftly served" is what most look for from this quartet of
"no-nonsense" (some say "sterile") noodle parlours, and
whilst the majority pronounces it "reliable for a decent,
quick meal", a few malcontents maintain the "bland"
offerings are "not worth a detour."

New World ●S　　　　　19　11　14　£20
1 Gerrard Pl., W1 (Leicester Sq.), 020-7434 2508; fax 020-7287 8994
■ "Go early or late to miss the crowds" at this "massive"
(600 seats!) Chinatown eaterie, which has been "smartened
up recently"; it's "ideal for dim sum first-timers" thanks to its
rolling delectables "as tasty as in China", but it also offers
a thick menu of "great" Cantonese dishes; "brisk staff",
including "very sweet trolley ladies", complete the picture.

Nico Central　　　　　　18　14　17　£38
35 Great Portland St., W1 (Oxford Circus), 020-7436 8846;
fax 020-7436 3455
☑ It's no longer linked with Nico Ladenis, but supporters
of this sedate Oxford Street venue find it hasn't suffered
for his absence, citing a New French menu that's "good",
if "restricted", and prices that are "alright if on expenses";
vocal dissenters call it "disappointing on all fronts",
disparaging "unimaginative" cooking and premises they
find "uninspiring from the outside" and "no better inside."

Nicole's　　　　　　　　19　19　19　£35
Nicole Farhi, 158 New Bond St., W1 (Green Park), 020-7499 8408;
fax 020-7409 0381
■ "One of the best 'shop' restaurants" in the West End is
this "sophisticated" basement eaterie in Nicole Farhi's Bond
Street store, where "elegant" Modern British–Med meals
provide shoppers with fortification "necessary before
venturing to buy"; not surprising, it's "expensive", but the
"wonderful people-watching" compensates – in sum, it's
"lovely for lunch" and "worth a try for dinner."

Nikita's ●　　　　　　　16　17　17　£39
65 Ifield Rd., SW10 (Earl's Court), 020-7352 6326; fax 020-7352 6969
■ "Remember to buy aspirin for your hangover before you
go" to this 30-year-old veteran on the Fulham-Chelsea
border, where the Russian food draws little comment beyond
the "highlights" – "blinis, caviar" – that pair nicely with the
free-flowing "vodka served in ice crates"; its "private
rooms behind red curtains" are "fun in large groups" (and
popular for stag parties): "you'll have the night of your life!"

Nirvana S | – | – | – | E |

277 Wimbledon Park Rd., SW19 (Southfields), 020-8780 2406;
fax 011-8989 4251

Formerly Rajput, this revamped, renamed and revitalised
Southfields Indian now sports a modern, minimalist interior
that serves as a suitable foil for the pricey, quality creations
of chef Ashok Patra, who most recently worked at Hotel
KC Residency in India.

Noble Rot | 18 | 19 | 16 | £40 |

3-5 Mill St., W1 (Oxford Circus), 020-7629 8877;
fax 020-7629 8878

☑ The award for "best restaurant name" goes to this
"trendy, California-style" eaterie near Regent Street that
produces "surprisingly good" Modern European cooking,
though the "cool, smooth", celebrity-rich members' bar in
the basement is "really the place to be" (it gets "raucous as
the night goes on"); "frosty" service gets the thumbs-down:
"need a course in customer relations"; N.B. as oenophiles
know, noble rot is a mould beneficial in wine-making.

NOBU S | 26 | 21 | 20 | £56 |

Metropolitan Hotel, 19 Old Park Ln., W1 (Hyde Park Corner),
020-7447 4747; fax 020-7447 4749

☑ "Clink chopsticks" with "celebs and foodies" at this "altar
of gastronomy" in Park Lane's Metropolitan Hotel, where
the "magical" Japanese–South American cuisine is "a
constant revelation" worth "mortgaging the house" for;
this "creative star" does have its critics, though, who carp
about "arrogant" service and a "plain-Jane" interior "noisy"
"enough to wake dead fish", but the fact that it's "still
impossible to get a reservation" speaks volumes: "there
are some things in life that simply have to be tried"; P.S.
most common question: "where is the linen cupboard?"

Noor Jahan ◑ S | 19 | 14 | 18 | £27 |

2A Bina Gardens, SW5 (South Kensington), 020-7373 6522

◼ It's "noisy" and the "tables are on top of one another",
but this nearly 40-year-old Indian veteran near Gloucester
Road remains a "neighbourhood" fixture beloved for its
"good, honest curry" ("best *saag* ever") that's considered
simply "splendid"; given that the place is always "very
busy", who can blame the "efficient" staff if they're "helpful"
but "not particularly warm"?

North Pole S | ▽ | 14 | 12 | 12 | £26 |

131 Greenwich High Rd., SE10 (Greenwich B.R.), 020-8853 3020;
fax 020-8853 3501

☑ This "decent gastro-pub in a bleak area" of Greenwich
is much-appreciated in the neighbourhood for its popular
ground-floor bar and first-floor eaterie serving "good"
Modern British fare, which is a local "favourite for Sunday
lunch"; N.B. a basement champagne bar opened post-
Survey called, you guessed it, South Pole.

Noto　　　　　　　　　　　16 | 10 | 14 | £19
Bow Bells House, 7 Bread St., EC4 (Mansion House),
020-7329 8056 ⊅
2-3 Bassishaw Highwalk, EC2 (Bank/Moorgate), 020-7256 9433;
fax 020-7588 5656

■ They have the same name (and owner), but these two "friendly" City Japanese venues have different menus: the Moorgate spot serves "top-quality sushi" and other "decent" traditional dishes, whilst the Bread Street branch is a "very quick" noodle bar and has no license; both are credited with "fresh food at very good prices."

Notting Hill Brasserie **S**　　　20 | 19 | 19 | £38
92 Kensington Park Rd., W11 (Notting Hill Gate), 020-7229 4481;
fax 020-7221 1246

■ "Much less stuffy then the last restaurant here" (Leith's), this "airy", "comfortable" and "down-to-earth" Notting Hill "newcomer" has made a "nice" start with its "upmarket, original" Modern British cooking; whilst it makes a fine choice for a "romantic dinner", denizens also consider it "very good for weekend brunches."

Noura ●**S**　　　　　▽ 18 | 18 | 19 | £32
16 Hobart Pl., SW1 (Victoria), 020-7235 9444; fax 020-7235 9244

■ Although it hasn't yet been discovered by many surveyors, those who know it consider this "great, bustling" newcomer a "fashionable" addition to Victoria, thanks to its "delicious" Lebanese cuisine served all day and "good prices."

OAK ROOM
MARCO PIERRE WHITE ●　　25 | 23 | 23 | £57
Le Meridien Piccadilly, 21 Piccadilly, W1 (Piccadilly Circus),
020-7437 0202; fax 020-7851 3141

☑ "All the splendour" of this "impressive dining room with many chandeliers" in Piccadilly's Le Meridien Hotel strikes admirers as the "ultimate lap of luxury", and though MPW is no longer in the kitchen, chef Robert Reid's "breathtaking presentations" of "sublime" New French dishes earn lavish "accolades" (despite last year's menu simplification); a "disappointed" few report "imperious" service amid a "huge, empty room", but they are outvoted by the majority that finds meals here "glorious", "unique experiences."

Odette's **S**　　　　　　21 | 21 | 19 | £39
130 Regent's Park Rd., NW1 (Chalk Farm), 020-7586 5486;
fax 020-7580 0508

■ "Take a lover" to this "oh-so-romantic" Primrose Hill "oasis" that "continues to be chic" after more than "20 years", thanks in no small part to the "special intimacy" of its "splendid, original" dining room (candlelight and gilt "mirrors everywhere"); the "innovative" Modern British cuisine also adds to its staying power, as well as the "fabulous basement [wine bar] in which to drink champagne."

Odin's
21 | 22 | 21 | £41

27 Devonshire St., W1 (Baker St.), 020-7935 7296; fax 020-7493 8309

■ "Still a landmark of civility", this "grown-up" Marylebone eaterie (next door to sib Langan's Bistro) is a "haven of discretion and tradition" known for its "good, old-fashioned" Anglo-French cooking delivered with near-"faultless service" amid a "warm, clubby interior" filled with art; it's "good for business" or "a quiet atmosphere."

Old Delhi S
22 | 15 | 19 | £32

48 Kendal St., W2 (Marble Arch), 020-7723 3335; fax 020-7258 0181

■ It's relatively little-known among surveyors, but this rather elegant, wood-panelled venue near Marble Arch is judged by those in-the-know to produce downright "fantastic" Indian-Persian cuisine, with "great service" to boot; a live harpist on Wednesday and Saturday nights (when a £2 cover charge is levied) adds to the endorsement.

Oliveto ●S
18 | 12 | 14 | £27

49 Elizabeth St., SW1 (Sloane Sq./Victoria), 020-7730 0074; fax 020-7824 8190

☑ This "casual", narrow "neighbourhood hangout" in Belgravia (a younger sib to Olivo) is a popular destination for "simple, well-prepared" Modern Italian fare, and whilst a few foes assert "prices are going too high for what you get", most don't mind much, given that the house speciality of "great pizzas" ensures they "never get bored."

Olivo S
19 | 15 | 17 | £33

21 Eccleston St., SW1 (Victoria), 020-7730 2505; fax 020-7824 8190

■ "Could be in a small village in Italy" say visitors to this "popular" ("still have to book") Victoria Italian, which serves "charming, simple" classic dishes at a "fair deal"; all told, it's a ray of "Sardinian sunshine" that keeps fans going "back again and again."

182 Mint
– | – | – | E

182 St. John St., EC1 (Angel/Farringdon), 020-7253 8368; fax 020-7253 8371

Few have commented on this "lively newcomer" near Smithfield with a Pacific-Rim menu, but there's a suggestion that the place "needs to make up its mind what it is": a "hangout" for locals or a destination for "serious" foodies.

115 at Hodgson's
– | – | – | E

115 Chancery Ln., WC2 (Chancery Ln.), 020-7242 2836; fax 020-7831 6113

A year after opening, this "bright" dining room above the Hodgson's Wine Bar near Covent Garden has distinguished itself with its "excellent" Modern British fare; detractors deem it "average", with "inconsistent service"; N.B. a new chef may outdate the above food rating.

1 Lombard Street　　　21 │ 18 │ 17 │ £44
1 Lombard St., EC3 (Bank), 020-7929 6611; fax 020-7929 6622
☑ "Fat cats" pounce on the more formal section of Soren Jessen's City "sophisticated", "well-designed" Modern British–French venue, where fans find the food "excellent" and foes feel it's "patchy" and "overrated"; on one point do all agree: it's "expensive" and best for a "business lunch."

1 Lombard Street Brasserie　　20 │ 20 │ 18 │ £37
1 Lombard St., EC3 (Bank), 020-7929 6611; fax 020-7929 6622
☑ There's an "uplifting buzz" at Soren Jessen's brasserie near the Bank of England, known for its "super bar" and "outstanding" Modern European fare that makes for "sleek lunching" for "elegant people"; the brassed-off opine the food is "disappointing" and the ambience "too noisy."

190, Downstairs at　　　17 │ 17 │ 17 │ £37
190 Queens Gate, SW7 (Gloucester Rd.), 020-7581 5666; fax 020-7581 8172
■ There's a "nice romantic atmosphere" at this "welcome haven" (in South Kensington's Bistro 190), where "friendly" staff serve "good" International fare and the "cool bar" is popular for sustenance before visiting the Royal Albert Hall around the corner.

192 ⊘Ⓢ　　　17 │ 14 │ 14 │ £33
192 Kensington Park Rd., W11 (Ladbroke Grove/ Notting Hill Gate), 020-7229 0482; fax 020-7229 3300
☑ The Modern British "food can be excellent" and the wine list offers "lots of cheap treasures", but it's more about "people-watching" at this "gossipy Notting Hill restaurant", where "wanna-bes hope to brush shoulders with someone famous"; though the jaded jeer the food's "hit-or-miss" and the service "sullen", fans feel this "old faithful" "still fills an important local function."

One-O-One Ⓢ　　　19 │ 16 │ 18 │ £45
Sheraton Park Tower, William St., SW1 (Knightsbridge), 020-7290 7101; fax 020-7235 6196
■ Though it's yet to be "discovered by London's restaurant-going crowd", this Knightsbridge hotel dining room offers a "surprisingly first-rate" French-seafood menu that includes "delicious fish dishes" delivered by "attentive" staff; those who don't find it so one-derful carp it's "overpriced."

OPIUM　　　19 │ 26 │ 18 │ £36
1A Bean St., W1 (Tottenham Court Rd.), 020-7287 9608; fax 020-7437 3500
■ This "hidden gem, or should I say den" off Oxford Street is an evocatively decorated spot with a "friendly doorman"; there's "surprisingly good [Vietnamese-French] food for a nightclub" (though a few critics contend the "service needs improving"), and most appreciate its "great late-night" features, including live cabaret acts.

Oriel 🅂 13 | 14 | 12 | £26
51 Sloane Sq., SW1 (Sloane Sq.), 020-7730 2804;
fax 020-7730 7966

▧ There are "better things to look at than the food" at this "hot spot in Sloane Square" that's "good for a quickie"; whilst the "mediocre" Eclectic fare inspires few, all agree it's "dependable when you can't think of anywhere else."

Orient ◕ 19 | 21 | 18 | £38
160 Piccadilly, 1st fl., W1 (Green Park), 020-7499 6996;
fax 020-7499 7779

▧ Featuring "fabulous artwork", this "stylish" first-floor newcomer in Piccadilly's China House attracts "glamorous people" with "lovely", "modern Chinese" cooking; doubters who find it "disappointing for these prices" can repair to the adjacent Clipper Bar for a consoling cocktail.

Original Tajine ▽ 20 | 15 | 18 | £27
7A Dorset St., W1 (Baker St.), 020-7935 1545

▧ "Spicy", "superb Moroccan peasant food at peasant prices" pleases the parsimonious at this Marylebone "find"; it's so "small" the staff must "squeeze between tables" to deliver your dishes (though they do so "with a smile").

ORRERY 🅂 23 | 21 | 21 | £48
55-57 Marylebone High St., W1 (Baker St./Regent's Park),
020-7616 8000; fax 020-7616 8080

▧ "Conran on a small but better scale" claim cognoscenti who consider this "light and lovely" Marylebone venue with a rooftop terrace "one of the best efforts" in Sir Terence's empire; "talented chef" Chris Galvin impresses with his "scrummy" New French fare ferried by "friendly", "sharp staff", and though some snipe it's "shamelessly expensive", more endorse it as a "great evening out."

Orsino ◑🅂 18 | 17 | 16 | £34
119 Portland Rd., W11 (Holland Park), 020-7221 3299;
fax 020-7229 9414

▣ It's "always a joy to visit" this "great neighbourhood Italian" in Holland Park announce amici of "Orso's more casual sister", known for "good food at a good price" (including its "excellent-value pre-theatre menu" at £15.50) and "service like clockwork"; opponents opine the fare's "average" and "inauthentic" and the setting's "cramped."

Orso ◑🅂 19 | 16 | 18 | £35
27 Wellington St., WC2 (Covent Garden), 020-7240 5269;
fax 020-7497 2148

▧ A "Covent Garden mainstay" pre- and post-theatre where the "dark basement setting belies" the "homey Italian food", this "classic" "still delivers" for devotees of its "varied menu" of "super food"; the "trendies" and "business clientele" create a "boisterous", "party" atmosphere and may have "too much fun to worry about forgetful service."

Oscar S
− − − E

*Charlotte Street Hotel, 15-17 Charlotte St., W1 (Goodge St./
Tottenham Court Rd.), 020-7907 4005*

The all-day dining area (with summer patio) of Fitzrovia's
smart new Charlotte Street Hotel serves "tasty" Modern
British fare, and although "service can be a bit slow", it's
growing in popularity as an "excellent drinks" option in a
competitive part of town.

Oslo Court
21 14 23 £37

*Charlbert St., Prince Albert Rd., NW8 (St. John's Wood),
020-7722 8795*

■ Even though "it comes from a bygone era" ("'60s − or is
it '50s?"), this "comforting" St. John's Wood eaterie remains
"a fun favourite for family celebrations" and "birthday
parties" featuring "huge portions of uncomplicated, but
carefully cooked" Classic French fare from a "consistently
good- value" prix fixe menu; a tip: "book well in advance."

Osteria Antica Bologna S
18 13 15 £29

*23 Northcote Rd., SW11 (Clapham Junction B.R.),
020-7978 4771; fax 020-7978 4771*

◪ This Battersea trattoria makes a "good local" due to its
bustling "family atmosphere" and "dependable, robust
Italian fare", though some insist it "overdoes the garlic and
herbs" and aesthetes admit the "decor's a bit tired."

Osteria Basilico S
21 17 18 £28

*29 Kensington Park Rd., W11 (Ladbroke Grove),
020-7727 9957; fax 020-7229 7980*

■ "It's impossible to get into" this "amazing little Italian
in Notting Hill", where the "great food and wine", the
"charming", "bustling" atmosphere and "people-watching"
make for an "excellent experience"; though the waiters
may be "grumpy", the "crammed"-in patrons are positively
jovial over the "reasonable prices."

Otto Dining Lounge
− − − VE

215 Sutherland Ave., W9 (Maida Vale), 020-7266 3131

"Still needs to get its act together, but on the right track"
sums up this glass-fronted, dinner-only newcomer in Maida
Vale with a short Modern European menu; proponents
contend the "decor and service are excellent", and the
nightly DJ in the "stylish cocktail lounge" is a big draw.

OXO TOWER ●S
19 23 16 £44

*Oxo Tower Wharf, Barge House St., SE1
(Blackfriars/Waterloo), 020-7803 3888; fax 020-7803 3838*

◪ "Watching the sunset over London is very cool" vouch
vista-philes of the "magnificent view" from this top-floor
South Bank landmark; supporters say the Modern British
fare is "exceptional" as well and admire the "towering
style" of the "modern" interior; naysayers pronounce the
food "patchy" and the service "sloppy."

Oxo Tower Brasserie ◐ S   17 | 21 | 15 | £35
Oxo Tower Wharf, Barge House St., SE1
(Blackfriars/Waterloo), 020-7803 3888; fax 020-7803 3838
◪ Boosters "keep going back for the view and buzz" at this "steely-chic" brasserie adjacent to Oxo Tower Restaurant on the South Bank, where "unfussy" Med–Pacific Rim cooking, "brisk service" and "relaxed" atmosphere get a thumbs-up; bashers bemoan the "bland", "formula cuisine", suggesting "it's better for a drink" (especially on the terrace).

Ozer Restaurant & Bar ◐ S   20 | 20 | 19 | £35
4-5 Langham Pl., W1 (Oxford Circus), 020-7323 0505;
fax 020-7323 0111
◪ For a "wonderful evening out", take "lots of friends" to sample "all the delicious starters" at this Modern Ottoman (read: Turkish) near Oxford Street; the "luxurious" decor provides a fitting backdrop for "excellent" food with options that are "great for vegetarians", all at "reasonable prices", but a minority maintains the fare's "nothing special."

Pacific Oriental   16 | 15 | 15 | £35
1 Bishopsgate, EC2 (Bank St.), 020-7621 9988; fax 020-7929 7227
◪ "City types still love this" Bishopsgate spot with a "busy downstairs bar" (beware "ear-splitting acoustics") serving snacks and a "comfortable" first-floor dining room featuring "imaginative" Pacific Rim dishes; if a few feel the "food isn't up to scratch", most rate it a "nice business-lunch venue."

Paell'ya S   – | – | – | M
811-813 Wandsworth Rd., SW8 (Clapham Common),
020-7627 5151; fax 020-7720 9969
A large, glass-fronted Wandsworth newcomer opposite a snooker hall, this functional, modern eaterie offers a Spanish menu of tapas as well as 12 paellas, all of which go down better with a sippable selection from the Iberian wine list.

Palm Court S   20 | 23 | 19 | £32
Le Meridien Waldorf, Aldwych, WC2 (Covent Garden),
020-7759 4001; fax 020-7240 9277
■ The elegant, all-day dining room in the Le Meridien Waldorf is "as reliable as ever", with "solicitous service" and a near-"faultless" Modern British menu; the real "story", though, is the famed afternoon tea, consumed to the strains of a harpist during the week and orchestra on weekends.

Paparazzi ◐   12 | 12 | 11 | £24
Paparazzi Lounge, 9 Hanover St., W1 (Oxford Circus),
020-7355 3337; fax 020-7355 3338
Paparazzi Lounge Cafe, 58 Fulham Rd., SW3
(South Kensington), 020-7589 0876 S
◪ "You end up dancing on the tables" with "wanna-bes dreaming of Hollywood" at this pair of "fun" Italians in South Kensington and off Regent Street, but when it comes to the cooking, "good" is as good as the comments get.

PARADE S
26 | 20 | 20 | £37

18-19 The Mall, W5 (Ealing Broadway), 020-8810 0202; fax 020-8810 0303

■ This "exemplary" Ealing venue "puts overpriced, over-hyped restaurants to shame" by virtue of its "superb" Modern British cuisine that uses "imaginative ingredients" yet tries "nothing too clever"; a few warn of "variable service", but most wish this "best-kept secret" would "stay unknown forever"; P.S. the £15 three-course lunch provides "excellent value."

Parisienne Chophouse S
– | – | – | E

3 Yeoman's Row, SW3 (Knightsbridge), 020-7590 9999

Yet another Marco Pierre White venture, this stylish newcomer in large Knightsbridge premises (formerly occupied by Chez Gerard) aims to raise the standard of Classic French bistro cooking in the capital; a three-course £13.50 prix fixe Sunday lunch menu is proving popular.

Parsee S
– | – | – | E

34 Highgate Hill, N19 (Archway), 020-7272 9091

It's been an encouraging debut for this "buzzy" Highgate "new baby" of the Café Spice Namaste group, where chef Cyrus Todiwala lets loose "amazing" dishes in the Parsee tradition (Indian with Persian influences), a cuisine that, it's claimed, can be found in no other restaurant in Europe.

PASHA ●S
19 | 24 | 17 | £36

1 Gloucester Rd., SW7 (Gloucester Rd.), 020-7589 7969; fax 020-7581 9996

☑ "Incense sets the mood the minute you walk into" this "beautiful" South Ken eaterie, and "cosy cushions" enhance the "pure romance" quotient; the "tasty" Moroccan fare and "exciting wine list" also elicit praise, and though the "dour" service puts a damper on the experience for some, the belly dancer might mollify them.

Pasha ●S
18 | 17 | 18 | £25

301 Upper St., N1 (Angel/Highbury & Islington), 020-7226 1454; fax 020-7226 1617

■ With a "glamorous" setting ("like *Arabian Nights*") and "the latest Middle Eastern pop music", this "plush" Islingtonian provides a "great atmosphere" in which to loll while partaking of "good Turkish food"; even those who find it "Europeanised" admit it's still "fun."

Passion S
– | – | – | E

119 Shirland Rd., W9 (Maida Vale), 020-7289 5667

A first solo venture from Craig Thomas ("ex Marco Pierre White"), this "new face" in Maida Vale – a "starved neighbourhood" – has quickly established a local following, more in response to Thomas' "very classy" Modern British cooking ("splendid fish, subtle soufflés") than the "uncomfortable, but attractively simple decor."

Passione
| 22 | 14 | 20 | £34 |

10 Charlotte St., W1 (Goodge St.), 020-7636 2833;
fax 020-7636 2889

■ "Choosing from the menu is almost traumatic – it's all so delicious" insist the impassioned of this "consistently brilliant" Modern Italian in Fitzrovia, where "wonderful" mushrooms are a house speciality; "knowledgeable waiters" may help you decide, though the "cramped seating" could be distracting; the biggest gripe, however: the place is "now so popular, you can't get in."

Patara S
| 22 | 16 | 19 | £29 |

9 Beauchamp Pl., SW3 (Knightsbridge/South Kensington),
020-7581 8820; fax 020-7581 2155
181 Fulham Rd., SW3 (South Kensington), 020-7351 5692;
fax 020-7351 5692

■ "My heart and stomach belong" to this popular pair of "excellent Thai" eateries in South Ken and Knightsbridge that serves "scrumptious", "consistent" fare – though timid tongues should "watch out for the hot dishes"; "great-value" prix fixe menus curry favour with bargain-hunters.

Patisserie Valerie S
| 19 | 13 | 14 | £16 |

8 Russell St., WC2 (Covent Garden), 020-7240 0064;
fax 020-7240 0064
105 Marylebone High St., W1 (Baker St./Bond St.),
020-7437 3466; fax 020-7734 6133
44 Old Compton St., W1 (Leicester Sq.), 020-7935 6240;
fax 020-7935 6543
215 Brompton Rd., SW3 (Knightsbridge), 020-7823 9971;
fax 020-7589 4993

■ "Oh, those delicious pastries", they're an irresistible temptation to spend time in "cake paradise" at these "noisy" cafes that also purvey Franco-Italian snacks; "brusque" service and "cramped" seating are bug-bears, but they're a small price for "dreams of chocolate and whipped cream."

Peasant, The ●
| 16 | 15 | 14 | £24 |

240 St. John St., EC1 (Angel/Farringdon), 020-7336 7726;
fax 020-7251 8525

■ This "pleasantly converted restaurant" above "an equally agreeable" Victorian pub in Clerkenwell offers "enjoyable", "straightforward" Mediterranean food "promptly served"; even though it's "not as Italian as it used to be" (new owners may be the explanation), it all comes "at a good price."

Pellicano S
| ▽ 21 | 14 | 21 | £31 |

19-21 Elystan St., SW3 (South Kensington), 020-7589 3718;
fax 020-7584 1789

■ A "wonderful touch with pasta" and other Italian offerings, coupled with a "very welcoming" atmosphere, makes this "cool, bright" newcomer "a home run"; it may be located on a "jinxed site" (formerly Icon) near Chelsea Green, but given its assets, it's likely to change all that.

People's Palace S   17 | 17 | 18 | £32
Royal Festival Hall, level 3, South Bank Ctr., SE1 (Charing Cross/Waterloo), 020-7928 9999; fax 020-7928 2355

☑ A royal *oui* for the "fascinating view of the Thames" (but "get a window seat") from this "spacious", high-ceilinged eaterie in the South Bank's Royal Festival Hall, where subjects enjoy "surprisingly good", "imaginative" Modern British–European cooking served by "helpful and pleasant staff"; even those who say it isn't "tops" admit it can make an "excellent pre- or post-concert" dinner.

Pepper Tree S   19 | 11 | 16 | £16
19 Clapham Common Southside, SW4 (Clapham Common), 020-7622 1758; fax 020-7622 1758

■ You get "just the right kick" from the "delicious" Thai fare on offer at this "stark", yet "cheerful" Clapham spot; since the curries and other dishes come at "value prices", it gets "unbelievably busy", and as "you don't book" (at dinner), diners are urged to "eat, not linger" – just as well, since you must "squeeze in on long tables."

Perc%nto Restaurant Bar S   ▽ 18 | 18 | 16 | £33
26 Ludgate Hill, EC4 (St. Pauls), 020-7778 0010; fax 020-7778 0013

☑ Playing the percentages is the team behind Il Convivio, and they've come up with what some reckon is "the best newcomer in the City", a bi-level eaterie near St. Paul's serving Modern Italian food; whilst a few find it "pricey", "attentive service" and a "fascinating wine list" satisfy.

Pescatori   18 | 14 | 17 | £33
57 Charlotte St., W1 (Goodge St.), 020-7580 3289; fax 020-7580 0539
11 Dover St., W1 (Green Park), 020-7493 2652; fax 020-7499 3180

■ The fishermen who supply these two Mediterranean seafooders in Charlotte Street (over 40 years old) and in Mayfair hook "consistently good" fish that arrive onto diner's plates "fresh and delicious"; it all comes at a "fair price", including the £17.50 set lunch – though service can be "a bit slow" during the crowded midday hours.

PÉTRUS   27 | 22 | 23 | £56
33 St. James's St., SW1 (Green Park), 020-7930 4272; fax 020-7930 9702

■ Marcus Wareing is earning thunderous "bravos" for his "sublime", "flawless" New French cooking served in an art-filled St. James's dining room that makes for a "powerful, yet understated experience", which some consider "well up to the standard of his mentor, Gordon Ramsay"; a few sour grapes gripe it "lacks atmosphere", but with Mr. Wareing at the top of his game and the "discreet" service, you can expect an "exceptional" meal; P.S. the "almost biblical wine list" is "wonderful for the rich!"

Pharmacy S
15 | 17 | 13 | £40

*150 Notting Hill Gate, W11 (Notting Hill Gate), 020-7221 2442;
fax 020-7243 2345*

"Keep taking the tablets and hopefully things will
improve" scoff snipers of this "kitschy" Notting Hill eaterie
that's "not the place to be seen" it once was and that
earns ire for its "arrogant" bedside manner; it's given
booster shots by those who praise the "cool" ground-
floor bar and airy, "arty" first-floor dining room where
"imaginative" Modern British can be at least "decent."

Phoenicia ● S
20 | 11 | 17 | £29

*11-13 Abingdon Rd., W8 (High St. Kensington), 020-7937 0120;
fax 020-7937 7668*

"Simply delicious Lebanese food" is what draws diners
to this "very friendly" Kensington veteran, safe in the
assumption that "everything is excellent"; perhaps it "needs
better atmosphere", but you don't hear those lining up for
the popular Sunday lunch buffet (under £15) complaining.

Phoenix Bar & Grill S
21 | 20 | 20 | £34

*162-164 Lower Richmond Rd., SW15 (Putney Bridge),
020-8780 3131; fax 020-8780 0019*

"Worth trying to find" say supporters of "Sonny's sister" in
Putney that "still delivers" "unfussy" Modern British nosh;
head-scratchers insist it's "inexplicably successful", citing
"inconsistent food" and service.

Phoenix Palace ● S
– | – | – | M

*3-5 Glentworth St., NW1 (Baker St.), 020-7486 3515;
fax 020-7486 3401*

"Not many are aware" of this new, unassuming Chinese
in Marylebone, but those in-the-know are "impressed" with
its "good dim sum" and other multiregional fare, including
bargain prix fixe menus that start at £5.50 for lunch.

PIED À TERRE
25 | 19 | 22 | £56

*34 Charlotte St., W1 (Goodge St.), 020-7636 1178;
fax 020-7916 1171*

"Perfection without the pretension", this "small" Fitzrovia
"gem" is where Shane Osborn's "imaginative, sophisticated"
New French cooking is "as good as it gets", aided by
"relaxed, but professional service"; whilst a few contrarians
conclude it "lacks charm" and object to "sardine-like"
seating, most agree this "cosy" spot "deserves more
praise" – particularly for the "great", 750-strong wine list.

Pierre Victoire ● S
12 | 10 | 11 | £20

*5 Dean St., W1 (Tottenham Court Rd.), 020-7287 4582;
fax 020-7287 4579*

Friends of this "cheerful" Soho French bistro feel it still
serves "simple", "good food", and whilst those who find it
less than victorious avow the eats "vary enormously", all
agree "you can't knock the price."

Pie²Mash S   –|–|–| E
9-11 Jamestown Rd., NW1 (Camden Town), 020-7482 2770;
fax 020-7482 2777
Although few have commented on this glass-fronted
Camden Town brasserie, the feedback is mixed: pie-tasters
promote the "fab" British cooking and its "good" ambience
(as well as prix fixe menus from £15), whilst crusty types
criticise the "cold decor" and "charmingly useless staff";
either way, it's early days for this laid-back youngster.

Pitcher & Piano   11 | 12 | 11 | £17
40-42 William IV St., WC2 (Charing Cross/Leicester Sq.),
020-7240 6180 S
18-20 Chiswick High Rd., W4 (Stamford Brook),
020-8742 7731 S
69-70 Dean St., W1 (Leicester Sq./Tottenham Court Rd.),
020-7434 3585
4-5 High St., SW19 (Wimbledon), 020-8879 7020;
fax 020-8879 3659 S
8 Balham Hill, SW12 (Clapham South), 020-8673 1107;
fax 020-8675 2228 S
214 Fulham Rd., SW10 (Earl's Court/South Kensington),
020-7352 9234 S
871-873 Fulham Rd., SW6 (Parsons Green),
020-7736 3910 S
316 King's Rd., SW3 (Sloane Sq.), 020-7352 0025;
fax 020-7352 1652 S
68 Upper St., N1 (Angel), 020-7704 9974 S
200 Bishopsgate, EC2 (Liverpool St.), 020-7929 5914
Additional locations throughout London
■ "A bar that happens to serve food" is the key to this chain
of "airy", "happy" drinking dens that are "monopolised by
office escapees after 5.30 PM", leading some to suggest
"picture yourself elsewhere"; whilst the Eclectic fare is
"no great shakes, it's fine" for a "casual" snack – "but
after a few pints, who really cares?"

PIZZA EXPRESS ◑ S   16 | 14 | 15 | £17
9-12 Bow St., WC2 (Covent Garden), 020-7240 3443;
fax 020-7240 3443
137 Notting Hill Gate, W11 (Notting Hill Gate), 020-7229 6000
35 Earl's Court Rd., W8 (High St. Kensington), 020-7937 0761;
fax 020-7938 4981
29 Wardour St., W1 (Leicester Sq.), 020-7437 7215;
fax 020-7494 2582
46-54 Battersea Bridge Rd., SW11 (Earl's Court/Sloane Sq.),
020-7924 2774
363 Fulham Rd., SW10 (Fulham Broadway), 020-7352 5300
895-896 Fulham Rd., SW6 (Parsons Green), 020-7731 3117;
fax 020-7371 7884
7 Beauchamp Pl., SW3 (Knightsbridge), 020-7589 2355;
fax 020-7589 5159

(continued)

PIZZA EXPRESS

The Pheasantry, 152-154 King's Rd., SW3 (Sloane Sq.),
020-7351 5031; fax 020-7349 9844
125 Alban Gate, London Wall, EC2 (Moorgate/St. Paul's),
020-7600 8880; fax 020-7600 8128
Additional locations throughout London

■ "You know what to expect" at this "trustworthy, familiar" pizza chain that's "in a league of its own" when it comes to "relentlessly good" Italian staples; a few malcontents think the "formula" is "in need of a revamp", but the majority is unequivocal: "got it just right."

Pizza Metro S | 23 | 13 | 19 | £25 |

64 Battersea Rise, SW11 (Clapham Common/Clapham Junction B.R.), 020-7228 3812; fax 020-7738 0987

■ Despite its "recent expansion" into adjacent premises, the "probability of getting a table" is still low at this "excellent" Battersea Italian with its "crazy staff" serving the "best wood-fired pizzas" in London and other "genuine Neapolitan food"; whilst the general "chaos" unsettles some, others find it "fun if you're in the mood."

Pizza on the Park ◐ S | 16 | 15 | 15 | £21 |

11 Knightsbridge, SW1 (Hyde Park Corner), 020-7235 5273;
fax 020-7236 6853

■ "The pizza-and-jazz thing makes a nice combo" say those who dig the "evening entertainment" of live music at this "friendly" pizzeria on Hyde Park Corner, and even if there are "no surprises" on the menu, there's enough "lovely" food to "tempt the senses."

Pizza Organic S | 15 | 11 | 14 | £16 |

100 Pitshanger Ln., W5 (Ealing Broadway), 020-8998 6878
20 Old Brompton Rd., SW7 (South Kensington), 020-7589 9613;
fax 020-8397 5556 ◐

■ A healthy "feel-good factor" pervades this pair of "very pleasant" organic pizzerias in South Kensington and Ealing that have many "favourably impressed", not least by the "cheap" Italian menu; some surveyors slice back that they're "not as good as" the mainstream competition.

Pizza Pomodoro | 17 | 14 | 14 | £21 |

51 Beauchamp Pl., SW3 (Knightsbridge), 020-7589 1278;
fax 020-7247 4001 S
7-8 Bishopsgate Churchyard, EC2 (Liverpool St.),
020-7920 9207; fax 207-7920 9206 ◐

■ "Live music" and "great, cheap pizza" "will cheer up anyone" at this "lively" Italian duo in Knightsbridge and the City; though they're "cramped" and "loud", it's "worth it for the people-watching."

Pizzeria Castello | 18 | 10 | 15 | £18

20 Walworth Rd., SE1 (Elephant & Castle), 020-7703 2556; fax 020-7703 0421

■ This "jewel in Elephant & Castle" might look "rather dated", but it's "always busy" ("booking essential"), filled with "savvy South Londoners" enjoying "great pizzas and other Italian food" at "extremely reasonable" prices; N.B. live salsa on Monday evenings.

PJ's Bar & Grill ◐ [S] | 15 | 16 | 15 | £27

52 Fulham Rd., SW3 (South Kensington), 020-7581 0025; fax 020-7581 0019

■ Still a place "to see and be seen", this Chelsea haunt has a "good vibe" and earns its spurs with a "wonderful American" menu; the "disappointed" call it "overpriced" but concede it's a "convenient" meeting place, especially during "happy hour."

PJ's Grill ◐ [S] | 15 | 13 | 15 | £27

30 Wellington St., WC2 (Covent Garden), 020-7240 7529; fax 020-7836 3426

◪ "Step into downtown USA" yell yankophiles of this Covent Garden grill where the "surprisingly good" American-biased International fare comes "at a reasonable price"; views on service swing from "excellent" to "lacklustre."

Place Below | ▽ 19 | 13 | 12 | £13

St. Mary-le-Bow Church, EC2 (St. Paul's), 020-7329 0789

■ The "ecclesiastic simplicity of the decor" is to be expected at this "worthy" self-service eaterie in the Norman crypt of a church near St. Paul's, serving "tasty, inventive Vegetarian" fare that's a cut above; a sandwich and coffee bar has been added.

Planet Hollywood ◐ [S] | 10 | 15 | 11 | £24

13 Coventry St., W1 (Leicester Sq./Piccadilly Circus), 020-7437 7639; fax 020-7734 0835

◪ "Tacky but likeable", this "noisy" Piccadilly branch of the international "film-themed" chain features "hearty burgers" and other Californian fare in "U.S.-size portions" at "decent prices"; some merciless critics contend the "dog has had its day and needs putting down", but the fact that "the kids love it" gets a thumbs-up from parents.

Poissonnerie de l'Avenue ◐ | 21 | 17 | 19 | £45

82 Sloane Ave., SW3 (South Kensington), 020-7589 2457; fax 020-7581 3360

■ This "old-fashioned" Brompton Cross Classic French–seafooder "sticks to its last with splendid consistency", preparing "great", "unmessed-about fish"; though the demographically inclined insist it "needs an injection of young people" to balance out the "captains of industry" and "old money", the prevailing view is that this "class" joint still "works well."

Pollo Bar ●⬛⌀　　　　12 ┃ 4 ┃ 7 ┃ £12
20 Old Compton St., W1 (Leicester Sq.), 020-7734 5917

⬛ "Cash-strapped students" throng this "very central, very cheap, very cheerful" (and very old) Soho Italian "haven" serving "basic, low-budget grub" that's strong on veggie options; its "grotty interior" doesn't promote "lingering meals", but it's "good for late-night nosh."

Polygon Bar & Grill ⬛　　　20 ┃ 19 ┃ 17 ┃ £28
4 The Polygon, Clapham Old Town, SW4 (Clapham Common), 020-7622 1199; fax 020-7622 1166

⬛ This "pretty", "stylish" venue in Clapham "continues to serve an interesting line" of Pacific Rim–Eclectic fare, including a "nice, big brunch" and an early-bird menu (5.30–7 PM); "service comes with a smile" and patrons smile back, especially during the "excellent-value happy hour" at the "neat bar."

Pomegranates ●　　　18 ┃ 15 ┃ 17 ┃ £38
94 Grosvenor Rd., SW1 (Pimlico), 020-7828 6560; fax 020-7828 2037

⬛ Loyalists "love the old-world charm" of this "comfortable" Pimlico "time warp" with its "wonderful atmosphere of faded opulence" and "delicious", "off-the-beaten-track" Eclectic fare; though a few think it "misses", many regulars remonstrate "everyone should go at least once!"

Poons ⬛　　　17 ┃ 11 ┃ 13 ┃ £23
4 Leicester St., WC2 (Leicester Sq.), 020-7437 1528; fax 020-8458 0968 ●
27 Lisle St., WC2 (Leicester Sq.), 020-7437 4549; fax 020-8458 0968 ●
Royal National Hotel, 50 Woburn Pl., WC1 (Euston/Russell Sq.), 020-7580 1188; fax 020-8458 0968 ●
Whiteley's Shopping Ctr., 151 Queensway, W2 (Bayswater/ Queensway), 020-7792 2884; fax 020-8458 0968

⬛ "Cheap and high quality – a London anomaly" say supporters of this Chinese quartet spread across town (from Bayswater to Euston), and comments are also all over the map: "delicious" and "perfect for pre-theatre" vs. "run-of-the-mill" and "variable"; however, proponents poontificate "just eat and enjoy."

Poons in the City　　　16 ┃ 12 ┃ 14 ┃ £26
2 Minster Pavement, Mincing Ln., EC3 (Monument/ Tower Hill), 020-7626 0126; fax 020-7626 0526

⬛ The basement of a modern City tower block makes an "interesting setting" for this old-fashioned Chinese, which is not on many surveyors' radar screens; those in-the-know go for "good food" in "nice surroundings"; N.B. in addition to the formal dining room is an all-day cafe for quick snacks and takeaway.

Pope's Eye 💳 21 | 8 | 17 | £28

108 Blythe Rd., W14 (Olympia), 020-7610 4578
277 Upper Richmond Rd., SW15 (East Putney), 020-8788 7733

◪ The "spartan interiors" ("like someone's front room") of this dinner-only duo in Putney and Olympia are "not your usual restaurant environments", but then neither is the habit of offering a "limited menu" of "good steaks, fine salads and heart-warming desserts"; a few declare "don't bother", as the food "ought to be much tastier"; N.B. dishes other than beef are available if ordered in advance.

Porters ☾ [S] 13 | 12 | 13 | £24

17 Henrietta St., WC2 (Covent Garden), 020-7836 6466; fax 020-7379 4296

◪ "When you're hungry and want simple, inexpensive [Traditional] British food", Lord Bradford's modest Covent Garden eaterie fits the bill with its "comfort" menu of "great pies", "stodgy desserts" and a "good range of beers"; non-traditionalists knock the "ordinary" fare as a "caricature of English cuisine."

porters bar [S] ▽ 11 | 10 | 11 | £14

16 Henrietta St., WC2 (Covent Garden/Leicester Sq.), 020-7836 6466
21-22 Poland St., W1 (Oxford Circus), 020-7287 1817; fax 020-7734 7585

■ Under the same ownership as Porters restaurant, this pair of bright, modern bars in Covent Garden and Soho provides a "good place to chill out" or "drop in while shopping" to snack on "reasonable bar food" from a competitively priced Eclectic menu.

Portrait [S] 17 | 21 | 14 | £27

The National Portrait Gallery, 2 St. Martin's Pl., WC2 (Charing Cross/Leicester Sq.), 020-7312 2490; fax 020-7925 0244

■ "A haven after art indigestion" applaud aesthetes of the National Portrait Gallery's smart, rooftop eaterie that boasts a "fabulous view" over Trafalgar Square, Whitehall and beyond; whilst most appreciate "good, clean" Modern British cooking (from caterers Searcy's), critics pan it as "not great", but "well-spaced tables" ensure its appeal for business lunches; N.B. dinner served on Thursday and Friday only.

Potemkin ▽ 19 | 21 | 21 | £30

144 Clerkenwell Rd., EC1 (Farringdon), 020-7278 6661; fax 020-7278 5551

◪ Supporters claim this warming Clerkenwell newcomer (named after the lover of Catherine the Great) is "the first decent, authentic Russian restaurant in town" with "caviar at its best", although a few revolutionaries reveal the food's "hugely overpriced"; a list of 120 vodkas and many unusual Eastern European beers makes the ground floor bar a "very dangerous" place!

Pret à Manger ⊘ | 17 | 12 | 16 | £8 |

421-422 Strand, WC2 (Charing Cross), 020-7240 5900;
fax 020-7836 6558 **S**
140 Bishopsgate, WC2 (Liverpool St.), 020-7377 9595;
fax 020-7377 2641
122 High Holborn, WC1 (Holborn), 020-7430 2090;
fax 020-7831 7002
7 Marylebone High St., W1 (Baker St./Bond St.),
020-7935 0474; fax 020-7935 0636
163 Piccadilly, W1 (Piccadilly Circus), 020-7629 5044;
fax 020-7629 4085 **S**
298 Regents St., W1 (Oxford Circus), 020-7637 3836;
fax 020-7580 9949
100 Tottenham Court Rd., W1 (Warren St.), 020-7631 0014;
fax 020-7580 1805
80 Kings Rd., SW3 (Sloane Sq.), 020-7225 0770;
fax 020-7581 5719 **S**
27 Islington High St., N1 (Angel), 020-7713 1371;
fax 020-7713 1373
28 Fleet St., EC4 (Temple), 020-7353 2332; fax 020-7353 3426
Additional locations throughout London
■ "Butties really don't get better than this" rave those ready
to eat "superior sandwiches" that "actually make you feel
good" at this "convenient", widespread chain known for its
"integrity" ("unsold given to the homeless") and "cheerful
service"; a few dissenters wish they'd "go easy on the
dressings" and find them "*un peu cher.*"

Prince Bonaparte **S** | 17 | 13 | 15 | £18 |

80 Chepstow Rd., W2 (Bayswater/Notting Hill Gate),
020-7313 9491; fax 020-7792 0911
■ "A better-than-most pub dining experience", this "trendy,
friendly" "meeting place" just off Westbourne Grove offers
"a good vibe" and "hearty" Modern British cooking that
"never fails to satisfy"; it's best to go during "off-peak times",
though, as it can be "difficult to get a table."

Princess Garden ●**S** | 20 | 17 | 19 | £43 |

8-10 N. Audley St., W1 (Bond St.), 020-7493 3223;
fax 020-7629 3130
◪ The "Mayfair formality" appeals to business diners as
much as the "excellent" multiregional fare at this Chinese
venue from the Zen group, which also features live piano
music and a large party room for banquets.

Prism | 19 | 19 | 16 | £41 |

147 Leadenhall St., EC3 (Bank/Monument), 020-7256 3888;
fax 020-7256 3883
◪ Looked at through one lens, the setting is "impressive"
and "fabulous" at this City banking hall, whilst others see it
as "impersonal"; so too, the Modern British cooking, viewed
as "wonderful" in some corners, though critics chide they
"could do so much better"; new chef Colin Layfield may
generate more consistent enthusiasm.

Prospect Grill ● ▽ 21 19 21 £27
4-6 Garrick St., WC2 (Leicester Sq.), 020-7379 0412;
fax 020-7836 3936

■ "A steady hand is in the kitchen" at this "intimate" Theatreland eaterie that's "popular for lunch and pre- and post-curtain" thanks to its "succinct", "rewarding" menu of "simple" Anglo-American grill dishes; better yet, the booths and banquettes offer a "sense of privacy", so you can keep your post-show critiques among yourselves.

Pucci Pizza ● S ⇄ 13 6 10 £20
205 King's Rd., SW3 (Sloane Sq.), 020-7352 2134;
fax 020-7352 0585

■ "Lambos outside" and "loud music" inside help fashion the "insane atmosphere" at this "classic" pizzeria; "if you're cruising the King's Road, it's a pit stop" where you can "charge up for a night out" on the "good pizzas" that always come with a side order of "top" people-watching.

Pug S 22 18 17 £31
66-68 Chiswick High Rd., W4 (Stamford Brook/
Turnham Green), 020-8987 9988; fax 020-8987 9911

☑ You "don't have to traipse all the way to the West End" for "terrific" Modern British cooking in a "relaxed atmosphere" say admirers of this Chiswick bar, lounge and dining room from the owners of Depot; the less-enamoured claim it's "uninspired looking" and can get "unbearably noisy."

Purple Sage 17 15 15 £27
92 Wigmore St., W1 (Bond St.), 020-7486 1912; fax 020-7481 1813

☑ "Fresh, arty, studio-type decor" creates a "California-esque atmosphere" at this large, "informal" eaterie near Oxford Street serving traditional-style Italian food; given that it "fills up" in the evening and can sometimes get "too noisy", some consider it "better for lunch."

Putney Bridge Restaurant S 21 22 18 £45
1 Embankment, Lower Richmond Rd., SW15 (Putney Bridge),
020-8780 1811; fax 020-8780 1211

☑ "Now the food matches the view" at this Putney riversider that's "improved from a couple years back" thanks to chef Anthony Demetre's "innovative", "good-quality" New French cooking; "minimalist-size portions" keep guests wondering "how they get away with very high prices."

Quaglino's ● S 18 20 16 £38
16 Bury St., SW1 (Green Park), 020-7930 6767; fax 020-7839 2866

☑ Terence "Conran's institution" in St. James's is "still glamorous (despite the hicks from the sticks)", boasting a "lively buzz"; whilst blasé types are a bit "bored with the menu" of "dependable" Modern British cuisine, the majority finds its "simplicity equals culinary success"; however, be warned "shouting is necessary" in this "warehouse" (and the "fab bar"), and the "erratic service" can be "S-L-O-W."

Quality Chop House ●🅢　　　21　14　18　£30
94 Farringdon Rd., EC1 (Farringdon), 020-7837 5093;
fax 020-7833 8748

◪ "You should be well-upholstered" because "the seats aren't" at this Farringdon eaterie with "original Victorian decor" and bench "seating" that "encourages conversation with others" – as well as "sore posteriors"; a "terrific range" of "down-to-earth" Anglo-French bistro food is "beautifully cooked", and the "informed, swift service" wins acclaim when the place is "busy", but note the "prices are no longer for the working class."

Queens, The 🅢　　　　　　▽　19　12　16　£21
49 Regent's Park Rd., NW1 (Chalk Farm), 020-7586 0408;
fax 020-7586 5677

◪ This small, low-key Primrose Hill gastro-pub (a Builders Arms sibling) is "great for a boozy Sunday lunch", with "good, well-presented food" from a "reasonably priced" Modern British (with a touch of French) menu; but foes find a few shortcomings: the "wines could be better", and more "money needs to be spent on decor."

Quilon　　　　　　　　　　▽　21　18　21　£34
41 Buckingham Gate, SW1 (St. James's Park), 020-7821 1899;
fax 020-7828 5802

◪ Near Buckingham Palace adjacent to the Crowne Plaza London St. James resides this stylishly modern Indian dining room (from the owners of the Bombay Brasserie) specialising in the coastal cuisine of Kerala; whilst not many voters are familiar with this upscale entry, those who've tried it report "notably" tasty dishes and "very good service and atmosphere", vowing to "definitely return."

Quincy's　　　　　　　　　　16　13　18　£29
675 Finchley Rd., NW2 (Golders Green), 020-7794 8499

◪ A longtime "friendly local" hangout in Finchley known for its "nicely arranged" Modern British food that always "tastes good", this "cosy" standby has a few fearing it "has perhaps lost its way" a bit since changing hands in '99; N.B. it's now dinner only.

Quo Vadis ●　　　　　　　　21　18　18　£43
26-29 Dean St., W1 (Leicester Sq./Tottenham Court Rd.),
020-7437 9585; fax 020-7736 7593

◪ "Grown-up" and "good for any occasion", this "plush, comfortable" Soho eaterie, another in the Marco Pierre White stable, is where "great art" is found both on the walls (including some of MPW's own creations) and on the plate, in the form of "exceptional" Modern British cooking; never mind if a few in the been-there-done-that set yawn "how boring."

Rain
20 | 20 | 15 | £31

303 Portobello Rd., W10 (Ladbroke Grove), 020-8968 2001;
fax 020-7449 6961

■ "Float in deep blue tropical ambience" at this "small corner of Thailand" in Notting Hill, where diners are immersed in a "dreamy", "ultra-cool atmosphere" as they sample "consistently" "terrific" Pan-Asian cooking from a former Vong chef, Sameer Vaswani (who's also the owner).

Rainforest Cafe §
11 | 20 | 13 | £22

20 Shaftesbury Ave., W1 (Piccadilly Circus),
020-7434 3111; fax 020-7434 3222

■ "You may get to meet Tarzan" at this "gimmicky", "fun" simulated tropical rainforest in Piccadilly that looks "like a theme park" – "great to distract naughty children" – and whilst the "boringly average" American fare has few friends, the no-booking policy provokes even greater frustration: "you spend time" (and, inevitably, money) "waiting in the shop" with the little ones.

Randall & Aubin §
20 | 16 | 15 | £25

14-16 Brewer St., W1 (Piccadilly Circus), 020-7287 4447;
fax 020-7287 9317
329-331 Fulham Rd., SW10 (Fulham Broadway/
South Kensington), 020-7823 3515; fax 020-7823 3991

■ Ed Baines' distinctive "rotisserie and seafood" concept is "now in two locations": the "cramped, noisy" Soho original, a former butcher's shop where diners "sit and watch comings and goings" atop "awkward bar stools", and the new Chelsea sibling, which "has changed the format" to a more modern, stylish rendition ("looks so cool"); both provide "fab", "fresh" fare.

Rani §
▽ 19 | 14 | 15 | £24

7 Long Ln., N3 (Finchley Central), 020-8349 4386;
fax 020-8349 4386

■ "Great vegetarian cooking" suffused with "extraordinary flavours" is the raison d'être of this bright, unpretentious, family-run Indian eaterie in Finchley, which specialises in homestyle, slow-cooked Gujarti dishes; N.B. reservations are recommended for dinner.

Ransome's Dock §
21 | 17 | 18 | £35

35-37 Park Gate Rd., SW11 (Sloane Sq.), 020-7223 1611;
fax 020-7924 2614

■ Those who follow the progress of Martin Lam's "popular" Modern European docksider in Battersea assert that at a decade old it "has gotten better with age", refining its "excellent combination of a relaxed atmosphere and super food" made of "great ingredients affectionately handled"; an added attraction is the encyclopaedic and "fascinating wine list."

Rasa [S] 23 15 18 £26

6 Dering St., W1 (Bond St./Oxford St.), 020-7629 1346; fax 020-7491 9540
5 Charlotte St., W1 (Tottenham Court Rd.), 020-7637 0222; fax 020-7637 0224
56 Stoke Newington Church St., N16 (Stoke Newington B.R.), 020-7249 1340; fax 020-7249 4692 ◐
55 Stoke Newington Church St., N16 (Stoke Newington B.R.), 020-7249 0344; fax 020-7249 4692

■ The "food comes from the heart" at these "excellent vegetarian Indians" in Stoke Newington and the West End, which cook up "inventive" Keralan dishes "delicately prepared" and served by "charming" staff that can be "a tad slow" but "helpful in explaining the dishes"; though the budget-minded balk at "expensive" prices, even they concede it's "a very nice way to try Indian cuisine"; N.B. the Charlotte Street branch also serves seafood.

Ravi Shankar [S] 19 11 15 £14

133-135 Drummond St., NW1 (Euston), 020-7388 6458; fax 020-7388 2494
422 St. John St., EC1 (Angel), 020-7833 5849; fax 020-7388 2494

■ Those "who appreciate something a bit different and aren't hung up on comfort" will feel at home at this "cheery" vegetarian Indian duo on the City fringes that offers "great cheap eats"; the St. John Street branch is BYO and has an "eat as much as you like" lunch buffet for a "bargain" £4.50.

Real Greek, The 23 18 19 £33

15 Hoxton Mkt., N1 (Old St.), 020-7739 8212; fax 020-7739 4910

■ "Is this what made Greece a great civilisation?" wonder worshipers of Theodore Kyriakou's "traditional" regional Greek cooking "elevated to haute cuisine" at this "cosy" spot in Hoxton Market that's credited with "introducing a completely new" "concept" of Hellenic food to London; despite grumbles about the out-of-the-way "location", consensus is it "succeeds remarkably well"; P.S. the "Greek wine list is a revelation (as is the hangover it produces)."

Rebato's ▽ 19 15 19 £24

169 S. Lambeth Rd., SW8 (Stockwell), 020-7735 6388

■ Venturers south of Vauxhall Bridge find "very authentic" Spanish food in pleasantly "dated, nostalgic" environs at this "good tapas bar" with an airy, mirrored restaurant at the back; regulars urge "choose the daily special", though there's also a £15.95 set menu.

Red Bar & Restaurant – – – E

5 Kingly St., W1 (Oxford Circus/Picadilly), 020-7434 3417; fax 002-7434 3418

This yearling restaurant/bar spread over two Soho floors offers a Modern British menu with a French twist from Bobby Gutteridge (ex-Alfred); as the name alludes, the stylised, industrial decor features deep red colouring.

Red Cube Bar & Grill ◐ 18 | 19 | 16 | £40

1 Leicester Pl., WC2 (Leicester Sq.), 020-7287 0101; fax 020-7851 0807

◪ "You can't avoid having a good time" at this Leicester Square private members' club/restaurant (which recently changed owners), according to addicts of the "good, filling" International cuisine, which well "suits" its "glamorous, glitzy setting"; N.B. there's a DJ nightly in the club, which is also open to diners.

Redmonds [S] 23 | 15 | 21 | £34

170 Upper Richmond Rd. W., SW14 (Mortlake B.R.), 020-8878 1922; fax 020-8878 1733

◪ Its "stark, noisy" setting may not endear it to many surveyors, but no matter: Redmond Hayward's "fine", "mainstream" Modern British cooking (specialising in game in season) is the main attraction at this "nice", little-known East Sheen eaterie with "good, personal service"; though it's "pricey" for the area, denizens glad to have it in the neighbourhood don't seem to mind much.

Red Pepper [S] 20 | 12 | 16 | £25

8 Formosa St., W9 (Warwick Ave.), 020-7266 2708

■ "Shame about the squashed surroundings", but it's "worth it" for some of the "best pizzas in London" and other "lovely", "simple Italian food" is the consensus on this "immensely popular" Maida Vale outpost of the 'coloured food' group (Purple Sage, etc.) that's "run and patronised by Italians"; those who find it "too cramped for an enjoyable evening", however, can always use the "take-out" option.

Reubens [S] 15 | 11 | 14 | £24

79 Baker St., W1 (Baker St.), 020-7486 0035; fax 020-7486 7079

■ The "authentic home cooking" is "not adventurous", but this simple Marylebone Jewish deli with "a real family atmosphere" is among the only options in town for "good kosher" classics like "great salt beef and tongue" and "real, honest Reuben sandwiches"; even if it strikes a few wallet-watchers as "too pricey", none can quibble with the "large portions."

Rhodes in the Square 23 | 19 | 19 | £44

Dolphin Square Hotel, Dolphin Sq., Chichester St., SW1 (Pimlico), 020-7798 6767; fax 020-7798 5685

◪ In a "midnight-blue ship"-like "room to love or loathe" ("intimate" vs. "business venue") within Pimlico's Dolphin Square Hotel, celebrity chef Gary Rhodes produces "interesting" and "superb" British cuisine – including "some of the dishes from his TV series" – helped along by "attentive", "charming service"; that said, the less-impressed, who find it "overpriced", vow "won't go down that Rhode again."

RIBA Café – – – M

Royal Institute of British Architects, 66 Portland Pl., W1 (Regent's Park), 020-7631 0467; fax 020-7307 3743

Designed by Conran & Partners and catered by Milburns, the handsome Florence Hall on the first floor of the Royal Institute of British Architects offers an impressively airy pit stop near Oxford Street for brunch and lunch from an International-Eclectic menu.

Rib Room & Oyster Bar [S] 22 19 21 £51

Hyatt Carlton Tower, 2 Cadogan Pl., SW1 (Knightsbridge/ Sloane Sq.), 020-7858 7053; fax 020-7823 1708

◪ "Heaven on a plate" is how devotees describe the "quality" British cuisine at this "red-meat haven" with an oyster bar in Knightsbridge's Hyatt Carlton Tower, a "throwback" serving what hard-core fans call the "best roast beef in Europe"; whilst for many the sight of "chefs preparing meals" in the open kitchen is a "delight", snipers slam the "spacious dining room's" "hotel"-decor.

Riccardo's ◐ [S] 18 13 14 £25

126 Fulham Rd., SW3 (Gloucester Rd./South Kensington), 020-7370 6656; fax 020-7244 6401

■ A "perfect neighbourhood haunt" in Chelsea, it's "always hectic" on account of its "consistently good" Tuscan cuisine served in trademark "small portions", encouraging diners to "try multiple dishes"; if the "laid-back" service can be "erratic", it's "very welcoming for young children."

Richard Corrigan at Lindsay House 23 19 21 £51

21 Romilly St., W1 (Leicester Sq./Piccadilly Circus), 020-7439 0450; fax 020-7437 7349

■ "Located in a fantastic townhouse" in Soho, this "homey", "nicely old-fashioned" dining room is the place where chef Richard Corrigan demonstrates "a mastery of his art" with "gutsy" Modern Irish cooking "for true foodies"; further praise goes to the "excellent" wine list ("impossible to choose a bad" bottle) and "incredibly accommodating", if "stiff", service; P.S. yes, it all "comes at a price."

Richoux [S] 14 13 12 £19

41A S. Audley St., W1 (Bond St.), 020-7629 5228; fax 020-7493 2204
172 Piccadilly, W1 (Green Park/Piccadilly Circus), 020-7493 2204; fax 020-7495 6658
86 Brompton Rd., SW3 (Knightsbridge), 020-7584 8300; fax 020-7589 8547
3 Circus Rd., NW8 (St. John's Wood), 020-7483 4001; fax 020-7483 3810

◪ This "quaint" quartet of "casual" tearooms around town is "good in a hurry" or for a "shopping break", given that it serves "breakfast and tea all day", along with other "reliably bland" but satisfying "snacks"; protesters point to "ho-hum" decor and sometimes "moody" service, whilst more bitter bashers brand it a "tourist-targeted rip-off."

Riso [S] 18 | 15 | 17 | £27
76 South Parade, W4 (Chiswick Park), 020-8742 2121; fax 020-8742 2121
◪ After undergoing a small expansion into next-door premises, this Italian in a "rather odd location" in Turnham Green can now fit in more fans of its "fantastic, fresh and simple" cuisine; whilst some still think it's "let down by the plain interior", regulars from the neighbourhood just "hope the standards are maintained" at this "good local."

RITZ RESTAURANT ◐ [S] 22 | 25 | 23 | £54
Ritz Hotel, 150 Piccadilly, W1 (Green Park), 020-7300 2370; fax 020-7907 2681
■ "Brings back memories of that golden time between the wars" muse "nostalgic" visitors to this "splendid dining room" in Piccadilly's historic Ritz Hotel, whose "luxurious" interior is "opulence defined", with "impeccable service" and "excellent" Classic French–British cuisine that are "nothing less than one would expect"; whilst a few cynics mutter "if only the food matched" the "beautiful" decor, the majority pronounces the place "pure perfection" "when you want to be spoiled" (at "Ritz prices", of course).

Riva [S] 23 | 14 | 18 | £40
169 Church Rd., SW13 (Hammersmith), 020-8748 0434; fax 020-8748 0434
◪ It might reside in a "converted shop in Barnes" that "needs decoration", but Andrea Riva's "crowded" eaterie wins accolades all the same with its "honest", "visually" "delightful" Modern Italian cuisine; undoubtedly it's "a fun place", though some disgruntled visitors suspect it's "more for locals, who get conspicuously better service."

RIVER CAFE [S] 24 | 20 | 20 | £47
Thames Wharf, Rainville Rd., W6 (Hammersmith), 020-7386 4200; fax 020-7386 4201
◪ "What more can anyone ask for?" wonder admirers of this "well-run ship" in "out-of-the-way" Hammersmith that's "still bringing them in" with its "absolutely fabulous" Modern Italian farmhouse cooking (or "*cucina rustica*") composed of ingredients whose "freshness bursts through"; whilst "fed-up" foes fume about "astronomical prices", a "boring setting" and "hype" that makes it "impossible to book", the majority affirms it's all "worth it in the end."

RK Stanley's 15 | 13 | 14 | £19
6 Little Portland St., W1 (Oxford Circus), 020-7462 0099; fax 020-7462 0088
■ For a "different slant on bangers 'n' mash", aficionados seek out this "tranquil" sausage "heaven" near Oxford Circus offering "good-value" British favourites washed down with beers from a "wide-ranging" list – no wonder "the boys love it!"; if it's "a bit variable", the "quite pleasant", updated '50s-"diner" decor is a further enticement.

Rocket ●

20 | 19 | 16 | £22

4-6 Lancashire Ct., W1 (Bond St.), 020-7629 2889;
fax 020-7629 2881

■ "Hidden away on a cobbled street" in Mayfair, this stylish, "delightful" bi-level bar/restaurant boasts a "lively" atmosphere that's "great for groups" thanks to its varied Mediterranean menu of "wonderful pizzas" and other "superbly prepared, unfussily presented" fare; best of all, it's "so cheap, you can eat there often."

Rock Garden ●S

13 | 10 | 11 | £22

6-7 The Piazza, WC2 (Covent Garden), 020-7836 4052;
fax 020-7379 4793

◪ "Wear earplugs" to soften the "rockin' good vibes" at this Covent Garden "theme" joint (with dancing) that proffers a "reliable", if "average", American-International menu and a "fab beer selection"; some claim it "no longer rocks" at night and attracts "only tourists", but indisputably it's still "great for kids"; N.B. live bands play on Sunday evenings.

Rodizio Rico ●S

18 | 10 | 15 | £22

111 Westbourne Grove, W2 (Bayswater/Notting Hill Gate),
020-7792 4035; fax 020-7243 1401

■ "Vegetarians need not apply" to this "most unusual" Bayswater "treat for carnivores", where the *churrascaria* dining concept "works well": it's a "true Brazilian-style barbeque" set up for "unique, unlimited meat-eating", wherein skewered meat–wielding waiters wander the dining room dispensing "beef and pork a-go-go", while diners help themselves to salad and side dishes at the buffet ("oba oba!").

Rosmarino S

21 | 18 | 20 | £35

1 Blenheim Terrace, NW8 (St. John's Wood), 020-7328 5014;
fax 020-7625 2639

■ "Zafferano's affordable cousin" in St. John's Wood "understands what customers want and like": "fabulous", "honest" Modern Italian cooking and "attentive service" in a "cute" space that "feels like Italy"; a handful of detractors reports "disappointing" experiences, but the majority is more than happy with this "great little gem" that's "much welcomed in the area" – as are hard-to-come-by tables on the "nice terrace."

Rotisserie Jules ●S

17 | 7 | 13 | £16

133A Notting Hill Gate, W11 (Notting Hill Gate), 020-7221 3331;
fax 020-7221 3736
6-8 Bute St., SW7 (South Kensington), 020-7584 0600;
fax 020-7584 0614

■ A "simple, well-executed formula" succeeds at these "bright", basic spit-roast specialists in South Kensington and Notting Hill, which are "perfect if you don't feel like cooking" and crave "tasty, cheap" chicken "on the run" ("they deliver" too); N.B. the Chelsea branch has closed.

Roussillon
23 | 19 | 22 | £45

16 St. Barnabas St., SW1 (Sloane Sq./Victoria), 020-7730 5550; fax 020-7824 8617

◪ "Talented" chef Alex Gaulthier's "inventive" New French cuisine is "the best" in "quiet" Pimlico, according to admirers of his "top-notch" "seasonal" menu in which "vegetables play a major role"; this "sophisticated" venue is "hidden away" in "one of London's most restful rooms", where the "attentive" staff makes diners "feel prized and treasured", even if a small, discontented minority counters the service is a bit "ragged."

Rowley's ●🅢
15 | 15 | 15 | £33

113 Jermyn St., SW1 (Piccadilly Circus), 020-7930 2707; fax 020-7839 4240

◼ Well over a quarter century old, this St. James's stalwart specialises in steak frites and other substantial selections from a "fair-value" British menu; "you get what you pay for" at this unassuming venue (housed in the building that was the original Walls Butcher Shop), a "fantastic standby" when a "rushed" business lunch or pre-theatre meal is called for.

ROYAL CHINA 🅢
24 | 14 | 15 | £27

13 Queensway, W2 (Queensway), 020-7221 2535; fax 020-7792 5752
40 Baker St., W1 (Baker St./Bond St.), 020-7487 4688; fax 020-7935 7893
68 Queen's Grove, NW8 (St. John's Wood), 020-7586 4280; fax 020-7722 0750
30 Westferry Circus, E14 (Canary Wharf), 020-7719 0888; fax 020-7719 0889

◼ "Although the wait can be eternal", this "garish" ("did they buy a bulk shipment of '80s disco decor?") Chinese foursome is well "worth it" given the "vast selection of superb", "authentic" Cantonese cuisine and what some consider "the best dim sum in town"; it's "reassuringly popular with Chinese customers" – "this place reminds me of home!" says one "born and raised in Hong Kong" – though "harried, impersonal service" can let the side down.

R.S.J.
18 | 12 | 16 | £33

13A Coin St., SE1 (Waterloo), 020-7928 4554; fax 020-7401 2455

◼ "In what could be your grandma's living room", this "rather jaded"-looking South Bank venue proffers "reliable" Modern British cooking that "works well without being outstanding", though the kitchen's handiwork risks being outshined by the "interesting" and "extensive" Loire Valley wine list; the general consensus is it "could be a topper if the decor and service matched the food."

Rudland & Stubbs　　19 14 17 £30
35-37 Greenhill Rents, Cowcross St., EC1 (Farringdon),
020-7253 0148; fax 020-7253 1534

■ It's somewhat "out of the way" on the edge of Smithfield Market, but this traditional, tiled seafooder boasts a menu of "excellent fish" as well as especially "good" daily specials based on yesterday's catch; it tends to be more of a lunch venue, however, and sometimes it can seem as if "no one's there at dinner."

RULES ●S　　21 22 20 £39
35 Maiden Ln., WC2 (Covent Garden), 020-7836 5314;
fax 020-7497 1081

☑ "After 204 years, it's still a gem" enthuse loyalists of this "relatively formal" Covent Garden "treasure" with a "wonderful", "very gamey" Traditional British menu that's "a bit pricey" but includes a "reasonable pre-theatre special" for under £20; although critics complain it "caters to tourists" and "out-of-towners" ("no trip to London is complete without eating here"), most agree it makes a "first-class business venue" and generally "rules in all departments."

Saga S　　▽ 22 16 25 £32
43 South Molton St., W1 (Bond St.), 020-7408 2236;
fax 020-7629 7507

■ The story here, nearly 30 years in the telling, is of an "unassuming" eaterie "nicely hidden away" near Bond Street with "very polite service" and "delicate", "fresh" dishes – most notably, "very good sushi and sashimi"; supporters "recommend it with a clear conscience", and the fact that it attracts "lots of Japanese" also tells the tale.

Saigon ●　　20 12 14 £27
45 Frith St., W1 (Leicester Sq./Piccadilly Circus), 020-7437 7109;
fax 020-7734 1668

■ "Taste the difference" at this Soho venue boasting "interesting Vietnamese cuisine" that aesthetes judge "unexpectedly good" considering the somewhat "haggard surroundings"; though the service continues to receive mixed views ("insistent" vs. "nice, gentle"), it's still "great for pre- post-theatre" dining with a prix fixe menu for under £17.

Saigon Times　　▽ 14 9 13 £28
17-22 Leadenhall Mkt., EC3 (Bank/Monument),
020-7621 0022; fax 020-7623 0028

☑ True, it's got little or "no atmosphere", but this Leadenhall Market brasserie is a useful City spot nonetheless, thanks to its unusual Vietnamese-French menu; it also serves traditional English breakfasts from 7.30 AM, while last dinner orders are at 9 PM.

Saint Bar & Restaurant   ▽ 13 | 13 | 10 | £28
8 Great Newport St., WC2 (Leicester Sq.), 020-7240 1551; fax 020-7240 0829

■ Nobody's rushing to canonise this "lively night spot" in Soho, since the consensus from the "cool people" who convene here is that it's "better for drinking than eating", though for those feeling peckish, the Pacific Rim "food is ok"; N.B. there's a cover charge for non-members on Fridays and Saturdays.

Sale e Pepe ●   18 | 15 | 17 | £36
9-15 Pavilion Rd., SW1 (Knightsbridge), 020-7235 0098

■ "Shouting waiters" bring a touch of comedy that's best appreciated if you bring "a sense of humour" to this "noisy", "frenetic" Italian "institution" in Knightsbridge; whilst it might not be everyone's cup of tea, when "hanging around Harrod's and it's time for dinner", have an "unpretentious meal" and a few laughs.

Salloos   21 | 14 | 17 | £39
62 Kinnerton St., SW1 (Hyde Park Corner/Knightsbridge), 020-7235 4444

■ This Pakistani-Indian's Knightsbridge mews location is a "charming" setting for "divine food" – a "wonderful place in a wonderful street"; it may be "a little pricey", but fans salloote it as a "really nice" eaterie where service is rendered "in a grand manner" by the "helpful" staff.

Salt House S   17 | 13 | 15 | £25
63 Abbey Rd., NW8 (St. John's Wood), 020-7328 6636; fax 020-7625 9168

■ "A previously grotty boozer" in St. John's Wood has been "transformed" into this "funky meeting place" where you'll find "surprisingly good", even "creative" Modern British pub fare; "at last, a good pub lunch in NW8" hurrah hungry hordes, whilst others praise the "willing, cheerful" service.

Salusbury Pub & Dining Room S   19 | 17 | 16 | £27
50-52 Salusbury Rd., NW6 (Queen's Park), 020-7328 3286

■ Bursting on the scene is this "bustling" Queen's Park gastro-pub that's made its mark by serving "cracking" Modern Italian food; it's "far better than you expect" from a local, so "put aside your preconceptions of the area" – in fact, it's "getting too popular" to turn up without reserving.

Sambuca ●   17 | 14 | 19 | £35
62 Lower Sloane St., SW1 (Sloane Sq.), 020-7730 6571; fax 020-7225 1210

■ "Extremely welcoming" "each time", this "jolly" trattoria near Sloane Square is, among other virtues, "a great place to take the parents"; the Traditional Italian menu is by most accounts "very reliable" (including "delicious pasta specials"), though thrill-seekers claim the "basic food" makes for an "uneventful" meal.

Sandrini ◐Ⓢ   18 | 18 | 18 | £40
260 Brompton Rd., SW3 (South Kensington), 020-7584 1724;
fax 020-7225 1210
◪ "They treat you as a long lost friend", engendering loyalty
to this "reliable" Brompton Cross eaterie for its "consistent",
"sometimes excellent" cooking ("wonderful seafood risotto
worth waiting for") and popular outside pavement tables;
unswayed by its charms, some claim "there are better
Italians" and that it's "expensive for what it is."

San Frediano ◐Ⓢ   15 | 14 | 15 | £34
62 Fulham Rd., SW3 (South Kensington), 020-7589 2232;
fax 020-7225 2982
◪ Those who think this famous South Ken venue "changes
every year" are not far wrong, with new management taking
over recently, introducing a new, "well-priced" Traditional
Italian menu, but keeping the same clean decor; it "deserves
more customers" say early commentators.

San Lorenzo ◐≠   19 | 19 | 17 | £45
22 Beauchamp Pl., SW3 (Knightsbridge), 020-7584 1074;
fax 020-7584 1142
◪ It's "always nice to see a famous face" at this nearly
40-year-old "romantic" Italian in Knightsbridge boasting
a "great atmosphere" ("fake tans and face-lifts" not
withstanding) and "classically fantastic" cuisine; a vocal
contingent finds it "below expectations", however,
complaining that the "indifferent" staff "looks after the
regulars only" – though "once you're 'in', the world is
yours"; P.S. some suspect the no-credit-cards "policy is to
keep out the riffraff."

San Lorenzo Fuoriporta Ⓢ   20 | 18 | 17 | £38
3A Worple Mews, SW19 (Wimbledon), 020-8946 8463;
fax 020-8947 9810
◼ "Has the ambience of a bustling city eaterie, with the
service of a family restaurant" is how fans sum up the
appeal of this attractive Wimbledon stalwart (run by the
same family as its Knightsbridge parent), where most laud
the "delicious" Modern Italian food and especially enjoy
"summer [dining] in the courtyard"; P.S. "it's *the* place to
see and be seen during the Wimbledon tennis period."

Santa Fe Ⓢ   15 | 14 | 14 | £23
75 Upper St., N1 (Angel), 020-7288 2288; fax 020-7288 2287
◪ For "a taste of Mexico", this "warm, bright" Islingtonian is
"worth a visit" according to fans who enjoy its "good"
Southwestern American cooking, but doubters, in equal
numbers, find the fare "disappointing" ("so much potential,
so little delivery"); however, the fact it's "hopping on
Saturday nights" with "loud music" speaks volumes; P.S.
it has a popular "Sunday brunch."

Santini ● S
         20 | 17 | 17 | £47

29 Ebury St., SW1 (Victoria), 020-7730 4094; fax 020-7730 0544

■ It's "a pleasure to eat" in this modern, "wonderful setting" near Victoria Station, where "well-sized portions" of "simple" but "excellent" Modern Italian cooking are bought for "silly prices" – but are deemed "well worth it" by connoisseurs; the staff "grant every wish" to their "loyal customers", who tend to be "on the older side."

Sarastro ● S
         10 | 22 | 14 | £28

126 Drury Ln., WC2 (Covent Garden/Holborn), 020-7836 0101; fax 020-7379 4666

■ "Forget the food" and enjoy the "decadence" and "bedlam" at this "bustling" Theatrelander where renditions of "live opera" "compensate" for any "shortcomings" of the "boring" Mediterranean menu; it's "worth booking a balcony" to get the most of the "eclectic atmosphere" ("it's like theatre in itself"), and further enticement is the "great" £10 pre-theatre menu; P.S. "check the loos" decorated with "pornographic art."

Sarkhel's S
         24 | 14 | 20 | £31

197-199 Replingham Rd., SW18 (Southfields), 020-8870 1483; fax 020-8874 6603

■ "Different, fresh", "first-rate regional" cuisine at "very reasonable cost for the quality" (e.g. £10 for the two-course dinner set menu) places this "modern", unassuming Southfields venue among the very "best Indians in London"; far-flung fans lament "too bad it's so far away"; P.S. it's "almost impossible to get a table on Saturdays", so book "in advance."

Sartoria ● S
         19 | 20 | 17 | £42

20 Saville Row, W1 (Oxford Circus/Piccadilly Circus), 020-7534 7000; fax 020-7534 7070

☑ There's a "tailoring theme" to the "cool, uncluttered decor" of Sir Terence Conran's "bright" eaterie in Saville Row, which proffers a Modern Italian menu that fans find "excellent" but doubters dismiss as "utterly unremarkable"; although the service too gets mixed reviews – "ace" vs. "rushed" – this "good standby" still makes the grade for "an informal business lunch" or dinner, or as a venue that "accommodates large parties easily."

Satsuma S
         17 | 14 | 13 | £19

56 Wardour St., W1 (Leicester Sq./Piccadilly Circus), 020-7437 8338; fax 020-7437 3389

☑ Boosters place this "versatile" Soho "hot spot" among the "best of the fashionable Japanese canteens" and rate it "great for a quick meal of fab food" – "delicious" sushi, "spicy noodles" – at a "decent price"; even though purists pout it's "not authentic enough" and lament the "limited menu", "muscley waiters" compensate; N.B. no reserving.

Sauce Organic Diner ▣   – | – | – | M
214 Camden High St., NW1 (Camden Town), 020-7482 0777;
fax 020-7813 5915
This all-day Camden diner (downstairs from Camden
Brasserie) with a juice/cocktail bar is an "enjoyable" "find"
for "delightful", "hearty organic grub" along the lines of
waffles, burgers (of both the beef and veggie variety) and
"brilliant smoothies"; the interior is cheerful and colourful,
but still there are a few grumbles about "student decor."

Savoy Grill   23 | 22 | 24 | £50
Savoy Hotel, The Strand, WC2 (Covent Garden/
Embankment), 020-7420 2065; fax 020-7420 2450
■ It's "fun spotting the famous" and "captains of industry"
at this "civilised" dining room in The Strand's Savoy Hotel,
which most consider "superb in every way", from the
"old-world", "impeccable service" to the "outstanding"
Traditional British–Classic French cooking ("never
disappoints") and "extensive wine list"; although the
budget-bound may balk at "absurd prices", few would
dispute this "classic" is "good to impress."

SAVOY RIVER RESTAURANT ◐▣   21 | 24 | 22 | £51
Savoy Hotel, The Strand, WC2 (Covent Garden/Embankment),
020-7420 2698; fax 020-7420 2450
■ "Grand dining with a river view" doesn't get much
better than the "very British experience" at this "elegant"
Strand dining room (circa 1889) in the Savoy Hotel offering
the utmost in "stiff-upper-lip" service and "faultless", albeit
"expensive" International cuisine; it's popular for power
breakfasts but is also a fine "romantic" choice, given the
live "music and dancing" on Friday and Saturday nights,
which makes it "perfect for an extravagant celebration."

Scalini ◐▣   21 | 15 | 19 | £41
1-3 Walton St., SW3 (Knightsbridge/South Kensington),
020-7225 2301; fax 020-7225 3953
■ This "crowded" Chelsea "institution" is "everything a
top-rate Italian should be", with a "terrific atmosphere",
"excellent" classic cuisine and servers who "always
remember you after a visit", and whilst a few feel it's "lost
something in the last couple of years", this "noise bomb" still
attracts the odd "famous face" and remains "enjoyable."

Scotts ▣   21 | 20 | 19 | £46
20 Mount St., W1 (Bond St./Green Park), 020-7629 5248;
fax 020-7499 8246
☑ "Certainly a treat", this "comfortably old-fashioned"
Mayfair stalwart (more than 150 years old) resides in a
"formal", "plush" ground-floor dining room that's home to
"first-class seafood"; though sceptics accuse it of "living on
past reputation" ("food has known better days"), there's
always the "wonderful jazz bar downstairs" where "the
cabaret adds a proper finale to an evening."

Searcy's at the Barbican 🇸
16 | 14 | 15 | £33

Barbican Ctr., Silk St. level 2, EC2 (Barbican/Moorgate), 020-7588 3008; fax 020-3822 7247

☑ "Post-concert" Barbican Centre visitors are something of a "captive audience" at this "quiet" eatery on Level 2 offering "tasty", "innovative" Modern British dishes (though bashers boo it "could do better"); service can range from "good" to "clueless"; N.B. a new chef may outdate the above food rating.

Seashell
18 | 10 | 15 | £20

49-51 Lisson Grove, NW1 (Marylebone), 020-7224 9000; fax 020-7724 9071

☑ "Nice to see it back" greet groupies who have monitored the "long refurbishment" of this Marylebone seafooder where "the traditional fish 'n' chips are as good as ever", although a few mutineers mutter it has "lost the plot"; either way, "you can't beat it for takeaway" – just remember, it can be "difficult to park with all those Rolls-Royces outside."

Shepherd's
19 | 18 | 20 | £36

Marsham Ct., Marsham St., SW1 (Pimlico/St. James's Park), 020-7834 9552; fax 020-7233 6047

■ Richard Shepherd's spacious, panelled Westminster eaterie has the air of a "slightly shabby club" for politicians (and there are "many in the place" from nearby Parliament), and the "consistently good" Traditional British fare is "perfectly executed", if "unexciting"; "excellent service" rounds out a "great lunch or dinner" experience.

Shimla Pinks
18 | 19 | 16 | £29

7-8 Bishopsgate Church Yard, EC2 (Liverpool St.), 020-7628 7888; fax 020-7628 8282

☑ In the "refreshingly different setting" of former Turkish baths near Liverpool Street, this "stylish" eaterie produces "gorgeous" Indian fare that "transports curry into the 21st century"; although malcontents malign the "slow service", most think this "City find" constitutes a "spicy surprise."

Shish ◑🇸
– | – | – | M

2-6 Station Parade, NW2 (Willesden Green), 020-8208 9292

This laid-back Willesden debutante serves as an ultra-modern setting for showcasing shish cookery (skewering, that is) in a counter-style dining area with a diverse menu spanning the Orient and the Mediterranean; upstairs is a more cosy bar serving health juices, cocktails and snacks.

Shoeless Joe's
11 | 12 | 11 | £24

Temple Pl., The Embankment, WC2 (Temple), 020-7240 7865; fax 020-7240 7867
555 King's Rd., SW6 (Fulham Broadway), 020-7610 9346; fax 020-7610 9414 🇸

(continued)
Shoeless Joe's
1 Abbey Orchard St., SW1 (St. James's Park), 020-7222 4707;
fax 020-7222 4709
Old Change Ct., EC4 (St. Paul's), 020-7248 2720 S
■ These "loud, brash" sports bars around town hit the mark
as "trendy party spots" with their "club-like" ambience,
though they're "not really geared up" for eating, as the
Eclectic fare is "nothing special"; in sum, it's the "selection
of beers" and mix of "ordinary and exotic clientele" that get
these places "buzzing"; N.B. at press time, a new location
is due to open on Dover Street in the autumn.

Shogun S   21 14 20 £48
Millennium Mayfair Hotel, Adam's Row, W1 (Bond St.),
020-7493 1255; fax 020-7493 1255
■ Raw-fish fans are hooked on this Mayfair hotel basement
dining room serving "top sushi" and other Japanese fare
that's "wonderfully prepared" by a "friendly chef"; the
"nice decor" and comparatively low prices are added
bonuses at this dinner-only venue; N.B. closed Mondays.

Shoreditch   14 15 14 £28
Electricity Showrooms S
39A Hoxton Sq., N1 (Liverpool St./Old St.), 020-7739 6934;
fax 020-7739 6451
⬚ The "off-putting decor" is not to everyone's taste at this
designer Hoxton venue that's more of a "trendy" bar with
"great" Modern European snacks than 'proper' dining
option; hardened naysayers claim the place is a "triumph
of style over substance", but others are adamant it's still a
"place to be seen."

Signor Sassi S   19 16 17 £36
14 Knightsbridge Green, SW1 (Knightsbridge), 020-7584 2277;
fax 020-7225 3953
■ "Noisy but nice", this Knightsbridge Traditional Italian
has been long known for its "old-fashioned", "charming
ambience"; an "exceptional lobster" dish stands out for
surveyors, who warn it's not always on the "good menu",
and though a few lament this place has "lost its touch",
more feel it's "always fun."

Signor Zilli ◑   19 15 17 £32
41 Dean St., W1 (Leicester Sq./Tottenham Court Rd.),
020-7734 3924; fax 020-7734 7786
⬚ Although it's a "great media haunt" run by TV chef
Aldo Zilli, this Soho trattoria manages to serve "lovely",
"unpretentious" Traditional Italian fare that's "not too
costly"; "delighted" diners who "can't live without
the lobster ravioli" don't mind being "squeezed" into
this "buzzy" spot.

Silks & Spice
| 17 | 15 | 16 | £22 |

95 Chiswick High Rd., W4 (Turnham Green), 020-8995 7991;
fax 020-8994 7773 S
23 Foley St., W1 (Goodge St./Oxford Circus), 020-7636 2718;
fax 020-7323 1927 S
561 King's Rd., SW6 (Fulham Broadway), 020-7736 2333;
fax 020-7736 0899
28 Chalk Farm Rd., NW1 (Camden Town/Chalk Farm),
020-7267 5751 S
Temple Ct., 11 Queen Victoria St., EC4 (Bank/Mansion House),
020-7248 7878; fax 020-7248 9595
42 Northampton Rd., EC1 (Farringdon), 020-7278 9983;
fax 020-7713 6783

◪ These Thai-Malaysian eateries threaded throughout the
city elicit sundry assessments: supporters praise the
"interesting" fare that's "excellent value" and served in
"atmospheric surroundings" by "fun staff", but opponents
opine the offerings are "just ok" and the "service tired."

Simply Nico
| 18 | 14 | 16 | £35 |

48A Rochester Row, SW1 (St. James's Park/Victoria),
020-7630 8061; fax 020-7828 8541
12 Sloane Sq., SW1 (Sloane Sq.), 020-7896 9909;
fax 020-7896 9908 S
London Bridge Hotel, 10 London Bridge St., SE1 (London Bridge),
020-7407 4536; fax 020-7407 4554 S
7 Goswell Rd., EC1 (Barbican), 020-7336 7677;
fax 020-7336 7690 S

◪ "Not a destination, but fine if you are nearby", this quartet
(not associated with Nico Ladenis) offers "better-than-
average" French fare: "some [dishes] very good, some
ordinary"; despite "aloof" staff, the "modern brasserie
setting" makes them a favoured "business-lunch" option.

Simpson's-in-The-Strand/
Grand Divan S
| 19 | 21 | 19 | £41 |

100 The Strand, WC2 (Charing Cross), 020-7836 9112;
fax 020-7836 1381

■ There's a "public-school feeling" to this Strand "old
faithful" (since 1828) "where MPs meet" and tourists
"experience olde England" through Traditional dishes like
"excellent roast beef"; though modernists mutter it's
"disappointing", loyalists cheer "long may it continue."

Simpson's-in-The-Strand/
Simply Simpson's S
| 19 | 18 | 19 | £34 |

100 The Strand, WC2 (Charing Cross), 020-7836 9112;
fax 020-7836 1381

■ The "pleasant" upstairs dining room of this Strand
landmark is more "upmarket" than the Grand Divan above
but offers a similar menu of "the best of [Traditional] British
fayre" that's strong on game; "old reactionaries" revel in the
"seamless service", adding "forget the wallet and enjoy."

Simpson's Tavern ▽ | 16 | 13 | 14 | £26 |
Ball Ct., 38½ Cornhill, EC3 (Bank), 020-7626 9985;
fax 020-7626 3736
■ Everything is "wonderfully old-fashioned (including the waitresses and furniture!)" at this lunch-only City institution that's clocked up nearly 250 years specialising in Traditional British grills and steamed puddings.

Singapore Garden S | 22 | 13 | 19 | £25 |
83 Fairfax Rd., NW6 (Swiss Cottage), 020-7328 5314;
fax 020-7624 2656
■ With the Gloucester Street branch closing, this "cheerful" Swiss Cottage venue is left to fly the flag solo, serving "well-spiced" Malaysian, Chinese and Indonesian food that's deemed "reasonably authentic"; a few feel it "looks tired" but insist the interior's "altogether satisfactory."

Singapura | 16 | 14 | 15 | £29 |
1-2 Limeburner Ln., EC4 (Blackfriars/St. Paul's), 020-7329 1133;
fax 020-7236 2325
78-79 Leadenhall St., EC3 (Aldgate/Tower Hill), 020-7929 0089
■ Expect "a touch of the Orient" at these "pleasant" City sisters serving "great", "pukka" Southeast Asian cooking from a "reasonably priced set menu"; both venues offer delivery, but Leadenhall Street is lunch only.

Six-13 S ▽ | 18 | 17 | 16 | £42 |
19 Wigmore St., W1 (Bond St./Oxford Circus), 020-7629 6133;
fax 020-7629 6135
■ This "stylish" Kosher-Fusion newcomer in Marylebone combines traditional elements with "high-cuisine standards" to create "unusual", "elegant" fare; if the service goes "a bit haywire" at times, the staff's "charm" makes amends.

Smiths of Smithfield – Dining Room | 18 | 19 | 17 | £30 |
67-77 Charterhouse St., EC1 (Farringdon), 020-7236 6666;
fax 020-7236 5666
☑ In a "funky warehouse" space is this Smithfield Market yearling that's as "close as you can get to NYC's TriBeCa"; the Modern British menu "pleases red-meat connoisseurs" but offers "plenty of other choices", including "fresh fish"; though some are "underwhelmed", more think the "great food" and "fab atmosphere" triumph over the "hype."

Smiths of Smithfield – Top Floor S | 21 | 20 | 19 | £40 |
67-77 Charterhouse St., EC1 (Farringdon), 020-7236 6666;
fax 020-7236 5666
☑ "Enjoy the view" from the "great terrace" at this "provocative newcomer" in Smithfield Market; the "healthy" Anglo–Pacific Rim fare includes rare-breed steaks and other "fantastically good" dishes that are "up to par" with the "sleek" setting; P.S. those who consider it "overpriced" should check out the £25 three-course Sunday lunch.

Smollensky's on the Strand 🅂   13 | 13 | 14 | £25

105 The Strand, WC2 (Charing Cross/Covent Garden),
020-7497 2101; fax 020-7836 3270 ◗

O₂ Ctr., 255 Finchley Rd., NW3 (Finchley Rd.), 020-7431 5007;
fax 020-7431 7533

☑ The food is "nothing special", but these "brash, fun" all-day American eateries on the Strand and Finchley Road (a "welcome addition") still attract "office parties" in search of a "loud" night out with "good [live] music"; on weekends, parents plop their kids into the "high chairs" and choose from a wide variety of "value"-priced eats.

Snows on the Green 🅂   17 | 12 | 15 | £32

166 Shepherd's Bush Rd., W6 (Hammersmith),
020-7603 2142; fax 020-7602 7553

■ This family-run Shepherd's Bush "find" offers "novel", "tasty" Modern British fare at a price judged "right for the quality"; whilst the rustic interior is "not very elegant", service is "pleasant" and most have "no real complaints."

Sofra ◗🅂   18 | 12 | 15 | £22

36 Tavistock St., WC2 (Covent Garden), 020-7240 3773;
fax 020-7836 6633
1 St. Christopher's Pl., W1 (Bond St.), 020-7224 4080;
fax 020-7224 0022
18 Shepherd St., W1 (Green Park), 020-7493 3320;
fax 020-7499 8282

■ "If passing by, it's silly not to drop in" for a "cheap" meal of "basic", "tasty" Turkish treats at these "cheerful" West End cafes; claustrophobes take issue with their "cramped quarters" ("not places to linger") but still recommend a "takeaway" order of "basic" mezze and some baklava "when in a hurry."

Soho House ◗🅂   18 | 19 | 17 | £34

Private club; inquiries: 020-7734 5188

☑ "Perfect for the Soho set, but not outsiders" may be the most accurate way to describe this private club, which counts "people-watchers", "lots of famous" faces and "beautiful women" as members; the Modern British "food is generally good" ("they do a wicked club sandwich" at the bar), but naysayers still think the place personifies "style over content."

Soho Spice ◗🅂   17 | 16 | 15 | £25

124-126 Wardour St., W1 (Leicester Sq./Tottenham Court Rd.),
020-7434 0808; fax 020-7434 0799

☑ "Generous portions" of "interesting" Indian cooking garner warm regard for this "lively" Soho Indian, which features a "vibrant" colour scheme and "lively" atmosphere; the fact that "everyone's under 30" is a good thing, since it "turns into a disco" on Friday and Saturday nights, when it's open late.

Solly's 🄢　　　　　18 | 10 | 13 | £23
148A Golders Green Rd., NW11 (Golders Green),
020-8455 2121
◪ Solid kebabs, shwarma and falafel as well as
"atmosphere with more than a taste of the Middle East"
attract a following for this "unpretentious" Golders Green
kosher Lebanese eaterie; the bill can be "expensive" and
service from "young staff" "is hit-or-miss", but the "reliable"
preparations mean many "still return."

Sonny's 🄢　　　　　21 | 19 | 21 | £34
94 Church Rd., SW13 (Hammersmith), 020-8748 0393;
fax 020-8748 2698
◼ "Imaginative, well-executed" seasonal Modern British
cooking, "efficient", "friendly" service and a "modern"
look that will make you feel "so relaxed, you'll want to put
your feet up" (but please don't) explain why this Barnes
eaterie "out in the 'burbs" is still "hugely busy."

Souk ◕🄢　　　　　16 | 21 | 14 | £20
27 Litchfield St., WC2 (Leicester Sq.), 020-7240 1796
◼ "Sitting cross-legged amongst cushions, drapes" and
other "fantastic" decorations while ogling the belly dancer
and inhaling "the wonderful, heady smell of incense" makes
for "great" "group" fun at this "cramped" Theatreland
Moroccan whose "cheeky" "entertaining" waiters come
"decked out in fezzes"; the edibles may "not be the best",
but the "party atmosphere" compensates.

Soup Opera ⇪　　　　　19 | 12 | 15 | £7
34 Villiers St., WC2 (Embankment), 020-7839 6300;
fax 020-7839 4162 🄢
18 Bloomfield St., EC2 (Liverpool St.), 020-7588 9188;
fax 020-7588 9103
17 Kingsway, WC2 (Holborn), 020-7329 1333;
fax 020-7379 1199
56-57 Cornhill, EC3 (Bank), 020-7621 0065;
fax 020-7621 0026
6 Market Pl., W1 (Oxford Circus), 020-7637 7882;
fax 020-7637 7869
Platform 8, King's Cross Railway Station, N1 (King's
Cross), 020-7713 1137; fax 020-7713 1362
Cabot Pl., concourse level, E14 (Canary Wharf DLR),
020-7513 0880; fax 020-7513 0890
2 Hanover St., W1 (Oxford Circus), 020-7629 0174;
fax 020-7629 0175
◼ The No. 1 Bang for the Buck in this *Survey* thanks to its
"souperb" soups and other "fresh, healthy" snacks such as
salads and sandwiches, this expanding chain of *potage*
specialists hits the spot, "especially in wintertime"; those
overwhelmed by the many choices to slurp from will be
pleased to know that "sampling is allowed."

Soup Works ⊭ | 19 | 9 | 13 | £7 |
29 Monmouth St., W2 (Leicester Sq./Tottenham Court Rd.),
020-7240 7687; fax 020-7379 7687
9 D'Arblay St., W1 (Oxford Circus/Tottenham Court Rd.),
020-7439 7687; fax 020-7287 5574
56 Goodge St., W1 (Goodge St./Tottenham Court Rd.),
020-7637 7687; fax 020-7637 7367
■ For "wholesome food on the hoof", a cure "for a hangover" or an "excellent", inexpensive "pre-theatre meal", consider these gourmet soup outlets where the "nice selection" includes interesting combos like chicken, sweet potato and coconut.

Southeast W9 🆂   ▽ | 18 | 14 | 15 | £21 |
239 Elgin Ave., W9 (Maida Vale), 020-7328 8883;
fax 020-7328 9879
■ A "Zen-like atmosphere" pervades this minimalist Maida Vale eaterie, which though not well-known among surveyors, offers a "good-value", "eclectic" Southeast Asian menu of "aromatic, flavoursome dishes" from various countries in the region; it also makes a "convenient" candidate for takeaway.

Spaghetti House | 13 | 10 | 14 | £19 |
24 Cranbourn St., WC2 (Covent Garden/Leicester Sq.),
020-7836 8168; fax 020-7395 0391 🆂
30 St. Martin's Ln., WC2 (Charing Cross), 020-7836 1626;
fax 020-7836 1606
20 Sicilian Ave., WC1 (Holborn), 020-7405 5215;
fax 020-7405 5210
74 Duke St., W1 (Bond St.), 020-7629 6097; fax 020-7629 6097 🆂
15-17 Goodge St., W1 (Goodge St.), 020-7636 6582;
fax 020-7580 7532 🆂
3 Bressenden Pl., SW1 (Victoria), 020-7834 5650;
fax 020-7834 5650
66 Haymarket, SW1 (Piccadilly Circus), 020-7839 3641;
fax 020-7930 7721 🆂
77 Knightsbridge, SW1 (Knightsbridge), 020-7235 8141;
fax 020-7235 8141
☑ These "lower-end Italians" around town are "not bad for a quick meal" – whether "after shopping" or "pre-theatre" – and if the fare of pastas and pizzas is "never outstanding", it's "so cheap", with generally "cheerful" service; N.B. "some [branches] are better than others."

Spago ◗🆂 | 19 | 12 | 12 | £22 |
183 Lavender Hill, SW11 (Clapham Junction), 020-7228 2660
6 Glendower Pl., SW7 (South Kensington), 020-7225 2407 ⊭
■ Here's a pair of "wood-fired pizza places" in South Kensington and Lavender Hill that offer "that Italian experience", complete with "beautiful (but clumsy) staff" and "macho Italian men [watching] football", not to mention the "wonderful", "great-value" pizzas with a seafood bent; overall, they're "ideal for low-key dates."

Spiga S
19 | 15 | 16 | £26

84-86 Wardour St., W1 (Leicester Sq./Piccadilly Circus),
020-7734 3444; fax 020-7734 3332 ☾
312-314 King's Rd., SW3 (Sloane Sq.), 020-7351 0101;
fax 020-7349 1488

■ "Bring earplugs" to this "lively", "cheerful" Soho Italian
with "cool, modern decor" and "good, robust" Italian
cooking that "never fails" (especially the "fantastic pizzas
from a wood-fired oven") and comes at a "good price for
the West End", although a few find it just "ordinary"; a
stylish second branch in Chelsea (with the obligatory
wood oven) opened post-*Survey*.

Spighetta S
19 | 13 | 16 | £26

43 Blandford St., W1 (Baker St.), 020-7486 7340; fax 020-7486 7340

◪ "In the [culinary] desert behind Selfridges" dwells this
"fun", "casual" Marylebone pizzeria (owned by the A-Z
group), which exudes a "young feel" and serves up
"reliable", "pleasant" Italian standards, including pizzas
from a wood-fired oven and "pastas worthy of exporting
to Napoli"; whilst snipers say it "suffers from being below
ground" ("uninteresting surroundings"), most don't seem
to mind much.

Spirit S
– | – | – | M

2-5 Carthusian St., EC1 (Barbican), 020-7253 6009;
fax 020-7336 0374

Split over two floors, this voguish, all-day Barbican
venue serves lunch and light evening snacks from an
International menu, as well as Sunday brunch; the
space hosts art exhibitions and invites DJs to perform four
nights a week (Wednesday–Sunday), while on Sundays,
any jockey can book a slot.

Spoon+ at Sanderson S
18 | 22 | 16 | £53

Sanderson Hotel, 50 Berners St., W1 (Goodge St./
Oxford Circus), 020-7300 1444; fax 020-7300 1479

◪ At this offshoot of Alain Ducasse's Parisian eaterie in Ian
Schrager's "very trendy" Sanderson Hotel in Bloomsbury,
the trademark "mix-and-match menu" divides diners: to
some it's a "very creative" way of eating "what you like with
what you like", but to others it's "horribly contrived" and
"overpriced"; either way, this "people-watching" paradise is
less "about eating [than] being seen eating", particularly
in the "amazing Long Bar", which looks like "a film set"; N.B.
the new '59-minute' lunch is perfect for clock-watchers.

Sporting Page S
15 | 14 | 15 | £16

6 Camera Pl., SW10 (Earl's Court), 020-7349 0455;
fax 020-7352 8162

■ This respectable Chelsea pub offers Modern British
cooking that's "nothing special" but "great if you can't be
bothered to cook", and the big-screen TV ensures a hive
of activity when major sporting events are taking place.

Sports Cafe ◐ [S] 9 | 13 | 9 | £21

80 Haymarket, SW1 (Piccadilly Circus), 020-7839 8300; fax 020-7839 8303

■ "It's all about the sports" transmitted on huge TV screens at this "cool place for the boys to relax" in Haymarket, where "massive portions" of American-style burgers and other "junk food" strike most as just "an afterthought"; it also serves as a "great spot for homesick U.S. sports fans" ("best place to watch the NFL").

SQUARE, THE [S] 26 | 22 | 24 | £58

6-10 Bruton St., W1 (Bond St./Green Park), 020-7495 7100; fax 020-7495 7150

■ "Other London restaurants should learn from" this "gorgeous, convivial" Mayfair "favourite", which "pleases even the most demanding of diners" with Philip Howard's "really stupendous menu" of "seriously grown-up", "world-class" New French cuisine, "excellent wine list to suit all tastes" and "impeccable", "professional service"; the "bill will take your breath away", but connoisseurs conclude it's "worth every penny" for such "all-round" "brilliance."

Sri Siam ◐ [S] 19 | 13 | 16 | £26

16 Old Compton St., W1 (Leicester Sq./Tottenham Court Rd.), 020-7434 3544; fax 020-7287 1311

■ "Ok, it's not Thailand, but it's pretty close" say supporters of this stark Soho eaterie's "authentic" and "reliable" Thai cooking, which has the added allure of being "cheap for the area"; whilst there's a suggestion that the service is sometimes "rushed" and "the noise level a little loud", all is forgiven in light of the "great-value pre-theatre" menu.

Sri Siam City 19 | 15 | 16 | £32

85 London Wall, EC2 (Liverpool St.), 020-7628 5772

◪ "Very good for City lunching" with some of the "best Thai" cooking around say supporters of this Sri Siam offshoot in an attractive basement setting at London Wall, though malcontents quip about needing a "microscope to see the portions"; N.B. the £15.95 set lunch has its followers.

Sri Thai 20 | 15 | 17 | £29

3 Queen Victoria St., EC4 (Bank), 020-7827 0202; fax 020-7827 0200

■ The youngest member of the Sri Siam trio is a "great business-lunch spot" in the City with "hot, spicy", "out-of-this-world" Thai food that's "worth every penny" and brought to table by "genuinely attentive servers"; fussier voters note there's an evening crowd of "annoying City types" "getting drunk", which may explain why it's considered "perfect birthday party material."

Stafford Restaurant, The 🅂 ▽ 23 | 20 | 24 | £45

The Stafford, St. James's Pl., SW1 (Green Park),
020-7493 0111; fax 020-7493 7121

■ There's an "old English style" to this "formal" dining
room in St. James's "lovely, hidden" Stafford hotel, where
admirers appreciate the "attentive service", "consistent",
albeit "pricey", Modern British–Classic French "comfort
food" and "soothing" environment; "excellent private
dining facilities" are also available.

Standard Tandoori ◐🅂 ▽ 18 | 9 | 14 | £20

21-23 Westbourne Grove, W2 (Bayswater), 020-7727 4818

■ "They reward the regulars with friendly service" at this
"excellent neighbourhood curry" house in Westbourne
Grove, a solid choice for "authentic" Punjabi fare from a
"very reasonably priced" menu; yes, the "decor is tired",
but veteran visitors advise "ignore it."

Starbucks 🅂 14 | 13 | 14 | £8

25A Kensington High St., W8 (High St. Kensington),
020-7937 5446
34 Great Marlborough St., W1 (Oxford Circus),
020-7434 0778
111 Marylebone High St., W1 (Baker St./Bond St.),
020-7486 9668
55-56 Oxford St., W1 (Tottenham Court Rd.), 020-7491 2183
809 Fulham Rd., SW6 (Parsons Green), 020-7371 9491
39 Abbeville Rd., SW4 (Clapham South), 020-8673 4004
123A King's Rd., SW3 (Sloane Sq.), 020-7376 4678
79 St. John's Wood, NW8 (St. John's Wood), 020-7586 4365
365 Cabot Pl. E., E14 (Canary Wharf), 020-7512 9530
Additional locations throughout London

■ "Formulaic, but a formula that works" is the scoop on
this "typically American" coffeehouse chain that's
"growing like fungus" around town; as far as the
"consistently" "very good coffee" is concerned, the
"addicted" declare "no contest", but the "great
atmosphere" that's a euphemism for "long queues" at
busy times, "limited food selection" (sandwiches, cakes)
and "expensive" prices are grounds for bitterness.

Star of India ◐🅂 20 | 16 | 17 | £33

154 Old Brompton Rd., SW5 (Gloucester Rd./
South Kensington), 020-7373 2901; fax 020-7373 5664

☑ It "needs a nip and tuck" decorwise, but still there's
a "magical atmosphere" at this "cramped" ("need a
shoehorn to get out!") South Ken Indian, possibly due
to the "fabulous aromas" and "palpable excitement"
generated by the kitchen's "authentic, delicious" and
"distinctive" handiwork; a three-point rise in its service
rating since the last Survey indicates that an increasingly
"friendly", "attentive" staff – and owner Reza Mahammad's
sense of "pure theatre" – meets with general approval.

Stepping Stone S
21 | 17 | 19 | £33

123 Queenstown Rd., SW8 (Clapham Common), 020-7622 0555; fax 020-7622 4230

■ It's a "stepping stone to food heaven" gush gastronomes of the "invariably delightful" Modern British cooking found at this "jewel" in Clapham that boasts "bright, modern decor" and "friendly" service that's "welcoming in a real way" and "tries hard"; all in all, it's voted a "terrific local" that's just the "place for Sunday lunch with the kids."

Sticky Fingers ●❍ S
13 | 14 | 15 | £22

1A Phillimore Gardens, W8 (High St. Kensington), 020-7938 5338; fax 020-7937 0145

◪ "Kids reign" at this "noisy", American-style Kensington diner that can seem like "a children's playground" and serves as an "ideal birthday [party] venue"; whilst those who find the eats "not very impressive" consider the wall-mounted Rolling Stones "memorabilia the best bit", overall it's "good family fun."

St. John
21 | 16 | 18 | £34

26 St. John St., EC1 (Farringdon), 020-7251 0848; fax 020-7251 4090

■ "Long live offal" cheer fans of this "treasure of compelling simplicity" in an old Smithfield smokehouse, where "genius" Fergus Henderson produces a Modern British menu that "specialises in the bits of animals you'd rather not know about"; the "gym-like atmosphere" may unsettle a few, but most rate the experience "genuinely challenging" (in a good way), albeit a "vegetarian's nightmare!"

Strada S
17 | 14 | 15 | £20

15-16 New Burlington St., W1 (Oxford Circus), 020-7287 5967; fax 020-7287 7607
175 New King's Rd., SW6 (Parsons Green), 020-7731 6404; fax 020-7731 1431
11-13 Battersea Rise, SW1 (Clapham Junction), 020-7801 0794; fax 020-7801 0754
8-10 Exmouth Mkt., EC1 (Farringdon), 020-7278 0800; fax 020-7278 6907

■ "Whilst still a secret" to some, this "brash", fast-growing chain of pizzerias owned by the Belgo group isn't likely to stay that way for long; "full of brio", it serves "great pizzas" and other Italian dishes with "interesting twists", and not surprising, it has "already" developed "a strong following" as somewhere "dependable for an evening with friends."

Stratford's S
▽ 23 | 14 | 21 | £35

7 Stratford Rd., W8 (High St. Kensington), 020-7937 6388; fax 020-7938 3435

■ This "cosy, elegant" Kensington townhouse makes a "serendipitous find" given its "great" Classic French menu of "mostly fish" dishes, paired with sauces that would "make a piece of cardboard taste good"; "excellent" service ("not intrusive at all") also gets the thumbs-up.

Stream ▽ 17 | 14 | 18 | £29

50-52 Long Ln., EC1 (Barbican/Farringdon), 020-7796 0070; fax 020-7796 0069

◪ Complete with chrome exterior and industrial interior, this Smithfield Market newcomer specialises (strangely enough) in molluscs and crustaceans – oysters, crab, mussels and the like – but early reports suggest mixed reactions: "keep it up" say some, but others gripe "badly run"; time will tell whether it becomes "a hit."

SUGAR CLUB S 22 | 18 | 19 | £41

21 Warwick St., W1 (Piccadilly Circus), 020-7437 7776; fax 020-7437 7778

◪ "There's a stark elegance" to this "classy" Soho eaterie that's "keeping to the same high standards even with the departure of Peter Gordon" (in 1999), the originator of its "inventive", "brave" International fusion menu known for "out-of-this-world combinations" of "eclectic ingredients from the East and West"; a few suggest the "old excitement is missing", but they are outvoted by those enamoured of this "happening", "accomplished" spot; P.S. "just make sure you're seated upstairs."

Sugar Reef ◑ 16 | 17 | 14 | £35

41-44 Great Windmill St., W1 (Piccadilly Circus), 020-7851 0800; fax 020-7851 0807

◪ This huge, "buzzy" establishment near Piccadilly Circus is a "combo of restaurant and nightclub", though "the latter seems to prevail as far as ambience goes" ("if you're older than 30, forget it"), which may explain why the Pan-Asian menu provokes conflicting reports ("quality" vs. "passable"); it's really all about the "great bar and dancing", so "if you want to show off your new Gucci outfit, go for it!"; N.B. it changed owners and got a new chef post-*Survey*.

Suntory S 24 | 18 | 21 | £55

72-73 St. James's St., SW1 (Green Park), 020-7409 0201; fax 020-7499 0208

■ "Divine", "aesthetic" but "ridiculously expensive" Japanese cuisine (sushi, sashimi and other classics) is what to expect at this "elegant", spacious St. James's stalwart (since '77) with "terrific service" that "blends into the background" ("lovely young ladies who cook at your table" notwithstanding); the majority reports "perfect experiences", particularly those on expense accounts.

Sushi Wong S ▽ 18 | 12 | 18 | £23

38C-D Kensington Church St., W8 (High St. Kensington), 020-7937 5007; fax 020-7937 0670

◪ It's a "pity about the decor", but this neon-lit, bi-level Kensington Japanese is a "pleasant" spot nonetheless for "good-quality sushi" and teppanyaki (downstairs), where "friendly, quick service" and "value" pricing help seal the deal for those who call it a "favourite."

Sway ◐ – | – | – | E

(fka 10 Covent Garden)

61-65 Great Queen St., WC2 (Holborn), 020-7404 6114; fax 020-7404 6003

After being sold post-*Survey* to the fast-expanding Chorian group (who have also snapped up Sugar Reef), this cool, modern spot in Covent Garden now features an easygoing ground-floor dining area with a Modern European menu (including its previous trademark rotisserie "chicken and sauces"), along with a lounge bar and two private-member bar areas.

Sweetings 21 | 15 | 18 | £32

39 Queen Victoria St., EC4 (Mansion House), 020-7248 3062

■ "Love or hate" it, this "idiosyncratic", "lunch-only" City "institution" (est. 1889) makes an "amazing" dining "experience", and whilst the "time-warp" atmosphere isn't to everyone's taste (especially the "uncomfortable seating"), most praise the "traditional, fresh fish", which is "not cheap, but good"; "you have to go, if only for the experience"; N.B. it was sold post-*Survey* by its owner of two decades, Patricia Needham, to the head chef, Patrick Molloy, who plans no changes.

Tabla [S] – | – | – | E

Dockmaster's House, Hertsmere Rd., E14 (Canary Wharf), 020-7345 0345; fax 020-7363 1013

Though not yet on many radar screens, this "nice building" (formerly the Dockmaster's House) at West India Quay houses an attractive newcomer producing contemporary iterations of Indian cuisine that satisfy some ("pleasant") more than others ("boring"); N.B. it's owned by the team behind the Cinnamon Club.

Tamarind ◐[S] 23 | 20 | 20 | £39

20 Queen St., W1 (Green Park), 020-7629 3561; fax 020-7499 5034

◪ "Superb Indian food" featuring "subtle", "sublime flavours" finds a "chic setting" in this "upscale" Mayfair eaterie that spins "new twists on traditional" Northern dishes, and whilst diners expect to "pay a lot" for the privilege, most feel it's "worth saving up for"; a few naysayers find the ambience "sterilised" and some servers "unhelpful", but most have only "excellent" "experiences" to report: "your best bet" for a "special occasion."

Tandoori Lane ◐[S] ▽ 19 | 13 | 18 | £20

131 Munster Rd., SW6 (Fulham Broadway/Parsons Green), 020-7371 0440

■ "Simple, wholesome" Indian food is the main attraction at this "cosy" Fulham curry house with "friendly" service, and if a few balk at somewhat "upmarket prices", there's always the takeaway option.

Tandoori of Chelsea ●S 20 | 16 | 20 | £28
153 Fulham Rd., SW3 (South Kensington), 020-7589 7617;
fax 020-7584 3168

■ The doorman "in traditional Indian garb" is a "precious" part of this "friendly, subterranean" Chelsea stalwart (circa '64) deemed "always dependable" thanks to its "solid" cooking and "very accommodating staff."

Tao 13 | 13 | 13 | £30
11-11A Bow Ln., EC4 (Mansion House), 020-7248 5833;
fax 020-7329 1446

◰ This "great lunchtime venue" for City folk boasts a "lively bar upstairs" and a stylish downstairs restaurant that benefits from the services of chef Bruce Warwick (ex The Groucho Club), who prepares "quality" European-Pacific fare; the outside courtyard is popular after work "in summer."

Tartuf ●S ∇ 20 | 16 | 19 | £15
88 Upper St., N1 (Angel), 020-7288 0954; fax 020-7288 0957

■ "Inspired", "cheap" Alsatian fare – most notably the pizza-like *tartes flambées* – is what's on offer at this "nice concept" eaterie in Islington with "the sweetest serving staff" and a relaxed atmosphere; "great if quantity comes before quality"; N.B. there's a terrace at the rear.

Tas ●S 20 | 14 | 18 | £21
33 The Cut, SE1 (Southwark), 020-7928 1444

■ "A simple formula well-executed" is the consensus on this "vibrant" Turkish spot in Waterloo that's something of "a jewel", with a "friendly staff" serving "interesting" cooking (including a "great vegetarian selection") at "reasonable prices"; best of all, despite being "very popular", it manages to "keep its feet on the ground."

Tate Gallery Restaurant S 18 | 19 | 16 | £27
Tate Britain, Millbank, SW1 (Pimlico), 020-7887 8825;
fax 020-7887 8902

◰ "Worth the trip, even if you don't enjoy the art" advise admirers of this "busy" basement dining room at the Tate at Millbank boasting a "beautiful" Rex Whistler mural and "decent" Modern British food; whilst a fussy few complain of "confused service", there's always the "surpassingly fine wine list" (400 labels).

TATSUSO 25 | 17 | 22 | £52
32 Broadgate Circle, EC2 (Liverpool St.), 020-7638 5863;
fax 020-7638 5864

■ It's "unbelievably expensive", but after all, this Broadgate Circle Japanese is among the "best in town", offering "fabulous" grill specialities in the teppanyaki room on the ground floor and "quality" sushi and sashimi in the "quieter" "downstairs" restaurant (there are also private tatami rooms); "charming", kimono-clad staff cater to every whim – except "after 9 PM", when some seem to "want to go home."

Teatro ●　　　　19　17　16　£41
93-107 Shaftesbury Ave., W1 (Leicester Sq.), 020-7494 3040;
fax 020-7494 3050
◪ There's "a buzz" at this first-floor Theatrelander (owned
by Lesley Ash and Lee Chapman), and the Modern
European cooking is "not too bad" either; if some find the
à la carte menu "too expensive", there's always the £11.50
lunch/pre-theatre set-price menu, as well as a recently
redesigned bar that's a "good place to spot stars"; N.B. a
second bar is for members only.

TECA　　　　21　18　20　£37
54 Brooks Mews, W1 (Bond St.), 020-7495 4774;
fax 020-7491 3545
◪ "Since A-Z [Restaurants] took it over", ratings for this
"civilised", "smart" eaterie in a Mayfair mews have moved
north, reflecting the fact that its "excellent" Modern
Italian cooking and "attentive service" have "improved a
lot"; whilst a dissatisfied few call it "too expensive" and
can't warm up to "somewhat coldish" decor, the majority
opines this "lovely" sleeper "deserves to succeed."

10 Devonshire Square　　　∇　17　18　21　£33
10 Cutlers Gardens Arcade, EC2 (Liverpool St.),
020-7283 7888; fax 020-7626 4859
◼ Few voters know this "cool"-looking, muralled City
basement that's only open for weekday lunches (it's
available for private hire in evenings), but those who do
praise its quite "good" British-Mediterranean cuisine;
N.B. new management took over in late 2000.

Tentazioni　　　　22　14　18　£38
Lloyd's Wharf, 2 Mill St., SE1 (London Bridge/Tower Hill),
020-7237 1100; fax 020-7237 1100
◪ "Great care is taken to welcome guests" with "a smile"
at this "sophisticated" eaterie set in a converted Butlers
Wharf warehouse, which proffers "delicious", "innovative"
Modern Italian cooking "beautifully presented" and
paired with "exceptionally fine wines"; whilst a handful is
dissatisfied with the "out-of-the-way location", the ayes
have it: an "impeccable dining experience."

Tenth Restaurant & Bar, The　　18　22　19　£41
Royal Garden Hotel, 2-24 Kensington High St., 10th fl., W8
(High St. Kensington), 020-7361 1910; fax 020-7361 1921
◼ "The best thing is the view" across Kensington
Gardens and beyond from this modern, 10th-floor dining
room of Kensington's Royal Garden Hotel, though the
few who comment also credit it for "surprisingly good"
Modern British–Eclectic food and dancing on Saturday
nights to live jazz music from a "good band"; though it's
something of a well-kept secret, those in-the-know call it
an "all-round favourite."

Terminus 🅂
| 14 | 14 | 12 | £28 |

Great Eastern Hotel, Liverpool St., EC2 (Liverpool St.), 020-7618 7400; fax 020-7618 7401

◪ There's a "railway theme" to the Conran Group's big, but "congested" (with "money brokers"), all-day brasserie in the Great Eastern Hotel by Liverpool Street Station, which defenders deem a "fairly polished formula" of "good" Modern British–International cooking and "lively service"; unhappy travellers (in large numbers) "don't like the feel of this place", however, citing "mediocre food", "noisy" acoustics and "disinterested staff", concluding "the UK train crisis extends to Terminus."

Terrace, The 🅂
| 19 | 21 | 18 | £38 |

Le Meridien Piccadilly, 21 Piccadilly, W1 (Green Park/ Piccadilly Circus), 020-7851 3085; fax 020-7851 3090

◪ This large, bright conservatory in the Le Meridien Piccadilly is somewhat underused, but those who know it consider meals here a "wonderful" "treat" with "fab" Classic French brasserie fare (overseen by Michel Rostang), even if there are a few murmurs that it's a bit "overpriced."

Terrace, The 🅂
| 22 | 17 | 19 | £36 |

33C Holland St., W8 (High St. Kensington), 020-7851 3081; fax 020-7851 3090

◪ "Go in the summer and sit outside" advise lovers of this "intimate" Kensington venue boasting an ever-changing menu of "lovely" Modern British cooking served by "great staff", as well as a terrace that's "ideal for" outdoor dining; if a few critics go away "disappointed", the majority insists this "tucked-away" spot "deserves to be better known."

Texas Embassy Cantina 🅂
| 14 | 14 | 15 | £21 |

1 Cockspur St., SW14 (Charing Cross/Piccadilly Circus), 020-7925 0077; fax 020-7925 0444

◪ "If you're hankering for Tex-Mex", "good, hearty Southwestern" eats await at this "noisy" Trafalgar Square entry that also offers an "abundance of tequilas"; even if some think it's "naff", "faux" and "tasteless", try telling that to the cowboys who rate it a "great" place to "soak up Coronas" and have a "party": "feels like a fiesta!"

Texas Lone Star ●🅂
| 11 | 11 | 12 | £22 |

50-54 Turnham Green Terrace, W4 (Turnham Green), 020-8747 0001; fax 020-8747 0001
154 Gloucester Rd., SW7 (Gloucester Rd.), 020-7370 5625; fax 020-7835 0677

■ It "looks authentic" and "makes an ok margarita" for those really "craving the Southwest", but aficionados affirm that this "tedious" theme duo in South Kensington and Turnham Green definitely is "not Tex, not Mex" – just "bland"; "quantity-over-quality" grub and "in-your-face service" aside, though, amigos appreciate that it's "good for teenagers" and "welcomes children."

T.G.I. Friday's ◐🅂　　　11 | 11 | 14 | £22
6 Bedford St., WC2 (Charing Cross/Covent Garden),
020-7379 0585; fax 020-7240 3239
96-98 Bishop's Bridge Rd., W2 (Bayswater), 020-7229 8600;
fax 020-7727 4150
25-29 Coventry St., W1 (Piccadilly Circus), 020-7839 6262;
fax 020-7839 6296

■ "Grown-up McDonald's" is how most see these "cheerful", "raucous" American-style burger bars with "great cocktails" and a "fab atmosphere" for when "there's a few of you" looking for a "noisy night out"; yes, the "wide choice" of "Yankee" food "could be better", but it suits those looking to "just pig out" or clear a "hangover"; P.S. "face-painting for kids at the weekend" goes down well.

Thai Kitchen　　　▽ 20 | 14 | 16 | £25
108 Chepstow Rd., W2 (Westbourne Park), 020-7221 9984

■ "Be warned, the food can be hot!" at this dinner-only Thai near Queensway that, whilst not well-used by surveyors, is credited with "very good" traditional cuisine by those who know it; sticklers for atmosphere might do better elsewhere, however, as the "spartan interior" doesn't exactly "inspire thoughts of Bangkok."

Thai on the River 🅂　　　21 | 19 | 19 | £36
4 Chelsea Wharf, 15 Lots Rd., SW10 (Fulham Broadway/
Sloane Sq.), 020-7351 1151; fax 020-7823 3390

■ It's "great if you can get a window seat" at this airy, "romantic" riverside Thai venue near Chelsea Harbour that provides "delicious food" amid "superb surroundings" featuring "wonderful" views (especially on the terrace); overall, it's voted somewhere "worth going for special occasions"; P.S. there's also a "good weekend lunch buffet."

Thai Pavilion ◐🅂　　　▽ 19 | 16 | 16 | £23
42 Rupert St., W1 (Leicester Sq./Piccadilly Circus),
020-7287 6333; fax 020-7587 0484

■ It's "hard to find" in the depths of Soho, but those who make their way to this "quiet", "cosy" Thai spread over three floors appreciate its "authentic" approach to "tasty food" served in "real Thai style"; the upper room has diners "sitting on the floor with cushions", which for the less limber can be "uncomfortable if you aren't used to it."

Thai Square ◐🅂　　　15 | 16 | 13 | £26
21-24 Cockspur St., SW1 (Charing Cross/Piccadilly Circus),
020-7839 4000

☑ Although some cynics think this spacious, "lavish" dining room inside the former Norwegian Embassy is "far from premier category", citing "mainstream Thai fare" and "difficult-to-find service", others appreciate the "good food" and "fun atmosphere"; maybe its "popularity" is due to the "bar downstairs" where "many Thais seem to go" for "lovely, fruity Asian drinks."

Thierry's 🗒   16 | 14 | 16 | £32

342 King's Rd., SW3 (Sloane Sq.), 020-7352 3365;
fax 020-7352 3365

■ This "casual neighbourhood bistro" in Chelsea makes a "reliable standby", thanks to its "authentic", "charming" French fare and "warm service"; whilst a few might quibble about "less-than-stunning decor" and claim it's "going off" the boil ("slow", "food can vary"), most denizens insist this laid-back "stalwart" is "perfect for a romantic dinner."

Tiger Lil's 🗒   14 | 13 | 13 | £22

75 Bishop's Bridge Rd., W2 (Bayswater/Queensway),
020-7221 2622
500 King's Rd., SW10 (Fulham Broadway/Sloane Sq.),
020-7376 5003; fax 020-7376 4002
16A Southside Clapham Common, SW4 (Clapham Common),
020-7720 5433 ☽
270 Upper St., N1 (Highbury & Islington),
020-7226 1118 ☽

■ "Choose your" plate of "ingredients" and then "watch as they furnace it in front of your eyes" at this "DIY" Asian trio in Chelsea, Islington and Clapham, which wins fans as a "cheap and cheerful" way of eating in "a group"; if a few naysayers find "the end result is not as great as expected" ("easier to cook at home"), "children love" the spectacle of "flames shooting up out of the pan"; N.B. a new Bayswater branch opened post-*Survey*.

Titanic ☽   12 | 15 | 11 | £37

81 Brewer St., W1 (Piccadilly Circus), 020-7437 1912;
fax 020-7439 4747

■ "All flash, little substance" is the general consensus on this "noisy" Piccadilly colossus where passengers report "sinking" experiences with the "mediocre", "expensive" Eclectic fare, "take-it-or-leave-it" service and clientele of "City boys" (and "girls") looking for "a night to remember" ("more cattle market than food market"); still, it's a "fun place", with "celeb-spotting" opportunities to boot; N.B. at press time, Marco Pierre White's involvement was not expected to continue into 2002.

Toast ☽🗒   16 | 16 | 14 | £29

50 Hampstead High St., NW3 (Hampstead), 020-7431 2244;
fax 020-7794 2333

■ In an "odd location" above "Hampstead tube station", this "trendy" eaterie boasting "cool-but-warm decor" and a "good-quality" Modern European menu is only open for dinner during the week, though on weekends neighbourhood denizens find it "great for brunch with the papers scattered around"; otherwise-satisfied surveyors report run-ins with "terrible service."

Toff's
| – | – | – | M |

38 Muswell Hill Broadway, N10 (Highgate), 020-8883 8656;
fax 020-8365 2540

Locals make big claims when it comes to the fish 'n'
chips fried up at this small cafe-cum-takeaway venue, a
Muswell Hill fixture since the '60s: "without a doubt, the
best in London" – or maybe even "the world"; that bold
boast goes uncorroborated, however, because this
modest ("forget the decor") veteran remains largely
unknown to surveyors.

Tokyo Diner ●S
| 16 | 11 | 13 | £17 |

2 Newport Pl., WC2 (Leicester Sq.), 020-7287 8777;
fax 020-7434 1415

☑ The "canteen-type atmosphere" is "a bit studenty", but
nonetheless this Chinatown Japanese endears itself as a
provider of "consistent, fresh sushi" that's "all you need"
for a "quick bite after work"; and whilst a few find it a "bit
disappointing" ("not authentic", "unfriendly" staff), no one
sneers at "cheap prices" and "great [bento] box sets."

Tom's Delicatessen S
| 21 | 15 | 14 | £17 |

226 Westbourne Grove, W11 (Notting Hill Gate),
020-7221 8818; fax 020-7221 7717

■ "Be prepared to queue", as there's a "lack of seating
space" in the cafe part of Tom Conran's "very cool",
all-day Notting Hill "place to be seen", which features
"great" Eclectic fare that's "so good" for "weekend
brunch" with "coffee and the papers"; those who think
it's just "too busy" these days can always make do with
"the deli" for "extra temptations to take away"; N.B. it's
now open evenings.

Tootsies S
| 14 | 11 | 14 | £17 |

120 Holland Park Ave., W11 (Holland Park), 020-7229 8567
35 Haven Green, W5 (Ealing Broadway), 020-8566 8200
148 Chiswick High Rd., W4 (Turnham Green), 020-8747 1869
35 James St., W1 (Bond St.), 020-7486 1611
48 High St., SW19 (Wimbledon), 020-8946 4135
147 Church Rd., SW13 (Hammersmith), 020-8748 3630
107 Old Brompton Rd., SW7 (South Kensington),
020-7581 8942
177 New King's Rd., SW6 (Parsons Green), 020-7736 4023
36-38 Abbeville Rd, SW4 (Clapham South), 020-8772 6646;
fax 020-8772 0672
196-198 Haverstock Hill, NW3 (Belsize Park), 020-7431 3812
Additional locations throughout London

■ "Does what it says on the tin" is the consensus on
the "formula" followed by this established chain of
"fun" American-style diners with "good burgers", "great
salads" and the like, all of which makes "exceptional
hangover food"; the main appeal is as a "great family
place" on weekends, when it gets "very noisy with kids."

Toto's ◐ 🅂   21 | 20 | 20 | £43
*Walton House, Walton St., SW3 (Knightsbridge), 020-7589 2062;
fax 020-7581 9668*
◪ "Elegant in the extreme" gush groupies of this "curiously
uncelebrated" venue in a Chelsea mews that provides
"truly outstanding", "artistically presented" Modern
Italian cooking to a "very glamorous" clientele ("where
the sugar daddies eat"); whilst there are isolated complaints
about "snooty" attitude from the staff, the majority sees it
as an "upbeat", "professionally run" outfit with the added
bonus of "garden tables" (at lunch only).

Trader Vic's ◐ 🅂   17 | 19 | 16 | £35
*Hilton Park Ln., 22 Park Ln., W1 (Hyde Park Corner),
020-7208 4113; fax 020-7208 4050*
■ "Corny to the max, but fun anyway" profess partisans
of this "totally nostalgic" (some say "old hat") "South
Seas"–themed stalwart (since '63) in Mayfair's Hilton
Park Lane hotel known for its "tiki"-style rum drinks and
"reasonable" Polynesian "munchies"; whilst "lackadaisical
service can dampen the mood like a monsoon", for most
this "timeless" "tropical" standby "can do no wrong"
as a "good meeting place."

Trafalgar, The 🅂   – | – | – | E
*The Trafalgar Hotel, 2 Spring Gardens, SW1 (Leicester Sq.),
020-7870 2900*
Hilton's handsome new hotel in Trafalgar Square with
impressive views over London boasts a hip, all-day lobby
bar (Rockwell) with a classic snack menu and over 100
American bourbons, as well as a cool, minimalist dining
room (Jago) with an International menu that errs on the
side of comfort food; the food operations are run in
conjunction with the Zeta team.

Tramp   14 | 16 | 17 | £51
Private club; inquiries: 020-7734 0565
◪ Cutting-edge types might consider this "pumping"
Piccadilly private nightclub slightly "out-of-date now",
but others happily "tuck in" to its "new", "improved"
Traditional British fare, noting that the "welcoming
waiters give great service" (a fact borne out by a rise in
ratings); never mind if those caught up in the "furiously
fast and fun" atmosphere claim it's "not a place for food."

Troubadour, The 🅂⇗   15 | 21 | 19 | £14
*265 Old Brompton Rd., SW5 (Earl's Court), 020-7370 1434;
fax 020-7370 0029*
■ "In the desert of Earl's Court" thrives this "quaint,
eccentric" coffeehouse that feels "like a [Parisian] Left
Bank cafe in the '60s" and is "always packed" with an "odd,
varied clientele" drawn to its "simple, reasonably priced"
Eclectic fare and live jazz, comedy and poetry sessions.

Truc Vert S – | – | – | M
42 N. Audley St., W1 (Bond St.), 020-7497 9988;
fax 020-7491 7717
Named after a French beach, this attractive restaurant-
cum-shop in Mayfair from the Villandry founders is a
bit of a tight squeeze in terms of seating; it's open all day,
offering a daily changing Modern French–Italian menu that
works for a "quick meal" or something more substantial,
and has the added benefit of wines charged at store
price plus £4.50 corkage.

Tuk Tuk Thai S 20 | 12 | 19 | £18
330 Upper St., N1 (Angel), 020-7226 0837
■ "A little more comfort wouldn't go amiss", but otherwise
this "brilliant little place" in Islington is hard to fault, given
its "consistently" "delicious" Thai cuisine packed with
"fresh ingredients and robust flavours"; "sweet, slightly mad
staff" and "seriously cheap" prices add to its appeal.

Turner's 21 | 17 | 19 | £42
87-89 Walton St., SW3 (South Kensington), 020-7584 6711;
fax 020-7584 4441
◪ It's "nice to see a famous chef so involved" in
proceedings (when he's not away on TV duty, that is) at
this "classy", "intimate" Chelsea stalwart owned by "lovely
bloke" Brian Turner, who "turns out fresh, inspired" Classic
French dishes; if sceptics scoff the place is "really nothing
special", citing "so-so service" and slightly "twee"
decor, all agree the "lunch-special menu" for under £18 is
"a terrific bargain."

Tuscan Steak ◑ ▽ 19 | 17 | 14 | £52
St. Martins Lane Hotel, 45 St. Martins Ln., WC2 (Leicester Sq.),
020-7300 5500; fax 020-7300 5501
■ In the space that was Saint M, inside the sleek St.
Martin's Lane Hotel in Theatreland, Ian Schrager introduces
Londoners to his successful Italian steakhouse chain
from Miami and New York, and early reports are positive:
a "high-quality" menu of "sumptuous dishes" designed
for "sharing", which is "expensive, but worth it"; critics
suspect "they've never been to Tuscany."

Tuttons Brasserie ◑ S 16 | 16 | 18 | £24
11-12 Russell St., WC2 (Covent Garden), 020-7836 4141;
fax 020-7379 9979
■ Given its "excellent location" and "good atmosphere"
(including alfresco seating), it's no surprise that this
"fun", easygoing Covent Garden brasserie is a tourist
staple, though it also makes a "safe bet" for locals "when
meeting up casually"; the International food is "nice", if
"no big deal", and the service is plenty "friendly."

Twelfth House S

| – | – | – | E |

35 Pembridge Rd., W11 (Notting Hill), 020-7727 9620;
fax 020-7243 1007

This quirky newcomer to Notting Hill features a small,
heavily mirrored upstairs restaurant where diners can
have their horoscopes or tarot cards read while tucking
into Traditional British fare, as well as a downstairs
cafe and bar.

Twentyfour

▽ | 19 | 21 | 18 | £32 |

Tower 42, Old Broad St., 24th fl., EC2 (Bank/Liverpool St.),
020-7877 2424; fax 020-7877 7788

◪ There's a "stunning view" across London from this
"hip", modern, 24th-floor restaurant (not to be confused
with a champagne bar on the 42nd floor) in Tower 42 on
Old Broad Street; surveyors busy gazing out the window
have little to say when it comes to the "great" Modern
European cooking from caterers Roux Fine Dining and
service that "never lets you down."

Two Brothers Fish

| 23 | 11 | 18 | £20 |

297-303 Regent's Park Rd., N3 (Finchley Central),
020-8346 0469; fax 020-8343 1978

◼ This modestly decorated, "cramped" Finchley venue
comes out "top of the class for fish 'n' chips", hence it's
"always packed" with "diners who come regularly" to
enjoy its "fabulous", "fresh" and "light" fried fare; "unless
you enjoy queuing, go before 7 PM" or make use of the
"fantastic takeaway" service.

Ubon by Nobu

| 23 | 22 | 18 | £50 |

34 Westferry Circus, E14 (Canary Wharf),
020-7719 7800

◪ Canary Wharf's "classy Nobu outpost" "has the potential"
to prosper, according to fans of its "fantastic" Japanese–
South American fusion menu (a "clone" of the Park Lane
original) and "lovely" setting featuring "stunning views
over the curve of the Thames"; whilst a fussy few find it's
"not up to standard yet", the majority calls this "classy"
newcomer simply "heaven" – and best of all, "you can
get a table without booking months ahead."

Union Cafe

| 17 | 14 | 16 | £27 |

96 Marylebone Ln., W1 (Bond St.), 020-7486 4860;
fax 020-7486 4860

◼ "Dead reliable" for "good", "simple" Modern European
cooking and "very nice service", John Brinkley's "bright,
airy brasserie" in Marylebone perhaps shines the brightest
when it comes to its "great" wine selection, which offers
"excellent value for the money"; P.S. regulars note it's
particularly "good for lunch."

Uno ◐ 17 | 15 | 16 | £22

1 Denbigh St., SW1 (Victoria), 020-7834 1001; fax 020-7932 0548

■ It serves "cheap, no-nonsense" Italian fare that's "reliable for quality" ("good pasta, great desserts"), and it happens to be "one of the few contemporary restaurants in Pimlico", so it's no surprise that this bi-level "neighbourhood" spot draws a crowd and "can get very noisy"; there are also "some interesting wines."

Upstairs at The Savoy ◐ 19 | 17 | 20 | £33

Savoy Hotel, The Strand, WC2 (Covent Garden/Embankment), 020-8836 4343; fax 020-7420 2450

■ Looking out over the main entrance of The Strand's Savoy Hotel, this upstairs bar/cafe is well-situated for spying, but it's also "a great little find" for relatively "reasonably priced" seafood with Asian accents (sushi is a specialty), and whilst a few think the kitchen "could be more creative", it remains a "great favourite" for the "perfect after-theatre supper."

Utah [S] 15 | 13 | 13 | £32

18 High St., Wimbledon Village, SW19 (Wimbledon), 020-8944 1909; fax 020-8944 1890

◪ "Lucky Wimbledon" cheer fans of this glass-fronted sib to Montana, Dakota et al., which serves up an extensive range of "good" New American fare; opponents assert it's "disappointing", however, citing merely "everyday eats" ("ostentatious menu descriptions" notwithstanding) and decor that looks "great from the exterior" but rather "minimalist and dull" once inside; P.S. beware "being put by the fire exit."

Vale, The [S] ▽ 20 | 12 | 16 | £26

99 Chippenham Rd., W9 (Maida Vale), 020-7266 0990; fax 020-7286 7224

■ An "ideal neighbourhood option" in Maida Vale, this "charming" Modern British eaterie in a conservatory setting wins friends with "top-quality", "imaginative", "daily changing" menu that's "terrific for the money"; if it's "rather empty" at times and "a bit draughty" in winter, locals confirm it's "certainly good for the area."

Vama ◐[S] 23 | 20 | 18 | £32

438 King's Rd., SW10 (Sloane Sq.), 020-7565 8500; fax 020-7565 8501

◪ "Rising well above the norm for Indian restaurants", this "lovely, romantic" World's Ender employs "fresh, distinct" ingredients and "unusual spices" in its "creative, out-of-the-ordinary" Northwest Indian cuisine, to "spectacular" effect; a less-convinced minority rejoins that it's "good, but not stellar", complaining of "slow-to-serve, quick-to-takeaway" service, but on balance, the ayes have it: "if you don't know Indian food, they'll make you a believer."

Vasco & Piero's Pavilion | 22 | 15 | 21 | £31 |

15 Poland St., W1 (Oxford Circus), 020-7437 8774; fax 020-7437 0467

■ "An informal, everyday place" in Soho, this family-run Italian hosts a "lively clientele" of "media types" who appreciate its "attentive" service and "good standard" of "simple, yet perfectly executed" dishes, mostly from the Umbrian region, which come at "great value" (for the area); if an unimpressed few quibble it's "not memorable", they're outvoted: "a real gem."

Veeraswamy ◐ [S] | 20 | 19 | 19 | £32 |

Victory House, 99 Regent St., W1 (Piccadilly Circus), 020-7734 1401; fax 020-7439 8434

◪ "Not just any old curry house", this "refreshingly different Indian" in "smart", "spacious", vibrantly hued Regent Street premises produces "interesting", "subtle" food that's "always a delight"; whilst a few think this stalwart (since 1926) is "a bit touristy" and has "lost its charm" since a "revamp" three years ago, the "smooth, considerate service" wins over all but the most curmudgeonly.

Vegia Zena [S] | 18 | 13 | 16 | £27 |

17 Princess Rd., NW1 (Camden Town/Chalk Farm), 020-7483 0192; fax 020-7483 0192

◪ A "great eating hideaway" that's a "well-kept secret in Primrose Hill", this "non-pretentious" Italian cooks up "authentic" classics ("Genovese" in spirit) that are brought to table by "warm" staff; disgruntled diners maintain it "sometimes gets it wrong" ("food a bit heavy"), but they're soundly outvoted by those who applaud this "jewel" and its "excellent value."

Verbanella ◐ [S] | 15 | 14 | 16 | £29 |

30 Beauchamp Pl., SW3 (Knightsbridge), 020-7584 1107; fax 020-7589 9662

■ It's "a bit old-fashioned" and "somewhat cramped", but this Italian "neighbourhood standby" in Beauchamp Place is "worth a look" for "reasonably priced", "well-thought-out" pastas and other "traditional" dishes delivered with "friendly, personalised service" (though its ratings are down since the last *Survey*); check out the "pretty good set lunch" menu at £12.50.

Vic Naylor ◐ | 17 | 16 | 16 | £27 |

38-42 St. John St., EC1 (Farringdon), 020-7608 2181; fax 020-7251 2697

■ There's a "good crowd and atmosphere" at this easy-going Smithfield gastro-pub, a popular source for "large portions" of "quality" British-Eclectic fare (including some of the "best sausage and mash in town"); what's more, film buffs consider it much "improved by association" after being featured in "*Lock Stock and Two Smoking Barrels*"; N.B. it recently expanded to include a separate rotisserie bar.

Viet Hoa ◐ [S] 21 | 6 | 12 | £16

70-72 Kingsland Rd., E2 (Old St.), 020-7729 8293; fax 020-7729 8293

■ "Above and beyond anything you'll ever get close to" for Vietnamese food in London, this "unique" canteen is definitely "worth the detour" to Shoreditch for "scrumptious", "authentic" and "fresh" cooking (most notably "fabulous pho" noodle soups); as for the "bleak", "spartan" interior, however, harsher critics call it downright "embarrassing" ("dingiest dive I've been to"), but that doesn't deter the "crowds" that fill this place regularly.

Villandry [S] 20 | 15 | 15 | £30

170 Great Portland St., W1 (Great Portland St.), 020-7631 3131; fax 020-7631 3030

◪ Those who "love the whole thing – store, bar, restaurant" – at this "classy" all-day venture on Great Portland Street single out the "quality produce that percolates through" its "imaginative", daily changing Modern British menu "that has real sparkle"; those who think it "could be better" bristle at the "disdainful" service and "outrageous prices"; N.B. the bar added last year is a popular destination.

Vine, The [S] ▽ 18 | 15 | 15 | £26

86 Highgate Rd., NW5 (Kentish Town B.R.), 020-7209 0038; fax 020-7209 3161

◪ "Utterly perfect for a relaxed lunch with friends", this laid-back, child-friendly gastro-pub in Kentish Town is well-loved by locals for its "zingy, fresh" Modern British–European fare; if a few carpers are slightly "disappointed", even they concede that the bartender's "homemade raspberry martinis are to die for!"; N.B. terrace tables prove very popular, even in winter, when they're covered.

Vingt-Quatre ◐ [S] 13 | 11 | 13 | £19

325 Fulham Rd., SW10 (South Kensington), 020-7376 7224

■ This "small", narrow Chelsea eaterie (recently refurbished) is open "around the clock" and serves Eclectic fare that most characterise as merely "simple and dependable", though "late-night desperados" "drunk and starving at 3 AM" think it "tastes like heaven"; it attracts a "good mix of people", ensuring the place is "always fun."

VONG ◐ [S] 23 | 21 | 20 | £46

Berkeley Hotel, Wilton Pl., SW1 (Hyde Park Corner), 020-7235 1010; fax 020-7235 1011

◪ "Fabulousness, but at a price" is the verdict on this "sophisticated" eaterie in Hyde Park Corner's Berkeley Hotel, where the legendary Jean-Georges Vongerichten's "imaginative", "beautifully presented" French-Thai fusion cuisine is deemed "extraordinary", the "stylish" setting "elegant" and the service "engaging"; still, a minority finds this "showy", "extremely pricey" "top" spot "a bit of a letdown", suggesting it's "time to re-boot the menu."

Voodoo Lounge ◐   12   16   13   £30

7-9 Cranbourn St., WC2 (Leicester Sq.), 020-7287 7773;
fax 020-7287 7774

■ This "fun" Leicester Square "hot spot" is more of a
nightclub than a restaurant, meaning that even though
it offers a menu of "average", "very filling" Eclectic
eats served "efficiently", most of its patrons are more
interested in its "great drinks and cocktails", not to
mention the "amazing cigar room."

Vrisaki   ∇   24   8   17   £23

73 Myddelton Rd., N22 (Bounds Green/Wood Green),
020-8889 8760; fax 020-8889 0103

■ "Utterly reliable", but "too busy for its own good" declare
diners enamoured with this Wood Green "traditional
Greek tavern" and its "excellent", "great-value" fare
(including "loads" of mezze) , which just "doesn't stop"
being served by "friendly" waiters to "more people in a
small space than ever witnessed"; a tip: "starve yourself
the whole day" before you visit.

WAGAMAMA S   18   14   16   £16

1 Tavistock St., WC2 (Charing Cross/Covent Garden),
020-7836 3330; fax 020-7240 8846
4A Streatham St., WC1 (Tottenham Court Rd.),
020-7323 9223; fax 020-7323 9224
26A Kensington High St., W8 (High St. Kensington),
020-7376 1717; fax 020-7376 1552
10A Lexington St., W1 (Piccadilly Circus), 020-7292 0990;
fax 020-7734 1815
101A Wigmore St., W1 (Bond St./Marble Arch),
020-7409 0111; fax 020-7409 0088
Harvey Nichols, 109-125 Knightsbridge, SW1
(Knightsbridge), 020-7201 8000; fax 020-7201 8080
11 Jamestown Rd., NW1 (Camden Town), 020-7428 0800;
fax 020-7482 4887

■ "Still the best budget noodle house around" for a
"cheap, quick" meal of "consistently good", "healthy"
Japanese fare, this "noodle-heaven" chain follows a
"great formula that really works"; keep in mind, though,
the "long, shared trestle tables are not places to linger":
expect to "queue" for a table and then "be rushed out";
P.S. it's "fun for kids" too.

Wakaba   ∇   21   14   17   £38

122A Finchley Rd., NW3 (Finchley Rd.), 020-7586 7960;
fax 020-7586 7960

■ Mr. Wakaba's minimalist, dinner-only Japanese in
Finchley successfully concentrates on preparing quite
"good" sushi and sashimi, and even though it may be
"very expensive" for some budgets, the fact that it's been
going strong since 1979 suggests a loyal following.

Wapping Food S ▽ 21 | 18 | 16 | £31

Wapping Hydraulic Power, Wapping Wall, E1 (Wapping),
020-7680 2080; fax 020-7680 2081

◪ Previously it was a hydraulic power station, but now
this "airy" space (with "all the machinery in place")
hosts a new "marvellously atmospheric" eaterie proffering
most "pleasant" Modern British fare from a daily changing
menu, along with an "excellent wine list"; all in all, it's a
"great addition to the culinary wilderness" of Wapping.

Waterloo Fire Station S 14 | 12 | 11 | £23

150 Waterloo Rd., SE1 (Waterloo), 020-7620 2226;
fax 020-7633 9161

◪ It's usually "a riot" at this "loud, lively" gastro-pub in a
converted fire station near Waterloo that's "becoming a
bit down at the heel"; whilst its raison d'être is not the
"consistent" Modern British fare, it's considered "one of
the best places" in the area for "grub in a gang."

Waterstones, Red Room 18 | 15 | 18 | £28

Waterstones, 203-206 Piccadilly, W1 (Piccadilly Circus),
020-7851 2464; fax 020-7851 2469

◼ "Shame it's not better supported" lament lovers of this
in-store eaterie "discreetly tucked away in the basement"
of Piccadilly's Waterstones bookstore, a "sufficiently
stylish" venue for "good-value" Modern British dining; N.B.
there's a bar and other eating options throughout the store.

Waxy O'Connor's Pub S 12 | 15 | 11 | £16

14-16 Rupert St., W1 (Piccadilly Circus), 020-7287 0255;
fax 020-7287 3962

◼ "The Disneyworld of Irish bars", this "buzzing", "noisy"
pub "well-situated" near Piccadilly Circus features a
labyrinth of theme rooms and proves popular with both
"tourists" and the pint-"after-work" crowd; even if the
traditional fare ("good oysters", a "fresh crock of mussels")
is "cheap", purists sniff it's "utterly inauthentic."

Well & Aquarium Bar, The S – | – | – | M

180 St. John St., EC1 (Farringdon), 020-7251 9363;
fax 020-7251 6611

A newcomer to Clerkenwell, this casual gastro-pub serves
Modern European fare from an open kitchen, while a
downstairs bar features wall-mounted tanks of tropical
fish; one major plus point is its pavement seating in summer.

Westbourne, The S 17 | 15 | 12 | £20

101 Westbourne Park Villas, W2 (Royal Oak/Westbourne Park),
020-7221 1332; fax 020-7243 8081

◼ "Getting a table can be difficult" at this "great gastro-
pub" in Westbourne Park, a local "surprise fave" on account
of its "cool atmosphere" and "good" Eclectic "pub grub"
at "wow prices" – but beware, "they often run out of dishes
fairly early"; in sum, it's a "hectic, very social spot."

White House, The ◐ [S] – | – | – | M

65 Clapham Park Rd., SW4 (Clapham Common), 020-7498 3388; fax 020-7498 5588

This white-fronted, impressive-looking, three-storey Victorian building in Clapham, which opened mid-*Survey*, features a casual restaurant/bar serving all-day International fare in tapas-style portions, as well as a members-only lounge, a roof terrace and three private dining rooms.

White Onion [S] 20 | 16 | 17 | £35

297 Upper St., N1 (Angel), 020-7359 3533; fax 020-7359 3533

◪ "Love it!" enthuse those enamoured of the "consistently excellent" French-Med cooking and "accommodating" staff at this "relaxing", high-ceilinged Islingtonian that even appeals to some as a "grand-occasion" option; vocal detractors who express "disappointment" (especially "in view of its great sisters, Purple Sage, Green Olive" et al.) particularly deride the "meagre portions", urging "more food, less pomp."

Wilton's [S] 21 | 20 | 22 | £52

55 Jermyn St., SW1 (Green Park/Piccadilly Circus), 020-7629 9955; fax 020-7495 6233

◪ "More like a club than a restaurant" approve admirers of this "formal", 270-year-old St. James's veteran replete with "old-world comforts", "impeccable service" and "wonderfully simple" Traditional British dishes (notably seafood and game); if some sceptics snipe the place "has grown slack", citing "indifferent food" and "staff spread thin" (a charge not borne out by ratings), their gripes fall on deaf ears amongst those who think this "classic" makes for "the perfect dining experience."

Windows on the World [S] 19 | 23 | 20 | £48

Hilton Park Lane, 22 Park Ln., W1 (Hyde Park Corner), 020-7208 4021; fax 020-7208 4144

■ "Breathtaking views of London" are the highlight of this 28th-floor bar/restaurant atop Mayfair's Hilton, where admirers report leaving "absolutely stuffed" with quite "good" Classic French fare served by "pleasant", "old-fashioned" staff; this retro spot is "neat for entertaining overseas visitors" seeking a "superb", "panoramic" view of town, though the less-enthused suggest it "could improve the food"; P.S. there's also "lovely dancing" on weekends.

Wine Factory 15 | 16 | 16 | £19

294 Westbourne Grove, W11 (Notting Hill Gate), 020-7229 1877

■ The "reasonable, simple" Modern Italian–Eclectic food (including "nice pizzas") gives diners "a good excuse for drinking" from the "good", "extensive and extremely cheap" selection of vinos proffered by this Notting Hill eaterie, where even though the menu is "a serious bargain" and the "staff friendly", most agree "it's really the wine list that brings" people in.

Wine Gallery S
13 | 13 | 15 | £21

49 Hollywood Rd., SW10 (Earl's Court), 020-7352 7572;
fax 020-7376 5083

■ In addition to a "mega-cool back garden", other virtues of this "mellow" Chelsea neighbourhood haunt include the "decent", "cheap" Modern British fare (though its food rating has slipped a bit since the last *Survey*) and an extensive selection of "good wine at reasonable prices"; overall it's a "splendid" choice "for a group or quiet dinner" – or somewhere "to get sloshed and enjoy good nosh."

Wine Library, The
▽ 14 | 12 | 15 | £29

43 Trinity Sq., EC3 (Tower Hill), 020-7481 0415;
fax 020-7488 3333

■ "There's no point going if you want to do any work in the afternoon", as this City venue in a former skittles alley is like "Disneyland for wine lovers", with a "great-value", 600-strong wine list (priced at retail plus £4 corkage) and an "accompanying buffet" of cheese, pâtés and other French nibbles deemed "just right to show off the wines"; N.B. it's now open for dinner until 8 PM.

Wiz S
18 | 18 | 18 | £32

123A Clarendon Rd., W1 (Holland Park), 020-7229 1500;
fax 020-7229 8889

◪ "Anthony Worrall Thompson presents a spin on traditional tapas" at his "fun" Notting Hill "concept for hip folks" proffering Eclectic small plates from "around the world" ("variety deserves kudos"); if a befuddled few find the menu "confusing" and "not exceptionally well-executed", they're outnumbered by enthusiasts of this "interesting, if cramped", bi-level venue, which makes an "awesome place for a group."

Wòdka ●S
18 | 14 | 17 | £29

12 St. Albans Grove, W8 (High St. Kensington),
020-7937 6513; fax 020-7937 8621

■ "Get ready to drink when coming" to this Kensington Eastern European, because as the name implies, it's known for its "unbelievable vodka selection, served ice cold"; whilst a handful report "less-than-memorable" fare ("wonderful pierogi" notwithstanding), boozers consider the Polish menu of "great home cooking" quite effective for soaking up the "assorted flavours" of firewater; P.S. "supermodel waitresses" are icing on the cake.

Wok Wok
15 | 13 | 14 | £19

7 Kensington High St., W8 (High St. Kensington),
020-7938 1221; fax 020-7938 3330 S
270 Chiswick High Rd., W4 (Chiswick), 020-8995 2100;
fax 020-8994 5697 S
10 Frith St., W1 (Leicester Sq.), 020-7437 7080;
fax 020-7437 3121 S

(continued)
Wok Wok
51-53 Northcote Rd., SW11 (Clapham Junction B.R.),
020-7978 7181; fax 020-7924 7329 S
140 Fulham Rd., SW10 (South Kensington/Fulham Broadway),
020-7370 5355; fax 020-7244 0600 S
Harrods, 87-135 Brompton Rd., SW1 (Knightsbridge),
020-7225 5951
67 Upper St., N1 (Angel/Highbury & Islington),
020-7288 0333; fax 020-7288 0284 S
30 Hill St., Richmond, W9 (Richmond), 020-8332 2646;
fax 020-8332 9171 S

☑ "Cheerful Asian food that doesn't break the bank" sums
up the appeal of this "funky" noodle-bar chain, which many
swear by for an "easy" meal or "when famished after the
cinema"; consider it "Asia's answer to Pizza Express",
even if a few sticklers suggest they could "do better."

Wolfe's Bar & Grill ● S | 15 | 11 | 16 | £29 |
30 Great Queen St., WC2 (Covent Garden/Holborn),
020-7831 4442; fax 020-7831 3769

☑ This Covent Garden stalwart receives polite notices as
a "useful" option (especially pre- or post-theatre) for "ok",
"reasonably priced" International fare, occasional problems
with service aside; nostalgics who find it "unremarkable"
and even "dull" insist it's "not the same as it used to be."

Wong Kei ● S ⊅ | 11 | – | 3 | £13 |
41-43 Wardour St., W1 (Leicester Sq./Piccadilly Circus),
020-7437 8408

■ "Insults come free of charge" and "add to the hilarity"
of this "bizarre" Chinatown eaterie that attracts "sado-
masochist diners" unfazed by the "world's surliest waiters";
if the "average Chinese food" is "disappointing", at
least it comes "cheap" and "fast"; N.B. a much-needed
refurbishment was completed post-*Survey.*

Woody's ● | ▽ | 15 | 15 | 13 | £31 |
41-43 Woodfield Rd., W9 (Westbourne Park), 020-7266 3030;
fax 020-7286 7070

☑ This comfortable, laid-back venue near the Westbourne
Park bus garage is "a restaurant/bar/disco combo": there's a
basement dance club, "great bar" on the ground floor and
first-floor restaurant with a relatively "high standard" of
American-Eclectic cooking.

World Food Café | ▽ | 17 | 11 | 13 | £15 |
14 Neal's Yard, 1st fl., WC2 (Covent Garden), 020-7379 0298;
fax 020-8992 0278

■ Globe-trotting cookbook authors Carolyn and Chris
Caldicott are the owners of this second-floor Covent Garden
space overlooking Neal's Yard, where "generous portions of
exotic" Vegetarian-Eclectic food find a devoted following; all
in all, it's a "peaceful" place for feeling "very healthy."

Yas ☽🅂 19 10 15 £20
7 Hammersmith Rd., W14 (Olympia), 020-7603 9148

■ "Yes for Yas" cheer fans of this small, 25-year-old BYO (and licensed) eaterie near Olympia serving "good, sophisticated" Persian fare that's "always delicious" and available "any time of the night", thanks to a 5 AM license; "drop in at 3 AM for starters, bread and tea."

Yatra ☽ 17 15 16 £33
34 Dover St., W1 (Green Park), 020-7493 0200; fax 020-7493 4228

☑ "Is it Indian, is it Thai?" – well, it's both at this "well-decorated", "cross-cultural" Pan-Asian eaterie in Mayfair that satisfies a wide audience with its "innovative, delicious" cooking and "good service"; "altogether a nice place" concludes the majority, which considers this an "interesting new" option for the area, even if a less-convinced few shrug "not worth the effort."

Yellow River Cafe 13 12 13 £22
12 Chiswick High Rd., W4 (Stamford Brook), 020-8987 9791 🅂
7 St. John's Wood High St., NW8 (St. John's Wood), 020-7586 4455 🅂
206 Upper St., N1 (Highbury & Islington), 020-7354 8833 🅂
10 Cabot Sq., E14 (Canary Wharf), 020-7715 9515; fax 020-7715 9528

☑ This expanding chain (owned by Shimla Pinks et al.) provokes conflicting views: to fans, it's a "reliable" option with a "well-thought-out" Pan-Asian menu that's "easy on the purse" (notably the lunch boxes), but foes find it has "more style than substance", lamenting "formulaic food" and "stern service"; either way, the involvement of "a chef of Ken Hom's stature" is an auspicious sign.

Ye Olde Cheshire Cheese 13 23 14 £21
145 Fleet St., EC4 (Blackfriars), 020-7353 6170; fax 020-7353 0845

■ "Take a step back in time" for a "taste of olde England" at this Fleet Street veteran that dates back to the 17th century; even though the consensus is that its traditional pub "food could be better" ("forgettable", "not so great"), the "unique atmosphere" – including its share of "smoke and blokes" – and "friendly staff more than compensate."

Yoshino ▽ 22 14 19 £26
3 Piccadilly Pl., W1 (Piccadilly Circus), 020-7287 6622; fax 020-7254 6751

■ "Tucked away" in an alleyway near Piccadilly, this diminutive, "delightfully authentic jewel" is usually "filled with Japanese" diners ("a good sign"), who seek out its "excellent-quality" cuisine and "wide range of sake"; "shhh! don't tell anyone" plead regulars; P.S. there are also "fantastic set meals" from £5.80 at lunch.

Yo! Sushi S
| 16 | 14 | 14 | £21 |

11-13 Bayley St., WC1 (Goodge St./Tottenham Court Rd.),
020-7636 0076
52 Poland St., W1 (Oxford Circus), 020-7287 0443 ◗
Selfridges, 400 Oxford St., W1 (Bond St.), 020-7318 3944;
fax 020-7318 3885
Harvey Nichols, Knightsbridge, 5th fl., SW1 (Knightsbridge),
020-7201 8641
O₂ Ctr., 255 Finchley Rd., NW3 (Finchley Rd.),
020-7431 4499
95 Farringdon Rd., EC1 (Farringdon), 020-7841 0785
☑ "Good, quick, fun" food when "time is short" is what
this "gimmicky" chain – dubbed the "McDonald's of
sushi" – is all about; and if the "novelty has worn off" for
some who cite "sky-high prices", "measly portions" and
"too-manufactured" edibles, even they can't deny the
appeal of the "cool conveyor belts" and robotic drinks
trolleys at this "great-for-children" "gadget heaven."

Yum Yum Thai S
▽ | 22 | 16 | 20 | £22 |

30 Stoke Newington Church St., N16 (Seven Sisters),
020-7254 6751; fax 020-7241 3857
■ "Everyone in Stokey loves this bustling, friendly Thai"
where loyalists proclaim they "could eat every night" on
account of its "delightful", "beautifully prepared" food –
"a sweet melody from the gods!" – at "reasonable prices",
and even if the "decor's a bit OTT, who cares?"; P.S.
"booking is essential at weekends."

ZAFFERANO S
| 25 | 19 | 21 | £47 |

15 Lowndes St., SW1 (Knightsbridge), 020-7235 5800
☑ Star chef Giorgio Locatelli "has gone" from the kitchen,
but this "chic", "secluded Belgravia" hot spot isn't suffering
for his absence: acolytes assert it's "still one of the best"
thanks to its "sophisticated", "spectaculous" Modern
Italian feats of pure "gastronomic delight", "excellent wine
list" and "gracious" service (not to mention "beautiful
people" clientele); a "disappointed" contingent claims
this "most perfect" place has "lost some of its magic",
though even critics can't deny its continued popularity –
it's "impossible to get in!"

ZAIKA S
| 25 | – | 21 | £38 |

1 Kensington High St., W8 (High St. Kensington),
020-7795 6533; fax 020-7937 8854
■ "An innovative modern approach to Indian cuisine"
distinguishes this "super-civilised" venue from Claudio Pulze
and chef Vineet Bhatia, which is voted the "best Indian in
London" ("on the planet"?) thanks to its "elegant, exciting"
and "artfully prepared" cuisine that "tastes as beautiful
as it looks"; N.B. it relocated post-*Survey* to Kensington.

Zaika Bazaar – – – E
2A Pond Pl., SW3 (South Kensington), 020-7584 6655;
fax 020-7584 6755

After the closure of El Rincon by top restaurateur Claudio
Pulze, his new venture on this tricky site builds on the
runaway success of Zaika, offering a straightforward
menu of simple Indian street food amid bright, soothing
settings resplendent with artefacts and colourful drapes
(all of which are for sale); there's also a big bar area
with comfortable seating.

Zamoyski S 18 11 18 £22
85 Fleet Rd., NW3 (Belsize Park), 020-7794 4792

■ It's "cramped" and can get "very, very noisy" (thanks to
the live Russian folk music), but this "charming" Belsize
Park "local restaurant" is a "fun" spot for "quaint, if
rather heavy", Polish–Eastern European "home cooking"
with a "frightening array of vodkas" to wash it down.

Zen Central ● S 18 15 17 £37
20 Queen St., W1 (Green Park), 020-7629 8089;
fax 020-7493 6181

◪ A "great all-rounder" assert supporters of this "calm,
understated" Mayfair sib of the Zen group boasting a
"good" atmosphere, "solid" Chinese cooking and
"reasonable service"; even if some rate the minimalist-
white room a bit "cold" ("'80s decor needs a touch-up")
and the menu "overpriced", all appreciate being able to
"get a table at the last minute."

Zen Chelsea ● S 20 16 17 £37
Chelsea Cloisters, 85 Sloane Ave., SW3 (South Kensington),
020-7589 1781; fax 020-7584 0596

◪ "I'd go more if it were less expensive" claim budget-
minded boosters of the Zen group's original venue, but "bar
the price", surveyors extol the "exquisite", "upscale"
Chinese fare ("superb lobster noodles") cooked up on this
Chelsea stalwart's stove; maybe it's "lost the buzz" it once
had, but it still rates as a local "favourite", particularly
for "special occasions."

Zen Garden ● S 20 17 18 £38
15-16 Berkeley St., W1 (Green Park), 020-7493 1381;
fax 020-7491 2655

■ "Tables are nicely spaced to allow quiet conversation"
at this "elegant", business-orientated Zen outpost in
Mayfair that's widely appreciated for its "varied and
excellent selection" of Cantonese cooking (including dim
sum) and "prompt service"; there's also a "great back
room for a party" (in fact, three rooms); P.S. ask about the
"dishes not listed on the menu."

ZeNW3 🖪 18 | 15 | 17 | £33
83-84 Hampstead High St., NW3 (Hampstead),
020-7794 7863; fax 020-7794 6956
■ "Once a trendsetter", this "lively" (if now somewhat "dated"-looking) Hampstead member of the Zen gang is still much appreciated for its "long, interesting and innovative menu" of "delicious" Chinese dishes "seasoned just right" ("so light and crispy") and boosted by "friendly service"; "a bit pricey" but "worth it" is the general conclusion.

Zeta ◑🖪 ▽ 15 | 19 | 15 | £33
35 Hertford St., W1 (Green Park/Hyde Park Corner),
020-7208 4067; fax 020-7208 4068
■ "Don't go for a quiet chat" to this "classy", "people-watching" venue next to the Hilton Hotel, because it's "crowded and noisy" at night thanks to the live bands, DJs and 3 AM license (most nights); it offers "nice" Asian–Pacific Rim "bar snacks" in the evenings, whilst on offer at lunch are 'liquid lunches' – fruit and vegetable juices, that is; N.B. a new sibling, Steam, is planned for Paddington in the autumn.

Ziani ◑🖪 20 | 15 | 17 | £35
45 Radnor Walk, SW3 (Sloane Sq.), 020-7351 5297;
fax 020-7244 8387
■ This "noisy, friendly" Chelsea Italian with "tightly packed" tables and "waiters [singing] opera" gives diners "a shot of adrenaline" along with their "good, solid" meals (pastas and other classic dishes); for most, "lively" experiences here are "always fun", though a few sensitive sorts find the "overcrowded" conditions and sometimes-"rushed" service hard to overlook.

Zilli ◑🖪 18 | 14 | 16 | £31
210 Kensington Park Rd., W11 (Ladbroke Grove),
020-7792 1066; fax 020-7734 7786
☒ Mixed reviews abound for this new Notting Hill offshoot of Zilli Fish: boosters proclaim it on a par with the original, thanks to "very good" Modern Italian seafood fare and "chirpy" staff; dissenters counter that, relatively speaking, it's "a real disappointment", with "absolutely no space to breathe" (that being the case, consider dining outside in warm weather).

Zilli Fish ◑ 20 | 15 | 16 | £33
36-40 Brewer St., W1 (Piccadilly Circus), 020-7734 8649;
fax 020-7734 7786
☒ Like all Zilli establishments, this "frenetic", "hip" Italian seafooder in Soho is "cramped" and "noisy", nonetheless, most praise the "great fish served with gusto", as well as the "must-try lobster spaghettini"; keep it in mind as a "place to start a night out", especially in summer, when "they open the [front] windows" so diners "can see the world pass by."

Zinc Bar & Grill 🌙 — 14 | 14 | 14 | £30

21 Heddon St., W1 (Oxford Circus/Piccadilly Circus), 020-7255 8899; fax 020-7255 8888

◪ "Usefully placed off Regent Street", this Conran-owned Modern European brasserie with Pacific Rim influences receives middling ratings and has its share of critics ("variable food", "functional surroundings"), but it does get some respect as a "nice place to meet with friends" and dine from a versatile menu (including prix fixe options) that "caters to different price levels."

Zizzi [S] — – | – | – | M

87 Allitsen Rd., NW8 (St. John's Wood), 020-7722 7296
231 Chiswick High Rd., W4 (Chiswick), no phone
20 Bow St., WC2 (Holborn), 020-7836 6101
35-37 Battersea Rd., SW11 (Clapham South), 020-7924 7311 🌙
35-38 Paddington St., W1 (Baker St.), 020-7224 1450 🌙
73-75 The Strand, WC2 (Charing Cross), 020-7240 1717; fax 020-7379 9753 🌙

This new, expanding pizza-and-pasta chain around town earns praise for its "fun", "friendly" approach and "fast, filling" Italian fare that's "always good value" – "great eat after eat" gush groupies; "tolerant staff" ensure they make an "excellent venue for children."

Zucca [S] — 18 | 15 | 16 | £28

188 Westbourne Grove, W11 (Notting Hill Gate), 020-7727 0060; fax 020-7726 0069

◪ "People-watching opportunities abound" at this "quality" Notting Hill Italian whose "stylish, minimalist decor" is complemented by a "limited", but "well-executed", list of offerings that range from pizzas and pastas to wood-roasted fish and meat; truth be told, regulars might even call it "excellent – if it had lower prices."

Zuccato 🌙 [S] — 18 | 17 | 17 | £23

O_2 Ctr., 255 Finchley Rd., NW3 (Finchley Rd.), 020-7431 1799; fax 020-7431 7198

◪ "A good choice for O_2 Centre" dining ("before or after the movies") declare boosters of this "fun, quick" Finchley Road coffee bar/Italian, which sports a retro '50s look, "value" menu and "friendly service"; N.B. the occasional live music performances have been discontinued.

Zuccato City — – | – | – | M

41 Bow Ln., EC4 (Mansion House), 020-7329 6364; fax 020-7329 6336

This Zuccato offshoot opened at press time in an attractive, terraced City location boasting a trendy ground-floor bar and downstairs trattoria serving Modern Italian fare and specialising in pizzas; dining in the secluded courtyard is restricted to lunchtime, but drinks can be taken outside in the evening.

F	D	S	C

AMBERLEY CASTLE, QUEENS ROOM [S] 20 | 27 | 21 | £40

Amberley Castle, Amberley, West Sussex, 01798 831998; fax 01798 831992

■ "So spectacular, you feel like royalty" gush admirers awestruck by the "medieval setting" of this 900-year-old Norman castle in Sussex (complete with battlements, portcullis and dry moat); whilst the "lovely" Eclectic cooking in the "beautiful dining room" doesn't quite rise to the level of the "wonderful" surroundings, the "incredible-value" set lunch at £15 (£45 for dinner) wins bravos – as does the "great style and skill" of "superb" servers.

Auberge du Lac [S] 22 | 21 | 20 | £46

Auberge du Lac, Brocket Hall, Welwyn, Hertfordshire, 01707 368888; fax 01707 368898

■ "A treat for those of us who live in the sticks!" (and also "worth leaving London for"), this "magnificent", 17th-century lakeside hunting lodge on the Brocket Hall estate in Hertfordshire boasts a "lovely" conservatory dining room with an "enjoyable atmosphere" and "superb" Modern French–European cooking (with Asian influences) that's "perfected by a fabulous wine list" with over 300 different bins.

Bear Hotel, The [S] 17 | 20 | 18 | £37

The Bear Hotel, Park St., Woodstock, Oxfordshire, 08704 008202; fax 01993 813380

◪ A 13th-century Oxfordshire former coaching inn is the "interesting location" (stone walls, exposed beams, etc.) of this "lovely restaurant" serving "good" Modern British–Classic French fare, including an "excellent Sunday lunch" for "parents to treat" their families; that said, critics think the "cooking never matches the reputation" it had before the "Granada takeover" (now part of Heritage Hotels), although ratings have hardly moved.

Beetle & Wedge [S] 23 | 20 | 21 | £40

Beetle & Wedge Hotel, Ferry Ln., Moulsford-on-Thames, Oxfordshire, 01491 651381; fax 01491 651376

■ "No need to beetle about, just linger and enjoy" this "wonderful riverside location" in an Oxfordshire boathouse with two eating options – the "comfy" boathouse itself and the more formal conservatory dining room – both offering similar, "fabulous" Anglo-French cuisine; it's deemed "very good all round" and particularly "a gem on a summer's day."

Bishopstrow House,   22 | 23 | 21 | £43
Mulberry Restaurant S
Bishopstrow House Hotel, Boreham Rd., Warminster,
Wiltshire, 01985 212312; fax 01985 216767
☑ Set in an elegant, creeper-clad Georgian country
house in a "quaint country town" in Wiltshire, this dining
room in the Bishopstrow House Hotel is the backdrop for
chef Chris Suter's "notable", "interesting" Modern British
cooking, which garners high marks but little comment
from surveyors; N.B. lighter meals are available in the bar
and in a conservatory overlooking expansive gardens.

Buckland Manor S   ∇ 23 | 23 | 24 | £51
Buckland Manor, Buckland, Broadway, Gloucestershire,
01386 852626; fax 01386 853557
☑ "A lovely experience in every way" gush groupies of this
"graceful" Cotswold country-house hotel (dating back to the
13th century) distinguished by handsome gardens; its light,
spacious dining room produces Traditional British cuisine
that's "pure pleasure" and served by an exceptionally
"attentive" staff; P.S. it's "great for Sunday lunch."

Chapter One Restaurant S   ∇ 21 | 16 | 17 | £43
Farnborough Common, Locksbottom, Kent, 01689 854848;
fax 01689 858439
☑ Mixed reports are tabled about this casual, understated
bar/brasserie in Kent: supporters tout it as somewhere
for "a great evening out", citing "beautifully presented"
Modern European cooking and "good service", but
others fondly recall "when it was the Fantail" Restaurant
(for 60 years, until 1996) and find this later incarnation
"expensive and noisy."

Charlton House,   ∇ 21 | 24 | 19 | £39
Mulberry Restaurant S
Charlton House, Shepton Mallet, near Bath, 01749 342008;
fax 01749 346362
■ It's not surprising that the "beautiful decor" at this
"very smart" country-house hotel in Somerset is all
Mulberry-designed, as the place was taken over by the
Mulberry founders five years ago; it features a small,
intimate dining room providing Modern British–Eclectic
dining "experiences" that devotees describe as "simply
perfect – and even better, [it's] not in London."

Cherwell Boathouse S   19 | 16 | 20 | £32
Bardwell Rd., Oxford, Oxfordshire, 01865 552746;
fax 01865 553809
☑ Although there's a sense this "lovely" riverside
boathouse on a stretch of the Thames in Oxfordshire
"has seen better days" (a winter refurb is planned), many
appreciate it as a "wonderful spot" for "imaginative"
Modern British cooking that makes people "feel good
about" life; overall, it's a handy "Oxford standby."

CHEWTON GLEN HOTEL, MARRYAT RESTAURANT [S] 25 | 23 | 26 | £55

Chewton Glen Hotel, Christchurch Rd., Chewton Glen, New Milton, Hampshire, 01425 275341; fax 01425 272310

■ "It's a privilege to eat here, and an even greater privilege to stay" at this "picturesque" country-house hotel in the New Forest, where "everything's run with military precision", including the "quiet", "formal" dining room that's home to "simply divine" British-French cooking that "exceeds expectations"; admirers are adamant this "gem" is "definitely worth the journey" (and the "expense"): "am I going back? – absolutely!"

CLIVEDEN HOTEL, WALDO'S 21 | 24 | 22 | £56

Cliveden Hotel, Taplow, Berkshire, 01628 607166; fax 01628 607166

◪ There's a "long leafy drive through the grounds" before arriving at this "really impressive" country-house hotel in Berkshire boasting a "pretty" basement dining room/bar that's "always a delight" to admirers of "very good" New French–Asian cooking and "impeccable" service; that said, dissenters deem the "food a little disappointing" and jest about "pompous staff" and "naff wallpaper", but on balance, the ayes have it: "worth saving up!"; N.B. there's a second, unrated eaterie overlooking the gardens.

Compleat Angler, Riverside Restaurant [S] 17 | 19 | 17 | £46

Compleat Angler, Marlow Bridge, Buckinghamshire, 01628 484444

◪ This "lovely spot" in Buckinghamshire, which makes a "blissful setting" on "a sunny afternoon", is a "very relaxing" place where supporters single out "fantastic cooking", "faultless service" and a "great ambience"; detractors are less upbeat, however, suggesting this Granada Heritage hotel suffers from "bland", "hit-or-miss" Modern British–Med cooking and also "needs smartening up."

Dining Room, The 24 | 17 | 20 | £35

59A High St., Reigate, Surrey, 01737 226650; fax 01737 226650 [S]

65 The Broadway, Haywards Heath, West Sussex, 01444 417755; fax 01444 417755

◪ It's a little "cramped" and could do "with comfy chairs", but TV chef "Tony Tobin's flair really shines" at this eaterie in Reigate with "first-class", "consistent" Modern British cooking and "knowledgeable young staff"; a minority dismisses it as "nothing special", but most credit it with being an "excellent find" in an "area with little to choose from"; N.B. Sussex "locals" will be pleased by the recent opening of a second location in Haywards Heath.

Eastwell Manor [S] 18 19 17 £44

Eastwell Manor Hotel, Eastwell Park, Ashford, Kent, 01233 213000; fax 01233 635530

◪ An "extraordinary experience" gush fans of this "gorgeous manor" house hotel in Kent with a grand, "old-fashioned" dining room serving "surprisingly good" Modern British food, accompanied by a live pianist (most meals); bashers take a contrary view, reporting "typical country-house fare" that, apart from the prix fixe menus (from £16.50 for lunch), is considered "overpriced."

FAT DUCK, THE [S] 24 19 21 £53

High St., Bray, Berkshire, 01628 580333; fax 01628 776188

◪ "Wear your brave hat" to this "relaxed" Berkshire pub/restaurant, as owner-chef Heston Blumenthal's "daring", "complicated" New French menu is "full of surprises" that "shouldn't work, but by Jove they do"; inevitably, some think the "wacky" cooking results in "a complete mishmash of flavours" (and "tiny portions"), but there's no doubt "Heston's artistry" – not to mention the "excellent wine list" – makes this "gem" "worth a special trip."

Feathers Hotel [S] 23 21 21 £38

Feathers Hotel, Market St., Woodstock, Oxfordshire, 01993 812291; fax 01993 813158

■ At the gates of Oxfordshire's historic Blenheim Palace is this "charming" hotel (dating back more than 300 years) that makes a "great weekend getaway", with a "restful", "romantic" atmosphere and "fantastic accommodation"; the "formal", quiet restaurant offers a "varied, interesting" Modern British–Classic French menu from Mark Treasure that's "expensive", but "wonderful", whilst "very good" snacks in the "relaxed" bar are "more affordable."

Fish [S] ▽ 19 14 17 £34

Old Mill Ln., Bray, Berkshire, 01628 781111

■ It's "a long way from the sea, but they know their fish" at this "very friendly", "relaxing" eaterie near Monkey Island in Berkshire, which offers a "good-value" Modern British menu based on the daily delivery of Cornish seafood; dinner reservations are essential, but it's also deemed "wonderful for Sunday lunch", when there's a special menu; N.B. not related to the Fish! chain.

French Horn [S] 22 22 22 £53

French Horn Hotel, Sonning-on-Thames, Berkshire, 01189 692204; fax 01189 442210

■ "Beautifully situated in gardens on the river", this "delightful, family-run" hotel near Henley is "simply superb" as far as most are concerned, with "excellent" Franco-British food ("worth going just for the duck") that a few find "pricey for what it is", although the £25 lunch is "not bad value"; brownie points go to the "very extensive wine list" – "read in awe and wonder!" – and "old-fashioned service."

GIDLEIGH PARK S　　　　26 | 23 | 24 | £57

Gidleigh Park Hotel, Chagford, Devon, 01647 432367;
fax 01647 432574

■ "Still the standard to measure against" according to
ardent admirers, this "charming countryside hotel" on the
edge of Dartmoor in Devon makes a "great place" for "a
weekend fling", with 15 bedrooms and "exquisite parklands"
"to walk in"; it's also a "fabulous experience to dine" in
the "comfortable" dining room with "garden" views,
where chef Michael Caines' "exciting", "fantastic" New
French cooking is matched by "top-notch service" and a
"spectacular wine list" (more than 500 labels strong).

GRAVETYE MANOR S　　　24 | 24 | 23 | £50

Gravetye Manor Hotel, East Grinstead, West Sussex,
01342 81567; fax 01342 810080

■ "Old-world charm combines with modern style" to
"superb" effect at this "magnificent" country-house hotel
in Sussex with a mile-long, rhododendron-lined driveway
and "beautiful" gardens ideal "to have drinks in"; in the
kitchen, chef Mark Raffan oversees a "super-creative
setup", producing "excellent" Modern British cooking
"served with care" by "unstuffy" staff.

HAMBLETON HALL S　　　25 | 23 | 24 | £53

Hambleton Hall, Hambleton, Oakham, Rutland,
01572 756991; fax 01572 724721

■ "Looking down to the lakes and countryside", this
"delightful restaurant" in an "exceptional" country-house
hotel by Rutland Water is praised for Aaron Patterson's
"heavenly", "immaculately cooked and presented"
Modern British fare that draws on "seasonal produce"
and is matched with a "comprehensive wine list"; though
"pricey" ("ouch!"), it's voted the "height of luxury, with
luxurious food to match."

Hartwell House S　　　20 | 21 | 20 | £48

Hartwell House, Oxford Rd., Aylesbury, Buckinghamshire,
01296 747444; fax 01296 747450

☑ Ninety acres of parkland surround this "lovely, relaxing
country-house hotel" in Buckinghamshire that counts
among its former residents King Louis XVIII (for five years
around 1810); when it comes to the "romantic" dining
room, however, respondents are of two minds: swooning
supporters cite "excellent" British cuisine, but others
find the offerings merely "ordinary" and something of a
"letdown" given the "beautiful setting"; all can agree the
£29 prix fixe lunch is "good value."

Hotel du Vin & Bistro S　　　23 | 21 | 21 | £39

Sugar House, Narrow Lewins, Mead, Bristol, 01179 255577
Crescent Rd., Royal Tunbridge Wells, Kent, 01892 526455;
fax 01892 512044

(continued)

(continued)

Hotel du Vin & Bistro

14 Southgate St., Winchester, Hampshire, 01962 841414; fax 01962 842458

■ "Please open more" of these "very comfortable", "convivial" hotels in Winchester, Tunbridge Wells and Bristol, urge admirers ("wish I had thought of it") who think three are not enough to "fill the need" for "simple, yet skillfully prepared" French bistro food (with some Med influences) and "inexpensive" wines, served by "staff who lack pomposity"; P.S. don't miss the "chance to stay in fab rooms."

HOTEL TRESANTON [S] 23 | 26 | 23 | £40

Hotel Tresanton, Lower Castle Rd., St. Mawes, Cornwall, 01326 270055

■ Surveyors lavish soaring ratings on this charismatic seaside hotel (owned by Olga Polizz of the Forte family) on the Cornish coast that's a good six-hour drive from London but makes an alluring destination with its "unbeatable terrace" looking out to sea and Modern British menu dominated (but not monopolised) by seafood from local producers; N.B. the hotel's 48-foot sailing yacht, The Pinicca, is available to hire.

Leaping Hare Vineyard Restaurant, The [S] – | – | – | E

Wyken Vineyards, Stanton, Bury St. Edmunds, Suffolk, 01359 250240; fax 01359 252372

This converted medieval barn surrounded by Suffolk vineyards is a "wonderfully individual setting" for Kenneth and Carla Carlisle's restaurant/cafe (with adjacent country store), which makes the most of "very fresh local ingredients" in its menu of Modern British–Californian dishes: "good effort" is the consensus; reservations are advisable in the restaurant, which is now open for lunch all week (dinner only served on Fridays and Saturdays).

Leatherne Bottel [S] 21 | 20 | 20 | £44

The Bridleway, Goring-on-Thames, Berkshire, 01491 872667; fax 01491 875308

■ "First-class" for a "fun lunch on a summer's day by the river" neatly encapsulates the appeal of this "gem of a place" on the edge of a "delightful" Berkshire village with "excellent" Modern British fare and service with "a real personal touch"; and if a minority detects "slipping standards", its not borne out in the ratings: most agree that this "idyllic" Thameside spot is "always enjoyable."

LE MANOIR AUX QUAT'SAISONS S

| 27 | 25 | 25 | £65 |

Le Manoir aux Quat'Saisons, Church Rd., Great Milton, Oxfordshire, 01844 278881; fax 01844 278847

■ "Enjoy being spoiled rotten" at Raymond Blanc's "absolutely exquisite" 15th-century Cotswold manor-house hotel featuring "magical grounds" and a "beautiful", formal dining room that delivers a "really stupendous experience" of "ravishing", "impeccable" New French cooking from chef Gary Jones with "lots of little surprises between courses"; if some balk at the "breathtaking bill", the "blissful" majority understands that at this "paradise for all the senses", "heaven has a price."

Le Petit Blanc S

| 20 | 17 | 19 | £34 |

The Promenade, Cheltenham, Gloucestershire, 01242 266800; fax 01242 266801
71-72 Walton St., Oxford, Oxfordshire, 01865 510999; fax 01865 510700
9 Brindley Pl., Birmingham, 01216 337333; fax 01216 337444 ●

☑ "There should be 50, not three!" suggest supporters of Raymond Blanc's trio of "informal" brasseries in Cheltenham, Oxford and Birmingham, which doesn't "take itself too seriously" while dishing out "wonderful", "smartly presented" French–Modern British bistro fare served by "efficient" staff; "sensible prices" and a "fun, lively" atmosphere round out the endorsement.

Le Poussin S

| – | – | – | VE |

Parkhill, Becullier Rd., Hyndhurst, Hampshire, 02380 282944; fax 02380 283268

In 1999, chef Alex Aitken moved Le Poussin from its home in Brockenhurst to take over the dining room at this hotel near Beaulieu, with encouraging results: fans proclaim it "outstanding in every respect" thanks to the "excellent" Modern British fare, "superb wine list" and "knowledgeable staff" who "recognise regulars"; some aim brickbats at the decor ("need to revamp"), but they are outvoted by those who consider it well "worth the drive", especially for a "delicious Sunday lunch"; N.B. its previous location now houses a low-key brasserie run by Aitken junior.

Le Talbooth S

| 20 | 22 | 19 | £48 |

Maison Talbooth Hotel, Gun Hill, Dedham, Essex, 01206 323150; fax 01206 322309

■ It's "a bit off-the-beaten-track, but well worth the effort" assert admirers of this "traditional", thatch-roofed, 16th-century Tudor-style venue in a "beautiful location" on the banks of the River Stour; the British fare is so "delicious" and the service so "friendly", many diners are tempted to "stay overnight" in one of 10 bedrooms and "enjoy a superb cooked breakfast."

Lucknam Park S
21 | 21 | 22 | £51

Lucknam Park Hotel, Colerne, Wiltshire, 01225 742777;
fax 01225 743536

☑ Set in a "delightful", 18th-century Palladium "country mansion" hotel on 500 acres of Wiltshire parkland, this formal, bow-fronted dining room (jacket and tie required in the evening) is home to "very well-presented" Modern British fare that most find "great" ("best roast beef in years"), if a bit on the "rich" side; N.B. a live guitarist adds to the atmosphere on weekend evenings, and a major refurb is planned from the end of 2001.

Lygon Arms, The S
20 | 22 | 20 | £50

Lygon Arms, Broadway, Worcestershire, 01386 852255;
fax 01386 858611

☑ Connoisseurs of "out-of-town dining" consider the Savoy Group's "historic" 16th-century coaching inn in the Cotswolds "a wonderful find" for its "very good", "well-prepared" Modern British cooking served in a "charming", "relaxing" setting (a barrel-vaulted dining hall with coats of arms, stags' heads, etc.) by "outstanding" staff for whom "nothing is too much trouble"; the less-enthused report "uninspired", "overpriced" food in a "gloomy" setting.

MALLORY COURT S
22 | 25 | 24 | £53

Mallory Court Hotel, Harbury Ln., Leamington Spa,
Warwickshire, 01926 330214; fax 01926 451714

■ Feels "like a private home" fawn friends of this "great country retreat" in a vine-covered Warwickshire hotel surrounded by beautifully tended gardens, which makes a "peaceful location" for "very good" (if "expensive") Classic French cooking featuring "lots of fresh ingredients" and "some clever twists"; "friendly service" and a "good" wine list add to the appeal.

Marsh Goose, The S
21 | 18 | 20 | £40

High St., Moreton-in-Marsh, Gloucestershire,
01608 653500; fax 01608 653510

■ "Thoroughly enjoyable" and "creative" Modern British cooking comes out of the kitchen at this "very cosy" eaterie spanning two rooms of a former Cotswold shoe shop, where the menu "changes often" and the "fab waiters" "really know what the food's about"; if a minority finds it's "nothing special", they're comfortably overruled by admirers of this "excellent out-of-town restaurant."

Merchant House
24 | 19 | 22 | £43

Lower Corve St., Ludlow, Shropshire, 01584 875438

■ "Well worth a marathon trek from anywhere" enthuse surveyors of this "cramped, overly warm" Shropshire eaterie in the centre of Ludlow, where chef "Shaun Hill delivers high-calibre, top-notch" Modern British dishes "at low prices" (£31 for dinner); at just seven tables, acolytes call it "small, but perfect."

Mr. Underhill's S
-|-|-| E

Mr. Underhill's, Dinham Weir, Dinham, Ludlow, Shropshire,
01584 874431
It's little known outside Shropshire, but this light, riverside
Ludlow restaurant with six modest bedrooms (often "full of
people") is deemed a "good setting" for chef Christopher
Bradley's "wonderful eats" from a £27.50 prix fixe New
French menu; "immaculate service" helps ensure a
"memorable evening" for many – but note, last orders are
at 8.30 PM; N.B. closed for lunch.

One Paston Place
▽ 25 | 19 | 23 | £41

1 Paston Pl., Brighton, West Sussex, 01273 606933;
fax 01273 645686
■ An "exotic mural lifts spirits in the elegant dining room"
of this "excellent place" in Brighton, which is "run by a
husband-and-wife team" (the Emersons) who provide
"superlative" New French cooking that's "elaborate,
yet stays just the right side of pretension"; overall, it's a
"charming", "warm" place "as good as many in London –
but without the price tag."

Pink Geranium S
▽ 21 | 18 | 19 | £45

25 Station Rd., Melbourn, Cambridgeshire, 01763 260215;
fax 01763 262110
■ "It's all a bit pink" (walls, chairs, etc.) at this "stylish",
thatch-roofed 16th-century cottage in a Cambridgeshire
village near Royston – a restaurant since 1942 – where chef
Mark Jordan prepares "simple", "consistent" Modern
British–New French fare; an "excellent Sunday lunch
venue" is the consensus.

RICK STEIN'S SEAFOOD RESTAURANT S
25 | 19 | 21 | £51

Riverside, Padstow, Cornwall, 01841 532700; fax 01841 532942
■ "A little piece of the West End in Cornwall" ("especially
the difficulty getting a table"), this "fish-lovers' paradise"
serves "fresh, unashamedly uncomplicated" Modern British
seafood, "supervised by the man himself": celebrity
chef Rick Stein, who runs this "top-class operation with
enthusiasm"; most happily overlook any shortcomings,
considering the "customer satisfaction" that comes de
rigueur at this "gem of a restaurant."

Royal Oak S
▽ 20 | 18 | 19 | £38

Royal Oak Hotel, The Square, Yattendon, Berkshire,
01635 201325; fax 01635 201926
☑ This pretty, wisteria-clad Berkshire restaurant (plus five
bedrooms) wins fans as a "quiet, calm" spot with "nice"
Modern British fare with French influences served in the
restaurant and a simpler, cheaper menu on offer in the
cosy brasserie; it's an "especially good setting" for a
"rustic day out."

Sir Charles Napier S
| 21 | 20 | 20 | £40 |

Spriggs Alley, Chinnor, Oxfordshire, 01494 483011;
fax 01494 485311

☑ "Cosy in winter, stunning in summer", this "slightly wacky", 18th-century Oxfordshire inn has a following who find it "worth the adventure to get there" ("middle of nowhere") for "consistently good" Modern British cooking "with some innovative touches" and a "true family welcome"; that said, others think it "needs more attention to detail", but on balance, most rate it really "very good for a country pub."

Stapleford Park S
| 20 | 22 | 21 | £48 |

Stapleford Park, Melton Mowbray, Stapleford,
Leicestershire, 01572 787522; fax 01572 787651

☑ "Magnificent setting" declare enthralled admirers of this "pretension-free country-house hotel" in a former stately home surrounded by 500 acres of rolling Capability Brown parkland in Leicestershire; also appreciated are the dining room's "delicious" Modern British cooking and "excellent service", though a "disappointed" few focus on the place's sporting and country pursuits (golf, tennis and horse riding); N.B. post-*Survey*, owner Peter de Savary sold out to hotelier Andrew Parker.

Stonor Arms S
▽ | 15 | 17 | 17 | £36 |

Stonor Arms Hotel, Henley-on-Thames, Oxfordshire,
01491 638866; fax 01491 638863

☑ "Watch this spot" advise those in-the-know about this cosy, 18th-century Oxfordshire coaching inn boasting an attractive restaurant, because it's "now under new management" (since February 2001); whilst some "hope they improve" things, anxious loyalists hope this popular "watering hole" maintains its "consistently good" Modern British cooking; N.B. refurbishments to the hotel and dining room are planned for late 2001.

VINEYARD AT STOCKCROSS S
| 24 | 23 | 23 | £57 |

Vineyard at Stockcross, Stockcross, Newbury, Berkshire,
01635 528770; fax 01635 528398

■ "If you like California wines, Sir Peter Michael's [Berkshire] hotel is the place", because there are 600 labels on the "pretty dining area's" impressive wine list, which complements the "intense natural flavours" of ex-L'Escargot chef Billy Reid's "terrific", "inventive" Modern British–Classic French cooking; if "pretentious service spoils" things for a few, the majority "really enjoys" this "sumptuous" venue.

WATERSIDE INN S   26 | 24 | 25 | £63 |

Waterside Inn, Ferry Rd., Bray-on-Thames, Berkshire,
01628 620691; fax 01628 784710

■ "Feel like royalty for a day" at this "idyllic setting" on the banks of the Thames in Berkshire, which offers "professionalism to a 'T'" when it comes to the "top-notch service" and Michel Roux's "awesome", "divine" French cooking that some say is "as perfect a meal as you could hope to get in the UK"; an added bonus is the "lovely" guestrooms for those who want to "stay over" – as a "special-occasion place", it's "very hard to beat."

Winteringham Fields S   ▽ 23 | 19 | 23 | £66 |

Winteringham, North Lincolnshire, 01724 733096;
fax 01724 733898

■ "Stuck in the most unprepossessing place" near the Humber in Lincolnshire is this "cluttered, yet characterful" restaurant (with 10 guestrooms), which has the feel of a "French country inn" and staff that "strike the right balance between formal and friendly"; there's widespread praise for chef-owner Germain Schwab's "precise", "memorable" New French dishes with "faultless textures"; this "local haven" just keeps "getting better."

Indexes

CUISINES
LOCATIONS
SPECIAL FEATURES

CUISINES

Argentine
El Gaucho (multi. loc.)
Gaucho Grill (multi. loc.)

Asian
Aquasia (SW10)
Asia de Cuba (WC2)
Bonjour Vietnam (SW6)
Cassia Oriental (W1)
Champor - Champor (SE1)
Cicada (EC1)
itsu (SW3)
Jim Thompson's (multi. loc.)
Rain (W10)
Singapura (multi. loc.)
Southeast W9 (W9)
Sugar Reef (W1)
Tao (EC4)
Tiger Lil's (multi. loc.)
Upstairs at The Savoy (WC2)
Wok Wok (multi. loc.)
Yatra (W1)
Yellow River Cafe (multi. loc.)
Zeta (W1)

Bangladesh
Ginger (W2)

Barbecue
Arkansas Cafe (E1)

Belgian
Belgo Centraal (WC2)
Belgo Noord (NW1)
Belgo Zuid (W10)
Bierodrome (multi. loc.)

Brasserie
Balans (multi. loc.)
Bluebird (SW3)
Brasserie Rocque (EC2)
Brasserie St. Quentin (SW3)
Bridge (EC4)
Browns Rest. (multi. loc.)
Café Delancey (NW1)
Café des Amis du Vin (WC2)
Café Flo (multi. loc.)
Cafe Rouge (multi. loc.)
Camden Brasserie (NW1)
Cantina Vinopolis (SE1)
Chez Gérard (multi. loc.)
Dôme (multi. loc.)
Elena's l'Etoile (W1)
House on Rosslyn Hill (NW3)
Joe's Brasserie (SW6)
Justin de Blank (SW1)
La Brasserie (SW2)
La Brasserie du Marché (W10)
La Brasserie Townhouse (WC1)
Langan's Brasserie (W1)
Le Metro (SW3)
Le Palais du Jardin (WC2)
Le Petit Blanc (multi. loc.)
L'Estaminet (WC2)
Luc's (EC3)
Mustards Smithfield (EC1)
Neat Brasserie (SE1)
Notting Hill Brasserie (W11)
1 Lombard St. Brasserie (EC3)
Oriel (SW1)
Oxo Tower Brasserie (SE1)
Pacific Oriental (EC2)
Quaglino's (SW1)
Randall & Aubin (multi. loc.)
Terrace (W1)
Tuttons Brasserie (WC2)
Union Cafe (W1)
Zinc B&G (W1)

Brazilian
Rodizio Rico (W2)

British (Modern)
Alastair Little (W1)
Alastair Little/Lancaster Rd. (W11)
Alfred (WC2)
All Bar One (multi. loc.)
Amphitheatre (WC2)
Anglesea Arms (W6)
Arcadia (W8)
Archduke (SE1)
Atlantic B&G (W1)

Le Talbooth (Essex)
LMNT (E8)
Lucknam Park (Wilts)
Lygon Arms (Worcs)
Marsh Goose (Glos)
Merchant House (Shrops)
Mesclun (N16)
Min's (SW3)
Mission (SW6)
Motcomb's (SW1)
Mustards Smithfield (EC1)
Naked Turtle (SW14)
Nicole's (W1)
Noble Rot (W1)
North Pole (SE10)
Notting Hill Brasserie (W11)
Odette's (NW1)
115 at Hodgson's (WC2)
1 Lombard St. (EC3)
192 (W11)
Oscar (W1)
Oxo Tower (SE1)
Palm Court (WC2)
Parade (W5)
Passion (W9)
People's Palace (SE1)
Pharmacy (W11)
Phoenix B&G (SW15)
Pie²Mash (NW1)
Pink Geranium (Cambs)
Portrait (WC2)
Prince Bonaparte (W2)
Prism (EC3)
Pug (W4)
Quaglino's (SW1)
Queens (NW1)
Quincy's (NW2)
Quo Vadis (W1)
Ransome's Dock (SW11)
Red Bar (W1)
Redmonds (SW14)
Rhodes in the Square (SW1)
Rib Room (SW1)
Richard Corrigan/Lindsay (W1)
Rick Stein's Seafood (C'wall)
Royal Oak (Berks)
R.s.j. (SE1)
Salt House (NW8)

Sauce Organic Diner (NW1)
Scotts (W1)
Searcy's at the Barbican (EC2)
Sir Charles Napier (Oxon)
Smiths of Smithfield - Din. (EC1)
Smiths of Smithfield-Top (EC1)
Snows on the Green (W6)
Sonny's (SW13)
Sporting Page (SW10)
Stapleford Park (Leics)
Stepping Stone (SW8)
St. John (EC1)
Stonor Arms (Oxon)
Tate Gallery Rest. (SW1)
10 Devonshire Sq. (EC2)
Tenth (W8)
Terminus (EC2)
Terrace (W8) (W8)
Titanic (W1)
Vale (W9)
Villandry (W1)
Vine (NW5)
Vineyard at Stockcross (Berks)
Wapping Food (E1)
Waterloo Fire Station (SE1)
Waterstones, Red Rm. (W1)
Wine Gallery (SW10)

British (Traditional)

All Bar One (multi. loc.)
Atrium (SW1)
Bear Hotel, The (Oxon)
Beetle & Wedge (Oxon)
Bentley's (W1)
Boisdale (SW1)
Buckland Manor (Glos)
Builders Arms (SW3)
Bush B&G (W12)
Butlers Wharf (SE1)
Chapel (NW1)
Chelsea Bun (multi. loc.)
Chelsea Kitchen (SW3)
Chelsea Ram (SW10)
Connaught Hotel, Rest. (W1)
Cow (W2)
Criterion Brasserie (W1)
Dan's (SW3)

Dorchester, Grill Room (W1)
Duke of Cambridge (N1)
Fatboy's Cafe (W4)
ffiona's (W8)
Fish! (multi. loc.)
Fortnum's Fountain (W1)
40° at Veronica's (W2)
Fox & Anchor (EC1)
Foxtrot Oscar (multi. loc.)
Freedom Brewing (multi. loc.)
French Horn (Berks)
George Bar (EC2)
Goring Dining Room (SW1)
Greens (SW1)
Grenadier (SW1)
Grumbles (SW1)
Guinea (W1)
Harrods (SW1)
Hartwell House (Bucks)
Honest Cabbage (SE1)
Joe Allen (WC2)
Just Around the Corner (NW2)
Justin de Blank (SW1)
King's Head, The (N21)
Langan's Brasserie (W1)
Langan's Coq d'Or (SW5)
Le Talbooth (Essex)
Maggie Jones's (W8)
Monkeys (SW3)
Odin's (W1)
Pie²Mash (NW1)
Porters (WC2)
porters bar (W1)
Quality Chop Hse. (EC1)
Richoux (multi. loc.)
Ritz (W1)
RK Stanley's (W1)
Rowley's (SW1)
Rules (WC2)
Savoy Grill (WC2)
Scotts (W1)
Shepherd's (SW1)
Simpson's/Strand/Grand (WC2)
Simpson's/Strand/Simply (WC2)
Simpson's Tavern (EC3)
Stafford (SW1)
St. John (EC1)
Toff's (N10)

Twelfth House (W11)
Vic Naylor (EC1)
Wilton's (SW1)
Ye Olde Cheshire Cheese (EC4)

Burmese

Mandalay (W2)

Chinese

Aroma Chinese (multi. loc.)
Bayee House (multi. loc.)
Cassia Oriental (W1)
Cheng-Du (NW1)
China City (WC2)
China House (W1)
Choys (SW3)
Chuen Cheng Ku (W1)
Dalchini (SW19)
Dorchester, Oriental (W1)
East One (EC1)
Feng Shang Floating (NW1)
Four Regions (SE1)
Four Seasons Chinese (W2)
Fung Shing (WC2)
Golden Dragon (W1)
Good Earth (multi. loc.)
Green Cottage (NW3)
Gung-Ho (NW6)
Hakkasan (W1)
Harbour City (W1)
Hunan (SW1)
Imperial City (EC3)
Jade Garden (W1)
Jen Hong Kong (W1)
Jenny Lo's Tea (SW1)
Jim Thompson's (multi. loc.)
Joy King Lau (WC2)
Kai (W1)
Kaifeng (NW4)
Lee Fook (W2)
Lee Ho Fook (W1)
Mandarin Kitchen (W2)
Mao Tai (multi. loc.)
Memories of China (multi. loc.)
Ming (W1)
Mr. Chow (SW1)
Mr. Kong (WC2)

Mr. Wing (SW5)
New Culture Rev. (multi. loc.)
New World (W1)
Orient (W1)
Phoenix Palace (NW1)
Poons (multi. loc.)
Poons in the City (EC3)
Princess Garden (W1)
Royal China (multi. loc.)
Singapore Garden (NW6)
Trader Vic's (W1)
Wong Kei (W1)
Zen Central (W1)
Zen Chelsea (SW3)
Zen Garden (W1)
ZeNW3 (NW3)

Chophouses
Black & Blue (W8)
Butlers Wharf (SE1)
Christopher's (multi. loc.)
El Gaucho (multi. loc.)
Gaucho Grill (multi. loc.)
Guinea (W1)
Parisienne Chophse. (SW3)
Pope's Eye (multi. loc.)
Quality Chop Hse. (EC1)
Rib Room (SW1)
Rules (WC2)
Simpson's Tavern (EC3)
Smiths of Smithfield - Din. (EC1)
Smiths of Smithfield-Top (EC1)
Tuscan Steak (WC2)

Coffeehouses
Aroma (multi. loc.)
Caffe Nero (multi. loc.)
Coffee Republic (multi. loc.)
Costa Coffee (multi. loc.)
Maison Bertaux (W1)
Patisserie Valerie (multi. loc.)
Starbucks (multi. loc.)
Troubadour (SW5)

Cuban
Asia de Cuba (WC2)
Cuba (W8)
Cuba Libre & Havana Bar (N1)
Havana (multi. loc.)

Danish
Lundum's (SW7)

Dim Sum
China City (WC2)
China House (W1)
Chuen Cheng Ku (W1)
Dorchester, Oriental (W1)
Golden Dragon (W1)
Hakkasan (W1)
Harbour City (W1)
Jade Garden (W1)
Joy King Lau (WC2)
Lee Ho Fook (W1)
Mr. Wing (SW5)
New World (W1)
Royal China (multi. loc.)
Zen Chelsea (SW3)
Zen Garden (W1)

Eclectic/International
Amberley Castle/Queens (W. Sus)
Andrew Edmunds (W1)
Aquarium (E1)
Arcadia (W8)
Archduke (SE1)
Archipelago (W1)
Attica (W1)
Aurora (EC2)
Axis (WC2)
Balans (multi. loc.)
bali sugar (W11)
Bankside (SE1)
Beach Blanket Babylon (W11)
Bibendum (SW3)
Bibendum Oyster Bar (SW3)
Bistrot 190 (SW7)
Blakes (NW1)
Blakes Hotel (SW7)
Blue Print Cafe (SE1)
Boardwalk (W1)
Books for Cooks (W11)
Brackenbury (W6)
Brasserie Rocque (EC2)
Bridge (EC4)
Brinkley's (SW10)
Browns Rest. (multi. loc.)

Woody's (W9)
World Food Café (WC2)

Fish 'n' Chips

Brady's (SW18)
Fish! (multi. loc.)
Geale's (W8)
George Bar (EC2)
Livebait (multi. loc.)
Nautilus Fish (NW6)
Rudland & Stubbs (EC1)
Seashell (NW1)
Sweetings (EC4)
Toff's (N10)
Two Brothers Fish (N3)

French (Bistro)

Bibendum Oyster Bar (SW3)
Bistro Daniel (W2)
Café Boheme (W1)
Café Delancey (NW1)
Café des Amis du Vin (WC2)
Café Flo (multi. loc.)
Cafe Rouge (multi. loc.)
Chez Gérard (multi. loc.)
Cork & Bottle (WC2)
Dôme (multi. loc.)
Elena's l'Etoile (W1)
Francofill (SW7)
Glaister's (multi. loc.)
Grumbles (SW1)
Hotel du Vin & Bistro (multi. loc.)
La Bouchée (SW7)
Langan's Bistro (W1)
Langan's Coq d'Or (SW5)
La Poule au Pot (SW1)
L'Artiste Musclé (W1)
L'Aventure (NW8)
Le Bouchon Bordelais (multi. loc.)
Le Boudin Blanc (W1)
Le Café du Marché (EC1)
Le Mercury (N1)
Le Metro (SW3)
Le Petit Blanc (multi. loc.)
Le Piaf (multi. loc.)
L'Escargot (W1)
Monsieur Max (Hampton Hill)
Mustards Smithfield (EC1)
Patisserie Valerie (multi. loc.)

Pierre Victoire (W1)
Quality Chop Hse. (EC1)
Rotisserie Jules (multi. loc.)
Tartuf (N1)
Thierry's (SW3)
Truc Vert (W1)

French (Classic)

Amandier (W2)
Auberge du Lac (Herts)
Aubergine (SW10)
Bear Hotel, The (Oxon)
Beetle & Wedge (Oxon)
Belair House (SE21)
Belvedere (W8)
Beoty's (WC2)
Brasserie St. Quentin (SW3)
Buckland Manor (Glos)
Chewton Glen, Marryat (Hants)
Chez Bruce (SW17)
Chez Gérard (multi. loc.)
Chez Max (SW10)
cheznico (W1)
Club Gascon (EC1)
Connaught Hotel, Rest. (W1)
Coq d'Argent (EC2)
Creelers (SW3)
Criterion Brasserie (W1)
Crivelli's Garden (WC2)
Drones (SW1)
Elena's l'Etoile (W1)
Feathers Hotel (Oxon)
French Horn (Berks)
Incognico (WC2)
John Burton-Race (NW1)
Just Around the Corner (NW2)
La Bouchée (SW7)
La Brasserie (SW2)
La Brasserie du Marché (W10)
Langan's Brasserie (W1)
La Poule au Pot (SW1)
La Tante Claire (SW1)
L'Aventure (NW8)
Le Bouchon Bordelais (multi. loc.)
Le Boudin Blanc (W1)
Le Café du Marché (EC1)
Le Colombier (SW3)

Kalamaras Taverna (W2)
Lemonia (NW1)
Real Greek (N1)
Vrisaki (N22)

Hamburgers

Arkansas Cafe (E1)
Babe Ruth's (E1)
Big Easy (SW3)
Black & Blue (W8)
Break for the Border (multi. loc.)
Cheers (W1)
Ed's Easy Diner (multi. loc.)
Fatboy's Cafe (multi. loc.)
Foxtrot Oscar (multi. loc.)
Hard Rock Cafe (W1)
Henry J. Bean's (SW3)
Joe Allen (WC2)
Kettners (W1)
Maxwell's (multi. loc.)
PJ's B&G (SW3)
PJ's Grill (WC2)
Planet Hollywood (W1)
Sports Cafe (SW1)
Sticky Fingers (W8)
Texas Lone Star (SW7)
T.G.I. Friday's (multi. loc.)
Tootsies (multi. loc.)
Vingt-Quatre (SW10)
Wolfe's B&G (WC2)

Hungarian

Gay Hussar (W1)

Ice Cream Parlours

Fortnum's Fountain (W1)
Harrods (SW1)
Marine Ices (NW3)

Indian

Bengal Clipper (SE1)
Bengal Trader (E1)
Bombay Bicycle Club (SW12)
Bombay Brasserie (SW7)
Cafe Lazeez (multi. loc.)
Cafe Spice Namaste (multi. loc.)
Chor Bizarre (W1)
Chutney Mary (SW10)
Chutney's (NW1)

Cinnamon Club (SW1)
Gopal's of Soho (W1)
Great Nepalese (NW1)
Kastoori (SW17)
Khan's (W2)
Khan's of Kensington (SW7)
Lahore Kebab (E1)
La Porte des Indes (W1)
Ma Goa (SW15)
Malabar (W8)
Malabar Junction (WC1)
Masala Zone (W1)
Mela (WC2)
Memories of India (multi. loc.)
Nirvana (SW19)
Noor Jahan (SW5)
Old Delhi (W2)
Parsee (N19)
Quilon (SW1)
Rani (N3)
Rasa (multi. loc.)
Ravi Shankar (multi. loc.)
Salloos (SW1)
Sarkhel's (SW18)
Shimla Pinks (EC2)
Soho Spice (W1)
Standard Tandoori (W2)
Star of India (SW5)
Tabla (E14)
Tamarind (W1)
Tandoori Lane (SW6)
Tandoori of Chelsea (SW3)
Vama (SW10)
Veeraswamy (W1)
Yatra (W1)
Zaika (W8)
Zaika Bazaar (SW3)

Irish

ArdRí at O'Conor Don (W14)
Conrad Gallagher (W1)
Richard Corrigan/Lindsay (W1)
Waxy O'Connor's (W1)

Italian (Contemporary)

Alba (EC1)
Al Duca (SW1)

Italian (Traditional)

Carluccio's Caffe (multi. loc.)
Cecconi's (W1)
Como Lario (SW1)
Condotti (W1)
De Cecco (SW6)
Del Buongustaio (SW15)
Diverso (W1)
Dorchester, Bar (W1)
Elistano (SW3)
Emporio Armani Caffe (SW3)
Friends (SW10)
Getti (SW1)
Il Falconiere (SW7)
Il Portico (W8)
La Bersagliera (SW3)
La Delizia (SW3)
La Famiglia (SW10)
La Fontana (SW1)
Little Italy (W1)
Luigi's/Covent Garden (WC2)
Made in Italy (SW3)
Marine Ices (NW3)
Mimmo d'Ischia (SW1)
Montpeliano (SW7)
Neal Street (WC2)
Osteria Ant. Bologna (SW11)
Pellicano (SW3)
Pizza Express (multi. loc.)
Pizza Metro (SW11)
Pollo Bar (W1)
Pucci Pizza (SW3)
Red Pepper (W9)
Riccardo's (SW3)
Riso (W4)
Sale e Pepe (SW1)
Sambuca (SW1)
Sandrini (SW3)
San Frediano (SW3)
San Lorenzo (SW3)
Scalini (SW3)
Signor Sassi (SW1)
Signor Zilli (W1)
Spaghetti House (multi. loc.)
Spago (multi. loc.)
Spighetta (W1)
Strada (multi. loc.)
Vegia Zena (NW1)

Verbanella (SW3)
Ziani (SW3)

Japanese

Abeno (WC1)
Aykoku-Kaku (EC4)
Benihana (multi. loc.)
Cafe Japan (NW11)
City Miyama (EC4)
Defune (W1)
Harrods (SW1)
Hi Sushi (multi. loc.)
Ikeda (W1)
Ikkyu (multi. loc.)
Inaho (W2)
itsu (multi. loc.)
Japanese Canteen (multi. loc.)
Jin Kichi (NW3)
Koi (W8)
Kulu Kulu Sushi (W1)
Matsuri (SW1)
Mitsukoshi (SW1)
Miyabi (EC2)
Miyama (W1)
Mju (SW1)
Moshi Moshi Sushi (multi. loc.)
Nobu (W1)
Noto (multi. loc.)
Saga (W1)
Satsuma (W1)
Shogun (W14)
Suntory (SW1)
Sushi Wong (W8)
Sway (WC2)
Tatsuso (EC2)
Tokyo Diner (WC2)
Ubon by Nobu (E14)
Wagamama (multi. loc.)
Wakaba (NW3)
Yoshino (W1)
Yo! Sushi (multi. loc.)

Jewish

Bloom's (NW11)
Reubens (W1)
Solly's (NW11)

Brown's Hotel, Rest. 1837 (W1)
Cafe de Paris (W1)
Cantina Vinopolis (SE1)
Chapter One (Kent)
Chapter Two (SE3)
County Hall (SE1)
Cow (W2)
Duke of Cambridge (N1)
English Garden (SW3)
Enterprise (SW3)
Foliage (SW1)
Footstool (SW1)
Granita (N1)
Gresslin's (NW3)
Ifield (SW10)
Ivy (WC2)
J. Sheekey (WC2)
Kennington Lane (SE11)
Le Caprice (SW1)
Le Pont de la Tour (SE1)
Lexington (W1)
Mash (multi. loc.)
Mezzo (W1)
Noble Rot (W1)
1 Lombard St. Brasserie (EC3)
Oriel (SW1)
Otto Dining Lounge (W9)
People's Palace (SE1)
Quo Vadis (W1)
Red Cube B&G (WC2)
Salusbury Pub (NW6)
Shoreditch Electricity (N1)
Sway (WC2)
Tao (EC4)
Teatro (W1)
Toast (NW3)
Twentyfour (EC2)
Union Cafe (W1)
Vine (NW5)
Zinc B&G (W1)

Moroccan

Adams Cafe (W12)
Ayoush (W1)
Julono (NW3)
Momo (W1)
Original Tajine (W1)
Pasha (SW7)
Souk (WC2)

North African

Adams Cafe (W12)
Ayoush (W1)
Laurent (NW2)
Levant (W1)
Momo (W1)
Original Tajine (W1)
Pasha (SW7)
Souk (WC2)

North American

Arkansas Cafe (E1)
Babe Ruth's (E1)
Big Easy (SW3)
Blues Bistro & Bar (W1)
Boardwalk (W1)
Break for the Border (multi. loc.)
Cactus Blue (SW3)
Canyon (Richmond)
Cheers (W1)
Chelsea Bun (multi. loc.)
Christopher's (multi. loc.)
Dakota (W11)
DKNY Bar (W1)
Ed's Easy Diner (multi. loc.)
Foxtrot Oscar (multi. loc.)
Hard Rock Cafe (W1)
Henry J. Bean's (SW3)
Idaho (N6)
Joe Allen (WC2)
Leaping Hare Vineyard (Suffolk)
Maxwell's (multi. loc.)
Montana (SW6)
Navajo Joe (WC2)
PJ's B&G (SW3)
PJ's Grill (WC2)
Planet Hollywood (W1)
Prospect Grill (WC2)
Rainforest Cafe (W1)
Reubens (W1)
Rock Garden (WC2)
Santa Fe (N1)
Smollensky's on Strand (WC2)
Sports Cafe (SW1)
Sticky Fingers (W8)
Texas Embassy Cantina (SW14)

Texas Lone Star (multi. loc.)
T.G.I. Friday's (multi. loc.)
Tootsies (multi. loc.)
Utah (SW19)
Wolfe's B&G (WC2)

Pacific Rim

bali sugar (W11)
Blakes Hotel (SW7)
Cinnamon Cay (SW11)
Cucina (NW3)
Denim (WC2)
Giraffe (multi. loc.)
I-Thai (W2)
itsu (W1)
182 Mint (EC1)
Oxo Tower (SE1)
Oxo Tower Brasserie (SE1)
Pacific Oriental (EC2)
Polygon B&G (SW4)
Saint Bar & Rest. (WC2)
Southeast W9 (W9)
Sugar Club (W1)
Yellow River Cafe (multi. loc.)
Zeta (W1)

Persian

Alounak (multi. loc.)
Dish Dash (W1)
Kandoo (W2)
Old Delhi (W2)
Yas (W14)

Peruvian

Fina Estampa (SE1)

Pizza

Ask Pizza (multi. loc.)
Basilico (multi. loc.)
Buona Sera (SW11)
Calzone (multi. loc.)
Cantina del Ponte (SE1)
Casale Franco (N1)
Condotti (W1)
Eco (multi. loc.)
Friends (SW10)
Harrods (SW1)
Il Forno (W1)
Kettners (W1)

La Delizia (SW3)
La Porchetta Pizzeria (multi. loc.)
Made in Italy (SW3)
Mash (multi. loc.)
Oliveto (SW1)
Orso (WC2)
Pizza Express (multi. loc.)
Pizza Metro (SW11)
Pizza on the Park (SW1)
Pizza Organic (multi. loc.)
Pizza Pomodoro (multi. loc.)
Pizzeria Castello (SE1)
Pucci Pizza (SW3)
Red Pepper (W9)
Riso (W4)
Rocket (W1)
Spago (SW11)
Spiga (multi. loc.)
Spighetta (W1)
Strada (multi. loc.)
Uno (SW1)
Wine Factory (W11)
Zizzi (multi. loc.)
Zucca (W11)

Polish

Baltic (SE1)
Daquise (SW7)
Wòdka (W8)
Zamoyski (NW3)

Russian

Caviar Kaspia (W1)
FireBird (W1)
Nikita's (SW10)
Potemkin (EC1)

Scottish

Boisdale (SW1)
Buchan's (SW11)
Creelers (SW3)

Seafood

Aquarium (E1)
Aquasia (SW10)
Back to Basics (W1)
Bah Humbug (SW2)

Belgo Centraal (WC2)
Belgo Noord (NW1)
Belgo Zuid (W10)
Bentley's (W1)
Bibendum Oyster Bar (SW3)
Bluebird (SW3)
Brady's (SW18)
Cafe Fish (W1)
Catch (SW5)
Chez Liline (N4)
Creelers (SW3)
Fish (Berks)
Fish! (multi. loc.)
Fishmarket (EC2)
Geale's (W8)
Greens (SW1)
Harrods (SW1)
Hotel Tresanton (C'wall)
Jason's (W9)
J. Sheekey (WC2)
Le Suquet (SW3)
Livebait (multi. loc.)
Lobster Pot (SE11)
Lou Pescadou (SW5)
Manzi's (WC2)
Moxon's (SW4)
190, Downstairs (SW7)
One-O-One (SW1)
Pescatori (multi. loc.)
Poissonnerie de l'Avenue (SW3)
Quaglino's (SW1)
Randall & Aubin (multi. loc.)
Rick Stein's Seafood (C'wall)
Rudland & Stubbs (EC1)
Scotts (W1)
Seashell (NW1)
Stratford's (W8)
Stream (EC1)
Sweetings (EC4)
Upstairs at The Savoy (WC2)
Well & Aquarium (EC1)
Wilton's (SW1)
Zilli Fish (W1)

South American

La Piragua (N1)

Spanish

Barcelona Tapas (multi. loc.)
Bar Madrid (W1)
Cambio de Tercio (SW5)
Cigala (WC1)
Don Pepe (NW8)
El Blason (SW3)
Galicia (W10)
Gaudí (EC1)
Harrods (SW1)
La Finca (multi. loc.)
La Mancha (SW15)
La Rueda (multi. loc.)
Lomo (SW10)
Meson Don Felipe (SE1)
Moro (EC1)
Paell'ya (SW8)
Rebato's (SW8)

Sudanese

Mandola (W11)

Swedish/Scandinavian

Garbo's (W1)
Lundum's (SW7)

Swiss

Movenpick Marché (SW1)

Thai

Bangkok (SW7)
Bedlington Cafe (W4)
Ben's Thai (multi. loc.)
Blue Elephant (SW6)
Blue Jade (SW1)
Blue Lagoon (W14)
Busaba Eathai (W1)
Busabong Too (SW10)
Chiang Mai (W1)
Churchill Arms (W8)
Elephant Royale (E14)
Esarn Kheaw (W12)
Exhibition Thai (SW7)
Fatboy's Cafe (multi. loc.)
I-Thai (W2)
Khun Akorn (SW3)
Mezzonine (W1)
Nahm (SW1)
Patara (multi. loc.)

Pepper Tree (SW4)
Silks & Spice (multi. loc.)
Sri Siam (W1)
Sri Siam City (EC2)
Sri Thai (EC4)
Thai Kitchen (W2)
Thai on the River (SW10)
Thai Pavilion (W1)
Thai Square (SW1)
Tuk Tuk Thai (N1)
Vong (SW1)
Yum Yum Thai (N16)

Turkish

Efes Kebab House (multi. loc.)
Istanbul Iskembecisi (N16)
Iznik (N5)
Ozer (W1)
Pasha (N1)
Sofra (multi. loc.)
Tas (SE1)

Vegetarian

Bah Humbug (SW2)
Blah! Blah! Blah! (W12)
Chutney's (NW1)
Cranks (multi. loc.)
Food for Thought (WC2)
Futures Café-Bar (multi. loc.)
Gate (multi. loc.)
Kastoori (SW17)
Lanesborough (SW1)
Mildreds (W1)
Place Below (EC2)
Rani (N3)
Rasa (multi. loc.)
Ravi Shankar (multi. loc.)
Six-13 (W1)
Soup Opera (multi. loc.)
Soup Works (multi. loc.)
World Food Café (WC2)

Vietnamese

Bam-Bou (W1)
Bonjour Vietnam (SW6)
Nam Long Le Shaker (SW5)
Opium (W1)
Saigon (W1)
Saigon Times (EC3)
Viet Hoa (E2)

LOCATIONS

CENTRAL LONDON

Belgravia

Beiteddine
Drones
Ebury Wine Bar
Grenadier
Grissini
Il Convivio
Lanesborough
La Tante Claire
Memories of China
Mimmo d'Ischia
Motcomb's
Nahm
Oliveto
One-O-One
Pizza on the Park
Rib Room
Salloos
Santini
Vong
Zafferano

Bloomsbury

Abeno
Alfred
Archipelago
Ask Pizza
Back to Basics
Bam-Bou
Bertorelli
Caffe Nero
Carluccio's Caffe
Chez Gérard
Cigala
Cranks
Dish Dash
Efes Kebab House
Elena's l'Etoile
Hakkasan
Ikkyu
La Brasserie Townhouse
Le Piaf
Malabar Junction
Mash

Nico Central
Oscar
Passione
Pescatori
Pied à Terre
Poons
Pret à Manger
Rasa
RK Stanley's
Silks & Spice
Soup Opera
Soup Works
Spaghetti House
Spoon+ at Sanderson
Villandry
Wagamama
Yo! Sushi

Chinatown

Aroma Chinese
China City
Chuen Cheng Ku
Fung Shing
Golden Dragon
Harbour City
Ikkyu
itsu
Jade Garden
Jen Hong Kong
Lee Ho Fook
Manzi's
Mr. Kong
New World
Poons
Tokyo Diner
Wong Kei

Covent Garden

Admiralty
Amphitheatre
Aroma
Asia de Cuba
Axis
Bank Aldwych
Belgo Centraal

Canary Wharf/Docklands

Babe Ruth's
Browns Rest.
Corney & Barrow
Cranks
Elephant Royale
Fish!
Four Seasons, Quadrato
Gaucho Grill
Moshi Moshi Sushi
Royal China
Soup Opera
Tabla
Ubon by Nobu
Wapping Food
Yellow River Cafe

Clerkenwell/Smithfield

All Bar One
Bierodrome
Bleeding Heart
Cafe Lazeez
Cellar Gascon
Chez Gérard
Cicada
Club Gascon
Cranks
Dibbens
Dôme
Eagle
East One
Fox & Anchor
Gaudí
Japanese Canteen
Le Café du Marché
Maison Novelli
Moro
Mustards Smithfield
182 Mint
Peasant
Potemkin
Quality Chop Hse.
Rudland & Stubbs
Silks & Spice
Smiths of Smithfield - Din.
Smiths of Smithfield-Top
Spirit
St. John

Strada
Stream
Vic Naylor
Well & Aquarium
Yo! Sushi

Greenwich/Blackheath

All Bar One
Chapter Two
Fish!
Le Piaf
North Pole
Starbucks

Shoreditch/Spitalfields

Bengal Trader
Cantaloupe
Great Eastern Din. Rm.
Real Greek
Shoreditch Electricity
Viet Hoa

South Bank

Bankside
Cafe, Level Seven
Cantina Vinopolis
Delfina Studio Cafe
Fina Estampa
Fish!
Honest Cabbage
La Finca
Neat
Neat Brasserie
Oxo Tower
Oxo Tower Brasserie
Simply Nico

Tower Bridge

Aquarium
Arancia
Bengal Clipper
Blue Print Cafe
Butlers Wharf
Cantina del Ponte
Champor - Champor
Foxtrot Oscar
Le Pont de la Tour
Tentazioni
Wine Library

Ma Goa
Memories of India
Naked Turtle
Phoenix B&G
Pope's Eye
Putney Bridge
Redmonds
Wok Wok

South Kensington

Ask Pizza
Bangkok
Bibendum
Bibendum Oyster Bar
Bistrot 190
Blakes Hotel
Bombay Brasserie
Cactus Blue
Café Flo
Cafe Lazeez
Caffe Nero
Collection
Crescent
Daquise
Exhibition Thai
Francofill
Il Falconiere
Joe's
Khan's of Kensington
La Bouchée
La Brasserie
Lundum's

Memories of India
Noor Jahan
190, Downstairs
Pasha
Patara
Pitcher & Piano
Pizza Organic
Rotisserie Jules
Sandrini
San Frediano
Star of India
Texas Lone Star
Tootsies

Wandsworth/Balham

Bayee House
Brady's
Chez Bruce
Dalchini
Foxtrot Oscar
Jim Thompson's
Kastoori
Le Piaf
Light House
Livebait
Nirvana
Pitcher & Piano
San Lorenzo Fuoriporta
Sarkhel's
Tootsies
Utah

WEST LONDON

Bayswater

Alounak
Al San Vincenzo
Al Waha
Amandier
Bistro Daniel
Coffee Republic
Fakhreldine Exp.
Four Seasons Chinese
40° at Veronica's
Ginger
Halepi
Inaho
I-Thai

Kalamaras Taverna
Khan's
L'Accento Italiano
Mandarin Kitchen
Mandola
Old Delhi
Poons
Prince Bonaparte
Rodizio Rico
Royal China
Standard Tandoori
T.G.I. Friday's
Tiger Lil's

192
Orsino
Osteria Basilico
Pharmacy
Pizza Express
Rain
Rotisserie Jules
Thai Kitchen
Tom's Deli
Tootsies
Twelfth House
Westbourne
Wine Factory
Wiz
Woody's
Zilli
Zucca

Olympia
Alounak
Cibo
Havelock Tavern
Pope's Eye
Yas

Shepherd's Bush
Adams Cafe
Anglesea Arms
Blah! Blah! Blah!
Brackenbury
Bush B&G
Cafe Rouge
Chinon
Esarn Kheaw
Snows on the Green
Zizzi

IN THE COUNTRY

Amberley Castle/Queens
Auberge du Lac
Bear Hotel, The
Beetle & Wedge
Bishopstrow, Mulberry
Buckland Manor
Chapter One
Charlton, Mulberry
Cherwell Boathouse
Chewton Glen, Marryat
Cliveden, Waldo's
Compleat Angler
Dining Room
Eastwell Manor
Fat Duck
Feathers Hotel
Fish
French Horn
Gidleigh Park
Gravetye Manor
Hambleton Hall
Hartwell House
Hotel du Vin & Bistro

Hotel Tresanton
Leaping Hare Vineyard
Leatherne Bottel
Le Manoir/Quat'Saisons
Le Petit Blanc
Le Poussin
Le Talbooth
Lucknam Park
Lygon Arms
Mallory Court
Marsh Goose
Merchant House
Mr. Underhill's
One Paston Place
Pink Geranium
Rick Stein's Seafood
Royal Oak
Sir Charles Napier
Stapleford Park
Stonor Arms
Vineyard at Stockcross
Waterside Inn
Winteringham Fields

SPECIAL FEATURES

All-Day Dining

Al Hamra (W1)
All Bar One (multi. loc.)
Alounak (multi. loc.)
Al Sultan (W1)
Al Waha (W2)
Aperitivo (W1)
Aroma (multi. loc.)
Ask Pizza (multi. loc.)
Babe Ruth's (E1)
Balans (multi. loc.)
Barcelona Tapas (multi. loc.)
Belgo Centraal (WC2)
Belgo Noord (NW1)
Bibendum Oyster Bar (SW3)
Big Easy (SW3)
Bistrot 190 (SW7)
Bloom's (NW11)
Browns Rest. (multi. loc.)
Café Delancey (NW1)
Café Flo (multi. loc.)
Cafe Lazeez (multi. loc.)
Cafe, Level Seven (SE1)
Cafe Pacifico (WC2)
Cafe Rouge (multi. loc.)
Caffe Nero (multi. loc.)
Calzone (multi. loc.)
Cantina Vinopolis (SE1)
Carluccio's Caffe (multi. loc.)
Casale Franco (N1)
Cheers (W1)
Chelsea Bun (multi. loc.)
Chelsea Kitchen (SW3)
China City (WC2)
Choys (SW3)
Chuen Cheng Ku (W1)
Coffee Republic (multi. loc.)
Condotti (W1)
Cork & Bottle (WC2)
Cranks (multi. loc.)
Crescent (SW3)
Crivelli's Garden (WC2)
Cuba (W8)
Cuba Libre & Havana Bar (N1)
Dôme (multi. loc.)
Down Mexico Way (W1)

Ed's Easy Diner (multi. loc.)
Efes Kebab House (multi. loc.)
Fakhreldine Exp. (multi. loc.)
Fifth Floor Cafe (SW1)
Food for Thought (WC2)
Fortnum's Fountain (W1)
Fox & Anchor (EC1)
Fung Shing (WC2)
George Bar (EC2)
Golden Dragon (W1)
Green Cottage (NW3)
Harrods (SW1)
Havana (multi. loc.)
Henry J. Bean's (SW3)
Hi Sushi (W1)
House on Rosslyn Hill (NW3)
Ikkyu (multi. loc.)
Il Forno (W1)
Imperial City (EC3)
Indigo (WC2)
Istanbul Iskembecisi (N16)
itsu (SW3)
Jade Garden (W1)
Jim Thompson's (multi. loc.)
Joe Allen (WC2)
Joe's Rest. (SW1)
Kettners (W1)
La Bouchée (SW7)
La Brasserie (SW2)
La Delizia (SW3)
La Finca (multi. loc.)
Lahore Kebab (E1)
La Mancha (SW15)
Langan's Brasserie (W1)
Langan's Coq d'Or (SW5)
La Piragua (N1)
La Rueda (multi. loc.)
Le Bouchon Bordelais (multi. loc.)
Lee Fook (W2)
Lee Ho Fook (W1)
Le Metro (SW3)
Le Piaf (multi. loc.)
Little Bay (NW6)
Little Italy (W1)

Maison Bertaux (W1)
Mandarin Kitchen (W2)
Maroush (multi. loc.)
Maxwell's (multi. loc.)
Melati (W1)
Memories of India (SW7)
Mildreds (W1)
Ming (W1)
Miyabi (EC2)
Mustards Smithfield (EC1)
Nachos (SW10)
Navajo Joe (WC2)
New Culture Rev. (multi. loc.)
New World (W1)
Noura (SW1)
Oriel (SW1)
Orsino (W11)
Orso (WC2)
Paparazzi (multi. loc.)
Patisserie Valerie (multi. loc.)
Pepper Tree (SW4)
Phoenicia (W8)
Pitcher & Piano (multi. loc.)
Pizza Express (multi. loc.)
Pizza on the Park (SW1)
Pizza Pomodoro (multi. loc.)
Pizzeria Castello (SE1)
PJ's B&G (SW3)
Planet Hollywood (W1)
Porters (WC2)
porters bar (multi. loc.)
Portrait (WC2)
Pucci Pizza (SW3)
Rainforest Cafe (W1)
Randall & Aubin (multi. loc.)
Richoux (multi. loc.)
Rock Garden (WC2)
Rotisserie Jules (multi. loc.)
Royal China (multi. loc.)
Rules (WC2)
Sauce Organic Diner (NW1)
Seashell (NW1)
Shoeless Joe's (multi. loc.)
Singapura (multi. loc.)
Sofra (multi. loc.)
Soho Spice (W1)
Solly's (NW11)
Southeast W9 (W9)

Spaghetti House (multi. loc.)
Sports Cafe (SW1)
Starbucks (multi. loc.)
Sticky Fingers (W8)
Terminus (EC2)
Texas Embassy Cantina (SW14)
Texas Lone Star (multi. loc.)
T.G.I. Friday's (multi. loc.)
Toff's (N10)
Tokyo Diner (WC2)
Tom's Deli (W11)
Tootsies (multi. loc.)
Truc Vert (W1)
Tuttons Brasserie (WC2)
Vic Naylor (EC1)
Vingt-Quatre (SW10)
Wagamama (multi. loc.)
Wolfe's B&G (WC2)
Wong Kei (W1)
Yellow River Cafe (multi. loc.)
Ye Olde Cheshire Cheese (EC4)
Yo! Sushi (multi. loc.)
Zaika Bazaar (SW3)
Zilli Fish (W1)
Zinc B&G (W1)

Breakfast/Brunch

(All hotels and the following
standouts; BR=breakfast;
B=brunch)
Abingdon (W8) (B)
Admiral Codrington (SW3) (B)
Admiralty (WC2) (B)
Aquarium (E1) (B)
Avenue (SW1) (B)
Balans (multi. loc.) (BR,B)
bali sugar (W11) (B)
Bank Aldwych (WC2) (BR,B)
Bank Westminster/Zander
  (SW1) (BR,B)
Beach Blanket Babylon (W11) (B)
Belvedere (W8) (B)
Bistrot 190 (SW7) (BR,B)
Bluebird (SW3) (B)
Bridge (EC4) (B)
Browns Rest. (multi. loc.) (B)

Bush B&G (W12) (B)
Butlers Wharf (SE1) (B)
Cactus Blue (SW3) (B)
Cafe at Sotheby's (W1) (BR,B)
Café Delancey (NW1) (BR)
Camden Brasserie (NW1) (B)
Cantaloupe (EC2) (B)
Canyon (Richmond) (B)
Carluccio's Caffe (W1) (BR,B)
Chelsea Bun (multi. loc.) (BR,B)
Chelsea Kitchen (SW3) (BR,B)
Christopher's (WC2) (B)
Chutney Mary (SW10) (B)
Coq d'Argent (EC2) (BR,B)
Cow (W2) (B)
Crescent (SW3) (BR,B)
Dakota (W11) (B)
Emporio Armani Caffe (SW3) (BR)
Engineer (NW1) (BR,B)
Fifth Floor Cafe (SW1) (BR)
Fortnum's Fountain (W1) (BR)
Fox & Anchor (EC1) (BR)
Giraffe (multi. loc.) (BR,B)
Harrods (SW1) (BR,B)
Honest Cabbage (SE1) (B)
Idaho (N6) (B)
Jason's (W9) (B)
Joe Allen (WC2) (B)
Joe's (SW3) (BR,B)
Joe's Brasserie (SW6) (B)
Joe's Rest. (SW1) (BR,B)
Kensington Place (W8) (B)
La Brasserie (SW2) (BR,B)
Langan's Coq d'Or (SW5) (BR,B)
La Porte des Indes (W1) (B)
Le Caprice (SW1) (BR,B)
Le Metro (SW3) (BR)
Lola's (N1) (B)
Manor (W11) (B)
Mash (multi. loc.) (B)
Montana (SW6) (BR,B)
Nicole's (W1) (BR,B)
Oriel (SW1) (BR)
Osteria Ant. Bologna (SW11) (B)
Patisserie Val. (multi. loc.) (BR,B)
PJ's B&G (SW3) (B)
PJ's Grill (WC2) (B)
Polygon B&G (SW4) (B)

Rain (W10) (B)
Ransome's Dock (SW11) (BR,B)
Richoux (multi. loc.) (BR)
Salusbury Pub (NW6) (B)
Simpson's/Strand/Grand (WC2) (BR)
Smiths/Smithfield-Top (EC1) (BR)
T.G.I. Friday's (multi. loc.) (B)
Tom's Deli (W11) (BR,B)
Truc Vert (W1) (BR,B)
Villandry (W1) (BR,B)
Vingt-Quatre (SW10) (BR,B)
Wiz (W1) (B)

Business Dining

Al Duca (SW1)
Atrium (SW1)
Aurora (EC2)
Avenue (SW1)
Bank Aldwych (WC2)
Bank Westminster/Zander (SW1)
Belvedere (W8)
Bentley's (W1)
Bibendum (SW3)
Bice (W1)
Blakes Hotel (SW7)
Blue Print Cafe (SE1)
Brown's Hotel, Rest. 1837 (W1)
Capital (SW3)
Caravaggio (EC3)
Caviar Kaspia (W1)
Cecconi's (W1)
Chewton Glen, Marryat (Hants)
cheznico (W1)
Christopher's (WC2)
Cinnamon Club (SW1)
Circus (W1)
City Rhodes (EC4)
Clarke's (W8)
Cliveden, Waldo's (Berks)
Club Gascon (EC1)
Connaught Hotel, Rest. (W1)
Dorchester, Grill Room (W1)
Dorchester, Oriental (W1)
Drones (SW1)
Elena's l'Etoile (W1)
Fakhreldine (W1)

Fifth Floor (SW1)
FireBird (W1)
Floriana (SW3)
Foliage (SW1)
Four Seasons, Lanes (W1)
Four Seasons, Quadrato (E14)
Glasshouse (Kew)
Gordon Ramsay/68 Royal (SW3)
Goring Dining Room (SW1)
Gravetye Manor (W. Sus)
Greens (SW1)
Hartwell House (Bucks)
Il Convivio (SW1)
Il Forno (W1)
I-Thai (W2)
Ivy (WC2)
John Burton-Race (NW1)
J. Sheekey (WC2)
Kai (W1)
Lanesborough (SW1)
Langan's Bistro (W1)
Langan's Brasserie (W1)
La Tante Claire (SW1)
La Trompette (W4)
Launceston Place (W8)
Le Café du Marché (EC1)
Le Caprice (SW1)
Le Gavroche (W1)
Le Manoir/Quat'Saisons (Oxon)
Le Pont de la Tour (SE1)
Le Soufflé (W1)
L'Incontro (SW1)
L'Odeon (W1)
L'Oranger (SW1)
Manzi's (WC2)
Memories of China (multi. loc.)
Mirabelle (W1)
Mitsukoshi (SW1)
Miyama (W1)
Nahm (SW1)
Neal Street (WC2)
Neat Rest. (SE1)
Nico Central (W1)
Nobu (W1)
Oak Room MPW (W1)
Odin's (W1)
One-O-One (SW1)
Orrery (W1)

Orso (WC2)
Oxo Tower (SE1)
Pétrus (SW1)
Pied à Terre (W1)
Poissonnerie de l'Avenue (SW3)
Princess Garden (W1)
Quaglino's (SW1)
Quo Vadis (W1)
Rib Room (SW1)
Ritz (W1)
River Cafe (W6)
Rules (WC2)
Santini (SW1)
Savoy Grill (WC2)
Savoy River Rest. (WC2)
Searcy's at the Barbican (EC2)
Shepherd's (SW1)
Shogun (W14)
Smiths of Smithfield - Din. (EC1)
Smiths of Smithfield-Top (EC1)
Square, The (W1)
Stafford (SW1)
Suntory (SW1)
Tamarind (W1)
Tatsuso (EC2)
10 Devonshire Sq. (EC2)
Terrace (W1)
Turner's (SW3)
Twentyfour (EC2)
Ubon by Nobu (E14)
Vong (SW1)
Waterside Inn (Berks)
Wilton's (SW1)
Windows on the World (W1)
Zafferano (SW1)
Zen Central (W1)

BYO

Alounak (multi. loc.)
Basilico (multi. loc.)
Bedlington Cafe (W4)
Blah! Blah! Blah! (W12)
Books for Cooks (W11)
Chelsea Bun (multi. loc.)
Food for Thought (WC2)
Kalamaras Taverna (W2)
Kandoo (W2)

Mandola (W11)
Monsieur Max (Hampton Hill)
Ravi Shankar (EC1)
Rotisserie Jules (SW7)
Tom's Deli (W11)
World Food Café (WC2)

Cheeseboard

Aurora (EC2)
Chewton Glen, Marryat (Hants)
Chez Bruce (SW17)
cheznico (W1)
Clarke's (W8)
Connaught Hotel, Rest. (W1)
Gordon Ramsay/68 Royal (SW3)
La Tante Claire (SW1)
La Trompette (W4)
Le Gavroche (W1)
Le Manoir/Quat'Saisons (Oxon)
Le Soufflé (W1)
L'Oranger (SW1)
Monsieur Max (Hampton Hill)
Oak Room MPW (W1)
Orrery (W1)
Pétrus (SW1)
Pied à Terre (W1)
Savoy River Rest. (WC2)
Smiths of Smithfield-Top (EC1)
Square, The (W1)
Waterside Inn (Berks)
Windows on the World (W1)

Dancing/Live Entertainment

(Check days, times and performers for entertainment; D=dancing; best of many)
Aix-en-Provence (W11) (jazz)
Archduke (SE1) (jazz)
Avenue (SW1) (piano)
Ayoush (W1) (belly dancer/DJ)
Baltic (SE1) (jazz)
Bankside (SE1) (jazz)
Bertorelli (W1) (piano)
Big Easy (SW3) (rock)
Bluebird (SW3) (piano)
Boardwalk (W1) (DJ)

Boisdale (SW1) (jazz)
Bombay Brasserie (SW7) (piano)
Break for Border (multi.) (D/bands/DJ)
Café Boheme (W1) (jazz)
Cafe de Paris (W1) (D/cabaret/DJ)
Cheers (W1) (D/DJ)
Chutney Mary (SW10) (jazz)
Coq d'Argent (EC2) (jazz)
Corney & Barrow (EC3) (bands/DJ)
County Hall (SE1) (jazz)
Cuba (W8) (D/bands/DJ)
Cuba Libre (N1) (D/DJ)
Don Pepe (NW8) (Spanish)
Dorchester, Bar (W1) (jazz/piano)
Dover Street (W1) (D)
Down Mexico (W1) (D/bands/DJ)
Efes Kebab (W1) (belly dancer)
FireBird (W1) (piano)
Goring Dining Room (SW1) (piano)
Havana (multi. loc.) (D/bands/DJ)
Home (EC2) (D)
Idaho (N6) (jazz/piano)
Joe Allen (WC2) (piano)
Julono (NW3) (belly dancer)
Kai (W1) (harp)
La Finca (multi. loc.) (D/DJ)
Lanesborough (SW1) (D/jazz)
Langan's Brasserie (W1) (jazz)
La Rueda (multi. loc.) (D/bands)
Le Cafe du Jardin (WC2) (piano)
Le Café du Marché (EC1) (jazz)
Le Pont de la Tour (SE1) (piano)
Le Soufflé (W1) (D/piano)
L'Odeon (W1) (jazz)
Lola's (N1) (jazz/piano)
Maroush (W2) (D)
Meson Don Felipe (SE1) (guitar)
Mezzo (W1) (D/bands)
Mirabelle (W1) (piano)
Montana (SW6) (piano)
MPW Brasserie (NW3) (jazz)
Mr. Wing (SW5) (piano/singer)
Naked Turtle (SW14) (jazz/magic)
Nikita's (SW10) (accordion/guitar)
Opium (W1) (D/cabaret)

Otto Dining Lounge (W9) (D/DJ)
Oxo Tower Brasserie (SE1) (jazz)
Palm Court (WC2) (D/band/harp)
Paparazzi (multi. loc.) (D/bands/DJ)
Pasha (SW7) (bands/belly dancer)
Pharmacy (W11) (D/DJ)
Pie²Mash (NW1) (jazz)
Pizza on Park (SW1) (cabaret/jazz)
porters bar (WC2) (jazz)
Potemkin (EC1) (singer)
Princess Garden (W1) (piano)
Quaglino's (SW1) (jazz/piano)
Rebato's (SW8) (piano/singer)
Red Bar (W1) (DJ)
Red Cube B&G (WC2) (DJ)
Rib Room (SW1) (piano/singer)
Ritz (W1) (D/band)
Rock Garden (WC2) (D/band)
Rodizio Rico (W2) (D)
Saint Bar & Rest. (WC2) (D/DJ)
Sarastro (WC2) (opera)
Savoy River Rest. (WC2) (D/band)
Shoreditch Electricity (N1) (D/DJ)
Smollensky's/Strand (multi.)
    (D/jazz/piano)
Soho Spice (W1) (DJ)
Souk (WC2) (D/belly dancer)
Spirit (EC1) (D)
Sports Cafe (SW1) (D)
Sugar Reef (W1) (D/jazz)
Tenth (W8) (D/jazz)
Titanic (W1) (D/DJ)
Trader Vic's (W1) (D/singer)
Troubadour (SW5) (varies)
Voodoo Lounge (WC2) (D/DJ)
Well & Aquarium (EC1) (D/DJ)
White House (SW4) (D/DJ)
Windows on World (W1) (D/band)
Woody's (W9) (D/DJ)
Zamoyski (NW3) (guitar/singer)
Zeta (W1) (D/band/DJ)

Delivery/Takeaway
(D=delivery; T=takeaway;
best of many)
Abeno (WC1) (T)
Al Hamra (W1) (D,T)
Alounak (multi. loc.) (T)

Al Sultan (W1) (T)
Arkansas Cafe (E1) (T)
Aroma Chinese (multi. loc.) (T)
Ask Pizza (multi. loc.) (T)
Aykoku-Kaku (EC4) (D,T)
Babe Ruth's (E1) (T)
Bangkok (SW7) (D,T)
Bayee House (SW15) (D,T)
Bedlington Cafe (W4) (D,T)
Beiteddine (SW1) (D,T)
Bengal Clipper (SE1) (T)
Bengal Trader (E1) (T)
Ben's Thai (WC1) (T)
Big Easy (SW3) (T)
Bloom's (NW11) (T)
Blue Elephant (SW6) (T)
Blue Jade (SW1) (T)
Bonjour Vietnam (SW6) (D,T)
Browns Rest. (W1) (T)
Busabong Too (SW10) (D,T)
Cafe Lazeez (multi. loc.) (T)
Cafe Spice Namaste (multi.) (D,T)
Calzone (multi. loc.) (T)
Cellar Gascon (EC1) (T)
Chelsea Bun (SW11) (T)
Chelsea Kitchen (SW3) (T)
Cheng-Du (NW1) (D,T)
China City (WC2) (T)
Chor Bizarre (W1) (D,T)
Chutney Mary (SW10) (D)
Chutney's (NW1) (T)
Como Lario (SW1) (T)
Condotti (W1) (T)
Defune (W1) (T)
DKNY Bar (W1) (D,T)
Ed's Easy Diner (multi. loc.) (D,T)
Esarn Kheaw (W12) (T)
Exhibition Thai (SW7) (T)
Fakhreldine Exp. (multi.) (D,T)
Fina Estampa (SE1) (T)
Four Regions (SE1) (T)
40° at Veronica's (W2) (D,T)
Friends (SW10 (T)
Garbo's (W1) (D,T)
Geale's (W8) (T)
Giraffe (multi. loc.) (D,T)

Dining Alone

(Other than hotels, coffee shops, sushi bars and places with counter service)

Special Features Indexes

Smiths of Smithfield-Top (EC1)
Square, The (W1)
Stafford (SW1)
Stapleford Park (Leics)
St. John (EC1)
Tabla (E14)
Vale (W9)
Waterside Inn (Berks)
Wilton's (SW1)
Winteringham Fields (N. Linc)
Wiz (W1)
Wòdka (W8)
Zafferano (SW1)

Historic Places

(Year opened)
1487 Bear Hotel, The (Oxon)
1598 Gravetye Manor (W. Sus)
1640 Compleat Angler (Bucks)
1667 Ye Olde Cheshire Cheese (EC4)
1700 Footstool (SW1)
1742 Grenadier (SW1)
1742 Wilton's (SW1)
1759 Simpson's Tavern (EC3)
1798 Rules (WC2)
1828 Simpson's/Strand/Grand (WC2)
1828 Simpson's/Strand/Simply (WC2)
1850 Cliveden, Waldo's (Berks)
1889 Sweetings (EC4)
1897 Connaught Hotel, Rest. (W1)
1906 Ritz (W1)

Hotel Dining

Amberley Castle, Queens Room
  Amberley Castle/Queens (W. Sus)
Auberge du Lac
  Auberge du Lac (Herts)
Bear Hotel
  Bear Hotel, The (Oxon)
Beetle & Wedge Hotel
  Beetle & Wedge (Oxon)
Berkeley Hotel
  La Tante Claire (SW1)
  Vong (SW1)
Bishopstrow House
  Bishopstrow, Mulberry (Wilts)
Blakes Hotel
  Blakes Hotel (SW7)

Brown's Hotel
  Brown's Hotel, Rest. 1837 (W1)
  Brown's Hotel, The Library (W1)
Buckland Manor
  Buckland Manor (Glos)
Capital, The
  Capital (SW3)
Charlotte St. Hotel
  Oscar (W1)
Charlton House
  Charlton, Mulberry (Nr. Bath)
Chewton Glen Hotel
  Chewton Glen, Marryat (Hants)
Claridge's Hotel
  Claridge's Bar (W1)
  Gordon Ramsay/Claridge's (W1)
Cliveden Hotel
  Cliveden, Waldo's (Berks)
Connaught Hotel, The
  Connaught Hotel, Rest. (W1)
Conrad Int'l Hotel
  Aquasia (SW10)
Crowne Plaza London St. James
  Quilon (SW1)
Dolphin Sq. Hotel
  Rhodes in the Square (SW1)
Dorchester, The
  Dorchester, Bar (W1)
  Dorchester, Grill Room (W1)
  Dorchester, Oriental (W1)
Eastwell Manor Hotel
  Eastwell Manor (Kent)
Feathers Hotel
  Feathers Hotel (Oxon)
Four Seasons Canary Wharf
  Four Seasons, Quadrato (E14)
Four Seasons Hotel
  Four Seasons, Lanes (W1)
French Horn Hotel
  French Horn (Berks)
Gidleigh Park Hotel
  Gidleigh Park (Devon)
Gore Hotel
  Bistrot 190 (SW7)
Goring Hotel, The
  Goring Dining Room (SW1)
Gravetye Manor Hotel
  Gravetye Manor (W. Sus)

"In" Places

Special Features Indexes

Original Tajine (W1)
Orrery (W1)
Orsino (W11)
Orso (WC2)
Oxo Tower (SE1)
Oxo Tower Brasserie (SE1)
Parisienne Chophse. (SW3)
Pétrus (SW1)
Pharmacy (W11)
PJ's B&G (SW3)
PJ's Grill (WC2)
Prism (EC3)
Putney Bridge (SW15)
Quo Vadis (W1)
Randall & Aubin (multi. loc.)
Real Greek (N1)
Richard Corrigan/Lindsay (W1)
Riva (SW13)
River Cafe (W6)
Rosmarino (NW8)
Saint Bar & Rest. (WC2)
San Lorenzo (SW3)
Shoreditch Electricity (N1)
Smiths of Smithfield - Din. (EC1)
Spiga (multi. loc.)
Spighetta (W1)
Spoon+ at Sanderson (W1)
Square, The (W1)
St. John (EC1)
Sugar Club (W1)
Sugar Reef (W1)
Tom's Deli (W11)
Ubon by Nobu (E14)
Vingt-Quatre (SW10)
Vong (SW1)
Voodoo Lounge (WC2)
Wagamama (multi. loc.)
Yo! Sushi (multi. loc.)
Zafferano (SW1)
Zaika (W8)
Zilli Fish (W1)

Late Dining – After Midnight

(All hours are AM;
* check locations)
Balans (multi. loc.) (3)*
Bar Madrid (W1) (3)

Blue Elephant (SW6) (12.30)
Boardwalk (W1) (1)
Café Boheme (W1) (3)
Cafe Lazeez (multi. loc.) (1)*
Cheers (W1) (3)
Cuba (W8) (2)
Denim (WC2) (1)
Dover Street (W1) (3)
Efes Kebab House (multi.) (2)*
Fakhreldine Exp. (multi. loc.) (1)
Havana (multi. loc.) (2)
Istanbul Iskembecisi (N16) (5)
Jen Hong Kong (W1) (3)
Joe Allen (WC2) (12.45)
Lee Ho Fook (W1) (1)
Le Mercury (N1) (1)
Little Italy (W1) (4)
Maroush (multi. loc.) (1)*
Mezzonine (W1) (3)
Mr. Kong (WC2) (2.45)
Paparazzi (multi. loc.) (1)
Smollensky's/Strand (multi.) (12.30)
Soho Spice (W1) (1)
Sports Cafe (SW1) (2)
Trader Vic's (W1) (12.30)
Vic Naylor (EC1) (1)
Vingt-Quatre (SW10) (24 hrs.)
Voodoo Lounge (WC2) (3)
Yas (W14) (5)
Zeta (W1) (1)

No Smoking Sections

Abeno (WC1)
Admiralty (WC2)
Amphitheatre (WC2)
Aquasia (SW10)
Archduke (SE1)
Archipelago (W1)
Arkansas Cafe (E1)
Aroma (multi. loc.)
Ask Pizza (multi. loc.)
Atrium (SW1)
Babe Ruth's (E1)
bali sugar (W11)
Baltic (SE1)
Bankside (SE1)
Base (NW3)

People's Palace (SE1)
Pepper Tree (SW4)
Pescatori (multi. loc.)
Phoenix B&G (SW15)
Pizza Express (multi. loc.)
Pizza on the Park (SW1)
Pizza Organic (multi. loc.)
Pizza Pomodoro (EC2)
Planet Hollywood (W1)
Quality Chop Hse. (EC1)
Rasa (W1)
Richoux (multi. loc.)
RK Stanley's (W1)
Rocket (W1)
Santa Fe (N1)
Sarkhel's (SW18)
Savoy River Rest. (WC2)
Scotts (W1)
Seashell (NW1)
Shepherd's (SW1)
Shish (NW2)
Silks & Spice (multi. loc.)
Smollensky's on Strand (WC2)
Snows on the Green (W6)
Solly's (NW11)
Southeast W9 (W9)
Spaghetti House (multi. loc.)
Spago (SW7)
Spighetta (W1)
Stafford (SW1)
Standard Tandoori (W2)
Stepping Stone (SW8)
Sugar Club (W1)
Tabla (E14)
Tandoori of Chelsea (SW3)
Tas (SE1)
Tate Gallery Rest. (SW1)
Tenth (W8)
Terminus (EC2)
T.G.I. Friday's (multi. loc.)
Tiger Lil's (multi. loc.)
Tootsies (multi. loc.)
Twelfth House (W11)
Two Brothers Fish (N3)
Ubon by Nobu (E14)
Union Cafe (W1)
Vale (W9)
Vineyard at Stockcross (Berks)

Vong (SW1)
Windows on the World (W1)
Wok Wok (multi. loc.)
Yellow River Cafe (multi. loc.)
Yoshino (W1)
Zamoyski (NW3)
Zizzi (W1)
Zuccato (NW3)

Noteworthy Newcomers

Aperitivo (W1)
Aquasia (SW10)
Archipelago (W1)
Attica (W1)
Baltic (SE1)
Bankside (SE1)
Basilico (multi. loc.)
Black & Blue (W8)
Bush B&G (W12)
Cecconi's (W1)
Champor - Champor (SE1)
Chives (SW10)
Cigala (WC1)
Cinnamon Club (SW1)
Cotto (W14)
Dalchini (SW19)
Don (EC4)
Drones (SW1)
Elephant Royale (E14)
Ginger (W2)
Gordon Ramsay/Claridge's (W1)
Hakkasan (W1)
I Cardi (SW10)
Just St. James's (SW1)
Kandoo (W2)
King's Head, The (N21)
La Trompette (W4)
Lemon Thyme (SW13)
Les Trois Garcons (E1)
LMNT (E8)
Manor (W11)
Masala Zone (W1)
Mju (SW1)
MPW Brasserie (NW3)
Nahm (SW1)
Neat Brasserie (SE1)
Neat Rest. (SE1)
Nirvana (SW19)
Notting Hill Brasserie (W11)

Noura (SW1)
182 Mint (EC1)
Opium (W1)
Oscar (W1)
Otto Dining Lounge (W9)
Paell'ya (SW8)
Parisienne Chophse. (SW3)
Parsee (N19)
Passion (W9)
Pellicano (SW3)
Perc%nto (EC4)
Phoenix Palace (NW1)
Pie²Mash (NW1)
Potemkin (EC1)
Pug (W4)
Red Cube B&G (WC2)
Shish (NW2)
Six-13 (W1)
Smiths of Smithfield-Top (EC1)
Spirit (EC1)
Truc Vert (W1)
Tuscan Steak (WC2)
Twelfth House (W11)
Ubon by Nobu (E14)
Wapping Food (E1)
Well & Aquarium (EC1)
White House (SW4)
Zaika Bazaar (SW3)
Zilli (W11)

Offbeat

Alounak (W2)
Aperitivo (W1)
Archipelago (W1)
ArdRí at O'Conor Don (W14)
Arkansas Cafe (E1)
Asia de Cuba (WC2)
Beach Blanket Babylon (W11)
Belgo Centraal (WC2)
Belgo Noord (NW1)
Belgo Zuid (W10)
Bierodrome (multi. loc.)
Blah! Blah! Blah! (W12)
Bloom's (NW11)
Blue Elephant (SW6)
Boisdale (SW1)
Books for Cooks (W11)
Cantina Vinopolis (SE1)
Cellar Gascon (EC1)

Chelsea Kitchen (SW3)
Chinon (W14)
Chor Bizarre (W1)
Club Gascon (EC1)
Delfina Studio Cafe (SE1)
Fish! (multi. loc.)
Food for Thought (WC2)
Footstool (SW1)
Garlic & Shots (W1)
Inaho (W2)
itsu (multi. loc.)
Jason's (W9)
Jenny Lo's Tea (SW1)
Jim Thompson's (multi. loc.)
Just Around the Corner (NW2)
Kaifeng (NW4)
Kulu Kulu Sushi (W1)
La Porte des Indes (W1)
Les Trois Garcons (E1)
Levant (W1)
LMNT (E8)
Lola's (N1)
Maggie Jones's (W8)
Mju (SW1)
Momo (W1)
Moro (EC1)
Moshi Moshi Sushi (EC2)
Mr. Wing (SW5)
Nahm (SW1)
Nancy Lam's Enak-Enak (SW11)
Navajo Joe (WC2)
Nikita's (SW10)
Ozer (W1)
Pharmacy (W11)
Pizza Metro (SW11)
Place Below (EC2)
Polygon B&G (SW4)
Quality Chop Hse. (EC1)
Rainforest Cafe (W1)
Richard Corrigan/Lindsay (W1)
Sale e Pepe (SW1)
Solly's (NW11)
Souk (WC2)
Spoon+ at Sanderson (W1)
St. John (EC1)
Sugar Club (W1)
Tate Gallery Rest. (SW1)
Tom's Deli (W11)

Troubadour (SW5)
Truc Vert (W1)
Twelfth House (W11)
Wagamama (multi. loc.)
Wapping Food (E1)
Wiz (W1)
Wok Wok (multi. loc.)
Yo! Sushi (multi. loc.)
Zaika Bazaar (SW3)

Outdoor Dining

(G=garden; P=patio;
PV=Pavement; T=terrace;
best of many;
see also Water Views)
Admiral Codrington (SW3) (P)
Aix-en-Provence (W11) (T)
Al Hamra (W1) (P)
Amandier (W2) (T)
Amphitheatre (WC2) (T)
Aquarium (E1) (T)
Aquasia (SW10) (T)
Archduke (SE1) (G,PV,T)
Archipelago (W1) (P)
Ark (W8) (T)
bali sugar (W11) (G)
Bam-Bou (W1) (P)
Beach Blanket Babylon (W11) (P)
Bedlington Cafe (W4) (PV)
Beetle & Wedge (Oxon) (G,T)
Belair House (SE21) (T)
Belvedere (W8) (T)
Bishopstrow, Mulberry (Wilts) (G)
Black Truffle (NW1) (G)
Boisdale (SW1) (P)
Brackenbury (W6) (P)
Brasserie Rocque (EC2) (T)
Bridge (EC4) (T)
Buckland Manor (Glos) (G,P)
Butlers Wharf (SE1) (T)
Cantina del Ponte (SE1) (T)
Cantinetta Venegazzu (SW11) (P)
Canyon (Richmond) (G,P,T)
Caraffini (SW1) (PV)
Casale Franco (N1) (P)
Cherwell Boathouse (Oxon) (T)
Chewton Glen, Marryat (Hants) (T)
Cigala (WC1) (P)

Coq d'Argent (EC2) (G,T)
Costa's Grill (W8) (G)
Cotto (W14) (PV)
Dakota (W11) (P)
Dan's (SW3) (G)
Daphne's (SW3) (G)
Depot (SW14) (P)
El Gaucho (SW3) (T)
Elistano (SW3) (PV)
Enterprise (SW3) (PV)
Fat Duck (Berks) (G,T)
Fifth Floor Cafe (SW1) (T)
Four Seasons, Quadrato (E14) (T)
Hambleton Hall (R'land) (G)
Hard Rock Cafe (W1) (T)
Havelock Tavern (W14) (G,PV)
Henry J. Bean's (SW3) (G,P)
Hotel Tresanton (C'wall) (T)
House on Rosslyn Hill (NW3) (T)
Hush (W1) (P)
Idaho (N6) (T)
Jason's (W9) (T)
Joe's (SW3) (PV)
Julie's (W11) (G,PV)
La Brasserie (SW2) (PV)
La Famiglia (SW10) (G)
Langan's Coq d'Or (SW5) (T)
La Poule au Pot (SW1) (P)
La Trompette (W4) (T)
Leaping Hare Vineyd. (Suffolk) (P)
Leatherne Bottel (Berks) (T)
Le Boudin Blanc (W1) (T)
Le Colombier (SW3) (T)
Le Manoir (Oxon) (G,P)
Le Pont de la Tour (SE1) (T)
Le Poussin (Hants) (G,T)
L'Oranger (SW1) (P)
Lundum's (SW7) (P)
Made in Italy (SW3) (T)
Mallory Court (Warwks) (T)
Mediterraneo (W11) (P)
Mirabelle (W1) (G,P)
Monza (SW3) (PV)
Moro (EC1) (PV)
Motcomb's (SW1) (PV)
MPW Brasserie (NW3) (T)
Oriel (SW1) (PV)
Orrery (W1) (T)

Parties & Private Rooms

(Any nightclub or restaurant
charges less at off-times;
* indicates private rooms
available; best of many)

Special Features Indexes

Power Scenes

Pre-Theatre Dining

(Call to check prices,
days and times)

Circus (W1)
Connaught Hotel, Rest. (W1)
County Hall (SE1)
Criterion Brasserie (W1)
Denim (WC2)
East One (EC1)
Food for Thought (WC2)
Footstool (SW1)
Fortnum's Fountain (W1)
40° at Veronica's (W2)
Frederick's (N1)
Goring Dining Room (SW1)
House on Rosslyn Hill (NW3)
Incognico (WC2)
Indigo (WC2)
Ivy (WC2)
Joe Allen (WC2)
J. Sheekey (WC2)
La Bouchée (SW7)
La Brasserie Townhouse (WC1)
Lanesborough (SW1)
Le Boudin Blanc (W1)
Le Cafe du Jardin (WC2)
Le Caprice (SW1)
Le Colombier (SW3)
Le Pont de la Tour (SE1)
L'Escargot (W1)
L'Estaminet (WC2)
Livebait (multi. loc.)
L'Odeon (W1)
Lola's (N1)
Manzi's (WC2)
Matsuri (SW1)
Mela (WC2)
Mezzo (W1)
Mezzonine (W1)
Mitsukoshi (SW1)
Mon Plaisir (WC2)
Moro (EC1)
Navajo Joe (WC2)
Oriel (SW1)
Orsino (W11)
Oxo Tower Brasserie (SE1)
Ozer (W1)
People's Palace (SE1)
Pescatori (multi. loc.)
Phoenix B&G (SW15)
PJ's Grill (WC2)

Planet Hollywood (W1)
Polygon B&G (SW4)
Porters (WC2)
Prospect Grill (WC2)
Quaglino's (SW1)
Richard Corrigan/Lindsay (W1)
Richoux (multi. loc.)
Rowley's (SW1)
Rules (WC2)
Savoy River Rest. (WC2)
Searcy's at the Barbican (EC2)
Simpson's/Strand/Grand (WC2)
Simpson's/Strand/Simply (WC2)
Smollensky's on Strand (WC2)
Sofra (multi. loc.)
Soho Spice (W1)
Stepping Stone (SW8)
Tamarind (W1)
Teatro (W1)
Upstairs at The Savoy (WC2)
Vama (SW10)
Vasco & Piero's (W1)
Veeraswamy (W1)
Villandry (W1)
Vong (SW1)
Waterloo Fire Station (SE1)
Zen Garden (W1)
Zinc B&G (W1)

Pubs/Sports Bars/ Microbreweries
(*Sports Bars)
Admiral Codrington (SW3)
Anglesea Arms (W6)
Archduke (SE1)
ArdRí at O'Conor Don (W14)
Babe Ruth's (E1)*
Blues Bistro & Bar (W1)*
Builders Arms (SW3)
Chapel (NW1)
Cheers (W1)
Chelsea Ram (SW10)
Churchill Arms (W8)
Cow (W2)
Duke of Cambridge (N1)
Duke of Cambridge (SW11)
Eagle (EC1)
Engineer (NW1)

Enterprise (SW3)
Fox & Anchor (EC1)
Freedom Brewing (multi. loc.)
George Bar (EC2)
Grenadier (SW1)
Guinea (W1)
Havelock Tavern (W14)
Honest Cabbage (SE1)
Lansdowne (NW1)
Mash (multi. loc.)
North Pole (SE10)
Peasant (EC1)
Prince Bonaparte (W2)
Queens (NW1)
Salt House (NW8)
Salusbury Pub (NW6)
Shoeless Joe's (multi. loc.)*
Sporting Page (SW10)*
Sports Cafe (SW1)*
Vic Naylor (EC1)
Vine (NW5)
Waxy O'Connor's (W1)
Westbourne (W2)
Ye Olde Cheshire Cheese (EC4)

Pudding Specialists

Alastair Little (W1)
Asia de Cuba (WC2)
Aubergine (SW10)
Aurora (EC2)
Belvedere (W8)
Bibendum (SW3)
Blakes Hotel (SW7)
Brown's Hotel, Rest. 1837 (W1)
Capital (SW3)
Chewton Glen, Marryat (Hants)
cheznico (W1)
City Rhodes (EC4)
Clarke's (W8)
Cliveden, Waldo's (Berks)
Club Gascon (EC1)
Connaught Hotel, Rest. (W1)
Fat Duck (Berks)
Fifth Floor (SW1)
Floriana (SW3)
Foliage (SW1)
Fortnum's Fountain (W1)
Four Seasons, Lanes (W1)
Glasshouse (Kew)

Gordon Ramsay/68 Royal (SW3)
Lanesborough (SW1)
La Tante Claire (SW1)
La Trompette (W4)
Le Gavroche (W1)
Le Manoir/Quat'Saisons (Oxon)
Le Soufflé (W1)
L'Oranger (SW1)
Maison Novelli (EC1)
Mirabelle (W1)
Monkeys (SW3)
Neat Rest. (SE1)
Nico Central (W1)
Nobu (W1)
Oak Room MPW (W1)
Orrery (W1)
Patisserie Valerie (multi. loc.)
Pétrus (SW1)
Richard Corrigan/Lindsay (W1)
Richoux (multi. loc.)
Ritz (W1)
River Cafe (W6)
Sartoria (W1)
Spoon+ at Sanderson (W1)
Square, The (W1)
Sugar Club (W1)
Vong (SW1)
Waterside Inn (Berks)

Quiet Conversation

Amandier (W2)
Aubergine (SW10)
Aurora (EC2)
Belair House (SE21)
Bentley's (W1)
Bice (W1)
Blakes Hotel (SW7)
Brown's Hotel, Rest. 1837 (W1)
Capital (SW3)
Cassia Oriental (W1)
Chewton Glen, Marryat (Hants)
cheznico (W1)
Chives (SW10)
Cliveden, Waldo's (Berks)
Connaught Hotel, Rest. (W1)
Creelers (SW3)
Dan's (SW3)
Dorchester, Oriental (W1)
English Garden (SW3)

Foliage (SW1)
Four Seasons, Lanes (W1)
Four Seasons, Quadrato (E14)
Goring Dining Room (SW1)
Greens (SW1)
Hartwell House (Bucks)
House (SW3)
Il Convivio (SW1)
Lanesborough (SW1)
La Tante Claire (SW1)
Launceston Place (W8)
Le Gavroche (W1)
Le Manoir/Quat'Saisons (Oxon)
L'Oranger (SW1)
Mitsukoshi (SW1)
Monkeys (SW3)
Neat Brasserie (SE1)
Oak Room MPW (W1)
Odin's (W1)
One-O-One (SW1)
Orrery (W1)
Pétrus (SW1)
Ritz (W1)
Roussillon (SW1)
Savoy River Rest. (WC2)
Scotts (W1)
Stafford (SW1)
Stonor Arms (Oxon)
Turner's (SW3)
Waterside Inn (Berks)
Wilton's (SW1)
Windows on the World (W1)

Romantic

Amberley Castle/Queens (W. Sus)
Andrew Edmunds (W1)
Aurora (EC2)
Belvedere (W8)
Blakes (NW1)
Blakes Hotel (SW7)
Blue Elephant (SW6)
Capital (SW3)
Caviar Kaspia (W1)
Chewton Glen, Marryat (Hants)
Clarke's (W8)
Cliveden, Waldo's (Berks)
Club Gascon (EC1)
Compleat Angler (Bucks)
Connaught Hotel, Rest. (W1)

Criterion Brasserie (W1)
Daphne's (SW3)
Drones (SW1)
Fifth Floor (SW1)
FireBird (W1)
Floriana (SW3)
Foliage (SW1)
Frederick's (N1)
French Horn (Berks)
Gidleigh Park (Devon)
Gordon Ramsay/68 Royal (SW3)
Gravetye Manor (W. Sus)
Hakkasan (W1)
Hartwell House (Bucks)
Julie's (W11)
La Famiglia (SW10)
Lanesborough (SW1)
La Poule au Pot (SW1)
Launceston Place (W8)
Leatherne Bottel (Berks)
Le Café du Marché (EC1)
Le Caprice (SW1)
Le Gavroche (W1)
Le Manoir/Quat'Saisons (Oxon)
Le Pont de la Tour (SE1)
Les Trois Garcons (E1)
L'Incontro (SW1)
L'Oranger (SW1)
Lundum's (SW7)
Lygon Arms (Worcs)
Made in Italy (SW3)
Maggie Jones's (W8)
Mirabelle (W1)
Momo (W1)
Monkeys (SW3)
Mr. Wing (SW5)
Nobu (W1)
Oak Room MPW (W1)
Odette's (NW1)
Odin's (W1)
Orrery (W1)
Pétrus (SW1)
Prism (EC3)
Richard Corrigan/Lindsay (W1)
Ritz (W1)
River Cafe (W6)
Roussillon (SW1)
San Lorenzo (SW3)

Savoy River Rest. (WC2)
Snows on the Green (W6)
Square, The (W1)
Waterside Inn (Berks)
Windows on the World (W1)
Zafferano (SW1)

Senior Appeal

Al Duca (SW1)
Belair House (SE21)
Belvedere (W8)
Bentley's (W1)
Bloom's (NW11)
Brasserie St. Quentin (SW3)
Cafe at Sotheby's (W1)
Capital (SW3)
Cassia Oriental (W1)
Caviar Kaspia (W1)
Cecconi's (W1)
Chewton Glen, Marryat (Hants)
cheznico (W1)
Cliveden, Waldo's (Berks)
Compleat Angler (Bucks)
Connaught Hotel, Rest. (W1)
Dan's (SW3)
Dorchester, Grill Room (W1)
Dorchester, Oriental (W1)
Drones (SW1)
Elena's l'Etoile (W1)
English Garden (SW3)
Floriana (SW3)
Foliage (SW1)
Fortnum's Fountain (W1)
Four Seasons, Lanes (W1)
Four Seasons, Quadrato (E14)
Gidleigh Park (Devon)
Glasshouse (Kew)
Gordon Ramsay/68 Royal (SW3)
Goring Dining Room (SW1)
Gravetye Manor (W. Sus)
Greens (SW1)
Hartwell House (Bucks)
Hotel du Vin & Bistro (multi. loc.)
House (SW3)
Il Convivio (SW1)
Ivy (WC2)
Jason's (W9)
John Burton-Race (NW1)
J. Sheekey (WC2)

Kai (W1)
Lanesborough (SW1)
Langan's Bistro (W1)
La Poule au Pot (SW1)
La Tante Claire (SW1)
Launceston Place (W8)
Leatherne Bottel (Berks)
Le Caprice (SW1)
Le Gavroche (W1)
Le Manoir/Quat'Saisons (Oxon)
Le Soufflé (W1)
L'Incontro (SW1)
L'Oranger (SW1)
Lundum's (SW7)
Lygon Arms (Worcs)
Manzi's (WC2)
Mimmo d'Ischia (SW1)
Mirabelle (W1)
Monkeys (SW3)
Motcomb's (SW1)
Neal Street (WC2)
Neat Rest. (SE1)
Nico Central (W1)
Noura (SW1)
Oak Room MPW (W1)
Odin's (W1)
One-O-One (SW1)
Orrery (W1)
Parade (W5)
Patisserie Valerie (SW3)
Pétrus (SW1)
Poissonnerie de l'Avenue (SW3)
Reubens (W1)
Rib Room (SW1)
Richoux (NW8)
Ritz (W1)
Rosmarino (NW8)
Rowley's (SW1)
Rules (WC2)
Sartoria (W1)
Savoy Grill (WC2)
Savoy River Rest. (WC2)
Scotts (W1)
Shepherd's (SW1)
Simpson's/Strand/Grand (WC2)
Simpson's/Strand/Simply (WC2)
Square, The (W1)
Stonor Arms (Oxon)

Tate Gallery Rest. (SW1)
Trader Vic's (W1)
Turner's (SW3)
Upstairs at The Savoy (WC2)
Waterside Inn (Berks)
Waterstones, Red Rm. (W1)
Wilton's (SW1)
Zen Central (W1)

Set Price Menus

Call to check prices, days,
and times; best of many)
Alastair Little (W1)
Alastair Little/Lancaster Rd. (W11)
Alloro (W1)
Amandier (W2)
Archipelago (W1)
Aroma Chinese (multi. loc.)
Aubergine (SW10)
Avenue (SW1)
Bam-Bou (W1)
Benihana (W1)
Bibendum (SW3)
Bice (W1)
Bistro Daniel (W2)
Blue Elephant (SW6)
Blue Jade (SW1)
Blue Lagoon (W14)
Brasserie St. Quentin (SW3)
Brown's Hotel, Rest. 1837 (W1)
Buckland Manor (Glos)
Butlers Wharf (SE1)
Cafe Pacifico (WC2)
Cantina Vinopolis (SE1)
Cantinetta Venegazzu (SW11)
Canyon (Richmond)
Caravaggio (EC3)
Cassia Oriental (W1)
Caviar Kaspia (W1)
Che (SW1)
Cherwell Boathouse (Oxon)
Chewton Glen, Marryat (Hants)
Chez Bruce (SW17)
Chez Gérard (multi. loc.)
cheznico (W1)
Chiswick (W4)
Chor Bizarre (W1)
Christopher's (multi. loc.)

Chutney Mary (SW10)
Cicada (EC1)
Cigala (WC1)
Cinnamon Club (SW1)
Circus (W1)
City Miyama (EC4)
Clarke's (W8)
Cliveden, Waldo's (Berks)
Club Gascon (EC1)
Compleat Angler (Bucks)
Creelers (SW3)
Dan's (SW3)
Defune (W1)
Del Buongustaio (SW15)
Dorchester, Grill Room (W1)
Dorchester, Oriental (W1)
Eastwell Manor (Kent)
Emile's (SW15)
English Garden (SW3)
Fat Duck (Berks)
Feathers Hotel (Oxon)
Feng Shang Floating (NW1)
Fifth Floor (SW1)
FireBird (W1)
Floriana (SW3)
Foliage (SW1)
Four Seasons, Lanes (W1)
Four Seasons, Quadrato (E14)
Gaudí (EC1)
Gidleigh Park (Devon)
Glasshouse (Kew)
Gordon Ramsay/68 Royal (SW3)
Goring Dining Room (SW1)
Granita (N1)
Gravetye Manor (W. Sus)
Grissini (SW1)
Hambleton Hall (R'land)
Hartwell House (Bucks)
Hotel du Vin & Bistro (multi. loc.)
Hush (W1)
Ibla (W1)
Idaho (N6)
Il Convivio (SW1)
I-Thai (W2)
Ivy (WC2)
Jason's (W9)
John Burton-Race (NW1)
J. Sheekey (WC2)

Mandalay (W2)
Marine Ices (NW3)
Masala Zone (W1)
Merchant House (Shrops)
Mildreds (W1)
Mju (SW1)
Moshi Moshi Sushi (EC2)
Mr. Underhill's (Shrops)
Nancy Lam's Enak-Enak (SW11)
Noto (EC4)
Pink Geranium (Cambs)
Portrait (WC2)
Pret à Manger (multi. loc.)
Rainforest Cafe (W1)
Rasa (multi. loc.)
RIBA Café (W1)
Rick Stein's Seafood (C'wall)
Royal Oak (Berks)
Rules (WC2)
Satsuma (W1)
Soup Opera (multi. loc.)
Soup Works (multi. loc.)
Spighetta (W1)
Stapleford Park (Leics)
Starbucks (multi. loc.)
Stonor Arms (Oxon)
Toast (NW3)
Tom's Deli (W11)
Truc Vert (W1)
Villandry (W1)
Wagamama (multi. loc.)
Yo! Sushi (multi. loc.)

Special Occasions

Asia de Cuba (WC2)
Aubergine (SW10)
Aurora (EC2)
Avenue (SW1)
Belvedere (W8)
Bibendum (SW3)
Blakes Hotel (SW7)
Blue Elephant (SW6)
Brown's Hotel, Rest. 1837 (W1)
Capital (SW3)
Cecconi's (W1)
Che (SW1)
Chewton Glen, Marryat (Hants)
Chez Bruce (SW17)
cheznico (W1)

Cinnamon Club (SW1)
Clarke's (W8)
Cliveden, Waldo's (Berks)
Club Gascon (EC1)
Compleat Angler (Bucks)
Connaught Hotel, Rest. (W1)
Criterion Brasserie (W1)
Daphne's (SW3)
Dorchester, Grill Room (W1)
Dorchester, Oriental (W1)
Drones (SW1)
FireBird (W1)
Floriana (SW3)
Foliage (SW1)
French Horn (Berks)
Glasshouse (Kew)
Gordon Ramsay/68 Royal (SW3)
Goring Dining Room (SW1)
Gravetye Manor (W. Sus)
Hartwell House (Bucks)
Hotel du Vin & Bistro (multi. loc.)
Il Convivio (SW1)
I-Thai (W2)
Ivy (WC2)
John Burton-Race (NW1)
J. Sheekey (WC2)
Lanesborough (SW1)
La Tante Claire (SW1)
La Trompette (W4)
Launceston Place (W8)
Leatherne Bottel (Berks)
Le Caprice (SW1)
Le Gavroche (W1)
Le Manoir/Quat'Saisons (Oxon)
Le Pont de la Tour (SE1)
Le Soufflé (W1)
L'Oranger (SW1)
Lundum's (SW7)
Mirabelle (W1)
Momo (W1)
Nahm (SW1)
Neal Street (WC2)
Neat Rest. (SE1)
Nobu (W1)
Oak Room MPW (W1)
Orrery (W1)
Pétrus (SW1)
Pharmacy (W11)

Pied à Terre (W1)
Quaglino's (SW1)
Quo Vadis (W1)
Richard Corrigan/Lindsay (W1)
Ritz (W1)
River Cafe (W6)
San Lorenzo (SW3)
Savoy River Rest. (WC2)
Smiths of Smithfield - Din. (EC1)
Smiths of Smithfield-Top (EC1)
Spoon+ at Sanderson (W1)
Square, The (W1)
Stapleford Park (Leics)
Ubon by Nobu (E14)
Vong (SW1)
Waterside Inn (Berks)
Windows on the World (W1)
Zafferano (SW1)
Zaika (W8)

Sunday Dining
(B=brunch; L=lunch;
D=dinner; plus most Asians)
Abingdon (W8) (B,L,D)
Admiral Codrington (SW3) (B,L,D)
Admiralty (WC2) (L,D)
Al Duca (SW1) (L,D)
Al Hamra (W1) (L,D)
Al Sultan (W1) (L,D)
Amberley Castle/Qns. (W. Sus) (L,D)
Anglesea Arms (W6) (L,D)
Ark (W8) (L,D)
Arkansas Cafe (E1) (L)
Asia de Cuba (WC2) (D)
Auberge du Lac (Herts) (L,D)
Avenue (SW1) (B,L,D)
bali sugar (W11) (L,D)
Bank Aldwych (WC2) (B,D)
Beach Blanket Baby. (W11) (B,D)
Beetle & Wedge (Oxon) (L,D)
Belair House (SE21) (L,D)
Belgo Centraal (WC2) (L,D)
Belgo Noord (NW1) (L,D)
Belgo Zuid (W10) (L,D)
Belvedere (W8) (L,D)
Bengal Clipper (SE1) (L,D)
Bentley's (W1) (L,D)
Bibendum (SW3) (L,D)

Bibendum Oyster (SW3) (L,D)
Bierodrome (multi. loc.) (B,L,D)
Big Easy (SW3) (L,D)
Bishopstrow, Mulb. (Wilts) (L,D)
Bistrot 190 (SW7) (B,D)
Black Truffle (NW1) (L,D)
Blakes Hotel (SW7) (B,L,D)
Bloom's (NW11) (L,D)
Bluebird (SW3) (B,L,D)
Blue Elephant (SW6) (L,D)
Blue Lagoon (W14) (L,D)
Blue Print Cafe (SE1) (L,D)
Brackenbury (W6) (L,D)
Bridge (EC4) (B,L)
Buckland Manor (Glos) (L,D)
Builders Arms (SW3) (L,D)
Busaba Eathai (W1) (L,D)
Butlers Wharf (SE1) (B,L)
Cactus Blue (SW3) (B,L,D)
Cafe Lazeez (multi. loc.) (L,D)
Cafe, Level Seven (SE1) (L)
Cafe Pacifico (WC2) (L,D)
Cambio de Tercio (SW5) (L,D)
Cantaloupe (EC2) (B)
Cantina del Ponte (SE1) (L,D)
Cantina Vinopolis (SE1) (B,L)
Cantinetta Venegazzu (SW11) (L,D)
Canyon (Richmond) (B,D)
Capital (SW3) (L,D)
Carluccio's Caffe (W1) (B,L,D)
Casale Franco (N1) (L,D)
Cassia Oriental (W1) (L,D)
Chewton Glen, Marryat (Hants) (L,D)
Chez Bruce (SW17) (L)
Chez Max (SW10) (L,D)
Chiswick (W4) (B,L)
Christopher's (WC2) (B)
Chutney Mary (SW10) (B)
Cinnamon Cay (SW11) (L)
Cinnamon Club (SW1) (B)
Compleat Angler (Bucks) (L,D)
Connaught (W1) (L,D)
Coq d'Argent (EC2) (D)
Creelers (SW3) (B,L,D)
Crescent (SW3) (B,L,D)
Criterion Brasserie (W1) (D)
Crivelli's Garden (WC2) (L)

Special Features Indexes

Marsh Goose (Glos) (L)
Masala Zone (W1) (L,D)
Mediterraneo (W11) (L,D)
Mela (WC2) (L,D)
Mezzo (W1) (L,D)
Mirabelle (W1) (L,D)
Monsieur Max (Hampton Hill) (L)
Montana (SW6) (B,D)
Montpeliano (SW7) (L,D)
Monza (SW3) (L,D)
Motcomb's (SW1) (B,L)
Nahm (SW1) (D)
Navajo Joe (WC2) (L,D)
Nobu (W1) (D)
North Pole (SE10) (B,L,D)
Odette's (NW1) (L)
Oliveto (SW1) (L,D)
Olivo (SW1) (D)
192 (W11) (L,D)
One-O-One (SW1) (L,D)
One Paston Place (W. Sus) (L,D)
Oriel (SW1) (L,D)
Original Tajine (W1) (D)
Orrery (W1) (L,D)
Orsino (W11) (L,D)
Orso (WC2) (L,D)
Osteria Basilico (W11) (L,D)
Oxo Tower (SE1) (L,D)
Oxo Tower Brasserie (SE1) (L,D)
Ozer (W1) (D)
Palm Court (WC2) (L,D)
Parade (W5) (L,D)
Parisienne Chophse. (SW3) (L,D)
Parsee (N19) (L,D)
Patara (multi. loc.) (L,D)
Patisserie Val. (multi. loc.) (B,L,D)
People's Palace (SE1) (L,D)
Pharmacy (W11) (B,L,D)
Phoenicia (W8) (L,D)
Phoenix B&G (SW15) (B,L,D)
Pink Geranium (Cambs) (L)
Pizza Express (multi. loc.) (L,D)
Pizza Metro (SW11) (L,D)
Pizza on the Park (SW1) (L,D)
PJ's B&G (SW3) (B,L,D)
PJ's Grill (WC2) (B,L,D)
Planet Hollywood (W1) (L,D)
Porters (WC2) (L,D)

Portrait (WC2) (L)
Putney Bridge (SW15) (L)
Quaglino's (SW1) (L,D)
Quality Chop Hse. (EC1) (B,L,D)
Rainforest Cafe (W1) (L,D)
Ransome's Dock (SW11) (B)
Redmonds (SW14) (B,L)
Red Pepper (W9) (L,D)
Rib Room (SW1) (L,D)
Riccardo's (SW3) (L,D)
Richoux (multi. loc.) (B,L,D)
Riso (W4) (L,D)
Ritz (W1) (L,D)
Riva (SW13) (L,D)
River Cafe (W6) (L)
Rodizio Rico (W2) (L,D)
Rosmarino (NW8) (L,D)
Rowley's (SW1) (L,D)
Royal China (multi. loc.) (L,D)
Royal Oak (Berks) (L,D)
Rules (WC2) (L,D)
Salt House (NW8) (L,D)
Salusbury Pub (NW6) (B,L,D)
Sandrini (SW3) (L,D)
San Lorenzo Fuoriporta (SW19) (L,D)
Santa Fe (N1) (L,D)
Santini (SW1) (D)
Sarkhel's (SW18) (L,D)
Sartoria (W1) (D)
Savoy River Rest. (WC2) (L,D)
Scalini (SW3) (L,D)
Scotts (W1) (L,D)
Searcy's/Barbican (EC2) (L,D)
Shogun (W14) (D)
Shoreditch Electricity (N1) (L,D)
Simpson's/Strand/Grand (WC2) (L,D)
Sir Charles Napier (Oxon) (L)
Smiths/Smithfield-Top (EC1) (B,L,D)
Smollensky's/Strand (WC2) (L,D)
Sofra (multi. loc.) (L,D)
Solly's (NW11) (L,D)
Sonny's (SW13) (L)
Souk (WC2) (L,D)
Spiga (multi. loc.) (L,D)
Spighetta (W1) (D)
Spoon+ (W1) (B,L,D)
Square, The (W1) (D)

Stafford (SW1) (L,D)
Stapleford Park (Leics) (L,D)
Star of India (SW5) (L,D)
Sticky Fingers (W8) (L,D)
Stonor Arms (Oxon) (L,D)
Stratford's (W8) (L,D)
Sugar Club (W1) (L,D)
Suntory (SW1) (D)
Tamarind (W1) (L,D)
Tandoori of Chelsea (SW3) (L,D)
Tate Gallery Rest. (SW1) (L)
Terminus (EC2) (L,D)
Texas Embassy (SW14) (L,D)
Texas Lone Star (SW7) (L,D)
T.G.I. Friday's (multi. loc.) (B,L,D)
Thierry's (SW3) (L,D)
Tom's Deli (W11) (B)
Tootsies (multi. loc.) (B,L,D)
Toto's (SW3) (L,D)
Trader Vic's (W1) (D)
Tuttons Brasserie (WC2) (L,D)
Utah (SW19) (B,L,D)
Vale (W9) (B,L)
Vama (SW10) (L,D)
Veeraswamy (W1) (L,D)
Villandry (W1) (B,L)
Vineyard at Stockcross (Berks) (L,D)
Vingt-Quatre (SW10) (B;L,D)
Vong (SW1) (L,D)
Waterside Inn (Berks) (L,D)
Wilton's (SW1) (L,D)
Windows on the World (W1) (B)
Wiz (W1) (B,L)
Zafferano (SW1) (L,D)
Zaika (W8) (L,D)
Ziani (SW3) (L,D)

Tea

(See also Hotel Dining;
best of many)
Atrium (SW1)
Berkeley Hotel (SW1)
Blakes Hotel (SW7)
Brown's Hotel (W1)
Cafe at Sotheby's (W1)
Capital (SW3)
Claridge's Hotel (W1)
Connaught, The (W1)

Dorchester, The (W1)
Emporio Armani Caffe (SW3)
Fifth Floor Cafe (SW1)
Fortnum's Fountain (W1)
Four Seasons Hotel (W1)
Goring Dining Room (SW1)
Harrods (SW1)
Julie's (W11)
Landmark Hotel (NW1)
Lanesborough (SW1)
Le Metro (SW3)
Mandarin Oriental Hyde Park (SW1)
Nicole's (W1)
One Aldwych Hotel (WC2)
Palm Court (WC2)
Patisserie Valerie (multi. loc.)
Portrait (WC2)
Richoux (multi. loc.)
Ritz Hotel (W1)
Savoy Hotel (WC2)
Stafford (SW1)
Tuscan Steak (WC2)

Teen Appeal

Aperitivo (W1)
Ask Pizza (W1)
Babe Ruth's (E1)
Basilico (multi. loc.)
Belgo Centraal (WC2)
Belgo Noord (NW1)
Benihana (multi. loc.)
Big Easy (SW3)
Blue Elephant (SW6)
Break for the Border (multi. loc.)
Browns Rest. (multi. loc.)
Buona Sera at the Jam (SW3)
Busabong Too (SW10)
Cafe Lazeez (SW7)
Cafe Pacifico (WC2)
Calzone (multi. loc.)
Cantina del Ponte (SE1)
Canyon (Richmond)
Casale Franco (N1)
Chelsea Bun (SW10)
Chelsea Kitchen (SW3)
Chelsea Ram (SW10)
China House (W1)
Chuen Cheng Ku (W1)
Chutney Mary (SW10)

Dakota (W11)
DKNY Bar (W1)
Dôme (multi. loc.)
Down Mexico Way (W1)
Ed's Easy Diner (multi. loc.)
Fish! (multi. loc.)
Foxtrot Oscar (W1)
Giraffe (multi. loc.)
Hakkasan (W1)
Hard Rock Cafe (W1)
Havana (multi. loc.)
Henry J. Bean's (SW3)
itsu (multi. loc.)
Jason's (W9)
Jenny Lo's Tea (SW1)
Jim Thompson's (multi. loc.)
Joe Allen (WC2)
Kettners (W1)
La Famiglia (SW10)
La Mancha (SW15)
Le Petit Blanc (multi. loc.)
Marine Ices (NW3)
Masala Zone (W1)
Mash (W1)
Maxwell's (multi. loc.)
Meson Don Felipe (SE1)
Montana (SW6)
Moshi Moshi Sushi (multi. loc.)
Movenpick Marché (SW1)
Nachos (SW10)
Navajo Joe (WC2)
New Culture Rev. (multi. loc.)
Oliveto (SW1)
Oxo Tower Brasserie (SE1)
Paparazzi (SW3)
Pitcher & Piano (multi. loc.)
Pizza Express (multi. loc.)
Pizza Metro (SW11)
Pizza on the Park (SW1)
Pizza Organic (multi. loc.)
Pizzeria Castello (SE1)
PJ's B&G (SW3)
PJ's Grill (WC2)
Planet Hollywood (W1)
Pret à Manger (multi. loc.)
Pucci Pizza (SW3)
Rainforest Cafe (W1)
Sauce Organic Diner (NW1)

Shoeless Joe's (multi. loc.)
Smollensky's on Strand (WC2)
Soho Spice (W1)
Soup Opera (multi. loc.)
Soup Works (multi. loc.)
Spiga (multi. loc.)
Spighetta (W1)
Sports Cafe (SW1)
Sticky Fingers (W8)
Texas Embassy Cantina (SW14)
Texas Lone Star (multi. loc.)
T.G.I. Friday's (multi. loc.)
Tiger Lil's (SW10)
Titanic (W1)
Tootsies (W11)
Uno (SW1)
Vic Naylor (EC1)
Vingt-Quatre (SW10)
Wagamama (multi. loc.)
Waterloo Fire Station (SE1)
Wok Wok (multi. loc.)
Wolfe's B&G (WC2)
Yellow River Cafe (multi. loc.)
Yo! Sushi (multi. loc.)
Zaika Bazaar (SW3)

Teflons

(Get lots of business, despite
so-so food, i.e. they have
other attractions that prevent
criticism from sticking)
All Bar One (multi. loc.)
Aroma (multi. loc.)
Beach Blanket Babylon (W11)
Café Flo (multi. loc.)
Cafe Med (multi. loc.)
Cafe Rouge (multi. loc.)
Caffe Nero (multi. loc.)
Coffee Republic (multi. loc.)
Corney & Barrow (multi. loc.)
Costa Coffee (multi. loc.)
Dôme (multi. loc.)
Ed's Easy Diner (multi. loc.)
Hard Rock Cafe (W1)
Kettners (W1)
Pitcher & Piano (multi. loc.)
Planet Hollywood (W1)
Rainforest Cafe (W1)

Richoux (multi. loc.)
Smollensky's on Strand (multi. loc.)
Starbucks (multi. loc.)
T.G.I. Friday's (multi. loc.)
Titanic (W1)

Visitors on Expense Accounts

Asia de Cuba (WC2)
Aurora (EC2)
Bank Aldwych (WC2)
Bank Westminster/Zander (SW1)
Belair House (SE21)
Bentley's (W1)
Bibendum (SW3)
Bice (W1)
Blakes Hotel (SW7)
Brown's Hotel, Rest. 1837 (W1)
Capital (SW3)
Caviar Kaspia (W1)
Cecconi's (W1)
cheznico (W1)
City Rhodes (EC4)
Clarke's (W8)
Cliveden, Waldo's (Berks)
Club Gascon (EC1)
Connaught Hotel, Rest. (W1)
Criterion Brasserie (W1)
Daphne's (SW3)
Dorchester, Grill Room (W1)
Drones (SW1)
Fifth Floor (SW1)
FireBird (W1)
Floriana (SW3)
Foliage (SW1)
Four Seasons, Lanes (W1)
Glasshouse (Kew)
Gordon Ramsay/68 Royal (SW3)
Gravetye Manor (W. Sus)
Great Eastern Din. Rm. (EC2)
Greens (SW1)
I-Thai (W2)
Ivy (WC2)
John Burton-Race (NW1)
J. Sheekey (WC2)
Kai (W1)
Lanesborough (SW1)
Langan's Brasserie (W1)
La Tante Claire (SW1)

Launceston Place (W8)
Le Caprice (SW1)
Le Gavroche (W1)
Le Manoir/Quat'Saisons (Oxon)
Le Pont de la Tour (SE1)
L'Incontro (SW1)
L'Oranger (SW1)
Maison Novelli (EC1)
Matsuri (SW1)
Mirabelle (W1)
Mitsukoshi (SW1)
Mju (SW1)
Nahm (SW1)
Neal Street (WC2)
Neat Rest. (SE1)
Nico Central (W1)
Nobu (W1)
Oak Room MPW (W1)
Odin's (W1)
One-O-One (SW1)
Orrery (W1)
Oxo Tower (SE1)
Pétrus (SW1)
Pied à Terre (W1)
Poissonnerie de l'Avenue (SW3)
Quaglino's (SW1)
Rhodes in the Square (SW1)
Ritz (W1)
River Cafe (W6)
Salloos (SW1)
San Lorenzo (SW3)
Santini (SW1)
Sartoria (W1)
Savoy Grill (WC2)
Savoy River Rest. (WC2)
Scotts (W1)
Shogun (W14)
Smiths of Smithfield-Top (EC1)
Spoon+ at Sanderson (W1)
Square, The (W1)
Suntory (SW1)
Tamarind (W1)
Tatsuso (EC2)
Turner's (SW3)
Twentyfour (EC2)
Ubon by Nobu (E14)
Vong (SW1)
Waterside Inn (Berks)

Wilton's (SW1)
Windows on the World (W1)
Zafferano (SW1)
Zaika (W8)
Zen Central (W1)

Water Views

Aquarium (E1)
Aquasia (SW10)
Beetle & Wedge (Oxon)
Blue Print Cafe (SE1)
Bridge (EC4)
Butlers Wharf (SE1)
Cantina del Ponte (SE1)
Canyon (Richmond)
Cherwell Boathouse (Oxon)
Compleat Angler (Bucks)
County Hall (SE1)
Depot (SW14)
Feng Shang Floating (NW1)
Fish! (E14)
Four Regions (SE1)
Four Seasons, Quadrato (E14)
French Horn (Berks)
Hambleton Hall (R'land)
Jason's (W9)
Leatherne Bottel (Berks)
Le Pont de la Tour (SE1)
Mr. Underhill's (Shrops)
Neat (SE1)
Neat Brasserie (SE1)
Oxo Tower (SE1)
Oxo Tower Brasserie (SE1)
People's Palace (SE1)
Putney Bridge (SW15)
Rick Stein's Seafood (C'wall)
River Cafe (W6)
Savoy River Rest. (WC2)
Thai on the River (SW10)
Ubon by Nobu (E14)
Waterside Inn (Berks)

Wine/Beer Only

Abeno (WC1)
Dalchini (SW19)
DKNY Bar (W1)
Eco (SW4)
Ed's Easy Diner (multi. loc.)
Gate (W6)

Hi Sushi (multi. loc.)
Ikkyu (WC1)
Jenny Lo's Tea (SW1)
Joe's Rest. (SW1)
Mildreds (W1)
Patisserie Valerie (multi. loc.)
Pepper Tree (SW4)
Randall & Aubin (W1)
Rotisserie Jules (W11)
Souk (WC2)
Tom's Deli (W11)
Truc Vert (W1)
Twelfth House (W11)
Viet Hoa (E2)
Wong Kei (W1)

Winning Wine Lists

Amberley Castle/Queens (W. Sus)
Auberge du Lac (Herts)
Aubergine (SW10)
Belvedere (W8)
Bibendum (SW3)
Brown's Hotel, Rest. 1837 (W1)
Cafe at Sotheby's (W1)
Cantina Vinopolis (SE1)
Cantinetta Venegazzu (SW11)
Capital (SW3)
Caravaggio (EC3)
Cecconi's (W1)
Cellar Gascon (EC1)
Che (SW1)
Chewton Glen, Marryat (Hants)
Chez Bruce (SW17)
cheznico (W1)
Christopher's (WC2)
Clarke's (W8)
Cliveden, Waldo's (Berks)
Club Gascon (EC1)
Connaught Hotel, Rest. (W1)
Cork & Bottle (WC2)
Crescent (SW3)
Criterion Brasserie (W1)
Dorchester, Grill Room (W1)
Drones (SW1)
Ebury Wine Bar (SW1)
Enoteca Turi (SW15)
Fifth Floor (SW1)
Foliage (SW1)
Four Seasons, Lanes (W1)

Gidleigh Park (Devon)
Glasshouse (Kew)
Gordon Ramsay/68 Royal (SW3)
Gravetye Manor (W. Sus)
Hotel du Vin & Bistro (multi. loc.)
Il Convivio (SW1)
John Burton-Race (NW1)
Lanesborough (SW1)
Langan's Bistro (W1)
La Tante Claire (SW1)
La Trompette (W4)
Le Gavroche (W1)
Le Manoir/Quat'Saisons (Oxon)
Le Metro (SW3)
Le Pont de la Tour (SE1)
L'Escargot (W1)
Le Soufflé (W1)
L'Incontro (SW1)
L'Oranger (SW1)
Mirabelle (W1)
Monkeys (SW3)
Neat Rest. (SE1)
Nicole's (W1)
Oak Room MPW (W1)
Odette's (NW1)
Orrery (W1)
Pétrus (SW1)
Pied à Terre (W1)
Prism (EC3)
Ransome's Dock (SW11)
Rib Room (SW1)
Richard Corrigan/Lindsay (W1)
Ritz (W1)
R.S.J. (SE1)
Sartoria (W1)
Savoy Grill (WC2)
Savoy River Rest. (WC2)
Square, The (W1)
Tate Gallery Rest. (SW1)
TECA (W1)
Turner's (SW3)
Vineyard at Stockcross (Berks)
Waterside Inn (Berks)
Wilton's (SW1)
Windows on the World (W1)
Wine Library (EC3)
Zafferano (SW1)

Young Children
(Besides the normal fast-food
places; * indicates children's
menu available)
Abingdon (W8)*
Al Hamra (W1)*
Aperitivo (W1)
Aroma Chinese (W1)
Ask Pizza (multi. loc.)
Babe Ruth's (E1)*
Balans (W8)
Bank Aldwych (WC2)*
Bank Westminster/Zander (SW1)*
Basilico (multi. loc.)
Belair House (SE21)
Belgo Centraal (WC2)*
Belgo Noord (NW1)
Belgo Zuid (W10)*
Benihana (multi. loc.)*
Big Easy (SW3)*
Bishopstrow, Mulberry (Wilts)*
Bloom's (NW11)*
Bluebird (SW3)*
Bombay Bicycle Club (SW12)
Bombay Brasserie (SW7)*
Bridge (EC4)
Buona Sera (SW11)*
Cafe Fish (W1)*
Café Flo (multi. loc.)*
Cafe, Level Seven (SE1)
Cafe Med (multi. loc.)*
Cafe Pacifico (WC2)*
Cafe Rouge (multi. loc.)*
Cafe Spice Namaste (E1)
Calzone (multi. loc.)*
Cantina del Ponte (SE1)*
Canyon (Richmond)*
Carluccio's Caffe (W1)*
Chapter One (Kent)*
Chapter Two (SE3)
Chelsea Bun (multi. loc.)
China House (W1)
Chiswick (W4)
Christopher's (multi. loc.)*
Chuen Cheng Ku (W1)
Chutney Mary (SW10)
Clock (W7)*
Como Lario (SW1)

Compleat Angler (Bucks)*
Cranks (W1)
Dakota (W11)*
Del Buongustaio (SW15)*
Don Pepe (NW8)*
Dorchester, Grill Room (W1)*
Eagle (EC1)
Eastwell Manor (Kent)*
Ed's Easy Diner (multi. loc.)*
Fifth Floor Cafe (SW1)
Fish! (multi. loc.)*
Florians (N8)
Fortnum's Fountain (W1)*
Frederick's (N1)*
Garbo's (W1)*
Gaucho Grill (NW3)*
Giraffe (multi. loc.)*
Glaister's (SW13)*
Hakkasan (W1)
Hard Rock Cafe (W1)*
Harrods (SW1)*
Henry J. Bean's (SW3)*
Honest Cabbage (SE1)
Hotel Tresanton (C'wall)*
House on Rosslyn Hill (NW3)*
Idaho (N6)
itsu (multi. loc.)
Jim Thompson's (multi. loc.)*
Julie's (W11)*
Just St. James's (SW1)*
Kensington Place (W8)
Kettners (W1)
Khan's (W2)
La Brasserie Townhouse (WC1)
La Famiglia (SW10)
Lanesborough (SW1)*
La Porte des Indes (W1)
Le Bouchon Bordelais (multi. loc.)*
Le Petit Blanc (multi. loc.)*
Le Piaf (multi. loc.)
Le Piaf (multi. loc.)*
Little Bay (NW6)*
Livebait (multi. loc.)*
Lou Pescadou (SW5)*
Lygon Arms (Worcs)
Mandalay (W2)
Marine Ices (NW3)*
Masala Zone (W1)*

Matsuri (SW1)
Maxwell's (multi. loc.)*
Mela (WC2)
Mitsukoshi (SW1)*
Montana (SW6)*
Nachos (SW10)
Naked Turtle (SW14)*
Navajo Joe (WC2)*
New Culture Rev. (multi. loc.)
North Pole (SE10)
Noura (SW1)
Oliveto (SW1)
Original Tajine (W1)
Oxo Tower Brasserie (SE1)
Palm Court (WC2)*
People's Palace (SE1)*
Pharmacy (W11)
Phoenicia (W8)*
Phoenix B&G (SW15)*
Pizza Express (multi. loc.)
Pizza Metro (SW11)
Pizza on the Park (SW1)
Pizza Organic (multi. loc.)*
PJ's B&G (SW3)
PJ's Grill (WC2)*
Planet Hollywood (W1)*
Porters (WC2)*
Quaglino's (SW1)*
Rainforest Cafe (W1)*
Redmonds (SW14)*
Red Pepper (W9)
Reubens (W1)
Riccardo's (SW3)
Richoux (NW8)*
RK Stanley's (W1)*
Rock Garden (WC2)*
Rodizio Rico (W2)*
Santa Fe (N1)*
Sarkhel's (SW18)
Sauce Organic Diner (NW1)*
Seashell (NW1)*
Shoeless Joe's (SW6)*
Sir Charles Napier (Oxon)*
Smollensky's/Strand (multi. loc.)*
Sonny's (SW13)*
Soup Opera (multi. loc.)
Soup Works (multi. loc.)
Spiga (multi. loc.)

Wine Vintage Chart 1985–2000

This chart is designed to help you select wine to go with your meal. It is based on the same 0 to 30 scale used throughout this *Survey*. The ratings (prepared by our friend **Howard Stravitz**, a law professor at the University of South Carolina) reflect both the quality of the vintage and the wine's readiness for present consumption. Thus, if a wine is not fully mature or is over the hill, its rating has been reduced. We do not include 1987, 1991–1993 vintages because they are not especially recommended for most areas.

	'85	'86	'88	'89	'90	'94	'95	'96	'97	'98	'99	'00
WHITES												
French:												
Alsace	24	18	22	28	28	26	25	23	23	25	23	25
Burgundy	24	24	18	26	21	22	27	28	25	24	25	–
Loire Valley	–	–	–	26	25	22	24	26	23	22	24	–
Champagne	28	25	24	26	29	–	24	27	24	24	–	–
Sauternes	22	28	29	25	27	–	22	23	24	24	–	20
California:												
Chardonnay	–	–	–	–	–	21	26	22	25	24	25	–
REDS												
French:												
Bordeaux	26	27	25	28	29	24	26	25	23	24	22	25
Burgundy	23	–	22	26	29	20	26	27	25	23	26	–
Rhône	25	19	26	29	28	23	25	22	24	28	26	–
Beaujolais	–	–	–	–	–	–	22	20	24	22	24	–
California:												
Cab./Merlot	26	26	–	21	28	27	26	24	28	23	26	–
Zinfandel	–	–	–	–	–	26	24	25	23	24	25	–
Italian:												
Tuscany	26	–	24	–	26	23	25	19	28	24	25	–
Piedmont	25	–	25	28	28	–	24	26	28	26	25	–